SELLING DYNAMICS

SELLING DYNAMICS

Robert Y. Allen • **Robert F. Spohn** • **I. Herbert Wilson**

Professor of Business
Northwestern Connecticut
Community College

Professor of Business
Northwestern Connecticut
Community College

Marketing Consultant

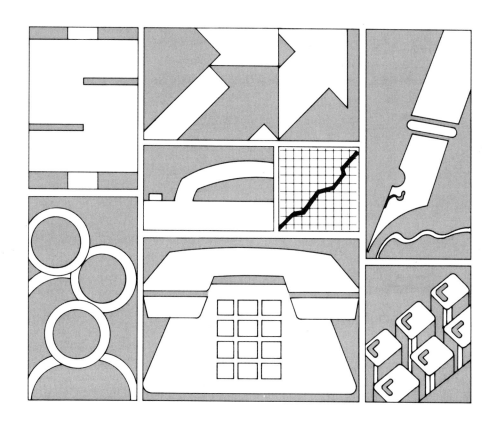

McGraw-Hill Book Company

New York • St. Louis • San Francisco • Auckland • Bogotá
Hamburg • Johannesburg • London • Madrid • Mexico
Montreal • New Delhi • Panama • Paris
São Paulo • Singapore • Sydney • Tokyo • Toronto

SELLING DYNAMICS

1 2 3 4 5 6 7 8 9 0 DOCDOC 8 9 8 7 6 5 4 3

ISBN 0-07-001161-3

This book was set in Serifa Lite by Bi-Comp, Incorporated.
The editors were Beth A. Lewis and Scott Amerman;
the designer was Jo Jones;
the production supervisor was Diane Renda.
The technical illustrations were drawn by J & R Services, Inc;
the nontechnical illustrations were drawn by Fredric Winkowski.
The cover was designed by Vernon Grant Associates.
R. R. Donnelley & Sons Company was printer and binder.

Library of Congress Cataloging in Publication Data

Allen, Robert Y., date
    Selling dynamics.

    (McGraw-Hill series in marketing)
    Includes index.
    1. Selling. I. Spohn, Robert F. II. Wilson, I.
Herbert. III. Title. IV. Series.
HF5438.25.A44 1984   658.8'5   83-11354
ISBN 0-07-001161-3

CONTENTS

viii

x

xvi

xviii

Preparing / Education, Training, and Previous Employment /
Writing Your Résumé / Finding the Jobs: Prospecting and the
Approach / Conducting Yourself during the Interview: The
Presentation / Follow Up on the Interview

Selling is a *dynamic* activity. Different selling situations are as varied and variable as the needs, wants, problems, moods, and aspirations of people themselves. No two are exactly alike. Because of this mosaic character of selling situations, a course in selling cannot be taught with the rigid guidelines of an exact science.

Our answer to that problem is twofold. In this text we present *principles* of selling, which remain constant in all situations. Along with the principles, we offer a great variety of *methods and techniques* for applying them to accommodate the individual selling situation. The principle is like the hub of a wheel; the methods and techniques are like the spokes.

We look at selling as a career—what it is, how it works, how to prepare for it, how to get into it. You will profit from this even if you never enter the selling profession. For the mastery of selling principles will further your success as an engineer or an accountant, executive or entrepreneur, politician, doctor, lawyer, scientist, or any chosen calling. In fact, selling skill will be useful in every phase of human relations—in society as well as in a career.

Another aspect of selling dynamics is the gradual development of the function over the centuries to meet the challenges of an ever-changing world. Although the basic principles do not change, there has been a continual quest for innovation in techniques to adjust to these changes and challenges. Selling today is as different from the selling of yesterday as the computer is different from the abacus. This text will concentrate on the latest techniques.

In an endeavor to combine the academic with the practical, the writing team that prepared *Selling Dynamics* was composed of two professors of marketing and a business executive who has been responsible for the training and direction of thousands of salespeople.

The first two chapters deal with the selling profession to provide you with background. The emphasis is that selling is a catalyst for the entire economy and for society in general. These chapters show that there are many dimensions to selling.

The next three chapters cover basic material that is preparatory to developing superior selling techniques. Developing communication skills, understanding buyers' motivations, and developing requisite sales knowledge are fully explained.

Chapters 6 through 13 are in many respects the essence of the book. Here the sales process is fully examined: prospecting, the preapproach, the approach, the sales interview, buyer resistance, and the close. In each chapter the basic process is described and many practical applications and examples are provided.

The next three chapters cover specific areas which are selling-intensive and offer many career opportunities: in-store and showroom (retail) selling, selling real estate, selling insurance, selling to industry, and selling to retailers.

PREFACE

The final four chapters of the book center around the person doing the selling: ethics and law, managing yourself and being managed, how to raise selling productivity, sales management, and getting started in selling.

A number of people assisted in the production of this book. We would like to thank the following staff at McGraw-Hill: John Carleo, Barbara Brooks, Carol Napier, Beth Lewis, Jim Armstrong, Scott Amerman, and Jo Jones. We would particularly like to acknowledge the many suggestions provided by Mary Drouin.

We would also like to acknowledge the suggestions of the following reviewers: Ray Burnett, Indiana University; Thomas Duda, Penn State University; Herbert Katzenstein, St. John's University; Richard Nelson, San Francisco State University; Harold Perl, County College of Morris; Art Rochlin, Miami-Dade Community College; Charles Schewe, University of Massachusetts; and Pablo Ulloa, Jr., El Paso Community College.

We also want to thank the many companies who cooperated in this venture.

We would especially like to thank our wives: Jane Allen, Barbara Spohn, and Maxine Wilson.

Robert Y. Allen

Robert F. Spohn

I. Herbert Wilson

SELLING DYNAMICS

CHAPTER OBJECTIVES

To explain the service functions that selling performs

To introduce the selling process so you will be familiar with it prior to its in-depth coverage in later chapters

To show you how selling can be used in many different situations

To point out some of the characteristics of selling as a career

CHAPTER OUTLINE

EVERYBODY SELLS

Nothing Happens Till Someone Sells Something.
Red Motley*

Everybody sells. You cannot spend a day in the modern world without continually selling and being sold, for selling is more than bringing about the exchange of money for goods or services. Selling is persuasion.

Every aspect of human relations is influenced by selling. You may be trying to persuade a consumer to purchase a garment or a business organization to install a new computer system. You may be presenting an idea to a board of directors or a plan for peace to nations. Whatever you achieve will depend in large measure on your ability to win acceptance and on your competence in the art and science of persuasion. This is selling.

"Nothing happens till someone sells something." The incandescent light, the telephone, and the airplane might still belong to humankind's dreamworld if someone had not persuaded someone to finance them, to produce them, to market them, to buy them. Without selling, antibiotics might still be languishing in a laboratory and Medicare might still be "in committee."

Selling advances human progress. It is just as important to sell people on being vaccinated as to develop the vaccine. That beautiful sports car on display in the showroom is doing nothing for anybody—it has to be sold to be useful.

The orders brought in by salespeople keep mines, factories, farms, forests, and fisheries humming. A store pays its rent and its employees' salaries with the proceeds of its sales. In our society, selling makes jobs.

So let's take a look at selling as a professional career—what it is, how it works, how to prepare for it, how to get into it—because today's selling differs as much from yesterday's selling as the computer differs from the abacus. Our endeavor will be to introduce you to selling as a possible career, but more than that, we will acquaint you with selling principles that will keep you in good stead throughout your life in any career you may choose.

*Red Motley—former salesman and president at Parade Publications, Inc.

SELLING IN PRACTICE

Do you want to help people? One way is to help them buy something. In the United States alone, approximately 230 million people and 12 million businesses and organizations are spending more than $2 trillion annually.

These people have all kinds of biological and psychological needs and wants. Buying intelligently helps them satisfy these needs and wants. Selling is a proud and purposeful career.

You're not a glib talker? That's okay. In modern selling, listening is at least as important as talking, often more so. Some of history's greatest salespeople—like Benjamin Franklin, for example—have been by their own admission short on eloquence.

You're not interested in selling people things they don't need? Good. There are so many things people *do* need that it would be a waste of time trying to sell them things they don't need. You're not a "born salesperson"? Nobody is. We're all born babies. Training determines the vocation, not birth.

Let's look at some situations where selling brings satisfaction to both the buyer and the seller. In each situation, try to put yourself in the position of the buyer and see whether or not a worthwhile service function was performed.

Assessing Needs

The experienced salesperson can be more aware of a buyer's needs than the buyer. Successful selling is based on making the buyer aware of hidden needs.

SELLING PROTECTS A DREAM

"Where do you want to be twenty years from now? What is your family dream?" asked Beverly Palmer, an insurance agent who was exploring the life insurance needs of Jack and Marian Nichols.

"Financial independence," they answered. "We want to pay off the mortgage on the house, see the kids through college, and have an equity in our nursery business."

"I know you're in the nursery business," said Palmer. "Is it all yours, or do you have interested associates?"

"It's half mine," replied Nichols. "Harold Lerner owns the other half."

"I asked," said Palmer, "because insurance has to be integrated into your total estate plan, and the more I know, the more intelligent my recommendations will be."

Two weeks later, Palmer delivered the certificates for the life insurance. At this time she asked whether the Hometown Nursery was a corporation or a partnership.

"It's a partnership," replied Nichols. "Why do you ask?"

"Well, I know you're in good health. You just passed an insurance medical exam. But what would happen if Lerner died?"

"I'd buy his half from his estate. He has the same call on my interest."

"Would it take a lot of money?"

"It sure would. I'm beginning to get your drift."

"If Lerner died tomorrow, would you have trouble financing the purchase of his interest?"

"If it happened tomorrow, yes."

"That's why I asked the first question, Mr. Nichols. The death of your partner could spike your family dream. How would you like to guarantee that dream?"

"How?"

"Partnership insurance. The Hometown Nurseries could take out insurance on your life and your partner's. If one of you dies, his estate is paid for his interest and the surviving partner owns the whole business."

"Funny we never got into that. Lerner is just as concerned as I am. He's a family man too."

A few weeks later Beverly Palmer closed on two $100,000 policies for the two partners in Hometown Nurseries. By uncovering an additional insurance need, she had provided total protection for the family dream of Jack and Marian Nichols.

Some prospects know exactly what they need; others think they know what they need; and still others, like Jack and Marian Nichols in the situation described above, have no idea that a need exists. A salesperson must be ready to recognize levels of need awareness and real needs. That means keen observation, thorough questioning, close listening, and careful analysis on the part of the salesperson.

And if you, the salesperson, cannot uncover a need unknown to the customer or properly interpret an apparent need, there will be no sale. Beverly Palmer effectively dealt with the apparent need for family life insurance for the Nichols family and then proceeded to uncover their need for partnership insurance. In doing so, she rendered a valuable service to her customer.

Information Dissemination

Not every buyer will be fully informed about the benefit or certain features of a product. Part of your job as a salesperson is to explain benefits and features so that the buyer can make an informed decision.

SELLING INCREASES GAS MILEAGE

Kurt Harnischberger has decided on the car he wants.

"Do you want cruise control?" asks the salesperson. "Just set it for the speed you want, and the car won't drop below that speed unless you step on the brake pedal."

"That's a frill I can do without. I see it's listed at a hundred dollars."

"About how many miles a year do you drive, Mr. Harnischberger?"

"Oh, about twenty-five thousand."

"Then you'll use about fifteen hundred gallons of gas. In addition to keeping you at the speed you want on the road, a constant speed level will give you between five and ten percent better gas mileage. At today's prices, that's a one-year saving of at least as much as you pay for the cruise-control feature and probably more."

"Not a bad idea. I'll take it."

Most people will seek information before making a decision, and buying means making a decision. In most situations, particularly if the purchase is an infrequent or major one, the more informed buyers are, the more comfortable they will feel about buying the product they are considering.

EXHIBIT 1.1
SOME PROS-
PECTS KNOW
WHAT THEY
WANT; OTHERS
NEED HELP

6

Everybody's dfferent. Some people will know more than others about a product they're thinking of buying. Their knowledge grows out of interest, from exposure to advertising and publicity, or from literature they've read on the subject. A stereo buff, for example, is apt to know volumes on the subject of stereo components.

But some buyers know little or nothing about the product or service they're looking for or the best way to use it. The qualified salesperson is an expert on the product or service sold and all factors surrounding its purchase and use. There are many classes of product or service where even the informed buyer needs more information before deciding to buy. Sometimes, the more knowledge the buyer has, the more questions he or she asks—intelligent questions on complex aspects of the purchase. To be a good salesperson, you must have needed information on tap.

Kurt Harnischberger almost passed up the cruise-control option for his new car. But an informed salesperson explained how this option could pay for itself in increased mileage per gallon of gasoline. By educating the buyer, the seller rendered a legitimate service to the buyer and increased the amount of the sale by $100.

Problem Solving

The salesperson is often called upon to help a customer solve a particular problem. Careful attention to the problem and good product knowledge produce a satisfactory solution for everyone.

THE SALESPERSON AS CONSULTANT

The five machines in Frank Baxter's small manufacturing business were overworked and drinking oil.

When Sam Jones, sales representative for Ace Industrial Supplies, called on Baxter to present the Ace line of industrial lubricants, he found a prospect who seemed to have a one-track mind.

"There's only one thing that interests me," said Baxter. "Price. I use so much oil and grease that it's killing me. What's your price?"

"Well, we have different lubricants for different machine requirements," replied Jones. "Each has a different price. How about letting me take a look at the operation to see what we would recommend for your specific needs?"

"Go ahead."

The investigation revealed that Baxter's machine temperatures were running very high and breaking down the lubricants too rapidly. A higher viscosity was needed.

When Jones explained this to Baxter, Baxter did not even ask the price. He simply said, "Send in a drum. We'll test it."

The recommended lubricant reduced grease consumption by 35 percent. Baxter was very pleased. Jones now enjoys whatever business Baxter has to place.

We could say that every purchase a buyer makes is intended to solve the problem of an unfulfilled need. But the intensity of the problem and the impor-

EXHIBIT 1.2
IN PRACTICE, SELLING IS USING THE SALESPERSON'S EXPERTISE TO SOLVE
PROBLEMS   (*Source:* Carl W. Cullen. Courtesy of Ex-Cell-O Corporation Manufacturing
Systems Company.)

tance of the salesperson's role in solving the problem vary. Even the buyer's
awareness of the problem depends on the situation.

As a salesperson, your task is to recognize both problems and their causes and
then prescribe a product or service to solve them. Knowing both your product and
service and creative ways to use them are musts. Sam Jones sold his industrial
lubricants to Frank Baxter because he understood the cause of Baxter's problem
and knew that his product would solve it.

Guidance

Even when seeing a need and knowing it will have to be filled sooner or later, a
prospective customer is still apt to hesitate. There always seem to be more facts
to gather before making the decision. In such a case, a good sales technique is to
advise the buyer about the advantages of acting now and the disadvantages of
putting off the decision.

SELLING GUIDES A FAMILY HOUSING DECISION

Three years ago the Burstens and the Johnsons had two things in common. Although
they did not know each other, both families lived in apartments. Each had around
$15,000 in savings.

At that time both the Burstens and the Johnsons decided it was time to buy a house. Both families were jittery about emptying their savings accounts and taking on a mortgage. But they decided to look anyhow and went their separate ways to real estate offices.

The Burstens did not find a house that met their needs exactly. They decided to wait. The Johnsons likewise could not find a house that matched their needs to a T. However, when they looked at one house that came close, the salesperson explained to them that owning it was better for them than living in an apartment. She advised that the house was a good investment. It would help them get ahead of the inflation spiral and into a better position as property values continued to rise, and the additional monthly costs would be offset by tax savings. The Johnsons bought the house with a $15,000 payment and a $60,000 mortgage. The Burstens kept their savings intact.

This year the same salesperson showed the Johnsons what really was their dream house. She knew what they wanted and had kept her eye out for it. The Johnsons fell in love with the house the minute they saw it. They sold their first house through the same salesperson and made a profit of $35,000. Their profit gave them enough to make a down payment on the $110,000 house they wanted.

In the meantime the Burstens earned approximately $6,000 in interest on their savings account, which barely kept pace with inflation.

The difference in the fortunes of these two families, so favorable to the Johnsons, was due to the guidance given by a salesperson who understood real estate, simple economics, and how to communicate effectively.

A smart salesperson has the buyer's best interests in mind. This could even mean advising the buyer *not* to buy the product or service right now. You hope that such guidance will bring positive results to the buyer so that a long-lasting relationship will develop.

In the case of the Johnsons and the Burstens, the Johnsons benefited from the salesperson's guidance. As a result, they had the financial capability and the confidence in their salesperson to purchase another house from her.

Ownership Transfer

Ownership transfer is the minimum requirement of selling—it is the basic sales service.

THE BASIC SALES SERVICE

Joyce Lanser was setting up a tax preparation service. She needed an electronic calculator. From her reading and her inquiries, she knew exactly the model she wanted to buy. All she needed was someone to buy it from.

Joyce called City Office Equipment and talked with salesperson Bill Maddio. After talking with Joyce about the machine she'd selected, Bill agreed that Joyce was right in her choice. He wrote up the order, completed a credit application, and arranged for delivery.

Bill's action was a service to the customer, the simple arrangement of ownership transfer. In its simplest form, a retail salesperson fills out a sales slip, takes the customer's money, and hands the customer the merchandise. More complex transactions, for example, those that occur in industrial selling, often require writing up product specifications, arranging long-term financing, and establishing an acceptable delivery date.

In much in-store retail selling, ownership transfer is the only service performed by the salesperson. In most other selling situations, however, some or all of the services we've mentioned—needs assessment, information dissemination, guidance, and problem solving—are required. Ownership transfer is then the last service performed . . . if the preceding services were performed well!

THE SELLING PROCESS

Selling is indeed a service that few of us can live without. When you buy, you are involved in a selling situation. When you are performing the service functions described earlier, of course, you are involved in selling. When you work at a nonselling job in an organization, you are working for an organization that is selling. (A charity calls it fund raising and a college calls it recruiting.)

Can selling be learned? Sure it can. Colleges teach selling. Many firms have formal sales training programs. But there is no universal formula for successful selling. There are too many different people selling too many different products in too many different situations to too many different buyers. On the other hand, there are established selling principles and time-tested techniques that successful salespeople have used. You need to apply these techniques and principles to suit the situation.

Of course, there is no substitute for experience in any effort—and selling is no exception. The formal study of selling, along with sales training programs that might be offered by employers, should provide the knowledge of the logical steps you need to make a sale.

At this point let's look at each of these steps briefly. We will cover each of these steps in detail later. (See Exhibit 1.3.)

Prospecting

Prospecting is the research stage of selling. Salespeople must pinpoint who is most likely to need their products or services. For example, if you are selling commercial meat-slicing machines, then butcher shops, delicatessens, and food

EXHIBIT 1.3
STEPS IN THE SELLING PROCESS

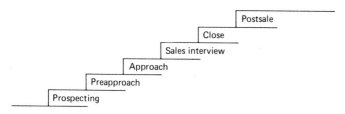

10

markets with meat and delicatessen departments are your most likely potential buyers, or *prospects*. Once you know your prospects, you can rank them by evaluating their needs and financial resources in relation to the products or services you offer. Those who need or want your products or services and are financially able to pay for them are called *qualified prospects*. Salespeople also prospect for new types of users or new uses for their products or services.

Good prospecting leads to more sales and less wasted effort. If you choose your prospects wisely, there's a good chance that many of them will take the time to discuss their needs with you.

The Preapproach

The preapproach is the preparation for selling. During this stage, you try to develop as much knowledge of your prospect as you can. For a business prospect, this includes finding out about the business itself—its nature and volume and who makes the buying decisions. For a consumer prospect, preapproach information includes such details as financial status, social status, marital status, and the like. This information helps you identify a prospect's needs, wants, and ability to pay. In selling situations where appointments are made, setting up a meeting—for example, making a telephone call to arrange a time and place—is part of the preapproach.

After the preapproach, you are now better prepared for the next steps in the selling process.

The Approach

Your first face-to-face encounter with the prospect—the approach—is the time for a favorable first impression. Your actions and words will pave the way for your sales interview. There are many types of approaches; the one you use and the benefits you stress during the interview depend on the information you've gathered during the preapproach and on the product or service you offer. Your approach also depends on whether you're calling on a new prospect or an established customer.

EXHIBIT 1.4
SMART PROS-
PECTING SEPA-
RATES PROS-
PECTS FROM
SUSPECTS

The Sales Interview

The sales interview allows you to gather even more information about the prospect and the prospect's need or needs. On discovering the need, you must get the prospect to agree that (1) the need exists, (2) the product or service your company sells will satisfy that need, (3) your company's product or service is the best for satisfying the need, (4) the cost-benefit analysis is positive, and (5) the prospect can afford the purchase.

This interview stage (sometimes called the *presentation*) is the real communication stage of selling. It involves asking the right questions and listening carefully to answers. It involves clear, concrete explanations, timely demonstrations, and the skillful handling of any resistance or objections by the prospect.

The Close

The close is the logical conclusion of the sales interview: It is the sale. It is the moment the prospect gives a verbal or written commitment to buy. A successful close depends, of course, on how successful you were during the preceding stages of the sales process. Most often an attempt to close will not be successful until there is agreement on the five basic issues listed in "The Sales Interview" section. Like the approach, there are many techniques for closing, and each varies with the circumstances of the selling situation.

The Postsale

During the postsale, you reassure the prospect—now the buyer or customer—that he or she has made the right decision. It's also the time when you follow up on the order to be sure, first, that delivery is made on time and, second, that the customer is satisfied with the product and is getting the most from it. The key to any salesperson's success often is repeat business. Proper attention to postsale details will ease your approach, interview, and close on the next sales call.

You can see that your success during each step of the sales process will determine your chance for success in later steps. If you have not selected the proper prospect during the prospecting stage, it's not likely that you will ever get to the postsale stage. If you prospect wisely, know your prospect's needs and your product's benefits, and communicate your knowledge, a closing follows naturally.

Now that we have been exposed to the selling process and have seen how selling helps people buy to satisfy their needs, let's look at how the concept of selling touches everything we do.

THE PERVASIVENESS OF SELLING

"We are all salesmen, every day of our lives. We are selling our ideas, our plans, our energies, our enthusiasms to those with whom we come in contact." This statement made by Charles Schwab, organizer and first president of U.S. Steel, more than half a century ago still holds true today. You are continually faced with situations in which the proper use of selling principles can be beneficial. Both your business dealings and your personal dealings can be more effective if you understand the application of selling to these situations.

Business Applications

Almost every aspect of business requires selling, both in dealings within the organization and in dealings with the many publics the organization serves. The design engineer has to get the design approved, the secretary has to convince someone that a new typewriter is needed, the copywriter has to convince the advertising manager that the copy meets the objectives of the organization's

EXHIBIT 1.5
CLOSING IS THE
BOTTOM LINE

advertising program. Of a more general nature, organizations must institute changes of all kinds and develop long-range plans.

Let's focus on gaining acceptance for change and gaining acceptance for a plan. Then to show the far-reaching, less obvious need for selling, let's look at how financiers sell.

Gaining Acceptance for Change   Any business or organization must make changes to survive. These changes are dictated by new competition, new markets, new legislation, new technology, and many other external and internal forces.

For example, until quite recently AT&T was sheltered from competition. New legislation and advanced technology have brought forth a host of competitors in the communications industry. As a result of this new competition, AT&T is changing from a staid, service-oriented telephone company to a marketing-oriented communications firm. This reorientation has necessitated many other changes within the organization.

One of the biggest problems faced by a manager is getting others to accept a change, especially when it directly affects their established practices or threatens their security. The change might be a new reporting system, a transfer to a new work location, a new company policy, or some other redirection.

Individuals affected by the change may be unaware of its benefits. In this case, you must sell the benefits by showing that the change will make the individuals' tasks easier to perform or will be personally beneficial in some other way. If the change does not offer a direct benefit, the individuals must be made aware of how the company will benefit, thus providing them with greater job security, higher dividend checks, or better profit sharing.

Gaining Acceptance for a Plan   Strategic planning has been one of the most popular terms heard within organizations for a decade or so. The strategic plan outlines the major course the organization will follow. RCA, after decades of growth through acquisition of nontechnical businesses, is now focusing on growth through what it knows best—technology. Somebody sold that plan. Years ago, Sears shifted its emphasis toward in-store retailing, which today accounts for almost 80 percent of sales of the largest retailer in the world. Somebody sold that plan. Strategic plans and all other subordinate plans have to be accepted and put into action. That takes selling.

Gaining acceptance for a plan calls into play all the principles of selling and almost every step of the selling process: researching and assembling facts, picking the right time to present the plan, presenting it, applying communication skills, anticipating and handling objections, and considering the special interests and personalities of those in a position to accept the plan.

Merging Corporations   J. Ira Harris of Wall Street's Salomon Brothers knew that Walter E. Heller International Corporation wanted to acquire a certain bank. He also knew that the deal had failed to materialize because of a disagreement between buyer and seller over the relative value of securities to be exchanged in the transaction. Harris called Heller's chief executive officer and proposed a solution: payment in cash. That was the answer. The bank was acquired.[1]

Behind the headline news of major corporate mergers are stories of the highest level of selling. Although J. Ira Harris and others who have effected the many mergers of the 1980s are called *investment bankers,* their strength is *selling.* They know finance and they know companies, but just as important, they know how to sell mergers.

Personal Applications

An understanding of selling principles can make you more successful and reduce the number of frustrations you encounter. You are continually faced with situations in which you must convince or persuade someone about something. How you go about it determines the outcome. Let's illustrate this by showing the need for selling in getting a job and in winning agreement on those many everyday issues that we all encounter.

Getting a Job   As a job seeker you must use all the skills that a salesperson would use in selling a product or service. The only difference is that you are selling your own services, so think of the employment market as a selling situation where the employer is the customer and you, the job applicant, are the seller.

The process of finding a job is similar to the salesperson's process of finding potential customers. You must determine where the job opportunities are, just as you must determine where potential customers are during the prospecting stage.

Once you know your best prospects, you should find out as much as you can about each prospective employer by reading articles that may have been written about the company and by asking people who may know. This is your preapproach. Your approach involves any materials you send in advance, such as a cover letter and résumé plus what you say when you enter the interviewer's office. Your approach will depend on how you found out about the job opening. "I'm Charles Everett. Karen Wilson, who works in your Accounting Department told me that Bigg & Co. needs some bright and ambitious sales representatives for your new Consumer Products Division" is an example of a good opening-line approach. Naturally, your appearance, manners, and mannerism also affect your approach . . . and your success in securing the position you seek.

During the job interview, you discuss the employer's needs and your ability to satisfy them. It is at this point that you must, if the match still exists, convince the employer that you are the person best qualified to fill the position.

Once there seems to be agreement on all points discussed during the interview, it's time to ask for and get the job. This is your close. A former student concluded an interview for a sales position with a major corporation by saying, "When do I start?" He started on the first of the month.

---

[1]"Ira Harris: Chicago's Big Dealmaker," *Business Week,* June 25, 1979, pp. 70–78.

14

Winning Agreement "I couldn't get my point across." "He wouldn't buy what I had to say." "She wasn't interested in my point of view." "I couldn't get him to go along with me." "We were on different wavelengths." "I turned her off." Do any of these statements sound familiar?

Do you come on strong, stressing your own concerns, ideas, and opinions, without considering the other person's self-interest or frame of reference? Do you tend to stress "I," instead of "you" or "we," when seeking another's cooperation or alliance?

The use of selling techniques can bring about more positive results. Most people are more receptive to you if they can identify with your idea, proposal, or problem. This requires your knowing and understanding what is important to them and then stressing that importance. For example, if the town is considering locating a dump (or, more euphemistically, a landfill) near your backyard, you are likely to get your neighbors' support in opposing it if you talk about the odious smell in *their* yards and the rodents that will attack *their* children. Placing emphasis on *your* yard and *your* children isn't as likely to get the neighbors all charged up to support you.

A CAREER IN SELLING

Selling has been around since people have been around. Early European empires owed much of their success to the traders (sellers) who brought them economic superiority. Early America survived and grew because peddlers brought life-sustaining and life-enriching products and services to its primarily rural population.

Throughout the years, selling has changed in terms of what is sold, how it is sold, the type of person doing the selling, and the objectives in making the sale. Along with these changes has come an increase in the respectability of selling as a career.

EXHIBIT 1.6
AN EARLY
SELLER

Let it be no secret that many of the positive results brought about by early selling were accompanied by a number of negative images resulting from questionable techniques of early salespeople. First, there were the peddlers foisting such things as Dr. Kikapoo's Snake Oil Remedy upon unsuspecting customers. And then for many years the stereotype of the salesperson was the outgoing, smiling, glib, affable person whose personality often helped sell a product to people whether or not they needed the product. This type is probably best characterized by Willy Loman, the washed-up salesman in Arthur Miller's *Death of a Salesman,* whose glad-handing, jocular manner wore thin as time passed. (See Exhibit 1.7.)

There are still snake oil peddlers and replicas of Willy Loman selling today, but the most successful contemporary salespeople are a different breed. Today's salespeople spread knowledge, solve problems, guide buying decisions, and satisfy needs. They manage sales territories and help the companies they represent grow.

Contemporary selling is less subjective than it was many years ago, less isolated from the rest of the marketing mix. In most fields of selling today, there is an

EXHIBIT 1.7
THE DEMISE OF WILLY LOMAN

Willy Loman was the tragic main character in Arthur Miller's play *Death of a Salesman*. Willy believed the only important ingredients for selling were a pleasing personality, good jokes, a smile, and contacts.

As the years passed, Willy continued to use this unsuccessful recipe that eventually led to ringing up zeroes in his sales territory and in his personal life. He told jokes and no one laughed; he smiled and no one smiled back; he no longer had his contacts. Unable to pay his insurance premiums, upset by his sons' unpromising futures, fired from his job, Willy took his own life.

overall plan of market cultivation, and the selling is coordinated with the rest of the marketing activities and with the organization's other functions. Increasingly, the salesperson is being required to cooperate in the interest of a bottom-line profit rather than be concerned strictly with obtaining orders.

In Chapter 2, the various types of sales positions will be surveyed, but first we will discuss here some of the characteristics of selling as a career. Once you have evaluated these aspects of selling and have assessed your personal objectives and characteristics, you will be in a better position to judge the relative merits of selling compared with other occupations.

Objective Evaluation

There are many fields where quality of performance and the resultant rewards are as variable and unpredictable as the number of people passing judgment. For example, who can say for sure, without any possibility of contradiction, how good is the performance of an artist, an office manager, a lawyer who prepares briefs, a civil engineer, a government official, or a health care administrator? Selling offers a singular advantage on this count.

As a salesperson, you typically have clearly defined goals, and your company has a reporting system that determines whether you have reached these goals. The goals center on sales dollars brought in. Usually included are actual sales compared with the goal, this year's sales compared with last year's sales, and other measures that consider how much profit results from those sales. There are other marks of merit or demerit in selling too, such as your cooperation with other departments, handling of service or complaint matters, reporting, expense control, and performing nonselling functions.

High Income

Competent salespeople have high incomes. Substantial five-figure incomes are common in sales, and six-figure incomes are also possible. (See Exhibit 1.8.) Many companies offer incentives for high performance. As a result, the more you

EXHIBIT 1.8
THE BIG MONEY IN SALES: TOP TEN SALESPEOPLE IN THE
UNITED STATES

Salespeople	Company	Annual earnings
Nicholas DiBari	Comdisco, Inc.	$674,253
John Slevin	Comdisco, Inc.	600,897
Irving Rousso	Russ Togs, Inc.	531,700
John Hill	Storage Technology Corp.	343,658
William McConner	Union Oil Co. of Calif.	339,666
Charles King	Standard Oil Co. of Ohio	334,790
David Tracy	Fieldcrest Mills, Inc.	288,577
Richard Barrie	Fabergé, Inc.	282,585
Benjamin Sampson	Cone Mills Corp.	265,375
Robert Lair	Cessna Aircraft Co.	242,749

Source: Adapted from Robert Levy with Mark Levenson, ''Willy Loman, Eat Your
Heart Out,'' *Dun's Revie,* December 1980, pp. 68–72. Based on a survey of publicly
held companies by *Sales and Marketing Management.*

sell, the more you earn. This means that your ambition and ability directly affect
your income. Of special importance to young salespeople is that pay is based on
how much you do for the company, not how long you have been employed. You
don't have to have gray hair to be rewarded.

Independence

In most sales positions, you are your own boss most of the time. You plan your
schedule, establish your own work habits, and develop selling techniques that fit
your personality and personal style.

You won't have a supervisor peering over your shoulder every time you make a
move. You're out there on your own, running your own little business—your
territory. A highly motivated, well-disciplined individual thrives on this kind of
independence.

Selling as a Career Path

Selling is a popular beginning for becoming a top corporate executive. Surveys
have shown that many executives began their careers in sales. (See Exhibit 1.9
for a sampling.) You may not reach the top, but if you want to try, selling is a good
way to begin your ascent.

Depending on your aspirations, a position in sales can be either an end in itself
or a stepping-stone to other positions within the company or to management
positions within the sales department. These options are open to you as a salesperson more than they are to most other employees of an organization, primarily
because your personal contacts inside and outside the organization are numerous
and your results are highly visible.

EXHIBIT 1.9
A SAMPLE OF THIS DECADE'S CHIEF EXECUTIVES
WHO CAME UP THROUGH SALES

Company	Chief executive
American Hospital Supply	Karl Bays
Avon Products	David Mitchell
Champion International	Andrew Sigler
Goodyear	Charles J. Pilliod, Jr.
Hershey Foods	William Dearden
Sunbeam	Robert Gwinn
Xerox	C. Peter McColough
IBM	John Opel
Merrill Lynch	Roger Birk
Monsanto	Jack Henley

There was a time when a salesperson had to be promoted to a management position to receive additional financial and status rewards. However, today most companies have career paths that enable a salesperson to remain in selling and still receive better titles, higher compensation, and other benefits that show a professional status. A typical progression in some companies is from sales trainee to salesperson to sales representative to senior sales representative.

In Chapter 2, you'll get a better idea of the types of sales careers to consider and see the kind of exposure salespeople have throughout the organization.

RECAP

Selling is a service function that assesses needs, disseminates information, solves problems, offers guidance, and transfers ownership.

The selling process involves a series of logical steps. These steps are prospecting, the preapproach, the approach, the sales interview, the close, and the post-sale.

Selling is an activity or skill that can be helpful in many situations. We can use it in our everyday business dealings and personal dealings whenever we are seeking agreement.

Selling provides excellent career opportunities. It scores high relative to other occupations with respect to providing objective evaluation, good income, independence, and advancement opportunities.

REVIEW QUESTIONS

1. Describe the five service functions of selling.
2. What are the steps, or stages, of the selling process?

3. How can selling help you gain acceptance for change?
4. Explain how getting a job is similar to making a sale.
5. Why is selling the pioneer of progress?
6. Why is a salesperson's performance evaluated objectively?
7. What are some financial incentives in selling?

DISCUSSION QUESTIONS

1. A teenager has just reached the legal age for obtaining a driver's license, but her father wants her to wait another year before getting it. How should she try to convince her father that she should get her license now?
2. To what extent can a politician use selling techniques in an election campaign?
3. Describe some instances where a salesperson has played a major role in your purchase decision.
4. Is selling a dead-end job? Explain.

LEARNING EXPERIENCES

1. Interview a salesperson to determine what he or she considers the most advantageous aspects of a selling career.
2. Attend a municipal meeting (board of aldermen, board of finance, etc.), and evaluate how proposals are presented.
3. Convince a nonbusiness student that he or she should take a course in selling.

CASES

JANE HANSEN

Jane Hansen is a receiving clerk who has worked for the same company at the same job for six years. She works a thirty-five-hour week and is almost certain that she will become a shift supervisor when her boss retires in five years.

Jane works so fast and efficiently that she usually completes her work by noon and has nothing to do for the rest of the day. She has been using the extra time at the plant to work on the development of a new materials-handling system.

Away from the job, Jane is an avid reader, being particularly fond of mysteries and biographical novels. She belongs to a bowling club and is its treasurer. She is single and enjoys meeting people. She finished high school with good grades, but that was the end of her formal education.

Jane is bored with her job and displeased with her income, although she knows she is being paid fairly for what she does. Several of her friends and coworkers have told her she is wasting her talents in her present job. Some have told her she should try selling. They think she would be good at it.

Questions

1. From the information given, what are the indications that Jane might be suited for selling?
2. What advantages might a selling career offer Jane that she is not getting from her present job?

THE WILMINGTON SCHOOL BUDGET

When the chairman of the Board of Education of Wilmington presented the school budget to the town, he received many queries from the audience about a $2000 item for summer school. This was the first time the board had opted to run a five-week summer session, and many people were unaware of the reason for its inclusion in the budget.

The small, 150-student school belongs to a regional school district. It has no facilities for vocational education, but the regional high school where the summer school is to be held has facilities that are unused during the summer months.

The courses, open to seventh- and eighth-graders, include basic reading, basic math, woodcraft, metalcraft, graphics, typing, and a few enrichment courses.

Twenty students have indicated an interest in the summer session. The operating costs will be borne by all six schools in the district on a pro rata basis.

Questions

1. Is the board chairman involved in a selling situation? Explain.
2. What aspects of the summer school do you think the voters would like most? Least? Explain.
3. How would you present the budget?

TWO

CHAPTER OBJECTIVES

To show how selling fits into marketing

To describe and emphasize the relationship selling must establish with other departments in the company

To explore the various types of sales positions

To describe the bases for determining sales territories

CHAPTER OUTLINE

Selling and Marketing
   The Marketing Mix
   Selling and Promotion
   Selling and the Product
   Selling and Pricing
   Selling and Distribution
Selling and Other Company Functions
   Selling and Production
   Selling and Finance
   Selling and Personnel
Sales Positions and Sales Territories
   Sales Positions Based on Channel of
     Distribution
   Sales Positions Based on Product or
     Service
   Sales Positions Based on Prospect
   Sales Territories
Recap
Review Questions
Discussion Questions
Learning Experiences
Cases
   Personal Computers
   3M = 48,000

20

SELLING IN PERSPECTIVE

All the world's a stage,
And all the men and women merely players.
Shakespeare*

As a salesperson you are at center stage, but a whole cast is supporting you. Know your part, but also know the parts of those supporting you. Work at getting the cooperation of all the people and the departments in your company so that the total effect is greater than the sum of the effects taken independently. This *synergism* will produce dynamic selling.

Your stage is your territory. It may be Broadway, off-Broadway, off-off-Broadway, or some little place in the boondocks. You may start in the boondocks, be discovered, and end up on Broadway. It depends on what you're selling, how you perform, and what kind of role you're playing.

The role you play depends a lot on what you are looking for in your career and what kind of product or service you sell. Some roles are tougher than others.

This chapter focuses on the other marketing activities and the other departments in the company that play supporting roles in the production of sales. It also explains the various kinds of sales positions (roles) and the territories (stages) that are assigned for carrying out the act of selling.

As You Like It, act 2, sc. 7.

SELLING AND MARKETING

You're the star, but not the only star, in most selling situations. Oh, if you gather your own grapevines, weave the grapevine wreath, and then go out and sell it yourself, you're the only star. This is not a typical selling situation, however. Most selling involves a blend of marketing activities performed by many specialists. Additionally, other departments in your company are behind the scenes developing the product or service, providing the financial resources, and supplying the people to provide the want-satisfying products and services you will sell. The selling activity is a part of the marketing function, and it interacts with the other elements of marketing and with other departments. They're all connected. (See Exhibit 2.1.)

The Marketing Mix

Marketing is a total system of business activities designed to plan, price, promote, and distribute want-satisfying goods and services to potential customers.[1] Some people think of marketing as selling. This assumes that there are no other marketing activities, which is not correct. Others think of selling and marketing as distinctly different and separate activities. This view omits selling as part of the marketing function, which is also not correct.

The activities performed by marketing are usually referred to as the *marketing mix*. The key elements of the marketing mix are promotion, the product (or service), pricing, and distribution. Selling relates to each part of the marketing mix. Let's see how.

Selling and Promotion

Promotion is the voice of marketing. You'll find as parts of the promotional mix all the activities that communicate with customers and prospective customers to influence them to buy. Selling is an important part of the promotional mix. The other parts are advertising and a wide range of sales aids called *sales promotion*. For the promotional mix to work, all these activities must support one another.

The Advertising Connection *Advertising* is communication that the advertiser pays newspapers, radio stations, and other media to transmit. Advertising is used to inform prospects about product features and benefits, to arouse awareness of needs, and to place the company and its product in a generally favorable light. Mass media advertising can reach large audiences, but advertising can also be directed toward specific groups through direct mail or selective placement (such as in an industrial magazine).

A company's advertising is designed to help its salespeople make sales. The content of the advertisement and its objective are based on many things, such as the product and the market. For industrial goods, such as valves, generators, and

[1]William J. Stanton, *Fundamentals of Marketing*, McGraw-Hill, New York, 1981, p. 4.

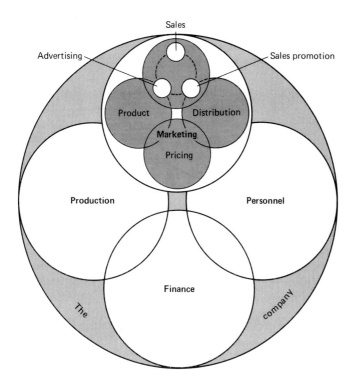

EXHIBIT 2.1
THEY'RE ALL CONNECTED

forklift trucks, advertising draws inquiries from companies who might become prospects for sales calls. For many consumer goods sold at stores, advertising persuades shoppers to choose the product from the shelves. As more products are sold from the shelves, the salesperson increases sales to the retailer to replenish those shelves. Procter & Gamble spends over half a billion dollars a year in advertising. It advertises Tide and Crest to consumers so they'll buy these products from the retailer and the retailer will "need" more Tide and Crest from Procter & Gamble. These products are also advertised in *Progressive Grocer* so that the retailer responsible for replenishing the shelves gets an additional message that may help the Procter & Gamble salesperson during the next sales call.

Advertising and selling should coordinate. The company's advertising should be aimed at those most likely to need the company's products or services. What's more, to be effective, the advertising program has to be consistent with the sales program. As a salesperson you must be aware and have up-to-date facts on the content of your firm's advertising program—its theme and its message.

This coordination is so important that sales managers usually participate in the development of the advertising program, and the salespeople receive copies of all advertising messages so that they know what prospects are seeing or hearing.

Your credibility and presentation can be destroyed if you don't know what's going on in the advertising program.

The Sales Promotion Connection   Sales promotion, which you can think of as a smorgasbord of sales aids, also supports the sales effort. Some common kinds of sales promotion are trade shows, samples, specialties, displays, and rebates. The aids might be used by the salesperson directly, be used through advertising, or stand alone. Let's look at these and see how they can help you as a salesperson.

• *Trade shows* are large gatherings of vendors of similar kinds of products. The purpose is to make it convenient for prospective buyers to "shop" at one place. The company's booth at a trade show is generally staffed by a representative from headquarters and/or a salesperson from the sales territory where the show is located. Sales can often be made at the show, but the primary purpose is to make contact with prospective buyers interested in having you call on them later. See Exhibit 2.3 for a sampling of the 9000 trade shows held annually.

• *Samples* are small quantities or pieces that represent the product you sell. Salespeople either give prospects a sample to try—a piece of cheese at the delicatessen—or show samples to prospects—fabric samples shown by an apparel salesperson. Samples help you sell because the prospect gets firsthand

EXHIBIT 2.2
PROSPECTIVE BUYERS ARE OFTEN FOUND AT TRADE SHOWS (*Source:* American Library Association. Used by permission.)

EXHIBIT 2.3
TRADE SHOW TRENDS FOR 1980

Show	Location	Registered attendance
International Concrete and Aggregates	Houston	5,549*
SAE Automotive Engineering	Detroit	19,155
National Home Center/Home Improvement	Dallas	14,026*
Office Automation Conference	Atlanta	5,223†
Pittsburgh Conference on Analytical Chemistry and Applied Spectroscopy	Atlantic City	5,000†
Assn. of Operating Room Nurses	Atlanta	5,714
Design Engineering	Chicago	22,715
National Plant Engineering and Maintenance	Chicago	21,860
Super Market Industry	Dallas	4,832†
Print '80	Chicago	57,251
AWS Welding	Los Angeles	7,966*
AFS Foundrymen's Casting	St. Louis	11,118
National Micrographics Assn.	New York City	8,791*
NRA Restaurant, Hotel-Motel	Chicago	54,028*
AMC Coal	Chicago	9,011
Offshore Technology Conference	Houston	86,965*
National Computer Conference	Anaheim	64,942*
Institute of Food Technologists	New Orleans	4,372*
International Machine Tool	Chicago	75,849
Water Pollution Control Federation	Las Vegas	5,114*
American Society of Civil Engineers	Hollywood, Florida	1,575*
Information Management/INFO '80	New York City	17,667†
ISA Annual Instrumentation Automation	Houston	16,175
Data Processing Management Assn.	Philadelphia	3,230*
PMMI Pack Expo	Chicago	30,878
Paint Industries	Atlanta	3,076
International Hotel/Motel and Restaurant Expos.	New York City	28,081*
American Assn. of Critical Care Nurses	Atlanta	3,593*
Radiological Society of North America	Atlanta	7,556*
Exposition of Chemical Industries	Chicago	9,345

*A comprehensive audience survey conducted by Exhibit Surveys, Inc. is available from the show producer.

† This figure represents the number of registrants from which the survey sample was drawn. It is not the total net attendance reported by the exposition management.

Source: Attendance figures by Exhibit Surveys, Inc., Middleton, N.J. Table reprinted with permission from *Industrial Marketing,* May 1981, p. 89. Copyright 1981 by Crain Communications, Inc.

exposure to the product. A sample can be used as a door opener in your approach to a prospect or as a sale clincher: "Here, try one before buying."

• *Specialties* are low-priced gifts that might serve as door openers, as conversation pieces, or as reminders of the company and its products. For years door-to-door marketers, such as Fuller Brush and Avon, have used specialties in approaching prospects. One golf ball salesperson would hand new prospects a square golf ball to get them thinking about the roll of a golf ball. Pens, calendars, and a host of other specialties are commonly used for the purposes mentioned.

• *Displays* are important at the point of purchase for consumer goods. They serve as the link between the advertising and the sale of the product. Those selling to retailers are interested in having good display material that will be used to promote the product. An important aspect of this sales job is to convince the retailer that using the display material will increase sales for all.

• *Rebates,* also looked on by some as price concessions, help close a sale. When the prospect is suffering from indecision, the $50 rebate for acting now could be the factor that closes the sale. Rebates gained renewed popularity recently when the automobile manufacturers offered them in an attempt to boost demand. Rebates are popular in many other industries, especially those involved in appliances and other *durable goods* which aren't purchased often.

You can see that sales promotion can help you from start to finish—from getting prospects to closing sales. Be aware of the sales aids your company has, and know how to use them effectively. As with advertising, sales promotion must be in step with the entire promotional program to pave the way for the sale.

Selling and the Product

The product or service itself is a big factor in the amount and kind of selling needed in the overall marketing mix. Industrial products, especially technical or complex ones, usually need more personal selling activity than most consumer goods. Consumer goods require varying amounts of selling. A suit requires more selling effort than a tube of toothpaste. The suit must be actively sold by the manufacturer or agent to the retailer, who then must have a salesperson help the customer make a selection. Toothpaste, on the other hand, only requires selling to middlemen. Advertising and sales promotion take over from there.

A new product is a source both of extra effort and extra rewards in selling. Because its features and uses are usually not familiar to the prospect, the new product needs a greater selling effort than the established product. This is the case particularly where the company is not well known. New products provide you with the chance to gain new prospects, develop new approaches, and increase sales to existing customers.

Selling and Pricing

The prospect's needs and the ability to satisfy those needs are usually governed by the exchange consideration—the *price*. High-priced products—fur coats, computers, and home security systems, for example—are products that take a sizable chunk of the prospect's budget. And they take a sizable chunk of selling effort. You have to work hard to convince the prospect that the need satisfaction is worth the money spent.

The concept of *relative price* is important. The relationship between the price of your product, competitors' products, and substitute products will affect both sales effort and type of presentation. When the price is relatively higher, quality, service, or other differences should offset the price disadvantage. If those advantages do not exist, the price disadvantages will squelch many potential sales.

The *quantity discount*, another pricing tactic that can affect selling, is a price reduction for large orders. For example, a buyer often gets a price reduction for buying many cases, rather than just a few units of a product. Quantity discounts help the salesperson increase volume where a need for larger quantities exists.

Selling and Distribution

Distribution is the system and the related activities that get a product to the customer at the right place at the right time. The system consists of channel members and physical distribution components. The *channel members* are the marketing intermediaries, or middlemen, who stand between the producer and the final buyer. The *physical distribution components* are storage and distribution facilities, inventory, and transportation. At this point we'll show how the physical distribution components affect your sales. Later in this chapter you'll find out about channel relationships.

Physical distribution plays a major role in determining the level of service you can give customers. Nearby warehouses, complete inventories, and efficient transportation are a salesperson's dream come true. Out-of-stock situations and slow deliveries can ruin an otherwise successful sale. You sell $1000 worth of merchandise to be delivered by next Tuesday, but only $600 worth is delivered the following Friday. This may result in your having to deal with a complaining customer or possibly having the customer cancel the $400 worth of merchandise that was back-ordered.[2]

Get to know how your company's distribution system works, and work with it. It's supposed to support your selling effort. A sale is not a sale until a product or service is delivered and paid for.

SELLING AND OTHER COMPANY FUNCTIONS

All companies have customers, products or services, money, and people. We've already seen that marketing, especially selling, deals primarily with customers. Production deals with the product, finance with money, and personnel with people. Larger companies have well-defined departments responsible for these functions. In smaller companies the lines of responsibility may not be formally drawn, but the functions still must be performed.

The relative importance of the functions also varies among companies. In a highly technical industrial-goods company, engineering is either an important part of production or a separate, but closely related, department. On the other hand, a wholesaler is usually not involved in manufacturing. Instead, the wholesaler must buy products for resale. If we were to stretch our imagination, we could see buying as the wholesaler's production function.

It's great when each department does its thing well and also cooperates with other departments. The ultimate, though, is when all departments are governed

---

[2]To back-order is to process an order or part of an order for later delivery when stock comes in.

by the philosophy and the practice of pleasing customers. This is what has made IBM, Xerox, General Foods, Procter & Gamble, and many other companies so successful. This is the kind of direction that helps you sell.

Selling and Production

If production did not manufacture the product, the salesperson would have nothing to sell. If the salesperson did not sell the product, production would not need to manufacture anything. It's a true chicken-or-egg dilemma: Which comes first? Let's just say that both are involved in production: Sales produces customers and production produces products or services.

Areas of production, such as scheduling and quality control, directly affect the selling effort. If sales gets orders for a hundred units a month and production turns out only fifty units a month, sales will be lost unless production schedules are adjusted. The same is true if the proper mix of sizes, colors, and styles produced is not in line with what is selling.

Often there are both planned and unplanned quality differences. Planned quality differences in products result from using different grades of material (for example, pine instead of cherry) to provide product variety at various price levels. Such a difference benefits sales. Unplanned quality differences result from defective merchandise or merchandise that does not meet planned standards. Whatever the reason, such a factor can cause lost sales and lost customers.

Cooperation and open communication between production and sales are vital. Production must turn out what the salesperson's customers want when they want it. Consumer demand must be forecast by the sales force—often in conjunction with marketing research—so that production can use its facilities effectively to meet the expected demand.

Selling and Finance

All decisions made by finance affect sales at least indirectly. Whether it's a decision to expand plant facilities or a decision to approve an increase in advertising expense, sales will eventually feel the effect.

The financial aspect most directly felt by sales is probably the company's credit policy. A liberal credit policy expands demand by making more money available for present purchases. It helps you overcome one of the principal objections raised by prospects: "I don't have the money now."

For consumer sales and many industrial sales, credit is convenient for the customer; credit allows the customer to take advantage of the benefits that the purchase will bring right away. Credit provides the retailer with the merchandise now and postpones payment until some of it has been sold, thus reducing the retailer's working capital requirement and providing the manufacturer's salesperson with an edge in making the sale.

During a slump in automobile sales, General Motors used low-rate financing to spur sales. Xerox salespeople have a competitive advantage because of the company's Xerox Equipment Equity Program (XEEP). This program allows customers to purchase Xerox products at interest rates 2 percentage points below bank rates.[3]

Selling and Personnel

Personnel's interaction with and influence on sales varies among firms. The personnel department may be involved with many activities, including wage and salary administration, personnel policies, recruiting, and training employees.

In many companies contacting and screening applicants for sales positions is the personnel department's responsibility, whereas sales management is often involved in the final hiring decision.

SALES POSITIONS AND SALES TERRITORIES

There are as many different types of sales positions as there are different types of marketing strategies. Marketing strategies are based on the types of products or services sold and the market served. So many variables exist that it's safe to say that no two sales positions are exactly alike. Nevertheless, in this section we'll explore a sampling of the many types of sales positions formed by differences in channels of distribution, products, and prospects. Then to give you a better idea of where a salesperson does the selling, we'll discuss sales territories.

Sales Positions Based on Channel of Distribution

In the long run the most important sale is the sale to the ultimate buyer, the user of the product or service. This buyer may be an individual consumer or an organization which will use the product or service in conducting its business or in manufacturing another product. Therefore, products and services must get to the end users in the *consumer market* or the *industrial market.*

The producer must decide on the most effective overall marketing strategy and the best path to reach these markets. Exhibit 2.4 depicts the channels commonly used. Since the thrust of the sales effort depends on the channel member you represent, let's explore the sales positions found in each channel.

Producers   The most distinguishing aspect of this type of position is that you are serving only one master: You are employed to sell the products of only one company. As you can see in Exhibit 2.4, the producer's salespeople may sell to a wholesaler (often called a *distributor*), a retailer, or directly to an end user, or consumer.

If you are selling to channel members, the selling does not stop there. You have to see that channel members sell to their customers. This often involves you in training their salespeople to sell your product. You can't sell them more if they

[3]Jeffrey A. Tannenbaum, "To Prop Sales, Xerox Gives Bargain Loans," *Wall Street Journal,* Jan. 8, 1981, p. 21.

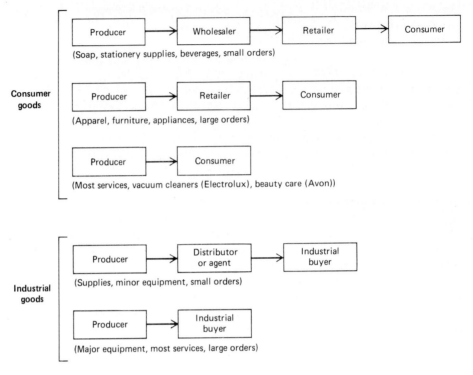

EXHIBIT 2.4
COMMON CHANNELS OF DISTRIBUTION

don't sell what they already have. To be successful in this type of selling it's important to be well-versed in all aspects of business so that you can relate to your customer's business problems and, if appropriate, play the consultant's role. (Selling direct to retailers is such a common type of sales position that Chapter 16 is devoted to this kind of selling.)

Direct selling All producers who don't use channel members must employ their own sales force to reach the end customer; this is called *direct selling*. Direct selling positions are found in both the industrial market and the consumer market. Most large companies selling to the industrial market use their own sales force to deal with the industrial buyer. IBM, Xerox, NCR Corporation, and U.S. Steel are examples. Companies selling business services, such as consulting, maintenance, and accounting, also use direct selling. Smaller companies may use direct selling, a distributor or an agent, or a combination of paths. This is a type of selling that requires knowledge of the product you sell and of the target businesses. (Industrial selling is such a vast field that Chapter 15 is devoted to it.)

Direct selling is not as common in the consumer market. Consumers have traditionally preferred to go to a store to buy, although recently they have been doing more buying through catalogs, such as those of L. L. Bean, Orvis, and

Sears. Also, most consumer goods are priced too low to cover the cost of a salesperson's call.

Vacuum cleaners (Electrolux, Health-Mor, Kirby), encyclopedias (World Book), and beauty care products (Avon) are notable examples of consumer goods sold direct, or door to door (as it is commonly called). Many products sold door to door are sold by part-time salespeople. This kind of selling has a high earnings potential for an energetic, enthusiastic individual, but it is one of the most demanding of all sales positions.

Consumer services are also sold direct. Insurance is the most noteworthy. Almost everyone needs some kind of insurance. (Part of Chapter 14 is devoted to this kind of selling.)

Wholesaling Intermediaries   These channel members are the links between the producer and the retailer for consumer goods and between the producer and the industrial buyer for industrial goods. Merchant wholesalers buy products from one or more producers and then resell to their customers. Those that sell to retailers are usually called *wholesalers,* and those that sell to industrial buyers, *distributors.* Additionally, *agents* are wholesaling intermediaries that do not buy (take title) but receive a commission from the producer.

As a salesperson you are usually responsible for selling to established customers in a specified geographic area. If you're selling for a wholesaler or a distributor, you could be selling hundreds or thousands of different products produced by dozens of manufacturers. It's difficult to know everything about all the products you sell. You have to service your accounts. Wholesalers have to manage or help their customers manage their inventory. They have to present new products that promise a fast turnover. Distributors must also look for new applications for the products they sell.

Agents are often seen as an extension of the manufacturer. On a commission basis, they usually represent a number of manufacturers of related products. Often called *manufacturer's representatives,* or *reps,* agents are especially prevalent in the industrial market and in the insurance industry. Agents usually sell the products and services of fewer manufacturers than merchant wholesalers, and they sell higher-priced products. For example, an industrial-supplies wholesaler is likely to sell cleaning supplies, whereas an agent is likely to sell certain types of industrial equipment.

Some manufacturers use both their own sales force and wholesaling middlemen. It's common for a manufacturer of consumer goods to use a wholesaler to sell to low-volume retailers and to sell direct to larger retailers. It's also common for a manufacturer of industrial goods to have its own sales force for reaching highly concentrated lucrative industrial markets and to use agents for opening up new territories or for selling to less concentrated markets.

Retailers   Sales positions in retailing vary considerably, depending on the type of store and the type of merchandise sold. In stores where self-service or self-selection is encouraged, the salesperson does little or no actual selling but performs primarily clerical functions. He or she is often referred to as a *salesclerk.*

On the other hand, there are retail sales positions requiring high levels of sales ability. Apparel, appliances, stereo equipment, and automobiles are among the types of merchandise usually sold by the complete salesperson. There are clothing stores, jewelry stores, and furniture stores that also have their salespeople make off-premises sales calls. Well-known jewelers travel across the country as salespeople with sample cases of goodies for wealthy customers. (You'll learn more about retail selling in Chapter 14.)

Sales Positions Based on Product or Service

If you were to read the employment ads in your newspaper, you would find ads for people experienced in technical sales, intangible sales, and a variety of specific categories. Why? Because sales positions call for different types of people with different characteristics and skills.

Sales positions can be classified by the nature of the product or service sold. *Tangibles* are typically physical products, such as clothing, appliances, valves, or machinery. *Intangibles* are typically nonphysical products or services, such as lawn care, consulting, bookkeeping, telephone answering, or a vacation. The distinction is not always clear-cut. For example, a vacation cruise to the Bahamas is sold on the basis of the tangible properties of the ship and the intangible service of the staff. "All products, whether they are services or goods, possess a certain amount of intangibility. Services like insurance and transportation, of course, are nearly entirely intangible."[4]

Tangibles Physical products can be displayed, stored, seen, touched, and demonstrated. You can use the characteristics of a tangible product advantageously in making a sale. Often the physical appearance of a sleek sports car, a luxurious fur coat, or a compact computer with video display will help make a sale. Many tangible products do not require the selling skill that is needed to sell intangibles. This is true primarily for low-unit-cost, nontechnical products, such as office supplies and many consumer goods.

Technical products, on the other hand, usually require selling skills and training considerably higher than that required for nontechnical products. This is often related to the intangibles connected with the physical product. For many types of technical products, *sales engineers* must fill the sales position. The sales engineer must be not only able to make the sale but also able to aid with the technical aspects of installation and use as well as the diagnosis and repair of malfunctioning products. Those selling avionics equipment must understand instrumentation, and those selling seismographs must understand geology.

Intangibles Most intangible products are services or benefits. The service industry is vast and growing. Since both consumers and businesses buy services, selling opportunities are expected to increase in these areas.

Generally speaking, since buyers perceive more risk in buying a service than in buying a product, intangible sales are more difficult to make. You're selling a promise that the service will be performed to the customer's satisfaction.

[4]Theodore Levitt, "Marketing Intangible Products and Product Intangibles," *Harvard Business Review*, May–June 1981, p. 94.

Put yourself in the customer's shoes. Suppose you're deciding between getting a new hat and a new short hairstyle for a special occasion. You could try on many hats, look in the mirror, and then make a decision to buy or not to buy. With the new hairstyle, however, you must make the buying decision first. Then the service is performed, and you look in the mirror. If you don't like the results, you're out of luck. Obviously, the hairstyle purchase is more risky, and you will need more ''selling'' before you buy it.

If you are selling intangibles, you have to gain your prospect's confidence in you and your service, and you must sell the reputation of the firm you represent. You must use your communication skills to explain something that can't be seen.

Sales Positions Based on Prospect

Every company has to sell to the customers it has and also get new customers. We refer to selling to established customers as *retention selling* and to finding new customers as *new business selling*. In most sales positions you will be expected to do both types. However, some companies have two different sales forces—one to call on established accounts and the other to prospect for new accounts.

Retention Selling   An established company has a solid base of regular customers that must be serviced. As part of a retention sales force, it's your responsibility to keep getting their business and to try to get more business from them. Regular customers have already been sold on your products and your company. You have to keep them sold.

Too many salespeople take their regular customers for granted—a routine of ''business as usual.'' This can't be done. Competition is courting your customer and trying to break up your marriage. You have to be on the alert for each customer's changing needs and help them satisfy those needs quickly and satisfactorily . . . before a competitor does. (See Exhibit 2.5.)

New Business Selling   Companies and their sales forces must continually seek new accounts. The company's survival depends on new customers both to replace lost customers and to provide growth. Regardless of the success of reten-

EXHIBIT 2.5
RETENTION SELLING

''If we had a chance to get a new customer or increase a current customer's volume, we'd choose the latter almost every time.'' These words of E. James Lowrey of Sysco Corporation, the biggest and most successful distributor of food to restaurants and institutions in the United States, reflect the thoughts of many marketers who stress the importance of retention selling.

Source: ''Sysco: Swallowing Its Competitors to Grow in Food Distribution,'' *Business Week*, Aug. 17, 1981, p. 117.

tion selling, some customers will be lost to competition, relocation, death (in the case of consumers), or business failure.

Some companies find it an advantage to have a new business sales force that calls on prospective accounts. Once the new account is secured, it's turned over to a salesperson responsible for repeat business.

Certain companies sell products or services that are not likely ever to be purchased again or frequently enough to require retention selling. Examples are fire engines (towns aren't likely to buy them more than every decade or two), encyclopedias (most families don't want a second set), and aluminum siding (it's supposed to last forever). For these companies it's either new business or no business.

Sales Territories

The company's total selling effort must be divided into manageable units called *territories*. In carving out territories, the company tries to make sure that it is reaching present and potential customers on a regular basis, keeping travel expenses at a minimum, and fully using the talents of each salesperson. Territories may be formed by geography, by customer, by product, or by a combination of these factors.

Geographic Basis Geography is usually the first consideration in setting up territories. The size depends primarily on the number of customers and potential customers. The salesperson for automatic plucking machines would have a large territory, because few chicken farmers in a local area are large enough to benefit from this kind of automation. On the other hand, the feed salesperson would have a smaller territory, because all chicken farmers are prospects.

The size of a territory may be as large as several states or as small as a portion of a city. It is common for a company to have three or four sales territories within a major city and only one or two for the rest of the state. For example, one salesperson for a specialty bakery sells to restaurants from 14th Street to 86th Street in New York City. Many salespeople have a sales territory consisting of just one customer, such as General Motors or AT&T. Publishers often have one or more salespeople selling textbooks to a large state university while other salespeople each sell to a dozen or more other schools.

Customer Basis Many companies sell their products to a wide range of customers having distinctly different needs and applications. This often calls for dividing territories so that these needs can be better served.

A major ingredient in successful selling is a thorough understanding of customers and their needs. The salesperson responsible for selling to a particular customer classification can develop a high level of expertise about the customer's business. In fact, sometimes the salesperson learns the customer's business so well that the customer makes a job offer.

When this method of assigning territories is used, national accounts might be segregated from other accounts, the original equipment manufacturers (OEMs) from replacement market customers, and one industry from another. Marketers of business systems such as electronic data processing (EDP), word processing, and telecommunications usually have industry specialists—banks, retailers, and manufacturers are handled by separate sales forces. The salespeople get to know the industry so well that they can propose the right product or system for the customer.

Product Basis   Many companies market complementary, or related, products or services that can be sold by the same salesperson. However, where the products are significantly different and require widely varying levels of expertise on the part of the salesperson, it is often necessary to have product specialists.

A company that sells both typewriters and sophisticated computer systems would not be maximizing its efforts if it were to use the same sales force to sell both lines. The salesperson most capable of selling the computer systems would be underutilized when selling less complex typewriters. On the other hand, the salesperson whose aptitude and training were most appropriate for selling typewriters might have difficulty selling the sophisticated systems. In this case, the company would have two salespeople call on the same account: one to sell typewriters and one to sell computer systems.

You can see that there are many different types of territories. Like so many aspects of selling, your territory is determined by many factors—product, market, marketing strategy, and so forth. Just like a farmer's field, your territory is yours to cultivate. You reap the rewards of your labors. Working your territory is like running your own little business.

RECAP

Selling is the business activity that brings home the bacon, but many other company activities help the selling effort. Selling relies on marketing and all other departments of the company. It's a big cooperative venture. All parts must work together to bring about successful results.

Sales positions vary with the type of product or service sold, the market served, and the marketing strategy used. Some sales positions are more demanding than others. Some require more background knowledge than others. This diversity in sales positions allows individuals to choose a position that suits their special talents and answers their aspirations.

Salespeople are assigned sales territories that define their areas of responsibility. The geographic scope of the market, the product, and the type of customer are all considered when territories are established.

REVIEW QUESTIONS

1. What are the elements of the promotional mix?
2. To what extent is advertising involved in selling a product?
3. How do new products help the salesperson?
4. How does the price of a product affect the sales effort?
5. How do out-of-stock conditions affect the salesperson's task?
6. What is the major distinction between selling for a producer and selling for an intermediary?

7. What is direct selling?
8. What is the difference between a merchant wholesaler and an agent?
9. Why might intangibles be more difficult to sell than tangibles?
10. Why are sales territories established?
11. Why might sales territories be assigned on a customer basis?

DISCUSSION QUESTIONS

1. George Burry, founder of Burry Biscuit Corporation (now a division of Quaker Oats), said, "No one eats around here until we make a sale." Discuss how Burry's statement relates to this chapter.
2. From the description of the different types of sales positions, which appeals to you most? Why?
3. Show the similarities between a sales territory and a legislative district in your state or a ward in your city.

LEARNING EXPERIENCES

1. Read the retail advertising in your local newspaper, go to the store, and refer to the advertisement for a stereo, tennis racket, food processor, or whatever it is you are interested in. Observe whether or not the salesperson is aware of the advertising message, including the paper in which it was run and the thrust of the appeal.
2. Talk with a salesperson (neighbor, relative, friend of the family, etc.). Find out how his or her company determines its sales territories and why.

CASES

PERSONAL COMPUTERS

The personal computer is the hot product of the 1980s. Industry analysts predict that within the next decade or so the personal computer will be as common as the home television and the office typewriter. More people are exposed each year to computer technology through high school and college courses and at work. Computer camps for children are springing up throughout the country. Personal computer prices are decreasing, technology is improving, and ease of operation is increasing—all signals for a potential mass market.

Large-scale, high-priced computer systems are sold by manufacturers' salespeople direct to users. The high price of these systems (often millions of dollars) justifies the cost of direct selling, and their special designs require a company-trained salesperson and supporting personnel to determine the customer's special needs and tailor the appropriate system. Selling low-priced, more standardized personal computers is different.

Dozens of companies have entered the personal computer sweepstakes to reach a potential market of millions of business and professional users and tens of millions of consumers. Radio Shack is selling its TRS-80 computers through its 8000 retail stores. Apple Computers is selling its Apples through more than 2000 independent stores, including department stores. IBM and Digital Equipment Corporation have opened their own stores. Many of those already in the personal computer business aren't sure whether they are using the best marketing strategy, and those planning entrance are searching for the best way to reach the vast potential market.

Questions

1. Should direct selling to consumers be considered? Explain.
2. Some producers are using and others are considering using office-machine distributors for selling to the business and professional market. What are the advantages and the disadvantages of this channel?
3. Is the selling effort required for personal computers similar to that required for selling televisions and/or for selling typewriters? Explain.

3M = 48,000

Many people think that *Scotch tape* is the generic name for a clear adhesive tape. Many people also incorrectly use the term *xeroxing* when they mean copying. Minnesota Mining & Manufacturing Co. (3M) would like the public to recognize that Scotch is the 3M brand of tape and that 3M also makes copiers. Equally important, the company wants its salespeople and its customers to know these facts.

Sales territories for 3M's 6500 salespeople are product-based. There are thirty-seven autonomous divisions, each selling separate product lines. In all, the company sells over 48,000 products. A key problem with product-based territories is that the salesperson often is not familiar with the other company products, and for that matter, neither is the customer. This means that the person selling 3M coated abrasives may not be aware that 3M can also solve the customer's copying needs and probably many other needs.[5]

Questions

1. Should 3M realign its territories away from a product basis? Explain.
2. Explain how all salespeople might benefit if each were to be more concerned with and informed about each other's products.
3. Do you think advertising could help customers be more aware of 3M's many products?
4. How would you involve the salespeople in the advertising?
5. Read the article (see footnote) to find out what 3M did.

[5]Adapted from Sally Scanlon, "Try Patching That Copier with Our Scotch Tape, Sir," *Sales & Marketing Management*, May 18, 1981, pp. 38–44.

THREE

CHAPTER OBJECTIVES

To explain the basic sales communication model

To familiarize you with ten common communication barriers

To examine ways to avoid or overcome these barriers in sales situations

To acquaint you with various forms of communication

To help you improve your communication skills

CHAPTER OUTLINE

The Communication Model
  The Sender
  The Message
  The Receiver
  The Channel
  When Sender Becomes Receiver
Avoiding Some Common Barriers to
  Communication
  Mental Set
  Differences in Perception
  Prejudice
  Appearance
  Listening Habits
  Distractions
  Poor Organization of Facts and Ideas
  Lack of Prior Knowledge or Experience
  Vocabulary
  Emotions
Overcoming the Barriers
  Image and Appearance
  Voice
  Active Listening
  Building Empathy
  Observing Nonverbal Communication
Other Forms of Communication
  Written Communication
  Telephone Communication
Recap
Review Questions
Discussion Questions
Learning Experiences
Case
  Todd Thiebault

DEVELOPING COMMUNICATION SKILLS

Talk to us—communicate!

"Talk to us—communicate!" was the plea of a group of buyers to its sales representatives. The request came through loud and clear at a national industrial purchasing forum and was reaffirmed in telephone interviews with key purchasing departments around the country.[1]

Selling is communicating. A good salesperson is one who communicates effectively with his or her buyers. You have to understand who they are and where they're at so you can talk their language. You have to learn to listen skillfully and effectively. You have to learn to recognize some of the barriers to good communication so that you can avoid or overcome them.

In this chapter, we are going to deal with some of the general aspects of communication. We'll talk about what is involved in a communication model. We'll deal with some of the problem areas, or barriers, to effective sales communication. And we'll give you some ideas on how to communicate more effectively in sales situations. Chapters 9 and 10 will give you many practical sales applications to the general areas of communication which we discuss in this chapter.

---

[1]James Morgan, "The Big Problem Is Communication," *Purchasing*, Nov. 7, 1979, p. 78.

THE COMMUNICATION MODEL

Selling is persuasion, and it is accomplished through communication. *Communication* is the transmission of an idea or a thought from sender to receiver with a minimum loss of meaning. The object is to get through to the other person's mind. Communication is the single most essential element in the selling process. There are four major components in communication: the sender, the receiver, the message, and the channel. Diagramed, it would look like Exhibit 3.1.

The Sender

The sender is anyone who communicates a thought, an idea, an emotion, or a concept. A communication can be transmitted to the other person in a number of ways; for example, it may be expressed in a nonverbal manner through actions, which is often called *body language*. Body language primarily includes hand gestures, facial expressions, and posture. When nonverbal communication is through pictures, the message is said to be coded *graphically*. Graphic coding is used with some advertisements and road signs—for example, the new international road signs. Graphic coding is also found in a number of company trademarks. Some familiar graphic codings are shown in Exhibit 3.2.

The Message

The message is the thing you want to communicate. It is the content of the thought, idea, or concept expressed in a code the sender has chosen, either intentionally, accidentally, or merely out of habit. For example, you may want to persuade someone to buy a camera. The main message you must communicate is that the camera is for sale. The submessage is that it is worth buying and owning because it can preserve memories. Another submessage might be that it is a unique camera that offers extra benefits over other cameras, such as automatic

EXHIBIT 3.1
THE COMMUNICATION MODEL

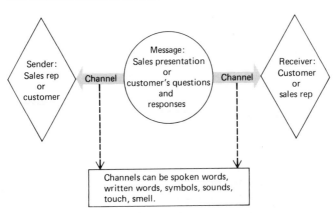

EXHIBIT 3.2
GRAPHIC CODING CAN BE FOUND IN MANY COMPANY TRADEMARKS, SUCH AS THESE
FAMILIAR ONES

focusing. And you might even communicate another submessage: special price
this week.

The Receiver

The receiver is the person to whom the sender directs the message. The components of sender and receiver are not fixed—both salesperson and prospect can
switch roles. For example, the salesperson (as sender) might be explaining a
special feature to the prospect (as receiver), or the prospect (as sender) explaining
a special need to the salesperson (as receiver). Remember that for communication
to exist, all four components of the model—the sender, the message, the receiver,
and the channel—must be present, at least to some degree. Therefore, the receiver must be willing and able to receive and understand the message in order
for communication to take place. Many people, including salespeople, don't realize this. They think that simply because they are talking, someone is listening.
But this isn't so. Think of the many times when someone said something to you,
but you never really heard it. In these cases, three of the four components were
present: the sender, the message, and the channel (face-to-face verbal communication, for instance). One component was missing: you, the receiver. The sound
waves might have bounced off your eardrums, but there was no communication if
your brain was not receiving the message. Listening is especially critical in
selling. Talking is not enough. It is the listening that makes or loses the sale in
many cases.

The Channel

The channel is the means through which the message is sent. There are a
number of possibilities: verbal, auditory, visual, tactile, and olfactory channels. As

the salesperson, you may choose a face-to-face situation to present a product or service verbally. Or you may choose a visual channel and send a letter (written message) with an accompanying pictorial brochure (graphic message). The use of touch may also be helpful with certain products—the prospect can feel the thickness (of carpeting), the softness (of fabrics), the durability (of a plastic), and so on. Smell would be an effective channel to communicate the features of products like foods, perfumes, and flowers.

Generally, communication is more effective when several channels are used. For example, a perfume salesperson would most effectively communicate the benefits of the product by employing several channels: by describing the product (speech and hearing), by showing the customer the attractive container and perhaps some supporting brochures (sight), and by letting the customer try the fragrance (smell).

When Sender Becomes Receiver

Now that we have examined the basic model of communication, let's look at how it varies in practice. In most selling communication, the sender and receiver continually change roles. The salesperson sends a message; the receiver listens and then sends a return message. This is shown in Exhibit 3.3. For example, the salesperson might transmit a message like, ''See how delicate this material is, Mrs. Fournier.'' Mrs. Fournier might reply, ''I am interested in a better quality fabric''; now Mrs. Fournier (the prospect) is the sender and the salesperson is the receiver. (By the way, let's hope the salesperson shows Mrs. Fournier a better grade of material.)

In actual practice the exchange between buyer and seller takes place without your consciously following a communication model. The only reason for the analytical approach in this chapter is that your understanding of the communication model can help you improve your communication strategy.

Communication based on your past patterns and habits may not be the most effective way. Understanding the model and its four components will help you develop a more effective sales communication strategy.

EXHIBIT 3.3
A COMMUNICATION EXAMPLE

Sender	Message	Receiver
1. *Salesperson*, explaining product or service	Benefits of ownership	*Customer*, listening to sales presentation
2. *Customer*, responding to salesperson	Wants, needs, objections	*Salesperson*, listening to customer's needs and objections
3. *Salesperson*, restating, clarifying features of product or service	Elimination of objections	*Customer*, accepting message and deciding to buy

AVOIDING SOME COMMON BARRIERS TO COMMUNICATION

The communication model is simple. The communication process may also appear to be simple, but it is not. In practice, good communication is difficult to achieve, and perfect communication—communication where there is no distortion of meaning—is almost never achieved. This is true whether we are talking about a wife communicating with her husband, a mother communicating with her child, an author communicating with a reader, or a salesperson communicating with a prospect. Many things create barriers to communication, and poor communication can lose a sale. The following happened to a colleague.

> "Well, now, it's so nice to be able to meet with you," said Mr. Gladston while heartily shaking the hand of the professor. Gladston was a salesperson for Inter-Continental Life Insurance Company, and he was meeting with Professor Milton to explain a new convertible decreasing-term policy he thought would interest the professor.
>
> "I'm interested in knowing how the benefits of this new policy compare with similar policies, and also how it fits in with my present protection program," said the professor.
>
> "We'll start right at the beginning," replied Gladston. "I'll take it step by step. Insurance can be very complicated, you know, and most people don't know beans about it."
>
> The professor quickly interrupted, "I realize it's complicated for most people, but we can skip the easy steps for me. Let's get to the heart of the question I asked. After all, I've taught insurance for over twelve years, and as a matter of fact, before that I worked for an insurance company."
>
> "Ah, yes, that's fine—very nice, indeed. Now, let's get on with it. First, let's look at these cartoon flash cards the company has prepared to illustrate the new policy."
>
> The professor interrupted, "Mr. Gladston, I've enjoyed meeting with you, but I've just remembered that I have an important faculty meeting to attend. Thank you for coming. I'll get in touch with you if I'm interested." With that, the professor excused himself and left the room.
>
> "What? But—wait! I haven't explained the policy yet! I'll make it very clear." Alone in the room, Gladston muttered, "That's the problem with selling insurance. It's too complicated for people to understand, and people are afraid of the unknown. Why, even the professor . . ."

In this case, Gladston's mental set interfered with his ability to listen. This inability to listen caused an inability to communicate and, in turn, an inability to sell. The interrelationship between communication and sales is that basic: Poor communication skills result in poor selling skills.

How can poor communication skills be avoided? By learning to recognize some of the common barriers to communication so that you can avoid them or work around them in relating to a prospect. The following sections include some common barriers you should learn to recognize and overcome. The list is not exhaustive; you can undoubtedly think of additional barriers from your own experiences.

EXHIBIT 3.4

Mental Set

Mental set is a term used by psychologists to describe preconceived or preformed attitudes. Some behavioral scientists refer to mental set as *psychological set*. A mental set may be useful in interpreting new experiences, but it can also interfere with your ability to receive messages accurately. Mental sets result from our developing mental patterns on the basis of past experiences. For example, quickly read the words in Exhibit 3.4. Do they look okay to you? If so, read the exhibit again, this time slowly—word by word. You probably noticed the extra word *the* in the triangle. The reason this would not be apparent the first time is that most people are accustomed (that is, have a mental set) to reading words in groups. Most do not often perceive single words.

The same is often true when we perceive people: We frequently judge a person by the group in which we meet him or her, and we may generalize on the basis of similar earlier experiences. In selling, you need to be aware of the presence of a possible mental set in presenting your product or service to your prospect. This can be a cause of communication breakdown that is apt to interfere with effective selling. For example, you are presenting a salary-deduction savings plan to a prospect. If the prospect is by nature a thrifty person, the mental set will help your sale because the prospect will be sympathetic to the message you are sending. If, on the other hand, your prospect is a spendthrift, the mental set presents a definite communication barrier, because the prospect is interested in spending, not saving.

EXHIBIT 3.5
MAKE SURE MENTAL SET DOESN'T CAUSE A COMMUNICATION BREAKDOWN

Differences in Perception

Because of individual differences and differences in past experiences, two individuals may see and interpret the same stimuli two different ways. For example, two witnesses at the scene of an accident, when later asked to recall what they saw, will frequently report different facts or sequences. This is due to differences in perception, which cause us to focus on those stimuli that are easiest for us to pick up because of our interest, background, or previous experience.

A very simple example is shown in Exhibit 3.6. Look at the cube, and with a pencil, outline the square that is the face of the cube (that is, the square or side which is closest to you). Then ask several classmates how they interpreted this figure. More than likely, some will have seen another side as the face. It is important to note that everyone in your class was exposed to the same stimulus: The lines are clearly shown and are identical in all copies of the text. However, some of you saw the side shaded in Exhibit 3.7a as the closest side (the dominant side), and some saw the side shaded in Exhibit 3.7b as the closest side. In other words, you perceived the same stimuli differently.

As a salesperson, you need to be aware of differences in perception. Once the differences, if any, have been determined, you can usually clear up matters with further explanation so that everyone perceives the same message.

Prejudice

Prejudice is another barrier to sales communication. It is closely related to mental set and differences in perception. In many respects it is more difficult to deal with, because it is emotionally steeped in one's background and subculture. Prejudice is an adverse judgment or opinion formed beforehand or without knowledge or examination of the facts.[2] Prejudice may be based on major factors, such as race, religion, skin color, sex, body build, or geographical differences. But it can also include "minor" things, such as hairstyle, type of dress, tone of voice, regional accent, etc. The important thing to remember about prejudice is that it is based upon generalizations that are erroneous.

Everyone hopes that prejudice will decrease with the passage of time. But this text is for today. As a salesperson you must learn to live with prejudice, to recognize it when you find it an obstacle to effective selling communication, and to deal with it. (This is covered in greater detail in Chapters 11 and 12.)

Appearance

By the term *appearance* we are referring to the visual impact of the two parties to the communication process: The salesperson (sender) has a visual impact on the prospect (receiver), and the prospect has a visual impact on the salesperson.

EXHIBIT 3.6

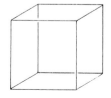

[2]William Morris (ed.), *The American Heritage Dictionary*, Houghton Mifflin, Boston, 1978, p. 1033.

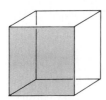 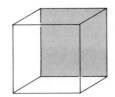

EXHIBIT 3.7

There are two things to remember about appearance. One is that the salesperson, knowing something about mental set and prejudice, can control his or her appearance to minimize the negative effects and to maximize the positive effects. (We'll discuss this in more detail in the next section of this chapter.) The second thing to remember is that the salesperson's own prejudice or mental set about the prospect's appearance may cause a communication breakdown if precautions are not taken.

A successful real estate broker once recalled a recent experience wherein her mental set against a prospect almost cost her the commission on a $200,000 house. She was sitting alone in the office on a quiet Sunday morning when her tranquility was broken by the roar of a Harley-Davidson motorcycle. A windblown, bearded driver hopped off, came into the office, and appeared somewhat out of place with his faded jeans and sweaty T-shirt. The realtor, assuming he had stopped to ask directions, was about to dismiss him when he asked whether she had any listings for contemporary-style homes in the $200,000 price range. There was, of course, considerably more discussion, questioning, and qualifying before she knew that she had an excellent prospect on her hands. The prospect was, in fact, a very successful pilot with a major airline who happened to enjoy dressing casually on the weekends. She sold him a house for $200,000. Multiply that amount times 6 percent if you would like to know how much a mental set about appearance could have cost her!

A similar experience happened to a yacht salesman, Larry White, at the Rex Marine Center, Inc. "This guy was here last year, but he dressed in old work clothes and everyone ignored him." It almost cost a $430,000 sale on a 50-foot Hatteras luxury cruiser. White added, "Just try to remember that sometimes that dirt under their fingernails is from burying money in the back yard."[3]

Listening Habits

"If you listen carefully—with your eyes and your brain as well as your ears—most prospects will tell you how to close them."[4]

[3]Tim Metz, *Wall Street Journal*, Oct. 8, 1981, p. 14.
[4]Alan N. Schoonmaker and Douglas B. Line, "Closing the Sale—A Special Report," *Sales and Marketing Management*, September 1977, p. 20.

Poor listening habits are one of the major causes of breakdown in verbal communication. If there is no listening, there will be no communication. Poor listening habits can hurt the salesperson in two ways. The first way is most obvious: If the prospective customer is not listening, the sales presentation is to no avail, and the sale will not be made. Therefore, it is important to get the prospect's attention before presenting the sales message. (Several ways of getting attention are described later in the chapters on the sales interview.) The second way that poor listening hurts is less obvious but just as important: The salesperson will miss valuable information which could be used to qualify the prospect and to determine what best fills the prospect's needs. Unfortunately, some salespeople perceive their role in the communication process as being exclusively that of sender. Some tips on effective listening are given in Exhibit 3.9.

Distractions

Any outside stimuli which are not related to communication are *distractions*. Distractions cause communication breakdown because they may cause the at-

EXHIBIT 3.8
APPEARANCES CAN BE DECEIVING; MAKE SURE IT DOESN'T PRECIPITATE A MENTAL SET OR PREJUDICE OR COST A SALE

EXHIBIT 3.9

SUCCESSFUL SALESPEOPLE ARE EFFECTIVE LISTENERS!

Some of our most successful salespeople are better listeners than talkers. This does not mean they cannot express themselves effectively. It means that they are listeners first and talkers second. In fact, there are many competent salespeople who are not spectacularly eloquent. But a successful salesperson who is not a good listener is a rarity. Here are some suggestions to help you become a more effective listener:

• *Listen with your mind as well as your ears.* Be like the owl rather than the rabbit. The rabbit, characterized by big ears, is not the smartest of creatures. The owl, with its tiny ears, is the symbol of wisdom.

• *Don't interrupt.* Your objective is to get the prospect talking, especially in the early stages of the interview when you are trying to listen and learn about the prospect's needs, wants, and problems. The more the prospect talks, the more you learn.

• *Listen with respect.* No matter how ridiculous a prospect's question or objection may seem to you, it is a serious matter to the prospect. Show your respect for the prospect's comments. Remember that it is volunteered information which will aid in the closing.

• *Remember your purpose.* You are trying to determine and satisfy a prospect's needs. All of your communication should lead up to this purpose. Impress your prospect with your product or service, not just your personal charm.

tention of the sender or receiver to wander. Typical distractions in personal selling include noise, interruptions, telephone ringing, uncomfortable temperature, and any other thing which is extraneous to the selling interview itself. The salesperson should make sure that the setting for the sales presentation has the fewest possible distractions.

Poor Organization of Facts and Ideas

Sometimes a receiver makes every effort to understand the message but can't because of the sender's failure to organize the facts and ideas properly. Lack of organization may be due to the sender's inability to organize logically, but more often it results from lack of preparation. In selling, lack of preparation is a problem that is easily solved. Familiarity with the product or service, familiarity with the presentation itself—whether it is memorized, outlined, or ad-libbed—and practice runs or rehearsals will help you present facts and ideas in organized and effective ways. (There are some suggestions for ways to organize in Chapters 9 and 10.)

Lack of Prior Knowledge or Experience

As a message sender, you may be well-organized and present the message clearly and still have a communication breakdown because of the receiver's lack of knowledge or experience. This lack might result from age, experience, or prejudice. For example, a child may have difficulty understanding certain adult experiences. Sometimes education is the problem. A prospect who is not an engineer might have difficulty understanding a very technical sales presentation for a turbo engine. Communication breakdowns can be minimized if you are aware of the prospect's background and tailor your presentation to the comprehension level of the prospect. One note of caution is in order here, however. Care must be taken to avoid "talking down" to the prospect. To do so usually builds resentment, which in itself can be a barrier to communication. There are ways to explain what must be explained without demeaning the prospect's status.

Vocabulary

Lack of a working vocabulary on either side, the sender's or the receiver's, can cause a communication breakdown. Vocabulary is an essential selling tool. To be an effective communicator in selling, you must use words which mean something to the buyer. This does not necessarily mean short words or long words. It means words that fit into the prospect's frame of reference, words the buyer is sure to understand. (See Exhibit 3.10.)

The salesperson is in a position to work on avoiding communication breakdown caused by vocabulary. Your selling vocabulary can be improved by participating in training programs in order to increase product knowledge and by participating in self-improvement programs (which might include personal and professional reading and formal educational courses).

EXHIBIT 3.10

"WORDS ARE BUT THE SKINS OF THOUGHTS"

So said Thomas Carlyle over a hundred years ago, and it is just as timely and true today as it was then.

The heart of effective communication is the degree to which the words *fit* the thoughts. The closer the fit, the better the communication.

When the bee stings you, a good, loud "Ouch!" fits your feelings and thoughts more aptly than saying softly, "I believe my skin has been pierced by an insect."

Generally, you should also avoid jargon, since jargon usually does not enhance the communication process. However, you may use jargon if it is the jargon of the prospect. For example, when you are selling to a retail account, *turnover* would be a useful word.

Emotions

Communication can be badly distorted or completely blocked by certain emotions. Fear and anger are the two emotions that most often interfere with good selling communication. A common fear met by salespeople is the buyer's fear of being cheated or being taken advantage of. These fears may be based on experiences the prospect has had with unscrupulous salespeople. Anger may enter into the sales process as a result of an unskilled or insensitive salesperson pressuring the prospect or making obvious attempts to manipulate him or her. As a salesperson, you should be sensitive to these emotions and reactions and learn to deal with them through honesty, good communication, and the establishment of trust.

OVERCOMING THE BARRIERS

Once you've learned to recognize some of the common barriers to good sales communication, you're in a better position to work at improving your communication. Probably the two most important rules to follow are *know your listener* and *know your purpose*. It is also important to know your subject, which is why all of Chapter 5 is devoted to this.

The reason it is important to know your listener and know your purpose is that you can adapt the variables of the sales communication process to them. You can work to overcome your mental sets so they don't cause a barrier, and you can try to avoid any known mental sets in your prospect. You can at least recognize and understand differences in perception between you and your prospect. For example, the purchase of a $75,000 house is a rather routine occurrence for an experienced real estate person, but to a first-time buyer, it is a huge financial decision and probably quite traumatic. Understanding the buyer's point of view will allow you to handle the sales process more skillfully. You will remember to calm the buyer's apprehension and treat the sale with respect for its importance to the buyer.

Similarly, if you can understand some of your own prejudices and work to avoid them, you'll increase the chances of good communication. Recognizing the prejudices of the prospect might help you steer the dialogue away from this potential barrier. Also, by remembering the purpose of your communication—to provide information and to make a sale—you will avoid the natural temptation to set the prospect straight about his or her prejudice. By keeping your purpose in mind, you are in a better position to organize your presentation so it will be clear, logical, and persuasive. (We talk a lot about this in the chapters on the sales interview.) Try to determine ahead of time how much knowledge and experience the prospect has so you can adjust your message accordingly. Try to choose a vocabulary that is readily understandable by the prospect, and be ready to adjust your level up or down after analyzing the prospect's reactions.

There are several important areas in effective sales communication where you are much in control. That is, you are in a position to improve yourself and thereby increase the chance of a successful sales interview. These areas include image and appearance, voice, active listening techniques, building of empathy, and observing nonverbal communication.

EXHIBIT 3.11
DON'T COMPLICATE THE SIMPLE; SIMPLIFY THE COMPLEX

52

Image and Appearance

Many people will argue that a person's wardrobe, grooming, and hairstyle provide superficial clues about that person and that they should be set aside so more important things about the person can be considered. Although this argument may be valid, it conflicts with reality in research concerning image and appearance and the effect they have on the first several minutes of the communication process.

The importance of appearance is indicated by activities in colleges and corporations. Recently, for example, over 200 MBA students at the Wharton School of the University of Pennsylvania crowded into a day-long seminar on executive dress. And corporations like Equitable Life and Flair make available professional advice on business attire.[5]

One of the most significant studies done relating to the importance of first impressions was conducted by A. S. Luchins. Luchins referred to these first impressions as the *primacy effect*. Under properly controlled experimental conditions, Luchins separated students into two groups: group E-I and group I-E. Group E-I was asked to read the following description of a young man named Jim:

> Jim left the house to get some stationery. He walked out into the sun-filled street with two of his friends, basking in the sun as he walked. Jim entered the stationery store, which was full of people. Jim talked with an acquaintance while he waited for the clerk to catch his eye. On his way out, he stopped to chat with a school friend who was just coming into the store. Leaving the store, he walked toward school. On his way out he met the girl to whom he had been introduced the night before. They talked for a short while, and then Jim left for school.[6]

They then read a second paragraph:

> After school Jim left the classroom alone. Leaving the school, he started on his long walk home. The street was brilliantly filled with sunshine. Jim walked down the street on the shady side. Coming down the street toward him, he saw the pretty girl whom he had met on the previous evening. Jim crossed the street and entered a candy store. The store was crowded with students, and he noticed a few familiar faces. Jim waited quietly until the counterman caught his eye and then gave his order. Taking a drink, he sat down at a side table. When he had finished the drink he went home.[7]

Group I-E, the second group, was asked to read the same two paragraphs, but in reverse order. After both groups had read the paragraphs in the order given to them, they were asked to write a personality sketch of Jim based on the information they had received. If you will look again at the paragraphs above, you will see that Luchins has described Jim in the first paragraph as being decidedly extroverted (E) and in the second paragraph as being decidedly introverted (I).

Most members of group E-I described Jim as being extroverted, whereas group I-E described Jim as an introvert. Luchins concluded that the primacy effect does exist. This means that the information presented *first* and received *first* is the

---

[5]Charles J. Rollo, "A Man's Guide to Dressing Well for Business," *Money*, February 1982, p. 85.
[6]A. S. Luchins, "Primacy Recency in Impression Formation," in Carl I. Hovland et al. (eds)., *The Order of Presentation in Persuasion*, vol. 1, Yale University Press, New Haven, Conn., 1957, pp. 33–34.
[7]Ibid.

EXHIBIT 3.12

DRESSING THE PART

A large part of the primacy effect (or first impressions) of salespeople is a direct result of their apparel. There has been much attention given to the effect of clothing. John T. Malloy, a clothing consultant, suggests the following specifically for salespeople.

> In addition to the general guidelines involving size, age, sex, race, socioeconomic background, geography, occupational orientation and product significance, there are some rules that some salesmen should adhere to, all the time. They are:

1. If you have a choice, dress affluently.
2. Always be clean; it is not always necessary to be obsessively neat, but it is imperative to be clean.
3. If you are not sure of the circumstances of a selling situation, dress more—rather than less—conservatively than normal.
4. Never wear any item that identifies any personal association or belief, unless you are absolutely sure that the person to whom you are selling shares those beliefs. This rule includes school rings, masonic rings, ties that are connected with a particular area, political buttons, religious symbols, etc.
5. Always dress as well as the people to whom you are selling.
6. Never put anything on your hair that makes it look shiny or greasy.
7. Never wear sunglasses, or glasses that change tint as the light changes. People must see your eyes if they're to believe you.
8. Never wear any jewelry that is not functional, and keep that simple. Big rings, bracelets, and gaudy cuff links are absolutely taboo.
9. If it is part of your regalia, always carry a good attache case.
10. Always carry a good pen or pencil, nothing cheap or junky.
11. [For men:] If you have a choice, wear an expensive tie.
12. Never take off your suit jacket unless you have to. It weakens your authority.
13. Whenever possible, look in the mirror before you visit a client.

Source: John T. Malloy, *Dress for Success,* Warner, New York, 1976, pp. 147, 148.

most decisive in forming general impressions. Subsequent encounters are influenced by this primacy effect. In selling you should make sure your primacy effect is as positive as possible.[8] (See Exhibit 3.12.)

Voice

In some respects, your voice has the same effect on the communication process as appearance does. The quality of your voice itself is part of your primacy effect.

---

[8]Incidentally, Luchins did find that the negative primacy effect could be lessened or eliminated by informing people of its effect and by warning them of the dangers of making snap judgments.

A good speaking voice generally enhances the content of your message, while a poor speaking voice usually detracts from it.

There are several components of voice quality over which we have some control, namely, volume, pitch, and articulation. You can work on these components to improve your speaking voice. For example, the pitch of your voice usually rises when you are nervous, and you tend to speak more rapidly. Both high pitch and rapid pace are distractions. To improve your pitch, listen to others speak— and to yourself. Notice how a high pitch is less attractive (except for adding emphasis and variety). Practice varying your pitch and find a comfortable, pleasant range. Read the following sentences aloud to a friend or into a tape recorder: "I want this sale" and "I'm really enthusiastic about our new product lines." Pay attention to the pitch. Try varying it. Was one way preferable to the other?

Volume is important so that you can be heard clearly. Although it normally is not a problem in a sales presentation to a single prospect, it may be a problem if you are presenting to a group. One common problem to watch out for is letting your voice trail off before the end of a sentence.

Articulation means how clearly you say each speech sound—particularly the consonants. Many of us become too lazy with our lips. *Want to* becomes *wanna*. *Going to* becomes *gonna*. *Selling* becomes *sellin*. Although you'll never get arrested for it, poor articulation can give the prospect an impression of sloppiness and poor attention to detail—images you want to try to avoid.

Active Listening

Earlier in this chapter we mentioned that poor listening can be a barrier to effective sales communication. Unfortunately, the emphasis in sales training programs is often placed on the act of *sending* the message, since speaking is the active part of the sales communication process. *Listening* appears to be the inactive part. We stress the word *appears* because, in fact, listening should be an active process.

Active listening is a process which employs many techniques. To actually listen, you have to concentrate on what the speaker is saying and try to ignore any distractions. Avoid the tendency to use listening time to formulate what it is you want to say as soon as the speaker stops talking. Instead, listen actively and, when the speaker pauses, acknowledge what it is she or he has said. A very positive form of acknowledgment is to paraphrase the main point the speaker has made. The act of repeating not only assures that you received the message accurately but also helps set it in your mind, thus enhancing the memory process for future recall. Additionally, paraphrasing generally flatters the speaker; most people like to hear you repeat what they have said.

Active listening aids the sales process immeasurably. It permits you to secure as much information as the speaker (customer or prospect) possesses or, at the least, is willing to share. Good listening skills please the buyer. People like to be acknowledged and listened to; it makes them feel worthwhile and important. It puts them in a positive frame of mind and therefore improves the relationship between the two parties to the sales process. A good relationship, in turn, pro-

EXHIBIT 3.13
HOW TO WIN A MILLION-DOLLAR CONTRACT WITHOUT SAYING A WORD

The electrical contracting company president was distraught. Three industrial electrical contractors had been given a chance to summarize their cases before a committee that would decide which supplier would get a million-dollar contract for all the electrical work in the new textile mill.

What a time to wake up with a severe attack of laryngitis! Nonetheless, she appeared at the meeting and sadly wrote on a pad, "I have lost my voice."

"I'll do the talking for you," said the textile company president. "Your technical data and quotations are already in, anyway." And he did so. All the electrical contractor did was smile and nod.

The *silent* salesperson was awarded the contract. She later confessed that if she had not lost her voice, she would have lost the contract. She had had a preconceived and inaccurate idea about the whole proposition. This only became clear when she heard the textile company president take her facts and present them from a different perspective.

"I discovered how it pays to let the other person do the talking."

vides a firm foundation to help make your sales techniques effective. (See Exhibits 3.13 and 3.14.)

Building Empathy

Empathy becomes possible if you mentally put yourself in the other person's shoes. In the selling situation, it is pretending you are the buyer. See the selling

EXHIBIT 3.14
THE TEN GREATEST SALESPERSONS—TEN GOOD LISTENERS

Robert L. Shook, chairman of the board of American Executive Corporation, made a study of leading salespersons and, in his book *The Ten Greatest Salespersons—What They Say about Selling*, made the following observation: "The ten greatest are all people who listen." In the same book, Shook quoted Joe Gandolfo, the salesperson who sold more than a billion dollars worth of insurance in one year, as saying, "Selling is ninety-eight percent understanding human beings and two percent product knowledge. . . . Asking a lot of questions and doing a lot of listening . . . that's the best way to understand people. . . . God gave you two ears and one mouth. . . . He meant for you to do twice as much listening as talking."

Source: Robert L. Shook, *The Ten Greatest Salespersons: What They Say about Selling,* Harper & Row, New York, 1978, pp. 25, 29.

process from your prospect's point of view. Empathy is a state of total communication with another person: an understanding of another's thoughts, feelings, and emotions at a particular moment. The salesperson should try to mentally reverse the normal role situation and say, "What would I want the salesperson to do for me if I were the prospect," or "What would I be hoping to get out of this transaction."

The first step in building empathy usually is building rapport. This can be done in several ways. For example, by a sincere smile, by bringing up a subject of common interest or of special interest to the buyer, by offering the person a seat or a cup of coffee, or through any other social amenity.

Observing Nonverbal Communication

Nonverbal communication is a catchall phrase to cover the areas of communication which cannot be classified as the spoken or written word. It includes hand gestures, facial expressions, body carriage, and posture. It also includes the use of *timing,* knowing when to ask for the sale; *silence,* knowing when to remain quiet and how to interpret a silence; and *tone of voice,* knowing what a change in tone means in reference to the content of the message.

Research suggests that nonverbal communication may more accurately reflect a person's true feelings than does verbal communication. Thus it can be said that we may use language as much to conceal as to reveal our true feelings and actions.

Posture can give you clues about a prospect (or can give the prospect clues about yourself). For example, a rigid posture with the head held stiffly erect, the arms pressed to the sides, and the muscles taut would signal tension or uncertainty. Posture can also relate to the degree of liking and acceptance. How much we like or accept someone may show in the degree to which we turn our legs and shoulders toward the other person. Attitude similarly can be indicated by *postural congruence*—the extent to which two or more people shift to maintain similar posture. Exhibit 3.15 gives you several examples of nonverbal signals.

OTHER FORMS OF COMMUNICATION

Written Communication

Written communication can be an integral part of the sales process. Letters written to obtain leads, preapproach sales letters, follow-up sales letters, and other correspondence are part of the total sales process. (This is covered in Chapter 7.) When writing a sales letter, the salesperson should be aware of the two basic aspects of the letter: the message itself and the package that carries the letter. The message should be well-organized, clear, and concise and should stress things of interest to the prospect—benefits. Obviously, care should be taken to observe the basic rules of grammar, punctuation, etc. The package includes selecting the appropriate stationery, properly spacing the message on

EXHIBIT 3.15
SOME CLASSIC NONVERBAL SIGNALS (*Source:* Courtesy of Gerhard Gshwandtner & Associates.)

Classic green light: Full speed ahead.

Classic yellow: Guarded and reserved.

Expressing superiority:
The hands say yellow.

The buyer in doubt:
Yellow again

Tension signals yellow,
and time for open questions.

Frustration, and very possibly no sale:
Another yellow

The yellow signal stand-off—
and no sale.

Meeting the buyer's
yellow signals with openness.

Red light: It might be too late to recover.

the page, and properly addressing the envelope. The importance of proper packaging to the reader of the letter is that it generates the first impression. He or she sees the overall effect of the letter before reading it. If it appears sloppy, it is apt to detract from the content.

Telephone Communication

Telephone communication is an important part of the salesperson's job (and is covered in more detail in Chapter 18). Obviously, a clear, audible, and courteous voice is an advantage during a phone conversation. Whether the salesperson is placing a call or answering a call, the use of his or her proper name and that of the company or affiliation is important. In placing calls, in order to appear prepared, use of notes may be helpful. Such preparation can help you avoid being sidetracked from the purpose of the call and leaving out necessary information. Similarly, when receiving calls, you'll find it helpful to take notes for future reference.

RECAP

Communication is the most essential element of the selling process. For communication to be effective, we must consider each of the four components of the model: the sender, the message, the receiver, and the channel chosen to transmit the message. This model is not static, and the sender and the receiver often switch roles.

With each of the four components, there can be several problem areas that create barriers to effective communication. The barriers include mental set, differences in perception, prejudice, appearance, listening habits, distractions, poor organization of facts and ideas, lack of knowledge or experience, vocabulary, and emotions. It is important for you to be able to spot and overcome each of these barriers.

A number of techniques can be used to improve your communication. One technique is to present the appropriate image through careful attention to appearance. Others are to develop better listening techniques, to build empathy, and to develop skills in observing and applying nonverbal communication.

Other forms of communication which are important to the selling process are written communication and telephone communication.

REVIEW QUESTIONS

1. How would you define communication?
2. Why is communication so basic to the selling process?
3. Diagram the communication model. Briefly describe each of the four parts. Give an example of each.
4. The text states that the communication model is not static. Why?

5. What is a communication barrier? Why are communication barriers important for the salesperson to understand?
6. What is the primacy effect?
7. Define mental set.
8. How can differences in perception be a barrier to communication? Give an example.
9. How does appearance relate to the communication process?
10. Can listening habits be a barrier to the communication process? If so, how?
11. Describe how poor organization of facts and ideas can be a barrier to communication. Describe also how lack of prior knowledge or experience can be a barrier to communication.
12. In what ways can vocabulary affect the sales communication process?
13. Give examples of emotions that may distort or inhibit effective communication.
14. What is meant by the term *active listening*?
15. Define nonverbal communication. Give several examples of nonverbal communication.

DISCUSSION QUESTIONS

1. From your own experiences, which communication model is more believable—verbal or nonverbal? What do you think is the cause of this?
2. "Mental set can be useful in interpreting new experiences, but it also can hinder one's ability to receive accurately." Discuss the above statement in terms of your own experiences.
3. Discuss the basic communication model. What changes would you make, if any, to adapt it better to the sales communication process?
4. "The primacy effect can help or hinder the sales communication process." Is this statement contradictory? What does it mean?

LEARNING EXPERIENCES

1. For a period of two or three days, keep a record of the nonverbal messages you observe. Compare your list with those recorded by your classmates. Which nonverbal messages appear most frequently?
2. Write a one-page case study of a communication failure that you recently have observed, read about, or been part of. Which of the barriers mentioned in this chapter was the basic cause? Could it have been avoided? If so, how?
3. Jot down the first impression you had of five of your classmates. Has your perception changed? If so, how?
4. Think of someone (preferably in your class) who gave you a false first impression. Briefly write your first impression. Then indicate what verbal and nonverbal messages you received to form this impression. Honestly indicate if any

mental sets or prejudices influenced your decision, and note them. Indicate what *changed* your impression. If you're feeling brave, ask the subject to do the same exercise for you!

5. Interview any experienced salesperson. Discuss communication and perception with that person. Ask the salesperson to elaborate on how he or she perceives buyers and selects cues in assessing them.

CASE

TODD THIEBAULT

Todd Thiebault is a sales representative for the Total Systems Communications Company. Total Systems is a small company that specializes in the communication needs of small- to middle-sized companies. It analyzes a client company's needs and proposes a system to meet those needs. The hardware for the system might include telephone fixtures, intercom systems, public address systems, two-way radios, computer terminals, and so on. Total Systems also designs or purchases the forms needed to expedite memos and reports.

Todd has been with Total Systems for a year and three months. His job is basically that of contacting prospective client firms and selling them on the need for Total Systems' analysis services. Todd enjoys his work. He was selected for this position partly because of his extroverted personality, his facility with words, and his excellent appearance. Todd had been active in a number of extracurricular activities while in college, including intramural sports and drama. He had the lead in several theatrical productions on the campus. Generally, he was well liked by his peers because of his ability to take charge of a situation and because he was never at a loss for words and could fill in any silence with a witty comment.

Perhaps because of all this, Todd had outstanding success in getting presentation interviews with his clients. He was able to dazzle them with his presentation and often got rave reviews for his performance. But Todd did not close as many sales as he could have. Although he had an excellent track record in getting the initial interview and impressing everyone with his presentation, his record for systems sold was not good. Jim Ryan, his sales manager, said, "It just doesn't make any sense. I'm not sure what is going wrong. Todd's a valuable salesperson, and I want to help him for his own sake as well as the company's. But I'm not sure where to begin."

Questions

1. Do you feel that there is a possible communication problem?
2. If you were called in as a consultant by Total Systems, what areas would you examine? Why?
3. What suggestions do you have to solve Todd's (and the company's) problem? Try to be as specific as possible.

FOUR

CHAPTER OBJECTIVES

To explain what motivates buyers and sellers and what they need from you as a salesperson

To examine the prospect's behavior from a psychological and a sociological point of view

To acquaint you with some of the psychological theories of Freud, Maslow, and Dichter

To introduce you to social class and its variables and the influence of groups and reference groups on individual buying behavior

To examine several other theories related to selling, including the life-cycle theory, the quadrant theory, and psychographics

CHAPTER OUTLINE

BUYER BEHAVIOR

I've dealt with thousands of men in my life, and the only one thing that stands out most clearly in my mind is that they were all different.

William Wrigley, Jr.*

Some people are ready to buy; they know what they want and when they want it. They've examined the competing products and alternatives before they come to the marketplace.

Others are just looking. They use the buying process as a way of gathering information about products or services. They take their time. They don't want to be pushed.

Still others use the buying process as a form of recreation. It's a challenge, a game. They like to match wits with every salesperson. But others are suspicious of salespeople. They see salespeople as the enemy and don't trust them.

The list of types of buyers and buyer behavior goes on and on. That's the purpose of this chapter. In this chapter, we will discuss buyer behavior from a psychological and a sociological point of view. We'll examine what motivation is and how it affects buyers. You'll see how different buyers are affected in different ways depending on their personality structure.

In this chapter, you will become acquainted with some of the psychological theories of Freud, Maslow, and Dichter, as well as the sociological theory of Warner. You will also become familiar with the life-cycle theory, quadrant analysis, and psychographics.

*William Wrigley, Jr., is the founder of Wrigley Chewing Gum.

64

SELLING AND BUYING

The other half of selling is buying. If you understand the process of buying, it makes selling much easier.

Most of the research in consumer motivation indicates that buyers generally buy a product not because of its features but because of the benefits they receive from the product. Benefits to a buyer are the product's or service's ability to meet certain needs. "What can this product do *for me*?" is the key question in the buyer's mind. You need to have an understanding of the process of need fulfillment and buyer behavior in order to sell. One way for you to learn about need fulfillment and buyer behavior is to examine the current theories in the behavioral sciences—specifically in psychology and sociology—that affect selling and buying.

Thomas Bonoma, professor of marketing at Harvard Business School, states that "seller awareness of and attention to the human factors in purchasing will produce higher percentages of sales. Only the most advanced companies recognize the psychology of buying as a major factor in improving account selection and selling results."[1]

TYPES OF BUYERS

There are many kinds of buyers, but the most useful way of classifying them is into three types: ultimate consumers, resellers, and industrial buyers. All of us act as ultimate consumers when we buy something for our own use or consumption. We are ultimate consumers when we buy cars, when we buy life insurance or homeowner insurance, when we buy food, and when we buy houses to live in. The list is endless. Resellers are buyers who buy a product for resale. Examples would be wholesalers and retailers. Industrial buyers, on the other hand, are buying a product or service which will be used primarily for producing other products or services or which will be used in the organization. Industrial buyers include manufacturers, raw-material processors, and farmers.

Behavioral Characteristics of Major Types Of Buyers

There are several ways that industrial buyers and resellers behave differently from ultimate consumers. This is natural, since their needs and their motivation are often different. Four major areas of difference between industrial buyers and resellers and ultimate consumers are as follows:

1. Industrial buyers and resellers are primarily motivated by economic considerations. They are interested in cost-benefit ratios, rate of return on investment, amortization schedules, etc. This is not to deny that they are not motivated by individual human factors, but it does suggest that the salesperson is safe to assume that a dominant motivation is economic.

[1]Thomas J. Bonoma, "Major Sales: Who Really Does the Buying? *Harvard Business Review*, May–June 1982, p. 111.

2. Industrial buyers and resellers usually make more rational or reasoned buying decisions than do ultimate consumers. Usually based on predetermined needs, these decisions are deliberate and well-planned. Impulse buying and buying based on emotion, colors, fashion, and fads—factors which frequently affect the ultimate consumer—are seldom factors in industrial buying decisions. An exception might be the decision making of a fashion buyer for a retail store.
3. Industrial buyers and resellers in larger companies are usually limited by company policy or procedures in the range of possible decisions they may make. For example, certain predetermined specifications (like tensile strength of steel, chemical composition of a solvent, or governmental regulations) may restrict the choices.
4. Industrial buyers and resellers are often restricted in their ability to make final buying decisions. In larger companies, decisions are often made by a committee or by higher-level management. Often the function of the industrial buyer, generally called a *purchasing agent,* is to gather, organize, and process information for a decision which will be made elsewhere in the organization.

The major focus of this chapter is on what motivates individuals in a buying situation and thus may more often apply to the ultimate consumer than to the industrial buyer. However, keep in mind that the person doing the actual buying, whether industrial buyer, reseller, or ultimate consumer, is usually influenced by other people and by psychological, sociological, and economic factors. It is the degree of importance of each of these factors that varies. (Selling to the industrial buyer is presented in detail in Chapter 15.)

WHAT IS MOTIVATION?

Motivation may be considered a driving force or a necessity to reduce a state of tension.[2] It is all those factors which make people act or move toward certain goals. Buyers are guided by many bases of motivation; some are physiological in their origin, some are psychological or sociological or economic in their origin, and many are combinations of the above.

An example of a physiologically based motivation is hunger. Hunger is actually a state of tension which is relieved by the act of eating. It is brought about by the body's biological need for nourishment; when you are hungry, you are motivated to eat. That is to say, your activities are directed toward the act of eating (or finding a suitable food and then eating it). If the motivation to eat were purely and simply physiological, you would be happy eating anything which could be safely eaten. Most often, however, this is not the case. Because of other existing bases of motivation, such as the sociocultural, psychological, and economic bases, you probably have a preference for certain types of food. For example, your basic motive to eat will be modified by social experiences and background. You may be motivated to seek out or prepare southern fried chicken, whereas another person

[2]Tension may be physiological, psychological, or social and may result from an unfulfilled need.

with the same basic hunger may prefer curried chicken on rice or chicken Tetrazzini served over pasta.

Economic bases of motivation can also be demonstrated by something as simple as where to eat. As an affluent consumer, you might be directed to an expensive restaurant known for its haute cuisine. As an economically minded consumer or one pressed for time, you might be more apt to head for a fast-food restaurant. The psychological bases of motivation may also come into play in fulfilling the need for food. You might have the need to satisfy a larger drive to eat in a fancy restaurant even though it means sacrificing expenditures in some other area. In this case, the prevailing motive would be psychological—perhaps the need to impress someone else or the need to support your psychological self-image. Whatever the reason, the physiological need to satisfy your hunger still exists, but it becomes subordinate to your psychological need to eat at an expensive restaurant.

From the examples you can see that the physiological drives are subject to psychological, social, and economic influences. Any digestible food will reduce hunger, but not all will satisfy the other needs like taste (socially determined) or status and self-image (socially and psychologically determined) or economy. The typical American will not eat horsemeat unless he or she is starving. However, he or she will readily eat corn right off the cob—to the disbelief of many Europeans who consider corn suitable only for livestock.

Differences between Needs and Wants

How often have you said to yourself or someone else, ''I need it, but I don't want it'' or ''I want it, but I don't need it''? Behaviorists often distinguish between the terms *need* and *want*. Salespeople should be aware of the differences, for they may be useful in making a presentation or in closing a sale.

A need can be defined as something (a product or a service) that a person cannot do without. Foods providing basic nutrition are needs. A want is something which is desired but which is not essential to the person's basic functioning. A person whose car *needs* a tune-up may *want* another car (but doesn't really need one). However, the person whose car just blew up on the turnpike *needs* another car, whether he or she *wants* one or not.

Sometimes in selling you can help a buyer turn a want into a need. For example, a buyer may want a new car but doesn't think she needs one. However, it is more than likely that this buyer needs to control her overall expenditures to keep them within her income. (Don't we all?) You may be able to capitalize on the need to economize and translate it into a need for a new car by demonstrating how the new fuel-efficient model will save money on gas and repairs over the long run.

PSYCHOLOGICAL EXPLANATIONS OF MOTIVATION

There are a number of psychological explanations of motivation. The most useful in explaining consumer buying behavior are the *psychoanalytical theory* of

Sigmund Freud, the *hierarchical need theory* of Abraham Maslow, the *personality structure and self-image theory* of Ernest Dichter, and some other general theories of motivation.

The Freudian Theory

Freud's psychological theory states that the personality is made up of three parts: the id, the ego, and the superego. Simply explained, the *id* is the pleasure-seeking and tension-reducing part of the mind which provides for great amounts of uninhibited energy. It is not encumbered by what is right or wrong; it does not concern itself with social restraints. Without regard to morals or ethics, it compulsively seeks pleasure and satisfaction.

The *ego,* or conscious self, imposes some constraints and rationality on the id. It is the part of the mind that provides rationality and helps the individual cope with reality. The ego leads to socially acceptable behavior and can be said to be

EXHIBIT 4.1
THE SALESPERSON HAS TO DEAL WITH THE OFTEN-CONFLICTING WANTS AND NEEDS OF BUYERS

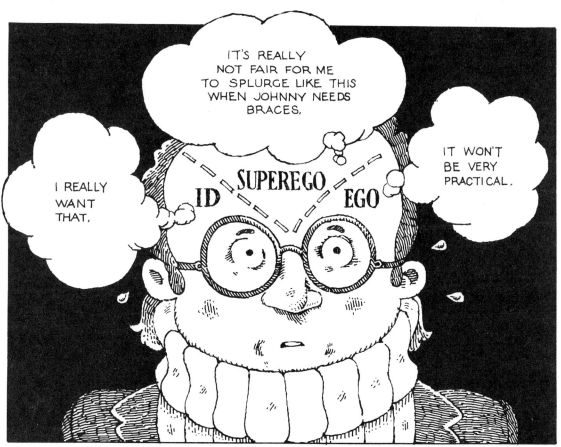

the rational part of the individual as it helps the individual weigh the practical consequences of an act rather than rushing into pleasure blindly.

The *superego* is described by Freud as the individual's conscience. It is the part of the mind which distinguishes between right and wrong. It is the ethical and moralistic mind.

Freud suggested that the mechanisms that lead to behavior are largely unconscious. Thus a person's behavior and motivation are based upon the interaction of the id, the ego, and the superego but in ways in which the person is not consciously aware. Motivation research relies upon clinical findings of psychiatrists and psychologists, and freudian psychology has played a dominant role in understanding buyer behavior over the years.

A significant implication from freudian theory for salespeople is that a person's real motive for buying a product may or may not be known to the person. That is, the real motive may be conscious or unconscious; the buyer may operate from different levels of awareness.

The freudian theory suggests that you, as a salesperson, might have to make the product appeal to the buyer's subconscious: to his or her dreams, hopes, or fears. It also suggests you must provide buyers with socially acceptable rationalizations for their purchasing to satisfy their superegos.

The Maslow Theory

Maslow's hierarchy of needs is a popular explanation of consumer behavior which adds to the salesperson's understanding of the multiple theories of motivation. Maslow's hierarchy consists of five levels of needs arranged in ascending order,[3] as shown in Exhibit 4.2.

The basic level consists of physiological needs, which would include the need for food and water. The next level is safety and security needs, which would include shelter (basic housing) and protection from perils (insurance, burglar alarms, fire alarms). The need for affection, belonging, and affiliation appear next. Examples of how these needs can be met in the marketplace are memberships in clubs and the purchase of cosmetics and grooming aids. The need for esteem and status come next. There are many examples of products or services which focus on fulfilling these needs: expensive executive housing, designer clothes, and certain imported automobiles. The highest level of need in Maslow's hierarchy is the one for self-actualization. This is the point at which the individual is seeking personal fulfillment for its own sake without regard for what others think. It is more difficult to think of specific products or services which meet this need. However, travel, certain publications, educational courses, and art and music products may, in part, fulfill one's need for self-actualization.

It is important to notice that the basis of the theory is that needs are arranged in hierarchical order, beginning with primary, or biologically oriented, needs and transcending these to social needs. The basic needs must be fulfilled, at least partially, before higher-level needs will become motivating forces. Thus an indi-

[3]Abraham H. Maslow, *Motivation and Personality*, Harper, New York, 1954.

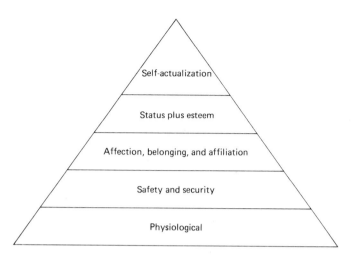

EXHIBIT 4.2
MASLOW'S HIERARCHY OF NEEDS   (*Source:* William C. Weaver,
Nicholas Ordway, and Dennis Tosh, "Satisfying Investment Needs,"
Real Estate Today, February 1979. Used by the permission of the
National Association of Realtors.)

vidual's behavior will focus on obtaining food as long as hunger is present. Not until this basic need is fulfilled will the individual's behavior be concerned with higher-level needs, such as those for esteem and status. For most consumers an adequate level of food must be assured before money will be allocated to higher-order needs for housing, clothing, companionship, and education.

You should also be aware that the same product or service (or group of products or services) may be presented to appeal to different levels of the prospect's needs. For example, housing can be presented to appeal to several needs. An astute salesperson would, of course, emphasize the features of the house in accordance with the level of need fulfillment at which he or she estimates the client to be. This level should be equivalent to the client's *buy button.* If the client appears to be operating at the safety and security level, a real estate salesperson can emphasize the rugged construction of the house, the solid burglar-proof exterior doors, and the low crime rate of the neighborhood. The appeal to the client at the next higher level, belonging and affiliation, would be to emphasize the closeness of the neighbors, the friendliness of the people in the town, and the fact that there are organized social clubs available to them. The appeal to the need for status could be made by pointing out that the property is located in an executive or professional neighborhood or that it has the latest designer kitchen. Selling a house on the basis of appealing to the need for self-actualization is somewhat more difficult. However, in this case, the salesperson should emphasize its uniqueness (not its similarity or closeness to others, which would appeal to a client operating out of a need for belonging), the space that would allow the client to do his or her "own thing," the privacy and quiet, etc. An imaginative salesperson who has determined that the client is operating at Maslow's highest

EXHIBIT 4.3
INVESTMENT HIERARCHY

Maslow's needs	Investment need fulfillment
Self-actualization	(a) Creation of something new (b) Extension of self through physical monument (c) Sense of ownership and territory
Esteem	(d) Status (e) Degree of control allowed (f) Appreciation (g) How investment fits in with overall goals
Belonging	(h) Legality (i) Degree of time required to manage for investment (j) Tax considerations (k) Adequate liquidity
Safety and security	(l) Cash flow (m) Stability of purchasing power (n) Stability of income (o) Adequacy of return (p) Safety of principle (q) Exposure to personal liability
Physiological	(r) Noninvestment expenditures for current consumption needs

Source: William C. Weaver, Nicholas Ordway, and Dennis Tosh, "Satisfying Investment Needs," *Real Estate Today*, February 1979.

level of need would do well to switch from trying to sell the client an existing home to arranging for a contract with an architect and a custom builder to allow the client to truly self-actualize and create his or her own house. (By the way, the commission from this type of sale is usually the same as that from selling an equivalently priced house.)

Exhibit 4.3 shows Maslow's hierarchy with a suggested investment hierarchy. This is an example of how a service can be sold to a client using the psychological theory as a backdrop for the method of the presentation. For example, the lower-level need for safety and security is met by presenting the investment in terms of stability of income and safety of principal. The need for esteem is met by emphasizing the sense of ownership, status of the investment, and appreciation. Self-actualization is shown by the creation of something new.

The Dichter Theory

The Dichter theory emphasizes the influence of four major attitudes in the buying process.[4] These attitudes relate to the client's self-image, which results from an interaction of mental age, family status, professional standing, and psychological income. This is shown in Exhibit 4.4. Mental age may differ from chronological

[4]Ernest Dichter, "How to Tailor Your Selling Identity to the Individual Prospect," *The American Salesman*, January 1959, p. 36.

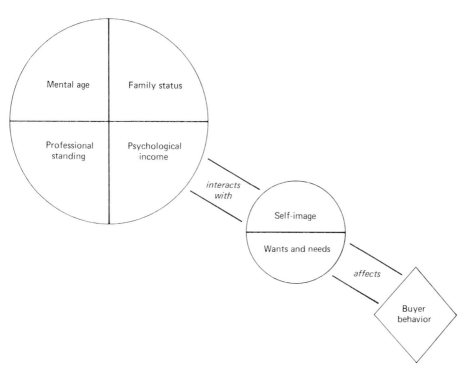

EXHIBIT 4.4
DICHTER'S THEORY

age: A person may wish to think of himself or herself as being older or younger. The component of self-image will affect many buying decisions, particularly those related to clothes or recreational products or services. Family status and professional standing are related to a sociological interpretation of the consumer. Psychological income may or may not relate to actual income. It refers to the attitude toward one's income, whether it is perceived as large, barely adequate, or insufficient.

Other Theories of Motivation

There are several other theories of interest to selling which we will briefly describe.

Some psychologists distinguish between primary and secondary motives. *Primary motives* are those prompted by basic needs and may be met by a variety of basic products. An example of a primary motive is hunger, which, as described above, can be met with any number of food products. *Secondary motives* are learned motives, which cause the behavior to be more discriminating. Thus the hunger may be for a specific food, such as a particular flavor of ice cream.

The same activity may come about from several different needs. For example, the needs for food, companionship, and status may be met by dining at a very prestigious restaurant with a group of close friends. In this way one can fulfill a primary motive for food and a secondary motive and selective appetite for gourmet food, along with other secondary motives of belonging and status while enjoying the company of good friends and the prestige of being seen at the right place by the right people.

In addition to the many motives which may be overlapping, motives may also exist at various levels of awareness. They may be conscious, preconscious, or unconscious. *Conscious motives* are those that a prospect is fully aware of and will usually be willing to discuss. *Preconscious motives* are those the prospect is aware of but is not willing to discuss or those that he or she is not fully aware of. An example is the purchase of an expensive imported car for which the preconscious motive is status but the rationalizations given to the salesperson are good engineering and safety. *Unconscious motives* are those of which a prospect has no awareness. However, psychologists feel that they may have some influence on behavior. Exhibit 4.5 illustrates how different levels of consciousness affect the buying decision. The outcome of this decision-making process is influenced by you, the salesperson.

The discussion of motives generally provides explanation as to why individuals behave as they do. Some of these motives are innate; others, perhaps the majority, are learned. Thus a good many motives are acquired as one becomes socialized in our society. Although members of our society share a great many motives, there are differences that are interesting to study. How the individual behaves as a member of a group, as well as how much influence the group has on the individual, is the field of concern of the sociologist and is important for you as a salesperson.

SOCIOLOGICAL EXPLANATIONS OF MOTIVATION

There is a relationship between the individual's needs and wants and basic motivations and those of the people with whom he or she associates or would like

EXHIBIT 4.5
LEVELS OF CONSCIOUSNESS—EXAMPLE OF MOTIVATION FOR A CAR DECISION

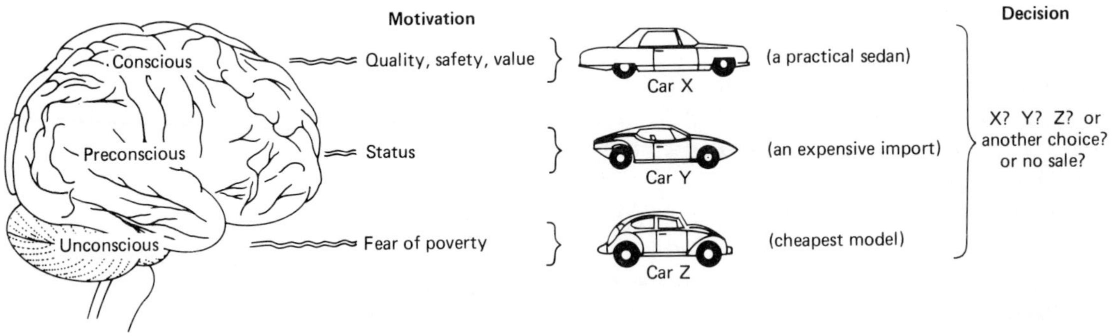

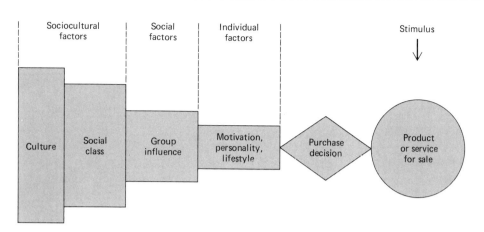

| Sociocultural factors | Social factors | Individual factors | | Stimulus |

EXHIBIT 4.6
FACTORS AFFECTING THE INDIVIDUAL'S BUYING PATTERNS   (*Source:* Adapted from Harold Kassarjian and Thomas Robertson, *Perspectives in Consumer Behavior*, Scott, Foresman, Glenview, Ill., 1968.)

to associate. These associations are the social class and the formal and informal groups of which he or she is part, or would like to be part.

Social Class

In the United States there are neither castes nor royalty. There are just subtle (sometimes not so subtle) differences in the way we live, think, act, and—of importance to the salesperson—buy.

You have probably heard many references to *class* in your everyday conversations, such as, "Inflation is hurting the middle class," "I'm just a working-class person," "He has no class," and "That was a low-class remark." These references to social class are somewhat informal and distorted offshoots of studies done by people like Lloyd Warner.

The importance of social class to the salesperson is in part due to its effect on the prospect's self-perception and values. This in turn affects lifestyle, which consequently affects buying patterns.[5] Exhibit 4.6 illustrates how social class and other social and individual factors affect buying patterns.

A Six-Class System   One of the traditional explanations of social class is that provided by Lloyd Warner. Although it is a theory developed more than a generation ago—since which time numerous social changes have occurred—it is widely referred to and is often the basis of other social-class theories. As a salesperson you will find it useful to be familiar with this theory in understanding

[5]H. Kassarjian and T. Robertson, *Perspectives in Consumer Behavior*, Scott, Foresman, Glenview, Ill., 1973, p. 67.

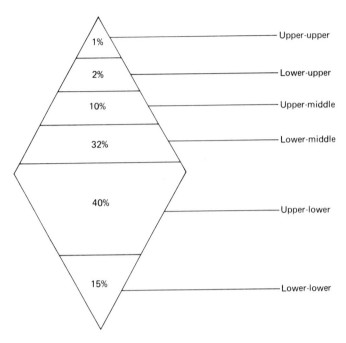

EXHIBIT 4.7
APPROXIMATE PERCENTAGES OF THE POPULATION FALLING
WITHIN WARNER'S SIX SOCIAL CLASSES

differences in buyer behavior. Warner defines a six-class system consisting of the upper-upper class, the lower-upper class, the upper-middle class, the lower-middle class, the upper-lower class, and the lower-lower class.[6] To update, the approximate percentages of the U.S. population that now fall into each class are shown in Exhibit 4.7.

It should be understood that there are no hard or distinct lines between classes; rather, they fall on a continuum of different characteristics and values. (See Exhibit 4.8.) Further, in the United States one's social class is subject to the possibility of movement: There are many examples of people moving from messenger to corporate president.

Notice that the lower-middle class and the upper-lower class are the two largest groups. Combined, they represent almost three-quarters of the population. Many contemporary social scientists refer to this combined group as the American middle class.

Variables of Social Class   Current literature indicates that there are several variables which influence social class. These are of use to the contemporary salesperson because they seem to be common to any of several theories of social

[6]Lloyd Warner, *Social Classes in America*, Harper & Row, New York, 1960, p. 70.

EXHIBIT 4.8
SOME SILLY OBSERVATIONS

- *Upper-class person:* Has elbow sticking through sleeve of Brooks Brothers sport jacket and doesn't care; might have patch sewn on jacket
- *Striving person:* Would be self-conscious about hole in sleeve; might have patch sewn on new jacket for effect; might even have bought it that way

- *Upper-class person:* Probably wouldn't watch corny TV shows; but if so, probably wouldn't hide the fact
- *Striving person:* Might or might not watch corny TV shows; but if so, would probably swear the family to secrecy

- *Upper-class person:* When talking to others about prominent friends, does not refer to them by name
- *Striving person:* When talking to others about prominent *acquaintances,* refers to them by name

- *Upper-class person:* Reads *The New York Times* because she wants to
- *Striving person:* Reads *The New York Times* to let the world know that she's informed

class. The variables are occupation, education, personal prestige, possessions, interaction, and value orientation.

Occupation   A person's occupation plays an important role in determining social status because it is fairly obvious to the observer and can be used to initially place a person. This is particularly true in a mobile society like ours in which we are unable to determine quickly the social background of those we meet. When a person is living in a part of the country where he or she did not grow up, family background is usually unknown. Many studies have shown a very definite pecking order in the status of occupation, with physicians, lawyers, business executives, and other professionals who have advanced degrees given higher status; office workers and small-business owners less status; and unskilled and unemployed workers little or no status.

Education   There is evidence that *education* plays an increasingly important role in American social-class structure. Higher status goes to those with graduate and professional degrees and to those who hold degrees from the more prestigious education institutions.

Personal prestige   The importance of personal prestige is often confirmed through comments from people, such as, ''She's a very successful lawyer,'' ''He's a highly skilled carpenter who does the best woodworking in this area,'' or ''He's the best salesperson Grace Company has seen in years." In cases like these, the individual is granted higher social status than his or her peers and, in some cases, than people in normally higher status occupations.

Possessions   This variable includes things such as houses, furniture, and automobiles, which also confer status.

Interaction   Interaction refers to "who visits with whom." This suggests that a true measure of social status is the social status of those who include you in their group. It is suggested here that whom you might invite to your house for dinner is not as important to your status as who invites you.

Value orientation   The final variable usually mentioned is value orientation, which includes ideas, concepts, time frame, attitude toward education, and philosophy of life.

While most sociologists don't include income as a variable, it is related to education, occupation, and possessions.

Keep in mind that exceptions abound. In selling, you must be careful to use this theory only as a clue to determining the actual needs of your prospect. If care is not taken, you can commit costly errors in making the wrong assumption about the buyer's class position. Unfortunately, the following incident actually happened.

> Scott, a tall, bearded black wearing paint-spotted jeans, a semiwhite T-shirt, and sandals, entered one of the east coast's best men's shops. A salesperson approached him and asked, "What are you looking for, Buddy?"
>
> "I'm not looking for anything, but you might show me your size-42 jackets," replied Scott.
>
> "Joe, take care of this guy. I'm going across the street to get a cup of coffee."
>
> With Joe's help, Scott bought a conservative gray suit and two tweed sport jackets, and Joe earned a commission that would pay for his coffee and more for many months to come. Because of a yen for a cup of coffee and an erroneous snap judgment, the first salesperson lost a commission and the opportunity to meet Professor Scott Calvin, one of the area's foremost artists.

Group Influences

Within the larger context of culture and social class, individuals are usually members of formal and informal groups. Every group can influence a person's behavior and buying decisions. (As an example, consider the effect your family or friends may have had on one of your own recent buying decisions.)

Formal groups are groups to which one belongs and which can be fairly easily identified.

"Phil, a sophomore at Andover, is a preppie." When Phil buys his clothing, you can almost be sure it will be within the confines of the accepted preppie look: Harris tweeds, button-down collars, etc.

"Marjorie has been with the law firm of Witherspoon and Carmudgeon for a year now, and I understand she is doing very well. She really fits in there." Marjorie's clothing and other buying decisions related to her lifestyle are most apt to be influenced by the conservative law firm with which she identifies.

Formal groups, then, include families, clubs, social organizations, educational institutions, places of employment, and other clearly defined groups. *Informal groups,* which also influence individual behavior and buying decisions, include social acquaintances and loosely formed groups in which there is some interaction between individual members.

The extent to which a group influences a buyer is also dependent on the degree to which the buyer belongs. Some individuals *actually* belong to a certain group (or social class), others *think* they belong to a certain group but in fact don't, and still others *would like* to belong to a certain group. In all three cases, the certain group will influence the individual's behavior. In fact, it could be argued that those who strive to belong to a group but don't yet belong would be most influenced by the group's norms.

Whether formal or informal, groups which influence individuals are known as *reference groups.* This suggests that the individual uses the group, either consciously or unconsciously, when making purchasing decisions.

THE LIFE-CYCLE THEORY

The life-cycle theory is predicated on the reasonable assumption that the prospect's buying behavior will be affected by whatever stage in the overall life cycle the prospect is in. Most literature and research seem to agree that there are five general life-cycle phases: the single young adult, the young married (or young household), the middle years, the empty nest, and retirement.

The *single young adult* is characterized by having a relatively large disposable income which will likely be spent on clothing, personal grooming, entertainment, travel, and so on. The *young married* refers to the beginning years of household formation. This phase usually involves marriage (thus its name), although in recent years it has come to include any type of joint-living arrangement. Characteristic buying patterns revolve around household purchases: furniture, appliances, and even houses. The second part of this phase often includes childbearing, with the obvious buying patterns it precipitates: baby equipment, toys, more furniture, and perhaps larger housing. In the *middle years* most adults are at the height of their careers and income. Buying patterns revolve around maintenance of a home (perhaps a newer, larger one), community recognition, and social status. Tuition for children is an important expenditure for some. The *empty nest* is similar to the middle years, except that the children have left the household, so the income, which is still at its peak, is more than adequate for many. Expenditures continue along the lines of the middle years but generally also include upgrading possessions (new, better-quality furniture, appliances, etc.) and spending more money on leisure activities (vacations, travel, and perhaps second or vacation houses). This affluent middle-aged group consists of big spenders, as marketers have discovered. Less eager than previous generations to leave their money to their children, this group tends to splurge on themselves.[7] *Retirement* is generally characterized by a decrease in income and a decline in buying. Buying patterns revolve around health maintenance, leisure activities and hobbies, and, for some, travel.

PSYCHOGRAPHICS

We've discussed several of the psychological determinants of buyer behavior. The collective synonym used for these variables in some of the literature is *psychographics*. Perhaps the major thrust of this concept is the recognition that buyers can be classified by a psychological state of readiness that results largely from lifestyle. This psychological readiness varies from individual to individual and may vary within the same individual buyer over a period of time.

Psychographics, often called *lifestyle analysis,* is useful in providing an understanding about the way consumers behave. For example, by using psychographic analysis, Needham, Harper, and Steers, the Chicago advertising agency, has identified ten major lifestyle classifications.[8] The numbers in parentheses show their estimate of the population within each.

- Thelma, the old-fashioned traditionalist (25 percent)
- Mildred, the militant mother (20 percent)
- Eleanor, the elegant socialite (17 percent)
- Candice, the chic suburbanite (20 percent)
- Cathy, the contented homemaker (18 percent)
- Herman, the retiring homebody (26 percent)
- Fred, the frustrated factory worker (19 percent)
- Dale, the devoted family man (17 percent)
- Scott, the successful professional (21 percent)
- Ben, the self-made businessman (17 percent)

Each of these lifestyle types is thought to have unique activities, interests, and opinions which affect individual product preferences and buying habits.

A Psychographic System for Sales

SRI International, a nonprofit think tank located in Menlo Park, California, has developed a psychographic system for categorizing customers based upon values and lifestyles. More than seventy major corporations, including General Electric, Citibank, General Foods, Lever Bros., and Standard Brands, have used this sys-

---

[7]*Wall Street Journal,* Apr. 16, 1979, sec. 1, p. 6.

[8]Peter W. Bernstein, ''Psychographics Is Still an Issue on Madison Avenue,'' *Fortune,* Jan. 16, 1978, pp. 78–84.

tem. Using psychological theories, SRI has isolated and labeled several types of consumers.[9] A summary of its classification follows:[10]

The Need-Driven   This classification includes "money-restricted" consumers who struggle just to buy the basics. This group is divided into two subgroups:

- *The survivors.* The old and poor who are out of the mainstream of society
- *The sustainers.* The young and angry who are struggling at the edge of society and will do anything to get ahead

The Outer-Directed   Accounting for two-thirds of the adult population, the outer-directed group makes up much of middle America. They conduct their lives so that others will think highly of them. This group can be broken into three subgroups:

- *Belongers.* Traditional, conservative, nostalgic, puritanical, unexperimental
- *Evaluators.* Ambitious, upwardly mobile, status conscious, competitive; also may be distrustful, having little faith that they will get a fair shake from the establishment
- *Achievers.* Leaders in business, the professions, and government; characterized by efficiency, status, comfort, the good life, and materialism

The Inner-Directed   This group buys products to meet inner needs, rather than for the opinion of others. Inner-directed consumers are expected to increase from approximately 33 million to 50 million by 1990 (and will then total approximately 28 percent of the adult population). There are three subgroups:

- *I-am-me's.* Young, zippy, impulsive, inventive, and individualistic
- *Experientials.* Want direct experience and involvement; concerned with inner growth and naturalism
- *Societally conscious individuals.* Attracted to simple living and smallness of scale; includes environmentalists and other conservationists; consumer-oriented

The Integrated   Merge the power of outer-directeds with the sensitivity of inner-directeds, and you get the integrateds. Psychologically mature, tolerant, assured, and self-actualizing, they total approximately 2 percent of the adult population.

THE QUADRANT THEORY

A method known as *quadrant analysis* will provide additional insight into why people behave as they do in relationship to salespeople. Quadrant analysis is a

---

[9]Niles Howard, "A New Way to View Customers," *Dunn's Review,* August 1981, p. 42.
[10]Ibid., pp. 43 and 44.

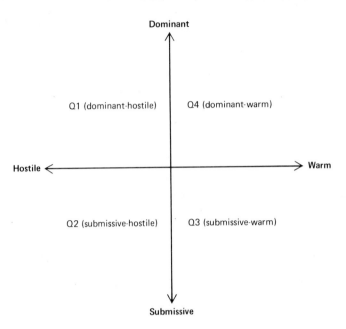

EXHIBIT 4.9
QUADRANT ANALYSIS SALES BEHAVIOR MODEL   (*Source:*
Adapted from V. R. Buzzota, R. E. Lefton, and M. Sherberg,
Dimensional Sales Model in ''What Makes a Sales Winner?''
Training Development Journal, November 1981, p. 74.)

way of categorizing patterns of behavior according to basic underlying motivations.[11] It has also been used to explain the varieties of sales behavior of salespeople.[12] The model measures two dimensions of behavior, and each dimension has
two opposite poles. Dominance and submissiveness are the opposite poles of one
dimension, warmth and hostility the opposites of the second dimension, as
shown in Exhibit 4.9.

It is thought that almost everyone can be described by these four qualities. The
dominant individual has a need to control others, whereas the submissive person
is willing to be controlled by others. The hostile person is insensitive to the needs
of others and has little regard for them, whereas the warm person is sensitive and
open to others.

The theory assumes that no one is completely at one pole (dominant or submissive, hostile or warm) but that people do tend to be predominantly one or the
other. Additionally, one's behavior may vary according to the role one is playing.
A person might be hostile at work but warm at home and in social situations.

The four quadrants, as shown in Exhibit 4.9, represent the four major personality types: Q1, the dominant-hostile; Q2, the submissive-hostile; Q3, the submis-
sive-warm; and Q4, the dominant-warm.

[11]Terry Sullivan, ''Mind Your Q's,'' *Real Estate Today,* April 1979, pp. 46–53.
[12]V. R. Buzzotta and R. E. Lefton, ''What Makes a Sales Winner?'' *Training and Development
Journal,* November 1981, p. 72.

Those high in dominance and warmth (the Q4s) make the best salespeople, because they deal with each buyer differently and according to individual needs. In terms of quadrant analysis, Q4s can tell which quadrant the buyer represents and respond accordingly. The following is a brief summary of ways to sell to the four personality types.

Selling to Q1s

Q1s (dominant-hostile) have great needs for esteem, recognition, and independence. Assertive themselves, they see other people as opportunistic and self-serving. The Q1s instinct is to be tough with salespeople. Belligerent talkers, Q1s make poor listeners and are often argumentative and eager to quibble over small points. Archie Bunker is TV's version of the perfect Q1.

To handle Q1s effectively, don't argue. Listen to them, and show that you are listening through body language. Keep good eye contact, and don't interrupt or appear impatient. Remember that if you make a Q1 appear small, you may win a point but lose a sale.

Q1s are usually more impressed with what they see than with what they hear, so your presentation should be visual and based on fact.

Selling to Q2s

Q2s (submissive-hostile) are largely motivated by security needs, and see other people as menacing and ready to take advantage of their submissiveness. Q2s are fearful, take few risks, and make decisions slowly. To be convinced of anything, they want logical proof.

The aggressive, forceful salesperson overwhelms Q2 buyers, who are particularly fearful of fast-talking salespeople. Q2s' refusal to speak often makes salespeople talk more to avoid an uncomfortable silence. Avoid moving or speaking too fast with Q2 buyers. Keep your distance physically, and give them plenty of space. You must be patient and reassuring to the Q2. Once trust has been established or reestablished, Q2 buyers usually accept your help willingly.

Selling to Q3s

Q3s (warm-submissive) are motivated by social needs and to a lesser degree by the needs of security and esteem. Warm and friendly, they believe everyone is basically good-natured.

Q3s have a strong drive to make friends with the salesperson; for them, a sales presentation is a social occasion. As a result, you cannot close Q3 buyers until you have first satisfied their social needs by responding in a warm and friendly manner. Let the Q3s attempt to make you a friend.

When attempting to close the Q3, avoid boring details. If they believe in you as a salesperson, they usually believe in your statements as well. The *assumptive close* often works with Q3 buyers: They want to please, so your assuming their willingness to buy can enable you to close.

82

Selling to Q4s

Q4s (dominant-warm) make decisions based on logic, not emotions. Businesslike in manner, they will be interested in specific data which support claims you may make in your presentation. Pragmatic and skeptical, Q4s want to see proof. Testimonial statements, charts and graphs, or reprints of articles written by authorities will be effective.

Presentations should be well-organized and well-prepared. Do your homework thoroughly. Your major ideas should flow smoothly and in a logical sequence.

OTHER CONTEMPORARY INFLUENCES

Additional factors influencing buyer behavior are extensions of the psychological and sociological theories already presented. Two that are important to those interested in sales are the influence of the family as a buying unit and the cultural change, which are affecting and will affect buyers.

Family Buying Units

For many people, the family has a strong and lasting influence on buyer behavior. Many buying decisions are made by the family operating as a buying unit. Most often, the husband and wife operate as a unit, although there is increasing evidence in recent years that children, particularly teenagers, are becoming part of the buying unit.

Questions you should try to answer regarding family buying decisions are: (1) Who is the actual decision maker? (2) Who will be using the product? and (3) Who makes the actual purchase? The answers to these questions will help direct your energies. The outcome of the situation will depend on the strength of the preferences of the individual members of the family, the degree of dominance and submissiveness of the individual members, the interaction between family members, and the amount of money each member is contributing to the purchase.

The questions are many, and the answers may be complex or obscure, but if you are sensitive in dealing with the family, you will be able to sense how a particular family operates and adjust your sales strategy accordingly.

Cultural Changes

Our culture, discussed in connection with sociological explanations of buyer behavior, is not static. The culture within which we operate and upon which we base our assumptions changes with the passage of time: New value systems replace the old, group and social class influence change, and people's needs and wants are modified. The following changes are important influences on buyer behavior. You should keep them in mind in determining your selling strategy.[13]

[13]Robert F. Spohn and Robert Y. Allen, *Retailing*, Reston Publishing, Reston, Va., 1977, p. 38; and William Stanton, *Fundamentals of Marketing*, 6th ed., McGraw-Hill, New York, 1981, p. 103.

Changing Family Influences These cultural changes include increased numbers of women entering the work force, institutional facilities for preschool children, an increased divorce rate, and geographical separation of extended families resulting from more children going to college and following careers that take them away from the hometown and the family homestead.

The Changing Role of Women Today's women have taken a role significantly different from their predecessors'. The increasing number of women in the labor force, in positions of business, political, and economic decision-making responsibility, means that women approach the buying decision with more money, more power, and more commitment.

Changing Attitudes toward Work Increasingly, people—especially young people—are not viewing work as the be-all and end-all of their lives. It has become perfectly acceptable, both socially and psychologically, to enjoy other things in life and to pamper oneself a little. In short, the puritan ethic regarding work and pleasure is changing.

Increased Leisure Time One result of our advanced technology has been a reduction of the hours in the typical workweek, leaving working people with more free time. Improved household appliances and earlier retirement have also contributed to this trend.

The Rising Influence of Educational Institutions A larger percentage of preschoolers are attending nursery schools, and an increasing number of adults are attending continuing education programs offered by colleges and other schools, with the result that a larger percentage of the population is spending more time in schools. This increasing influence of educational systems may also be a way of filling the vacuum left by weakened church and extended family ties.

RECAP

This chapter has outlined what motivates buyers and sellers and what they need from you as a salesperson. To be effective, you must learn to be sensitive to the differences in people's behavior as well as to your own actions. Train yourself to respond appropriately to the prospect who is communicating with you, arguing with you, appealing to you, or withdrawing from you.

We have analyzed the prospect's behavior from a sociological and a psychological point of view. Needs and wants are the basis of a prospect's motivation, and the fulfillment or meeting of needs and wants is your responsibility as a salesperson.

The major psychological theories discussed were Freud's psychoanalytic theory, Maslow's hierarchy of needs, and Dichter's personality structure and self-image. In addition, there was a general discussion of multiple and overlapping motives.

Warner's six-class theory and the six variables in social class, as well as the influence of groups and reference groups, are theories that affect individual buying behavior.

The life-cycle theory suggests that there are buying patterns which relate to the major, adult life cycle: the single young adult, the young married (or young household), the middle years, the empty nest, and retirement. The quadrant theory is based upon a behavior model with two biopolar dimensions: (1) dominant and submissive and (2) hostile and warm. According to this theory, every buyer can basically be described by one of the four quadrants created by the intersection of the poles.

REVIEW QUESTIONS

1. Define motivation. Give an example which will support your definition.
2. According to Freud, what is the id? the ego? the superego?
3. How do the id, ego, and superego affect buying behavior?
4. A popular explanation of consumer behavior is offered in Maslow's hierarchy of needs. Explain the five levels of motivation.
5. Can a salesperson present a product or service to different levels of needs of a prospect? Explain.
6. What theory emphasizes the influence of four major attitudes in the buying process? What are these attitudes?
7. What is the difference between a primary motive and a secondary motive?
8. Of what use can the theory of multiple motives be in selling?
9. Of Warner's classes, which constitute the bulk of our population?
10. What are the six variables of social class?
11. Why is occupation an important function of social status?
12. Do groups have any influence on buying decisions? How?
13. What are reference groups?
14. How does the life-cycle theory relate to consumer motivation?
15. Explain what quadrant analysis is. What are the two opposite poles of the two dimensions?

DISCUSSION QUESTIONS

1. Discuss the effects of motivation in your life. How does it affect you as an individual? as a student and/or worker? as a friend? as a buyer?
2. What are some of the reasons that education is becoming important in determining social status? Do you think that this will become more important or less important in coming years?
3. What assumptions, if any, may a salesperson make based on age? How does this relate to the life-cycle theory? Do you feel that the life-cycle theory as presented in the chapter could be modified to include any other phases?

4. Discuss the quadrant theory of consumer motivation. Describe your own behavior as a prospect in terms of one of the quadrants. Does this behavior agree with your overall, general behavior? Explain any differences.

LEARNING EXPERIENCES

1. Interview three other students who are taking this class with you. Ask them what they are seeking most at this point in their lives (i.e., what motivates them the most). Relate these responses to Maslow's hierarchy of needs as best you can. Are there any other theories presented in this chapter which would provide a better explanation?
2. Analyze the responses in Learning Experience 1 in terms of your own answer (i.e., what motivates you the most at this point in your life). Assuming that there are some differences, how would you explain them?
3. Visit with a cross section of salespeople in your community (a minimum of five), and ask them on what basis they determine buyer motivation. You may want to phrase the question as, "What makes people buy?" Do the responses seem to indicate that the salespeople understand the many bases of motivation?

CASES

FEMININE FASHION

Judy Aldeman and Kelly Kusuma ran Feminine Fashion, a women's clothing store in Amyville, a suburb of Atlanta. Judy and Kelly had met while students at New York University, where they had majored in retailing, with several courses in fashion and in sales. Both had been executive trainees at Lord & Taylor earlier in their careers.

Before opening the store, they had researched Amyville and the surrounding market area and had found that it consisted primarily of lower-middle-income people. They selected and priced their merchandise accordingly. Friends and associates were enthusiastic about their likelihood for success. They seemed to have the necessary ingredients: a flair for fashion and an understanding of the market.

The store was very sophisticated—and the display cases were exquisite. From all appearances, inside and out, you would never guess that they carried a moderately priced line of merchandise. The store appeared to have a good location in a busy retail area with ample traffic.

After the store had been open for several weeks, Judy and Kelly began to become concerned. A lot of people walked by and glanced in the window, but very few entered the shop. Those that did, seemed pleased—even a bit surprised—at the reasonable prices. They said that they would tell their friends about the store.

But Judy and Kelly were not satisfied, because sales were inadequate to cover costs. Word-of-mouth advertising was good in the long run, but they needed increased sales right away. Once they had a prospect in the store, they could sell—but they were not attracting enough prospects.

Questions

1. What do you feel is the basic problem?
2. What measures could Judy and Kelly take to correct the problem?
3. What does this case tell us about human behavior that would be useful in similar situations?

CAN WILLIAM PSYCH THEM OUT?

William watched intently as the prospects approached. . . . He didn't miss a detail. The husband was well-groomed and wearing an expensive-looking sport coat and slacks. The wife was equally well-dressed in a wool skirt and blazer. Somehow it added up to a confident, prosperous look.

William met them at the door of the showroom and chatted with them for a few minutes. He was getting excited, although he didn't let it show. He knew from his years of successfully sizing up prospects that this was a prosperous couple. He was seldom wrong about his hunches.

"We thought maybe you could help us," said the husband. "We're interested in a new car."

"Yes, and we're a bit confused because we haven't purchased one for several years," added the wife.

"This looks great," thought William to himself. Working for Hoffman Motors, he had a lot of latitude in what he could sell. Hoffman had a wide merchandise line, including Oldsmobile, which offered an economy model, BMW, and Rolls-Royce. He could show them cars costing from $8,000 to $175,000.

"I might add one thing," said the husband. "I'm ready to buy, but I don't enjoy shopping, and I enjoy a poor sales presentation even less. So let's get right to the point: What can you show me that will be—dollar for dollar—the best purchase for me?"

William was getting a nervous feeling in the pit of his stomach. He knew that if he made the right presentation, the sale was his—and it could be a substantial commission. But if he proceeded down the wrong track, it was all over. These were the type of people who would politely stand up, thank him for his time, and walk out the door to spend their dollars elsewhere.

William thought, "If I only knew what made them tick. Well, I suppose that's easy. They're about my age, and I think it's safe to assume that they want the same things out of life that I do. What motivates me must motivate them."

So William launched into his presentation based upon that assumption.

Questions

1. Do you think that William's assumption about what motivates this couple is correct?
2. What theory of motivation do you think might be most applicable here?
3. How would you sell to this couple?

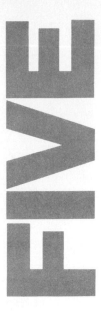

FIVE

CHAPTER OBJECTIVES

To illustrate why knowledge is important to
successful selling

To point out the kinds of sales knowledge a
salesperson should try to acquire

To identify the various available sources of
sales knowledge

To examine the ways in which sales knowledge can be used effectively

CHAPTER OUTLINE

SALES KNOWLEDGE

No ingenuity in framing arguements [sic], no artfulness in the marshaling of words, no mastery of the powers of persuasion, powerful as these agencies are, can compare for an instant with the plain truth-telling of the man who knows what he is talking about and has no aim except to impart his wisdom to others on the strength of which the public will cheerfully part with its money.*

To the scholar, knowledge for its own sake is reason enough to acquire it. To many individuals, knowledge enhances self-worth and gains the respect of others. To the salesperson, knowledge helps make sales.

Knowledge is the foundation for all other aspects of selling. No matter how articulate you are, you cannot communicate if you have nothing to say.

In this chapter, we look at the knowledge you need and how you can acquire it so that you can execute the selling process more effectively.

*Reprinted from a 1911 copy of *Mills Supplies Industrial Distribution*, in *Industrial Distribution*, October 1980, p. 35.

THE IMPORTANCE OF SALES KNOWLEDGE

Sales knowledge means knowing your product, your company, the competition, the market, and general business conditions. A thorough understanding of these key areas gives you confidence and credibility and provides the basis for developing effective sales presentations and handling objections.

Confidence

In selling, confidence is a major factor in attaining success. You must be convinced that your prospect can benefit from your product or service, and you can be convinced only if you understand your prospect's needs, the features of your product, the ability of your company to provide the product and necessary services effectively, and the relative merits of your product when compared with the competition.

Credibility

As a salesperson, you must avoid a credibility gap in dealings with customers. For a sale to be made, the prospect must believe in you and the company you represent. If you do not appear to be knowledgeable about the products and services of your company, it will destroy your credibility when an attempt is made to show the prospect the benefits of your product.

A salesperson is usually the most frequent or the only contact the prospect has with a company. Many prospects consider the salesperson and the company synonymous. If you as a salesperson don't know what you are doing, it is likely that the prospect will assume that no one else in the company knows anything either, including those who manufacture the product.

Sales Interviews

In many cases, the seller has several products, each one designed to meet a specific customer need. Also, each product has features that are of more concern to one customer than to another. As a salesperson, you must be able to select the most appropriate product for the customer. During the sales interview, you will explain the product's capabilities in terms of how it meets the prospect's needs. The better the match between capabilities and needs, the more likely it is that a sale will result. Without a thorough understanding of your product line, you will find that the proper match is difficult to make. For example, the prospect needs a machine with adjustable cutting knives. You don't know whether your firm's machine is adjustable or whether an adjustable machine can be specially ordered. You will lose this sale. Your lack of knowledge will create an unnecessary obstacle to your presentation.

Objections

Often, a prospect has misconceptions about your product, company, or competition. These misconceptions are likely to be presented by a prospect as an objection to buying. If you also have misconceptions owing to inadequate knowledge, the objection is compounded. For example, a prospect might say, "I need steel construction because it is stronger than wood." As a knowledgeable salesperson, you would respond by saying, "Laminated wood is as strong as steel," and then show the results of stress tests to prove your point. (See Exhibit 5.1.)

KINDS OF SALES KNOWLEDGE

The kinds and amount of knowledge required for selling are infinite. The greater the breadth and depth of knowledge, the more opportunities for its effective application. Knowledge of sports, gardening, astronomy, and so on can be most useful in developing relationships with customers having similar interests. It is essential, however, that as a salesperson you have knowledge about the key areas: your product, your company, the competition, the market, and general business conditions.

EXHIBIT 5.1
FROM WHICH SALESPERSON WOULD YOU BUY?

Prospect's question	Reply: Salesperson A	Reply: Salesperson B
What is this suit made of?	Let's see. The label should tell us. Oh, yeah, 50% Dacron and 50% wool. That's popular this year.	50% Dacron and 50% wool, a blend that looks natural yet has wrinkle-resistant qualities provided by Dacron.
What happens to the motor if the machine overheats?	I wouldn't worry about that if I were you. That wouldn't happen, but if it did, I'm sure we would stand behind it.	It shouldn't, but as an added precaution, there is an automatic shutoff that prevents serious overheating.
How do your flaffels compare with Fliffel's flaffels?*	Ours are much better.	Our flaffels are automatic and theirs are semiautomatic. Ours are 100% steel construction and theirs are 80% steel and 20% plastic. Our guarantee is for 2 years and theirs is 1 year.
Do you service what you sell?	Sure.	Our own service department is on 24-hour call. We provide scheduled maintenance and emergency service. Our service people have been with our company for an average of 17 years.

*A flaffel can be anything you want it to be.

The Product

The importance and the amount of product knowledge required depend on the nature of the product, the type of customer, the type of sales position, and other factors pertinent to the overall selling situation. The sales engineer is usually expected by both the company and the customer to have a high level of product knowledge. People who sell services also usually need a high level of knowledge. What they know about the service and how they communicate this information will essentially become the product in the mind of the buyer. On the other hand, the salesperson for a drug wholesaler, who sells thousands of different products, cannot be expected to excel in product knowledge for each item. Regardless, a relatively high level of product knowledge will help salespeople in all sales categories. Let's look at some of the useful things to know about the product.

How It Was Developed Some products are "me too" products, and some have been pioneered by a particular firm. A product developed as a result of a customer's idea shows that your company listens to its customers. If your product was the first of its kind to come on the market after ten years of intensive research, testing, and development, both your firm and the product have earned much credibility.

Any significant facts about a product's development can be used as either selling points or points of interest. For example, Denton Mills got the idea for its Dr. Dentons sleepwear from Frank Stanton, a foreman in a woolen mill back in the 1890s, who decided to sew feet in long johns. Procter & Gamble got the idea for Pampers from a Procter & Gamble engineer, who struggled with the diaper-changing chore while babysitting for his grandchild. Besides having story value, the presentation of this kind of information can imply that everyone in the company is thinking about a better way to satisfy buyers' needs.

What Goes into the Product The materials used in the product and the manufacturing process are often of concern to the prospect. The fact that your product is handcrafted and made of natural material, such as leather, can be a selling point. On the other hand, the use of a machine-made synthetic in your product could also be considered a positive feature. The custom machinery might assure uniform construction, and the synthetic material might be more durable or have some other quality that is noteworthy. (See Exhibit 5.2.)

The reason for using a particular material in the construction of the product often provides the opportunity to introduce a benefit or turn an objection into a selling point. For example, more plastic is being used in cars. Plastic is anathema to many customers because they consider it cheap and because it is not biodegradable. However, one of the principal reasons it is used is to reduce weight. The net result is fuel economy. By knowing this, you can shift the discussion from plastic to lower operating costs—a benefit for the buyer.

For a service, the background and capabilities of the people performing the service should be known. Their education and special training will help assure the buyer that the service will be performed expertly. For example, the fact that a

EXHIBIT 5.2
EXAMPLE OF CRAFTSMANSHIP

Carson's, a North Carolina furniture maker, limits automation and assembly-line techniques. Rather than increasing production speed by having separate craftsmen cover the cushion, arms, and back with cloth, each craftsman covers the entire piece of furniture. This ensures that cloth patterns are properly fitted and that each craftsman is personally committed to the product.

Source: "High Point, N.C.: The Furniture Makers Are Coming Unglued," *The New York Times*, Mar. 15, 1981, p. 4F.

financial management consultant has an M.B.A. and has spent twenty years at a major accounting firm makes the service more salable.

Differentiating Features   Besides knowing as much as you possibly can about your product or service, find out what makes it different from others. Is it more durable? Why? Is it more versatile? Why? Does it have a better guarantee? Just keep asking yourself and other company employees questions such as these, and you should come up with a rather long list for most products and services. Use the plus points in your sale, but remember that to be worth talking about, a differentiating feature must benefit the customer. Although the feature of the product or service is what provides the benefit, it is the benefit that sells the customer. Try to think in terms of differentiating *benefits*.

Applications and Uses   Knowing what a product is made of, how it is made, and what its special features are will provide a sound basis for product knowledge. However, the product's applications and uses are equally important. For years Arm & Hammer baking soda was used for just baking (and perhaps occasional tooth brushing). Now you can find it soaking up odors in refrigerators and traveling down drainpipes. What are the various uses of your product or service, and how is it used? How else might it be used? These questions focus on the different types of benefits that can be derived from a product's different uses. In effect, you are prospecting for new uses with existing customers.

Many products and services offer multiple benefits, depending on the buyer's needs. For example, an insurance policy can provide death benefits for the insured's beneficiary, life benefits for the insured, an education for the insured's children, and a bequest to the insured's alma mater. A television can be an entertainment receiver, a vehicle for playing electronic games, and a babysitter. The more uses your product or service has, the more benefits it can provide. Get to know all its existing uses, and try to think of new uses for it.

Learn how to use your product. You'll feel much more comfortable telling your prospect how easy it is to operate if you know how to operate it yourself. If a demonstration is important in your presentation, know how to operate the product correctly. If you are selling a service, get to know how the service is performed. If possible, use the service yourself to get a firsthand understanding.

The Company

Buyers are concerned about the source, which is the company, as well as the product. The company you represent can be more important to the buyer than the product. Just as your sales knowledge gives you credibility, your company gives your product or service credibility. You have to sell your company, and the only way you can do this is by knowing something about it. Besides the general knowledge you should have about your company, you should know about its policies regarding order handling and delivery, credit, and servicing.

General Knowledge   When the company was founded, who founded it, whether it is privately or publicly owned, whether it has any operating subsidiaries, and its annual sales and profits are all things you need to know. Besides helping you understand the company's decisions and policies, this knowledge can be used effectively during a sales interview. For example, if you say that your company has been in business for fifty years, your prospect will know that you are not representing a fly-by-night outfit. This, in turn, gives credibility to your promise that your company can fulfill your customer's needs. If your company is relatively young but has a noteworthy growth record, this, too, can be used advantageously. "Yes, we are relatively new to this business, but our sales have doubled every year for the past three years" is a statement that can give even the most skeptical prospect some confidence in your company. Most buyers will assume that your company wouldn't be experiencing this phenomenal growth without doing something right.

Information about your company's distribution strategy, community consciousness and involvement, and so forth is also valuable. If you are calling on a full-service retailer and another division of your company sells to discount store chains, you had better know it and be prepared to defend this dual distribution strategy. If your company doesn't sell to discount chains and your competitor does, this, too, should be known and used advantageously.

Even knowing how your company got its name or named its products can be of interest to your customer, make you look smarter, and add to a point you may want to make in your sales presentation. Apple Computer, for example, is a name that could stump even the most imaginative person. The name *Apple* was chosen because cofounder Steve Jobs eats only fruit and because the company didn't want to give its computer an imposing technical name.

Order Processing and Delivery Systems   Know exactly what happens to an order from the time the prospect says "yes" to the time delivery is made. Know how to fill out an order form and how to route it. Know which departments or offices the order passes through and the names of the people responsible at

There's a lot of Vermont in every tap we make.

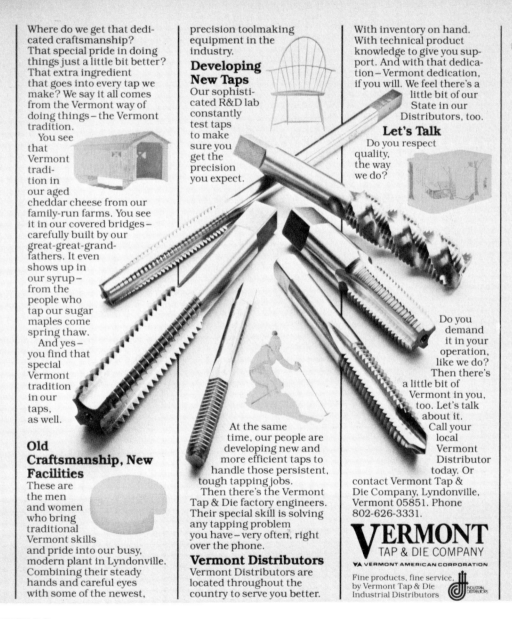

Where do we get that dedicated craftsmanship? That special pride in doing things just a little bit better? That extra ingredient that goes into every tap we make? We say it all comes from the Vermont way of doing things—the Vermont tradition.

You see that Vermont tradition in our aged cheddar cheese from our family-run farms. You see it in our covered bridges—carefully built by our great-great-grandfathers. It even shows up in our syrup—from the people who tap our sugar maples come spring thaw.

And yes—you find that special Vermont tradition in our taps, as well.

Old Craftsmanship, New Facilities

These are the men and women who bring traditional Vermont skills and pride into our busy, modern plant in Lyndonville. Combining their steady hands and careful eyes with some of the newest,

precision toolmaking equipment in the industry.

Developing New Taps

Our sophisticated R&D lab constantly test taps to make sure you get the precision you expect.

At the same time, our people are developing new and more efficient taps to handle those persistent, tough tapping jobs.

Then there's the Vermont Tap & Die factory engineers. Their special skill is solving any tapping problem you have—very often, right over the phone.

Vermont Distributors

Vermont Distributors are located throughout the country to serve you better.

With inventory on hand. With technical product knowledge to give you support. And with that dedication—Vermont dedication, if you will. We feel there's a little bit of our State in our Distributors, too.

Let's Talk

Do you respect quality, the way we do?

Do you demand it in your operation, like we do? Then there's a little bit of Vermont in you, too. Let's talk about it. Call your local Vermont Distributor today. Or contact Vermont Tap & Die Company, Lyndonville, Vermont 05851. Phone 802-626-3331.

VERMONT
TAP & DIE COMPANY
VA VERMONT AMERICAN CORPORATION

Fine products, fine service, by Vermont Tap & Die Industrial Distributors

---

EXHIBIT 5.3
KNOWLEDGE ON TAP: AN ADVERTISEMENT GIVING THE SOURCE CREDIBILITY   (*Source:* Vermont Tap & Die Company)

each step along the way. Know how the product is physically handled and transported to your prospect. And know who to contact if a problem arises.

In even the most efficient order-processing systems, there are snags that can hinder the processing of your customer's order. Be sure the order has a successful start in its journey toward completion by filling it out completely and accurately and forwarding it in the correct manner. If there is a problem at any point, your knowledge of the systems will help you solve it.

Two big problems for salespeople involve shipping—shipping nothing because goods are out of stock and shipping incorrectly. Shipping incorrectly might involve the wrong product, the wrong amount, the wrong size, the wrong color, the wrong time, or the wrong place. The salesperson has to follow up on such problems to keep the customer's confidence—and business.

Out-of-stock merchandise is usually *back-ordered*. This means that it will be shipped when available. Follow up to find out approximately when it will be shipped, and pass this information on to your customer. You may be able to substitute a product that is available.

Your company must balance the need for a high level of customer service and an economical delivery system. The trend is for customers to shift the responsibility (and cost) for carrying inventory to the supplier. This means many are looking for a shorter order cycle, which involves faster delivery. You have a responsibility to your company to make profitable sales and to your customers to satisfy reasonable service requirements.

Get to know your company's delivery methods and schedules, and make sure your customer also knows them. Know which kinds of orders are shipped directly from the factory and which are shipped from a local warehouse. For services, know the realistic starting and completion dates for delivering the service. By knowing your company's policies and capabilities, you can avoid many troublesome situations. Far too often, sales reps make promises to their customers that either they can't meet or they can only meet at a considerable expense to their company.

Here are some things to keep in mind about delivery:

• Work with your customer to determine normal purchase requirements and safety stocks. This means knowing how much your customer needs until the next scheduled delivery, with an allowance for unusual demand (*safety stock*).

• Find out what size order is most economical for your company and your customer. Carload shipments are less expensive than less-than-carload shipments, whether your company uses its own transportation or public transportation. And, more important, your customer will usually benefit from a quantity discount.

• Plan your sales calls so that there is enough lead time to assess the customer's needs, process the order, and assure a timely delivery. Regardless of how well you coordinate the order—delivery cycle—unplanned deliveries may be necessary. Know how to handle these emergencies to satisfy a customer. It could mean personally delivering the product or simply knowing how to make arrangements to send a delivery out on the next bus or the next airplane. Melvin's

Pharmacy in Great Barrington, Massachusetts, has bagels for its customers because an inventive salesperson figured out how to get them there: Every Sunday morning a Bonanza bus heads north from New York City with its belly full of bagels.

Credit Policies Credit expands the money supply. As the money supply expands, the chances for sales expand. Your company's credit policies will affect your ability to close sales and increase orders.

Some companies deal with new customers on a cash-on-delivery (c.o.d.) basis until the customer proves financial capability over a period of time. Other companies offer a limited amount of credit at the beginning of the business relationship. In either case, if the creditworthiness of a customer improves, more credit is allowed.

The salesperson is usually responsible for filling out the customer's credit report. This is sent to the company's credit department, where it will be scrutinized. Based on the information provided, credit terms are either offered or refused to the customer. If credit is offered, a line of credit is established, and this credit line is communicated to the customer and the salesperson.

The line of credit is the maximum amount of credit purchases permitted. The salesperson should review each customer's financial status periodically and submit the proper paperwork to increase the customer's credit line when the circumstances warrant doing so.

To many salespeople, the credit department is the enemy because it turns down requests for credit by customers who do not qualify. In fairness, the salesperson must realize the following:

1. Credit department personnel are evaluated on their prudence in granting credit.
2. The company's success is determined by dollars received, not by orders and deliveries.

An understanding of credit policies and procedures and cooperation with the credit department will bring about the best results for the firm and, ultimately, for *all* employees of the firm.

EXHIBIT 5.4
SERVICE CAN MAKE THE DIFFERENCE

Servicing Not all repairmen are as lonely as Maytag repairmen are alleged to be. Even the highest-quality products produced by the most reputable companies require routine maintenance and occasional emergency repair. Dependable after-sale service for those types of products and services requiring it builds strong company reputations and repeat sales.

In today's technological society, many products need scheduled maintenance and are subject to breakdowns if not properly maintained. Examples are typewriters, automobiles, computers, cash registers, lawnmowers, and printing presses. Many prospects for these types of products are more concerned about the service they will receive than any other aspect, including price and special features.

Service begins with the warranty, which makes the seller responsible for the repair or replacement of defective parts for a specified time period after purchase. Understand the provisions of warranties so that you can explain them to your prospects and can enforce their compliance by your service department.

Some companies also sell service contracts. Some contracts run parallel to the warranty and exclude malfunctions caused by customer negligence, some are in lieu of a warranty, some are only maintenance contracts, and some are for protection beyond the warranty period.

If your service is good and you know it, you can use this knowledge to your advantage. Many apparel salespeople have sold suits because they knew the store's tailor could alter the suit to the customer's satisfaction. Also, in the insurance industry, the good reputation of a company's claims service has helped make many insurance sales.

The Competition

In many sales interviews, the buyer will want to talk about competitive products. He or she is often in the position of deciding *which*, not *whether*, meaning which product to buy, not whether to buy or not to buy. Competitors are the other *whiches*.

Even consumers, who tend to be more impulsive than professional buyers, want to look at their options before leaping into a proposition that's costing them money. Professional buyers, such as purchasing agents and buyers for retail stores, in particular, will rarely make a buying decision before comparing the offerings of various sources.

Your responsibility is to make sure the information a buyer has about the competition is right and to supply missing information. Sometimes a buyer compares apples with oranges when comparing your product with the competition's. For example, he or she might say that your price is too high, not realizing that your price includes options that the competition charges extra for. Your knowledge of competition will clear up this misconception. Professional buyers usually have catalogs and price lists of several suppliers. If they don't have all the information they need before making a buying decision, you can supply the information. In fact, many companies provide their salespeople with catalogs that contain cross-references to competitive products. These catalogs give the sales rep knowledge about competition and can be shared with the buyer.

Knowledge of the competition's calling patterns and delivery schedules can be most helpful. Timing is a crucial element of any selling strategy. If your competition has infrequent or irregular calling patterns, you might be able to make inroads by attentively calling on your competitor's customers. You have an opportunity to get orders from a competitor's customers when they are out of the competitor's product and are waiting for a delivery. Attentiveness can get short-term sales with potential long-term results.

Competition includes more than just those who are selling products and services having characteristics similar to yours. It includes generically different products and services that compete for the prospect's dollar and satisfy broad needs.

For example, the boat salesperson is competing not only with other brands of boats, but also with a country club membership and a Caribbean vacation. The salesperson of newspaper advertising space is competing not only with other newspapers but also with TV and other advertising media.

The Market

In Chapter 4 we addressed the behavioral aspects of buyers. In this section we address the need to know about the market in terms of the industry served and the geographical aspects of the territory.

Most reps who sell to retailers and industrial accounts need a considerable knowledge of the prospect's business—the industry and how the firms within the industry operate. This is why many companies align sales territories on an industry basis.

The kind of product needed and how it will be used vary among businesses. For example, a manufacturer might want a computer primarily for process control, whereas a retailer might want it primarily for inventory control. Each requires a computer with special capabilities. The salesperson must understand manufacturing in one case and retailing in the other, in order to match the product and the need effectively.

By understanding the customer's business, you can recognize special problems and even use the appropriate terminology in communicating with your customer. Many companies include a comprehensive course in their customers' businesses as part of their training programs. For example, oil companies require that their salespeople learn about retail service station operations, including, in some cases, actually running a station. NCR Corporation has some of its sales trainees work in banks as tellers and in trust departments. Companies often hire salespeople who have worked in the industry to which they will sell.

General Business Conditions

You do not have to be an economist to be an effective salesperson, but you should have at least an understanding of basic economic principles and an awareness of both the national and local economies.

What does inflation mean to your company? To your customers' businesses? How does the high cost of money affect your company's credit policies or your customers' inventory levels? How would a change in the investment tax credit affect your customers' businesses? How will higher energy costs affect your customers' purchasing decisions? What effects do changes in populations have on your territory's economy? What effects do plant closings have? These are among the dozens of questions to which you should have answers. (See Exhibit 5.5.)

The economic realities of the 1980s have brought about lifestyle changes that have affected everyone. More laypeople are trying desperately to understand economics so that they can cope. In many schools throughout the country there is increasing demand for economics courses. Very often, one person's famine is

EXHIBIT 5.5
DON'T ASK, "HOW'S BUSINESS?"

Unable to compete with rising imports, Zenith, Sioux City's largest employer, moved its operations to Mexico. There were once 2000 employees making parts for stereo and television sets. When the plant closed, the remaining 1400 workers walked to the unemployment line.

The effect on the local economy was widespread. Many former Zenith workers left town to find employment elsewhere. Those who remained were primarily women workers whose families lost the second paycheck. According to the manager of Younkers Department Store, "People are buying their needs, but they aren't buying the extras."

The plant closing also affected local suppliers. One supplier had to reduce its employees by 75 percent because of the lost business.

Source: "Sioux City Still Suffers after Its Top Employer Moves Business Abroad," *The Wall Street Journal,* Apr. 5, 1979, p. 1.

another's feast. For every bond dealer who can't sell a bond or every insurance salesperson who can't sell a whole-life policy, there is a money fund manager picking up additional business. For every thermostat that is being turned down, there is a chain saw being turned on. The knowledgeable salesperson figures out which fork to use at the feast and which problem-solving technique to use during the famine.

SOURCES OF SALES KNOWLEDGE

You're familiar with the kinds of knowledge you need for confidence and credibility and to help you overcome objections and, ultimately, make the sale. Now it's time to look at some of the most valuable sources for obtaining that knowledge. All or most of these sources generally will be useful to you, regardless of the particular sales position you hold.

Sales Training Programs

Sales training programs vary in formality, length, and content. Most companies have some form of training for new recruits as well as for veteran salespeople. The initial training usually lasts at least a week and may last as long as two years. The depth of training varies with the nature of the sales position. Training for salespeople who sell specialty steel is much more extensive than training for those who sell standardized consumer goods.

Training never ends for the progressive salesperson or for the progressive company. Development and refresher programs are used to keep everyone sharp and up to date. Product knowledge and company knowledge are invariably part of a firm's training program. Films, cassette tapes, literature, lectures, and visits to company offices and plants are among the methods used. Some companies also require in-service training. The sales trainee is actually assigned to work in the plant, the warehouse, and in various company offices for a period of time to get "hands-on" experience. Field training is generally part of a training program.

Company Literature

Your company will generally have all kinds of informative material, ranging from one-page technical bulletins to lengthy sales manuals.

Typically, sales manuals are the most extensive information source produced by the company and usually include the following:

- Organization charts
- Company history
- Sales policies, including required reports
- Ordering procedures
- Credit department policies, procedures, and terms
- Servicing information
- Product information, including fact sheets, competitive information, and promotional activity

The firm's annual report, once considered nothing more than a troublesome annual undertaking to meet the legal requirements for publicly held corporations, has gained new status. Many annual reports are elaborate four-color booklets that contain a wealth of company and product information.

Advertising

Generally your company will inform you about an upcoming advertising campaign prior to its occurrence. Obviously, competition will not do this. Follow their advertising to see what they are saying about their products. You'll know what your customers are hearing, what your competition is stressing, and with which kinds of objections you might have to deal.

Test Results

There are three main testing arenas: your company's testing laboratory, your customers' testing laboratories, and independent testing laboratories. Most test results depict both absolute and relative merits. Tests conducted by independents, such as Consumers' Union and Underwriters' Laboratories, are highly regarded, and the results are distributed to a wide audience. Although tests conducted by customers such as Macy's and Penney's, who have their own testing laboratories, are directed toward their own particular objectives, these tests are informative and useful testimonials. Promotional considerations aside, test results are usually an objective source of product information.

Trade Shows

Your competitors are likely to have booths at the various trade shows sponsored by the industry. This is an excellent opportunity to inspect their products, watch their demonstrations, and receive their product literature. You might also observe which features they are stressing and which benefits they are emphasizing to the people visiting their booths, many of whom are your customers or prospects.

Customers

Customers generally tell salespeople what they like and what they dislike about the product or service. They also reveal much about competition. Listen attentively to what customers say, and gain this valuable knowledge. After using your product or service for a while, customers might also discover product features—good and bad—that you were unaware of or had minimized. Use the good features in your presentations to other customers. Bring any bad features to your company's attention, and prepare yourself to answer objections based on them.

Periodicals

Magazines published by trade associations and publishing houses are invaluable sources of information. *Business Week, Fortune, Sales and Marketing Management,* and *Business Marketing* are business publications that should be on your reading list. Publications dealing with your specific industry should also be read regularly, e.g., *Datamation, National Petroleum News, Chemical Week.* Find out what your customers are reading, and read the same literature. For example, if you sell to the grocery industry, your customers are probably reading *Progressive Grocer, Supermarket Business,* and *Frozen Foods.* Your company and your competition might also be advertising in these publications. By reading industry periodicals, you'll be better informed of your competition and of your customers' needs and interests. And your prospects will respect you for your interest.

Computer-Based Information Systems

The computer is being increasingly used in sales training programs, particularly for gaining product knowledge. Some companies have developed their own computerized inquiry systems. Using a terminal for access, you can interact with the computer to get product information.

Some companies are using packages that have been developed for subscribers. One system that is popular is Control Data Corporation's "Plato." Sales reps of subscribers can go to the nearest of Control Data's fifty information centers throughout the country to use a terminal. Among its subscribers are Merrell-National Laboratories and Cleveland Twist Drill Company.[1]

---

[1]"Plato's Wisdom," *Sales and Marketing Management,* June 1978, pp. 19–20.

EXHIBIT 5.6
READING FOR KNOWLEDGE (*Source:* McGraw-Hill, Inc.)

Associations

Besides the periodicals they publish, professional and trade associations provide industry surveys and compile statistics for their members. They also hold seminars and conventions that provide information about new technology and new governmental regulations.

Courses

Many companies encourage their salespeople to attend courses for the purpose of obtaining both general and specific knowledge. Larger companies often have their own schools for training new salespeople and retraining veterans. Most industries sponsor seminars and courses for their member companies. The Graduate Realtors Institute Course and the Life Underwriter Training Council Course are noteworthy examples.

College and university courses provide requisite knowledge for salespeople. Business-related and liberal arts courses are often encouraged. In many cases, companies completely or partially reimburse their employees for the expenses incurred in successfully completing courses.

EFFECTIVE USE OF SALES KNOWLEDGE

The way you use your knowledge will depend on the prospect with whom you are dealing. Some prospects are more benefit-oriented, some more feature-oriented. When a prospect has little concern for the technical aspects of the product, intricate technical details are not necessary. Don't feel that you have to dazzle your prospect with your knowledge.

Regardless of the amount of knowledge you have, there will be times when you do not have an answer for a prospect's question. In these cases, don't fake it. In most cases, you can refer to your catalog or manual for the answer or call the appropriate office at your company. Knowing where to go for information you do not have is as important as the information you have on tap.

RECAP

Knowledge is a prerequisite for successful selling. It breeds confidence and credibility, which help you make better sales presentations, and it enables you to make better replies to objections.

It is important to know how your product was developed, how it is made, and what it is made of; how it differs from other products; and how it can be used effectively by customers.

Knowledge of your company is essential. It is important to understand how orders are processed and delivered, how credit is granted, and how products are serviced after the sale.

Your search for sales knowledge should not stop at knowing your product and your company. The total sales information package should include knowledge of the competition, the market, and general business conditions.

Much of the required knowledge will be provided by your company through its sales training program and its literature. Additional knowledge can be acquired from reading, doing course work, and observing and listening to what is going on around you.

Get as much knowledge as you can, and use as much as you need for each selling situation.

REVIEW QUESTIONS

1. Why does knowledge help make sales?
2. What kinds of knowledge about the product or service should you have as a salesperson?
3. Why is it important to know your competition's calling patterns and delivery schedules?
4. How can you use knowledge of your company's history?
5. Do you need to know your company's order-processing and delivery systems? Explain.

6. Why should you understand the industry that you sell to?
7. Is it important for a salesperson to know something about economics? Why?
8. What kinds of information can you get from a sales manual?
9. Which test results are most effective in selling?
10. Should you use all your knowledge when dealing with a customer? Explain.

DISCUSSION QUESTIONS

1. "Knowledge is more than equivalent to force," said the English man of letters Johnson.[2] How do you interpret this statement in the context of selling?
2. "It's not what you know, but who you know" is a common saying. Does this apply to salespeople?

LEARNING EXPERIENCES

1. Visit a factory and view it from a seller's perspective. Look at the production process in terms of what you should know if you were selling the products being produced.
2. Read a few articles about a company that interests you. After reading the articles, list the information given in the article that might be useful in discussions with customers.

CASES

ENSON REBUFFED

Larry Enson called on Janice McCarthy, manager of Hawthorne Hardware. Enson's firm had added a new paint to its line of varnishes and stains. McCarthy was particularly interested in talking with Enson because one of her principal suppliers had gone out of the paint business, and she was interested in a replacement brand.

"We have a revolutionary new paint that is better than either Truecolor or Stayput," Enson assured his prospect.

"Well, let's not worry about Stayput, because they are now kaput," replied McCarthy. "How does you paint compare with Truecolor and some of the others I'm considering?"

"No kidding! Stayput is no longer in the paint business? To answer your question, our new paint is by far the best on the market."

[2]Samuel Johnson, *Rasselas*, chap. XIII, 1759.

"Is it an oil-based or a water-based paint, and what are its mildew-resistant qualities?"

"I think it comes as both oil-based and water-based, but I'll look it up to be sure. Yes. We have it in both forms. As for mildew-resistance qualities, I'm sure it's superb. Can I answer any other questions?"

"No. You can't," replied McCarthy.

Questions

1. Why didn't McCarthy want Enson to answer any more questions?
2. Was there anything wrong with Enson's referring to his sales manual to answer whether the paint was oil-based or water-based?
3. How would you restate Enson's replies?

PRESS INK COMPANY

Ellen Compton, sales rep for Press Ink Company, called on the *Midstate Journal,* her first sales call since completing Press Ink's sales training program. Homer Eddy, the production manager confronted her with the "rub-off" problem. He said that many of the *Journal's* subscribers had more ink going to their hands than information going to their brain.

Compton's first thought was to find out about the *Journal's* newsprint. She found that it had recently changed to a thinner, less porous newsprint to economize. She pointed this out to the production manager.

She further pointed out that the standard ink is a blend of 88 percent mineral oil and 12 percent carbon-black pigment. It does not contain the costly resins used in magazine publishing. Newspaper publishers balk at higher costs for ink and the cost of natural-gas baking ovens for curing paper to reduce or eliminate the rub-off problem.

Compton told Eddy that some newspapers had reduced rub-off significantly by using less ink but had received complaints from their elderly subscribers who couldn't read the lighter print. She also said that her company was trying to develop a water-based ink that would smear less than those currently on the market.[3]

Questions

1. Was it necessary to give the standard ink formula?
2. If you were Compton and, for some reason, were limited to giving only two pieces of information, which would you choose?
3. Are you impressed with Compton's knowledge? Explain.

[3]Adapted from ''Ay, There's the Rub: Big Stink over Ink Makes Press Rethink,'' *The Wall Street Journal*, Dec. 6, 1979, p. 1.

CHAPTER OBJECTIVES

To stress the importance of prospecting to the selling process

To describe the many methods used to obtain leads

To illustrate how leads are qualified

To show how prospects are arranged in priority order

CHAPTER OUTLINE

PROSPECTING

The secret of walking on water is knowing where the stones are.*

Herb Cohen

If you wanted to pick a ripe banana, where would you go? To Brazil or to Passaic, New Jersey? If you wanted to find a pot of gold, where would you look? Under the rainbow or over it? To find what you want, you have to go to the right place. The salesperson looking for a sale also must go to the right place.

Prospecting is the stage of the sales process that steers you in the right direction to make your efforts most effective. In this chapter, we'll take you to Brazil, help you set your sights under the rainbow, and show you where the good prospects are.

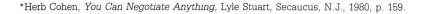
*Herb Cohen, *You Can Negotiate Anything*, Lyle Stuart, Secaucus, N.J., 1980, p. 159.

PROSPECTS

Prospects are people or firms that are likely to buy your product or service. Before gaining prospect status, these people or firms are called *leads* or *suspects*. Prospects who buy your product or service are called *customers*. Customers who usually satisfy their buying needs by purchasing from you are called *regular customers*. (See Exhibit 6.1.)

Different types of customers are also referred to by different terms. Individuals who buy products and most services for their own use or consumption are usually called *consumers*. Those who buy legal and tax services are referred to as *clients*. Those who buy medical services are referred to as *patients*. Those who buy for business purposes are referred to as either *customers* or *accounts*.

THE IMPORTANCE OF PROSPECTING

The status quo is unacceptable in selling. Most companies expect yearly sales increases from their salespeople, and most salespeople expect increases from themselves. This is accomplished by a combination of efforts to retain existing customers, increase sales to existing customers, and obtain new customers.

The loss of regular customers is unavoidable. Consumers die, move (the mobility rate is about 20 percent yearly), or enter new stages of the life cycle, thus no

EXHIBIT 6.1
TURNING LEADS INTO REGULAR CUSTOMERS

longer needing some products and services. Business customers are also lost for various reasons. They may go out of business. They change ownership or merge with other companies. They change the nature of their business and no longer need the product or service you sell. Additionally, of course, customers are lost as a result of dissatisfaction with the salesperson, the company, or the product or service.

New prospects are needed to replace lost customers and to add to existing business. There must be a reservoir of prospects at all times, because prospects lead to customers and customers provide sales revenue.

There is a direct relationship between prospecting effectiveness and closing effectiveness. Regardless of how much skill you have in the other facets of the selling process, your sales will be few and far between if you do not have good prospects to interview.

You don't have to be a gambler to understand and be influenced by odds. People postpone parties when the weather reporter predicts a nine-in-ten chance for a major snowfall. Basketball players bring the ball in toward the basket before taking a shot. They do this because they know that a much higher percentage of shots fall through the hoop from 10 feet out than from 25 feet out.

The salesperson's looking for a good prospect is like the basketball player's looking for a good shot. The chances for success become more favorable when qualified prospects are being called on by the salesperson. Good prospects give the salesperson a better shot at making the sale.

THE PROSPECTING PROCESS

Prospecting should be considered an extension of or part of the marketing research function. *Marketing research* involves gathering information about markets to determine the firm's product or service offerings. In most cases, however, the marketing research function defines general markets, not specific potential users. For example, the need for materials-handling equipment can be determined by looking at such factors as number of private and public warehouses, number of competing firms, and growth rates. The firm might estimate that it will get 5 percent of this market. It does not know the specific customers making up that 5 percent.

The research continues as the salespeople try to determine which potential customers will be part of the 5 percent figure. For most types of products or services, it is virtually impossible to know or to contact every single potential user. Therefore, a selection process must be undertaken. This process (prospecting) involves obtaining the names of potential users, qualifying the potential users, and making a priority list.

Obtaining Leads

The total number of potential users of the product or service you sell depends on many factors, most important of which are the nature of the product and the market segment you want to reach. Some products and services have a mass appeal, while others are more limited. The seller of individual life insurance could consider every name listed in the telephone directory a potential customer. The seller of leatherworking tools and machinery, on the other hand, could consider shoemakers, leather-craft shops, and saddlery shops as potential customers.

The first step in the prospecting process is getting the names of individuals or firms that might be potential candidates. These names are often called *leads*. There are many sources for obtaining leads. We'll tell you how to get leads later, after you have a better understanding of the process.

Qualifying Leads

In qualifying leads, you separate the wheat from the chaff. You take a good look at a lead and try to determine whether this person or firm qualifies for the time and cost involved in a sales interview. You must assess both the current and future needs, financial capabilities, and decision-making authority of the lead. If there is no need, the lead does not qualify as a prospect. If there is no money (including creditworthiness), there is no prospect. If there is no authority to make a purchasing decision, there is no prospect.

In the life insurance example, employed people with dependents, inadequate life insurance coverage, and some money would be prospects. Retired people without dependents would not be likely prospects. (They may, however, be prospects for an annuity if they have not prepared for outliving their assets.) In the leatherworking tools and machinery example, only those that are engaged in leather fabrication and repair activities would meet the need test. Those that only resell leather products would not be prospects at this time.

If money were no object in our exchange system, the prospect pool would expand considerably for most products and services. Since this is not the case, financial capability is an important aspect of qualification. For an individual, disposable or, preferably, discretionary income is a determining factor. For a business, positive cash flow and a high credit rating are factors.

When qualifying potential users of consumer goods, in many cases the individual with the need has the authority to make the buying decision. In some cases, however, the decision is made jointly by the consumer and another person (husband and wife, for example) or independently by some other person. When qualifying potential users of industrial goods or middlemen, buying authority becomes even more critical in prospecting. You might think you have a good prospect, when in fact the buying decision will be made by a central buying committee or a purchasing agent at the firm's headquarters. After you read about the sources of prospects, we'll give you additional thoughts about qualifying.

Ranking Prospects

During the qualifying process, some prospects score higher than others in meeting the criteria established for qualification. It is important to rank prospects in terms of urgency of need fulfillment and sales potential. Those who appear to have

EXHIBIT 6.2
STRETCHING SINGLES INTO HOME RUNS

Pete Rose became one of the highest-paid baseball players—his secret for success: singles. While many other players were swinging for home runs, Rose proceeded to hit more singles than any player in National League history.

Andy Gandolfo (no relation to "Billion Dollar" Joe Gandolfo) also spurned the home run when he began selling for the Metropolitan Life Insurance Company. As did his colleagues, he used the newspapers for prospecting. However, there was one major difference. His colleagues tried to get appointments to sell newlyweds life insurance, whereas Andy got appointments and sold newlyweds inexpensive renters' insurance policies.

His colleagues laughed at him for expending so much time and effort for the paltry $4 commissions received for these policies. However, as his colleagues continued to strike out on the phone, his renters' insurance policyholders became his prospects and subsequent clients for all their insurance needs, including life insurance. His singles became home runs.

an immediate need and a high potential volume would be your top priority, and those with a less immediate need and lower potential volume have a lower priority.

One thing to keep in mind is that those high on your prospect list may also be high on your competitors' lists. In addition, sometimes it's wise to go after prospects that don't have the potential for high-volume sales now but have good long-term potential. See Exhibit 6.2 for an example of this.

A system for ranking your prospects should be developed and reviewed regularly. A card system is commonly used. A card is prepared for each prospect (see Exhibit 6.3 for an example of a prospect card) and is placed in a prospect file. The cards can be color-coded or sequentially arranged to designate priority status.

SOURCES FOR PROSPECTS

There are numerous sources for prospects. Generally, the more sources used, the longer the prospect list. Most salespeople use a combination of sources to obtain maximum prospecting effectiveness. This section explains the principal sources that can be considered by almost all types of salespeople.

Referrals

A referral is usually the best source for prospects. Social and business contacts, satisfied customers, and other prospects are all excellent sources for obtaining names of individuals or companies that might buy your product or service.

NAME OF FIRM		CONTACT		
ADDRESS		TITLE		
		COMMENTS		
TELEPHONE NO.				
TYPE OF BUSINESS		SOURCE AND DATE OF LEAD		
TYPE OF NEED		PRIORITY: ☐ HIGH ☐ MEDIUM ☐ LOW		
PRESENT SUPPLIER(S)		ACTION TAKEN		
CREDIT RATING		DATE	PURPOSE	RESULTS
ESTIMATED VOLUME				
COMMENTS				

EXHIBIT 6.3
A PROSPECT CARD SHOULD BE PREPARED AND REVIEWED PERIODICALLY

Contacts   Both social and business contacts represent a vast reservoir of possibilities for new customers. Your personal contacts are often good prospects, but more important are the people your contacts know who might have the need for your product or service. Generally, the more influential the contact, the more likely it is that he or she will have clout and credibility in making referrals. Influential people are often considered to be centers of influence or opinion leaders.

Social contacts include friends, acquaintances, neighbors, relatives, and people met at social gatherings. Business contacts include the various merchants and professional people with whom you do business. Each of these is likely to want to cooperate by either buying from you or referring you to someone else who might buy.

Influential people like to be recognized as such and also like to test their perceived influence. This means that when you ask them for a favor, you are in turn doing them a favor. It is likely that they have worked hard and used their own contacts effectively to gain this position and now want to reap the benefits. The motive could be self-serving or altruistic, but it doesn't really matter to the individual seeking the favor.

What this means to the salesperson is that contacts can lead to sales prospects. Let everyone know what you sell, for whom you sell, and to whom you expect to sell.

Satisfied Customers   Satisfied customers are prospects for additional products and services that might be added to your line. The retailer who opens another store in your wholesaling territory is a top-priority prospect. The customer who purchases a second home is a prime prospect for any salesperson selling a product or service that would be needed in the second home as well as in the original home. Satisfied customers become regular customers.

In addition to being prospects for additional business, regular customers are sources for other prospects. The fact that your regular customer gives you repeat business would indicate that you have a positive relationship and that your customer is benefiting from your product or service. You can strengthen this relationship by giving such a customer extra service and attention. This may involve rushing an order or helping a customer solve a business problem.

In many cases, the completely satisfied customer becomes committed to helping you increase your sales. The best way for the customer to do this is to provide names of other individuals or businesses that are likely to become customers.

When regular customers are handled properly, the prospecting aspect of the salesperson's job is aided in three ways:

1. Fewer prospects will be needed to replace dissatisfied customers.
2. The customer is a prospect.
3. The customer provides names of potential prospects.

Other Prospects   Prospects who buy and prospects who do not buy are both sources of potential prospects. The salesperson who relies on prospects to secure additional prospects recognizes that the purpose of the sales interview is twofold:

1. To make the sale
2. To get the name or names of other people who might be interested in the product or service

This method of prospecting, referred to by many as the *endless chain,* is based on a geometric expansion of potential prospects. If two names are obtained from each prospect, each of whom supplies two more names, the result will be a prospect list that rapidly multiplies. (See Exhibit 6.4.)

Those who buy are often happy to refer you to their friends who might be in a position to benefit from your product or service. Some are so enthusiastic about their purchase that they want friends to share their enthusiasm and are willing to give you the names of those friends. Others give referrals for another reason. They may be somewhat uncertain about their purchase decision and want friends to buy also to support their decision. This feeling (called *cognitive dissonance*) is especially prevalent among buyers of expensive or new products. They take comfort in being able to say, "Harry Becker also purchased this kind of buggy whip, and you know that Harry has always been an astute predictor of the future."

Prospects who do not buy because they do not have an immediate need or sufficient financial capability might still be so impressed by your proposition that

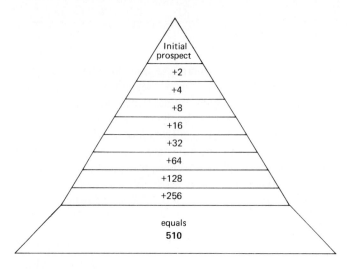

EXHIBIT 6.4
HOW TO GET 510 PROSPECTS

they want to do a friend a favor by having you pay him or her a call. This is a good reason why you should not oversell to the point of being *persona non grata*. If good rapport is maintained, the chances of a referral are increased.

Whether referrals come from contacts, regular customers, or prospects, the probability of success in converting a referral into a customer is improved if your source provides more than just a name. The best results occur when the source of the referral calls the prospect for you or provides you with a letter of introduction. The next best situation is to have permission to use the source's name when making the call on the prospect. Always ask for these aids. They will improve the approach to the prospect and increase his or her interest in hearing your presentation.

Other Salespeople

Once you have been in a sales territory for a period of time, you typically develop a camaraderie with the various salespeople representing other companies. It is likely that you will encounter them at service club meetings, at restaurants, or at the customer's place of business. These salespeople sell competitive and non-competitive product lines. In either case, a good relationship with them can lead to information that might be valuable in prospecting.

A salesperson who sells chain saws to a dealer network might inform you that a dealer is considering adding woodburning stoves to his merchandise mix. Here is a potential prospect you probably would not have known about otherwise. A salesperson who sells industrial supplies informs you that the purchasing agent at

XYZ Corporation experienced difficulty with the communication network when trying to get verbal approval for a purchase order. Thus the XYZ Corporation might be a prospect for your communication service. A competitor's salesperson mentions to you that her company cannot meet the new specifications for a customer. Your company may be able to meet the specifications, and you may have a prospect.

Cold Canvassing

Cold canvassing involves literally going from door to door, factory to factory, or office to office in search of prospects. The salesperson essentially qualifies the prospect on initial contact and hopes to either get agreement for an immediate sales interview or an appointment for an interview at a later time. It also includes canvassing by telephone.

The Girl Scouts (cookies), certain religious orders (booklets), and direct-sales companies (vacuum cleaners, encyclopedias, cosmetics, etc.) are common users of this prospecting method. It is employed for those products and services that are used by a wide range of the population, regardless of demographics or other characteristics of the total market.

Industrial salespeople also use cold canvassing as both a primary and a secondary source of prospects. An industrial cleaning supplies salesperson can call on every factory in an area: He or she assumes that every establishment either is being kept clean or should be. The prospecting call will reveal the "is" or "should be" status. The clean factory is a likely prospect for a new cleaning formula or perhaps for lower-priced supplies that will not compromise cleanliness. The dirty factory has an obvious need that would have to be broached in a delicate manner.

Even those who generally do not rely on this prospecting method use it to increase their selling productivity. There will be times when a prospect cancels an appointment for a sales interview or when you have an open time block for some other reason. You can use this otherwise unproductive time to make a cold call on a nearby potential prospect.

Cold canvassing should only be used for those types of products and services for which other prospecting methods are not practical and to fill time between calls to bona fide prospects. It is clearly the least efficient method of prospecting. Many cities have ordinances prohibiting canvassing, and both Oregon and Washington prohibit it throughout their states.[1] In Toronto, canvassing salespeople are required to have photo-identification cards.

Telephone canvassing is the least expensive and generally the least effective kind of canvassing. Companies selling inexpensive items use the telephone to make the sale. Other companies use the telephone primarily for the initial contact to determine whether the individual (or company) is a prospect. Salespeople using other prospecting methods also use the telephone to qualify the lead further and to make an appointment for a sales call.

---

[1]"Door-to-Door Dollars," *Forbes*, Aug. 6, 1979, p. 65.

118

Advertising and Inquiries

Placing the right kind of advertisement in the right medium is the first step. Handling the inquiries generated by advertising is the crucial second step. Let's look at the media commonly used to generate leads and then discuss how to handle the inquiries.

Advertising Media   The type of product you sell and the type of person or firm you want to reach will determine the advertising medium used. Some companies use a multimedia approach. Others find they can reach the target audience through one particular medium. Direct mail, print media, and broadcast media are the principal sources from which inquiries are received.

Direct mail   Some companies solicit by mail and make sales without the aid of a salesperson. The buyer simply sends the reply card along with a check and receives the merchandise. This direct-mail method is used primarily for inexpensive merchandise where the dollar risk is minimal.

For many types of products and services, the direct-mail package contains a description of the product or service and a reply card to be returned to the advertiser. The reply cards received by the advertiser represent potential prospects who might be called on by a salesperson.

Important to the success of direct-mail advertising is a good *current* list of people you want to reach. There are hundreds of firms that rent or sell lists of names they have acquired and cataloged. The lists usually rent for $30 to $60 per thousand names. Market Data Retrieval (MDR) is a company that lists 9 million businesses. You can reach the 432 barber schools they list, or the 50,347 barbershops, or just barbershops in California. MDR seeks leads for its service in *Business Marketing*. (See Exhibit 6.5.) So you see, everybody's out there prospecting—in this case, prospecting for firms that want to prospect.

Print media   The print media—newspapers, magazines, trade and professional journals, and so forth—are also used to develop prospect lists. Advertisements are placed in the publications most likely to generate inquiries. For example, the IBM Displaywriter System is advertised in *Business Week*. Interested readers are encouraged to inquire by either filling out the in-ad coupon or calling a toll-free number. Tubbs Cordage Company, on the other hand, is looking for industrial distributors to sell its products, so it advertises in the more specialized *Industrial Distribution*. Interested distributors may circle the appropriate number on the reader's card, which is sent to the publisher, who acts as a clearinghouse for the advertiser. (See Exhibit 6.6.)

Broadcast media   Radio and television are used to some extent for prospecting by getting inquiries primarily from consumers rather than from other kinds of buyers. Usually the address or the toll-free phone number of the advertiser is given for those desiring more information about the product or service or to place actual orders.

D&B HAS GAPING HOLES IN ITS BUSINESS LIST

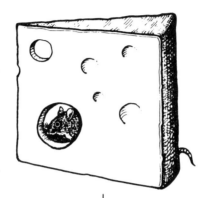

If you're really interested in reaching American business, you have to reach beyond D&B.

Because D&B has some very big holes in its business list.

Hole Number One: D&B omits hundreds of thousands of Retailers.

Hole Number Two: D&B lists almost 2,000,000 fewer Business and Professional Services than we do.

Hole Number Three: We've got 300,000 more Wholesalers than D&B.

Hole Number Four: D&B offers nearly zero names in the vital, dollar-spending Government Agency sector.

We have virtually the same businesses as D&B has, plus over 3,000,000 they don't have. 9,000,000 businesses in all.

Most of these 3,000,000 extra names are the smaller businesses salesmen can't afford to call on. But don't underestimate their importance to you.

Our customers tell us that these are the most mail-responsive businesses on our file.

If you rely on D&B you're missing a market that's the numerical equivalent of *all* the businesses in California, New York, Texas, Ohio, Pennsylvania, Illinois and Florida.

All our names are fresh. We crank over 50,000 new names into our computer every day.

Our service is fast. With a 95% guarantee of accuracy. And you can have our list for $35 a thousand or less. As you know, D&B charges $50 or more a thousand.

So, a phone call to MDR can dramatically increase your customer universe and could cut your list cost in half.

When you use MDR's business list you can put gaping holes in *your* competition.

EXHIBIT 6.5
PROSPECTING FOR PROSPECTS FOR PROSPECTING (*Source:* Market Data Retrieval.)

120

January 1982 Valid Thru 5/82 [ ][ ][ ][ ][ ][ ][ ]
(For Office Use Only)

Name _____

AFFIX PEEL-OFF LABEL
FROM FRONT COVER HERE

Title _____
Company _____
(Do not abbreviate)
Company Address _____
City _____ State _____ Zip _____
Telephone (_____)

Complete questions [1] [2] & [3], sign and date for your FREE copy of INDUSTRIAL DISTRIBUTION.

CIRCLE THE INQUIRY NUMBERS OF ITEMS ON WHICH YOU WANT MORE INFORMATION.

1	33	65	97	129	161	193	225	257	289	321	353	385	417	449
2	34	66	98	130	162	194	226	258	290	322	354	386	418	450
3	35	67	99	131	163	195	227	259	291	323	355	387	419	451
4	36	68	100	132	164	196	228	260	292	324	356	388	420	452
5	37	69	101	133	165	197	229	261	293	325	357	389	421	453
6	38	70	102	134	166	198	230	262	294	326	358	390	422	454
7	39	71	103	135	167	199	231	263	295	327	359	391	423	455
8	40	72	104	136	168	200	232	264	296	328	360	392	424	456
9	41	73	105	137	169	201	233	265	297	329	361	393	425	457
10	42	74	106	138	170	202	234	266	298	330	362	394	426	458
11	43	75	107	139	171	203	235	267	299	331	363	395	427	459
12	44	76	108	140	172	204	236	268	300	332	364	396	428	460
13	45	77	109	141	173	205	237	269	301	333	365	397	429	461
14	46	78	110	142	174	206	238	270	302	334	366	398	430	462
15	47	79	111	143	175	207	239	271	303	335	367	399	431	463
16	48	80	112	144	176	208	240	272	304	336	368	400	432	464
17	49	81	113	145	177	209	241	273	305	337	369	401	433	465
18	50	82	114	146	178	210	242	274	306	338	370	402	434	466
19	51	83	115	147	179	211	243	275	307	339	371	403	435	467
20	52	84	116	148	180	212	244	276	308	340	372	404	436	468
21	53	85	117	149	181	213	245	277	309	341	373	405	437	469
22	54	86	118	150	182	214	246	278	310	342	374	406	438	470
23	55	87	119	151	183	215	247	279	311	343	375	407	439	471
24	56	88	120	152	184	216	248	280	312	344	376	408	440	472
25	57	89	121	153	185	217	249	281	313	345	377	409	441	473
26	58	90	122	154	186	218	250	282	314	346	378	410	442	474
27	59	91	123	155	187	219	251	283	315	347	379	411	443	475
28	60	92	124	156	188	220	252	284	316	348	380	412	444	476
29	61	93	125	157	189	221	253	285	317	349	381	413	445	477
30	62	94	126	158	190	222	254	286	318	350	382	414	446	478
31	63	95	127	159	191	223	255	287	319	351	383	415	447	479
32	64	96	128	160	192	224	256	288	320	352	384	416	448	480

Primary Business Activity (check one)   REV 03/81
☐ 01 General Line Distributor
☐ 02 Specialist Distributor
☐ 03 Combination Distributor
☐ 04 Mfg. Agent/Rep
☐ 05 Importer/Exporter/Broker

Employment Data:
Number of employees at this location _____
Is this location a Company — (Please Check)
☐ Headquarters   ☐ Branch
Number of salesmen at this location?
Outside Sales _____
Inside Sales _____

Main Product Lines Normally Stocked At This Location
(Check all that apply)
☐ A. Cutting Tools and Abrasives
☐ B. Mechanics Tools and Accessories
☐ C. Powered Shop Equipment and Quality Control
☐ D. Pipe, Tubing Valves and Fittings
☐ E. Fluid Power Hydraulic/Pneumatic
☐ F. Power Transmission Products
☐ G. Bearings
☐ H. Materials Handling Equipment
☐ J. Industrial Rubber and Plastic Products
☐ K. Fasteners
☐ L. Electric and Electronic
☐ M. Safety and Security Supplies
☐ N. Contractors Supplies and Accessories
☐ P. Maintenance Repair and Operating Items
☐ Q. Welding Equipment and Supplies
☐ R. Facility Maintenance and Supplies

What Is The Average Value of Inventory At This Location?
☐ A. Less than $25,000
☐ B. $25,000 - 49,999
☐ C. $50,000 - 99,999
☐ D. $100,000 - 299,999
☐ E. $300,000 - 499,999
☐ F. $500,000 - 999,999
☐ G. $1,000,000 - 4,999,999
☐ H. $5,000,000 +

Signature _____
Date _____

EXHIBIT 6.6
PUBLISHER'S REPLY CARD (*Source: Industrial Distribution.*)

Handling Inquiries   Systems for handling inquiries range from sophisticated centralized systems that require salespeople to report the results of the lead they receive to no system at all. The following depicts what a well-managed system would look like:

1. The inquiry is received by the advertiser directly from the inquirer or from the advertising medium acting as a clearinghouse.
2. Additional literature is sent to the inquirer about the product or service.
3. Qualifying information concerning specific needs is obtained through a telephone call to the inquirer or through the return of a reply card sent to the inquirer with the literature. Financial qualifying may be done now, or later, by the salesperson.
4. Data for qualified leads (prospects) are sent to the salesperson.
5. The salesperson responds by calling on prospects and then reports the results of the initial call and follow-up calls.

The interests of the company are served best when inquiries are turned into sales. Unfortunately, inquiries serve disparate interests. Publishers are judged by the number of inquiries generated by their publications, and the advertiser's advertising department is often judged by the number of inquiries that come in from its advertisement. The quantity of inquiries tends to increase if it is easy for the reader to inquire by circling numbers on reader's cards or making a toll-free call. Many of these inquirers clearly are not serious prospects. Some companies do not include toll-free numbers because they feel that those with serious intent will pay the dollar or two for the call. Piper Aircraft is one company that dropped its 800 number and increased both responses and sales.

The seriousness of an inquiry can be determined only by following up on it. Many interested inquirers complain that they never receive a response or that they receive information too late. This is the fault of the inquiry-handling system. The result is that salespeople are denied potential prospects.

Many aspects of inquiries are beyond your control. But you do have control over the leads sent to you. Follow up on them, and keep a record of the results of your follow-up even if your company doesn't require your feedback. If your company requests that you report back, do so. It will help your company assess the relative merits of the various inquiry sources and might improve the qualifying process. In the long run, the quantity and quality of leads you receive may increase.

Company Employees

Every company employee is likely to be a source for prospects. Their friends and neighbors are usually aware of their company affiliation and often pass along information which might be beneficial to the salesperson's prospecting endeavor.

Company service people can be particularly helpful. They are in contact with customers to perform routine maintenance and to make repairs. They are aware of the remaining useful life of the product they are servicing and the extent to which it is acceptable for satisfying the customer's changing needs. A customer is likely to say, "This machine has probably seen better days. It has worked hard and long to keep up with the increasing demand." This customer could be a prospect for a replacement sale, an upgrade sale, or an additional sale.

Delivery people uncover all kinds of information that might be valuable for prospecting. They get to see places and people that salespeople might not get to see. They go to the warehouse and talk with warehouse employees who might make comments, such as, "I wish Ace Corporation's deliveries were as reliable as yours" (Ace is a competitor that has a share of the business), "Ace's cartons are difficult to handle," or "Ace products don't move out of this place as fast as yours do." Such statements should be conveyed to you because they indicate that Ace's customers might be a likely source of prospects.

Delivery people are also in a position to pick up information from their counterparts for competing companies. Information exchanged at coffee shops and diners where they meet can be revealing. If they understand that they, too, can employ the observation method, then prospecting is aided.

In companies that stress a marketing orientation for all employees, the salespeople benefit by being helped in all aspects of selling, particularly prospecting. It is important that you maintain a favorable relationship with nonsales employees so that they are encouraged to cooperate with you.

Observation

Every day you are exposed to all kinds of information. The newspapers you read, the people with whom you have conversations, and even the areas through which you travel are among the many sources. By keeping your eyes and ears open, you are able to pick up information that might be helpful in prospecting.

The newspaper is a principal source of prospects for some salespeople. Their targets include the engagement announcements that list tomorrow's newlyweds, who will need a multitude of products and services for the big event and postwedding living. Photographers, banquet managers, and insurance salespeople are among those who see these people as prospects. Even the classified section of the newspaper is replete with potentially valuable information. One insurance agent studies the help-wanted ads to see what employee benefits are being offered. If health benefits are not offered, the employer can be considered a prospect for a group medical insurance package or the employees can be considered prospects for individual plans.

Every time an individual's (or a business's) circumstances change, new needs are likely to follow. We hear every day about those who are pregnant, are moving, have inherited money, and so forth. To most people, this is just interesting gossip. To the astute salesperson, this can be valuable information for adding to a prospect list. (See Exhibit 6.7.)

While you are traveling through your territory, it is wise to keep your eyes open for more than just oncoming cars. If you are like most salespeople, you are apt to

EXHIBIT 6.7
PROSPECTING THROUGH THE NEWS

The news	Who cares?
Mrs. Jones is pregnant for the first time.	Diaper Service Realtor (larger house?) Maternity shop Insurance agent Attorney (will? guardian?)
The Littles are moving.	Moving company Realtor Tag Sale Enterprises
The Rich's have inherited a fortune.	Investment counseling service Realtor Travel agent Car dealership Local furrier Everyone with something to sell!
Hilton's store was robbed.	Police Ketchems Security Systems Insurance agent Guard service Guard-dog-training service

spend one-quarter to one-third of your time in your car. Most salespeople can make valuable observations while traveling between accounts. Some do most of their prospecting this way. Both house painters and siding salespeople look for peeling paint on houses. Moving companies look for *for sale* signs. Fenestration engineers (window salespeople) look for energy-inefficient windows on buildings.

Trade Shows

There are hundreds of trade shows conducted every year throughout the country. They are sponsored by industries such as the National Association of Home Builders, the National Micrographics Association, and the National Material Handling Association. Companies rent exhibit space to display and demonstrate new and existing products.

Many manufacturers of industrial goods use the trade show as their principal method of prospecting. Those attending the show are primarily buying influences, which means they make buying decisions or participate in making buying decisions for their companies. A study conducted by the Trade Show Bureau reveals that 83 percent of the buying influences at exhibits had not been called on by the exhibitor during the previous year. "The 83% average illustrates strongly that effective exhibits are reaching the hidden buying influences."[2]

The purpose of the trade show is twofold:

1. To make sales at the show
2. To qualify prospects for follow-up calls

It is important that as much information as possible about the buyer's needs and other buying influences in the company be obtained so that the on-premises sales call will be more productive.

Research

There are various publications and sources that provide pertinent information about industries and companies within those industries. The inexpensive *Standard Industrial Classification Manual* published by the U.S. Government Printing Office uses a hierarchical method of providing data by standard industrial classifications (SIC). These SIC codes allow the salesperson to zero in on the companies within any segment of a given industry.

SIC codes are four-digit numbers. The first two digits represent the major group, such as manufacturing firms (20 to 39) or professional services (80 to 89). The third digit represents the industry group, the fourth digit the specific industry. (Exhibit 6.9 illustrates some SIC codes.)

Other publications such as *Thomas' Register* and *Mac Rae's Blue Book* are also most helpful in prospecting. *Mac Rae's,* for example, lists all U.S. manufacturers alphabetically by company name, by trade name, and by product classification.

---

[2] "Trade Shows: Where Exhibitors Call on You—A Special Report," *Sales & Marketing Management,* Aug. 20, 1979.

EXHIBIT 6.8
PROSPECTING UNDER A VARIETY OF CIRCUMSTANCES
(1) At a party; (2) with a customer; (3) in a library with directories; (4) on the telephone; (5) in the newspaper; (6) ringing doorbells; (7) at a child's baseball game.

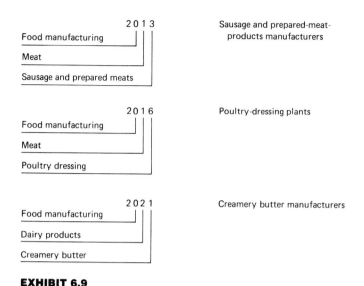

2013	Sausage and prepared-meat-products manufacturers
Food manufacturing	
Meat	
Sausage and prepared meats	

2016	Poultry-dressing plants
Food manufacturing	
Meat	
Poultry dressing	

2021	Creamery butter manufacturers
Food manufacturing	
Dairy products	
Creamery butter	

EXHIBIT 6.9
SIC CODE SAMPLES

Included is information on capital rating, approximate size, and telephone numbers of branch and sales offices. *Thomas' Register* contains similar information arranged geographically. For specific geographic areas, the Yellow Pages are widely used. Every telephone book has a business directory (Yellow Pages) containing vendors of products and services in the directory's geographic area. Since every business phone subscriber is entitled to be in the Yellow Pages, you're bound to find any business you're looking for. The problem is that if you're prospecting a wide market, you'll have to let your fingers do the *running* through the Yellow Pages. Another source is AT&T's *Business Directory*, which is an industrial sales and service guide.

Incidentally, the mailing-list firms mentioned previously use the Yellow Pages for developing their data bases for the direct-mail lists they rent. Also, buyers use the Yellow Pages when they are prospecting for sellers, making this directory a source for inquiries concerning many types of products and services.

AT&T's Market Reports can also be helpful for gaining general knowledge and identifying specific prospects. They contain U.S. Department of Commerce and U.S. Department of Labor statistics, reports from planning and zoning commissions, lists of manufacturers classified by number of employees, and so forth. You can get them from the local telephone office or from the chamber of commerce in your area. Additionally, chambers of commerce, banks, and public utilities have publications that may be useful to some salespeople.

Computer-assisted prospecting is becoming more widely used. A company searching for information about companies within a target industry can use terminals to access data bases containing relevant information. An example of this is the Lockheed Dialog information-retrieval system. This system provides access to Economic Information Systems' data bank of more than 100,000 manufacturing plants listed by SIC code, volume of sales and purchases, and so forth.[3]

HOW TO QUALIFY LEADS

How you go about qualifying a lead depends quite a bit on how you generate the lead and on the kind of product or service you're selling. The qualifying process is ongoing. You do as much as you can during the prospecting stage, then more during the preapproach stage, and, finally, more during the sales interview.

Referral leads generally are the easiest to qualify. The person doing the referring often has the information you need. All you have to do is ask. For example, assume you sell a data processing service and have just sold the service to Lillian Simmons, who has given you the name of Howard Stotto of Addens, Inc.

YOU: Mrs. Simmons, about how many employees does Addens have?
SIMMONS: About seventy-five to a hundred.
YOU: What would you say its sales volume is?
SIMMONS: It must be almost twice ours, and growing.
YOU: What's Mr. Stotto's position with Addens?
SIMMONS: Same as mine: chief accountant.
YOU: This information is very helpful. What kind of a person is Mr. Stotto?
SIMMONS: About forty, dynamic, conservative dresser.

Simmons has helped you qualify that lead. Number of employees (payroll processing) and sales volume (receivables, payables, inventory) indicate the need for more sophisticated data processing methods. Addens is growing, which indicates the business is successful and can probably afford the service (or can't afford not to have the service). According to Simmons, Stotto is dynamic, which along with his position in the firm indicates he'll have the buying authority.

You even got some preapproach information (covered in the next chapter) about Stotto. He's a conservative dresser. So when you approach him, leave your leisure suit in the closet.

Not all referrers will be as helpful and informed as Simmons. Nevertheless, for all types of referrals and leads from other salespeople and company employees, ask the person giving you the lead for information. If they can't give you some qualifying information, it isn't much of a lead.

For other types of leads, check, analyze, relate, and ask to get qualifying information.

Check the lead's credit rating at the local credit bureau or through Dun & Bradstreet's rating service, if necessary. Check what is listed in directories about the company and its personnel.

Analyze observable characteristics, such as lifestyle for a consumer and advertising for a firm. Size of house, kind of car, style of dress, and circle of friends may

[3]Jay Gould, "Panning Gold from Torrents of Data," *Sales & Marketing Management,* June 13, 1977, pp. 104–106.

indicate needs and purchasing power. A firm's advertising may indicate something about its concern for quality, its size, and so forth.

Relate similar leads to your experience. Try to see how the profile of one lead compares with the profiles of other leads you have followed up. There may be a pattern, such as renters being better prospects than homeowners, physicians better than dentists, colleges better than high schools, for the product or service you sell.

Ask the source of your lead questions, or ask the lead. You can ask further qualifying questions when you phone for your appointment.

PROSPECTING NEVER STOPS

Prospecting should be an ongoing activity. Use every opportunity to get the names of potential prospects and qualify them. Keep adding to your prospect list, and rearrange priorities as you add names. There are never enough good prospects.

Keep in mind that the success of the entire sales process begins with effective, diligent prospecting. Every day there are salespeople drinking a second, third, or fourth cup of coffee or cruising around their territories because they do not know on whom they should call next. A salesperson without a prospect is like a clotheshorse all dressed up with no place to go.

Prospecting is the beginning of the selling process and is an activity that must receive continual attention.

RECAP

Prospects are individuals, firms, or organizations that are likely to have the need, money, and buying authority for your product or service.

Prospecting involves obtaining names of potential users, qualifying those names, and listing prospects in priority order. There are numerous sources for prospects, including referrals, other salespeople, cold canvassing, inquiries, company employees, observation, trade shows, and directory research.

Prospecting opens the selling process. Intelligent prospecting is one secret of effectiveness in closing.

REVIEW QUESTIONS

1. Explain the relationship between leads, prospects, and customers.
2. During the qualifying process, what assessments about the lead must you make?
3. What factors determine the priority a prospect receives?
4. Explain why prospecting is so important to the selling process.
5. Why might your contacts be interested in helping you obtain prospects?

6. How does the proper handling of satisfied customers aid prospecting?
7. What are the ways used by advertisers to allow readers to respond to ads?
8. Why is a good inquiry-handling system important?
9. What kinds of things can the newspaper reveal that will help in prospecting?
10. What is the purpose of a trade show?
11. Explain what the digits in a SIC code represent.
12. Why are the Yellow Pages an important prospecting tool?
13. Does qualifying occur only during prospecting? Explain.

DISCUSSION QUESTIONS

1. Can you think of instances during which a salesperson has tried to sell you something when you were, in fact, not really a prospect? What made the salesperson think you were? What qualifying procedures were lacking?
2. Why do you do friends a favor? How would your reasons apply to giving referrals?
3. Explain the research methods you would use to make a major purchase (car, stereo, camera, etc.), and show any similarities to a seller's prospecting activities.

LEARNING EXPERIENCES

1. Interview a college coach (preferably the football coach), and ask about the recruiting methods used. What is the relationship of recruiting to prospecting?
2. Interview a salesperson, and ask how he or she develops a prospect list. What technique generally provides the best prospects?
3. Interview a personnel manager, and find out which prospecting methods are used for new employees, especially new salespeople.

CASES

RETAIL SECURITY SYSTEMS

Retail Security Systems (RSS) sells a variety of mirrors and cameras used for deterring and catching shoplifters. It markets its products in a three-state area in the midwest. About 90 percent of its customers are supermarkets.

The store security industry has grown rapidly during the past decade. Annual losses from theft, commonly called *shrink,* have been estimated at more than $10 billion. As inflation pushes up prices and erodes consumer purchasing power, customer theft is expected to be an even greater problem for the retail industry.

RSS's sales have not kept pace with the industry's sales increases. The sales manager has said that better prospecting methods should be developed by the sales force. Currently, customer referrals and inquiries from advertisements in a monthly trade magazine are the principal sources of leads.

Questions

1. Why do you think the sales manager concluded that better prospecting methods were needed?
2. Explain what other prospecting methods should be considered.

LEAD MANAGEMENT

Stock brokerage firms primarily use direct mail and print-media coupon ads to generate sales leads. Direct-mail response rates average 4 to 6 percent. For the print media (newspapers and magazines), a 1 percent response rate is considered quite good.

While response rates are a traditional yardstick for measuring advertising effectiveness, the ultimate concern of the brokerage firm is the number of respondents turned into customers. This is where many firms fail. Brokerage A converts only 3 percent of its leads from a particular source to customers. Brokerage B, using leads from the same source, converts 15 percent.

This information has been brought to the attention of the sales manager at brokerage A. The sales manager says that brokerage B's advertising elicits better-quality leads, but the marketing director says that brokerage B must be better at managing its leads.

Questions

1. What other statistic might give a clue about the quality of the leads?
2. How would you check the management of the leads?

SEVEN

CHAPTER OBJECTIVES

To acquaint you with the kinds of information you should try to obtain in advance of the selling approach

To pinpoint the kinds of information you should try to obtain at the outset of the interview

To provide a checklist to guide you in planning your approach

To cover the principles and methods that win sales interviews

To describe some special preapproach techniques for *re*-calls

CHAPTER OUTLINE

THE PREAPPROACH

> The secret of success is to be prepared for opportunity when it comes.
>
> Benjamin Disraeli

In all fields of human endeavor, success is directly related to diligent preparation behind the scenes. Disraeli's advice is especially valid for a salesperson's approach to a prospect. The better your *pre*approach, the better your chances for the attention and potential interest of your prospect.

This chapter will cover the fundamentals of the preapproach. When you have completed it, you will know how to apply these fundamentals to improve your odds for an easier approach, a more meaningful sales interview, and a successful closing.

PREAPPROACH DEFINED

The preapproach covers everything you do in advance of the approach and in the early stages of the sales interview to make your approach and the sales interview successful.[1]

The preapproach involves finding out all you can about the prospect, both as a buyer and as a person, to make sure you say the right things in your approach and selling effort. It means advance preparation to make sure your approach and presentation are meaningful to the prospect. It means utilizing proven devices to gain a proper sales hearing. It means the quest for an approach and selling strategy that will open the prospect's mind as well as the prospect's door.

Where does prospecting end and the preapproach begin? Selling is not an easily compartmentalized activity. The various steps in the selling process blend into each other and even sometimes change places. By and large, your preapproach begins when you start to think about a specific prospect. The general search for potential buyers that preceded this individual consideration was prospecting. In addition, the preapproach extends right into the early stages of the sales interview itself—since the distinguishing characteristic of the preapproach is establishment and confirmation of how to approach and sell to the specific prospect. The reason it is called the preapproach is to place emphasis on *the things you do in advance* of your approach—or selling commitment in the interview itself—until you know you are on track with the specific prospect. Expressed in another way, your preapproach is complete when you know enough about the prospect to start your close without fear of a backfire. (See Exhibit 7.1.)

For example, imagine you are an automobile seller. Your preapproach is complete when you know:

1. The buying objective of your prospect, i.e., price range, operating cost, convenience, status, credit accommodation, or other motivation
2. The right model to present to answer this motivation
3. Who will make or influence the buying decision, i.e., user, managers, spouse, employer, friends, etc.
4. The prospect's ability to finance the purchase
5. The prospect's buying habits or manner of decision making

This last item will serve as a guide as to how to conduct your presentation to conform to the prospect's frame of reference, speed of perception, and similar qualifications.

Says George Berkwitt, chief editor of *Industrial Distribution:* "Many salesmen make a beeline for the purchasing department before they know anything about the plant and its real needs. No attempt is made to see where and how their products are used or by whom—especially by whom. *Many of them overlook the unusual potential of the man or the woman in the shop to influence the ultimate decision to buy.*"[2]

---

[1] The terms *sales call* and *sales interview* are used interchangeably in this text. All sales interviews are sales calls. But at various times, the buyer calls on the seller; the seller calls on the buyer: or seller and buyer meet at another location, for example, at a business show or a fair.

[2] George Berkwitt, "The Real Influence," *Industrial Distribution,* January 1982, p. 37.

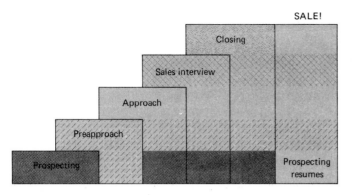

EXHIBIT 7.1
STEPS IN THE SELLING PROCESS

A TALE OF TWO SALES—THE PREAPPROACH MADE THE DIFFERENCE

Jason Whitaker knew he had to take out more insurance on his house. He had just added a second bathroom and a large family room. In addition, he had not increased his insurance coverage during seven inflationary years. So when insurance broker Sam Greenfield phoned for an appointment, Whitaker agreed to see him.

Just as Greenfield was starting his sales presentation, the phone rang. When it rang a second time, Whitaker told his secretary to hold all calls. However, partway through Greenfield's introductory statements, the phone rang once more.

"I must apologize," said Whitaker. "An emergency has come up, and I have to drop everything. Let's meet again next Thursday. By then I should be cleared away and free to talk."

But Greenfield never had the second interview. Because Jess Simmons, another broker, also knew Whitaker was a prime prospect. Only Simmons proceeded differently. He questioned the contractor who had done the job for Whitaker, hoping to find a special need or want that would give direction to his presentation.

"Whitaker is a strange duck," the contractor told him. "He's the big boss, but he gets in every morning at six. He opens the joint up."

Simmons phoned Whitaker and said, "I have some new information on home insurance that could be valuable to you. But I'm all booked with dates for a week ahead. Is it possible to see you early tomorrow morning?"

"How early?" asked Whitaker.

"You name it," said Simmons.

"Well, how about six-fifteen?" Whitaker chuckled as he spoke. He assumed *early* to Simmons meant eight-thirty or nine.

Simmons pretended to gulp. "I'll be there," he said.

At 6:15 the next morning there was no one on hand but Whitaker and Simmons. The stage was set for an uninterrupted sales interview. Moreover, it got off to a favorable start because Whitaker was amused at having gotten Simmons out of bed so early. You see, his early bird reputation was a secret source of pride to Whitaker.

When Greenfield phoned to confirm his new appointment, Whitaker apologized to him again. He already had a binder on his new insurance policy.

In the situation above, one salesperson got a couple of apologies. The other, because of advance work—a good preapproach—got the order. This really is a tale of two sales efforts, not two sales. Only one sales representative made a sale.

ELEMENTS OF A SOUND PREAPPROACH

Selling is a game of options. At each step in the selling process, you must decide between different courses of action. The more you know about the answers to the questions (shown in Exhibit 7.2), the more intelligent will be your choice of options. We call this *the selling question chain*.

The essence of the preapproach is to ascertain as much of this information as possible before the sales interview.

What makes one preapproach better than another? It depends on three elements and the skill with which the salesperson carries them out:

1. Research
2. Planning and preparation
3. Preapproach action

Research

The first essential of the preapproach is finding out all you can about the prospect both before the approach and in the early stages of the interview. The more information you obtain, the more comprehensive will be your strategy for approaching and selling this buyer.

Eleven Key Questions   The answers to these eleven key questions will start you off in your research.

1. What are the prospect's needs, wants, or special problems?
2. Which features of your product or service answer these needs, wants, or special problems?
3. What type of motivation is apt to influence the purchase?
4. If more than one person is involved, who will make the buying decision? Who will influence it? (In its simplest form, this question arises in a selling approach to a family. It can be far more complex when the prospect is a business organization, a government, or a university. See Exhibit 7.3.)
5. What are the names and titles of the buyer and anyone who may influence the buying decision? How does each prefer to be addressed? Will it be "Mr.," "Doctor," or "Charlie," "Mrs.," "Ms.," "Senator," "Mary," or something else?
6. What are the prospect's personality characteristics, hobbies, and special interests?

EXHIBIT 7.2
THE SELLING QUESTION CHAIN

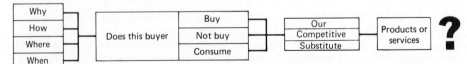

EXHIBIT 7.3

WHICH ONE TO SEE?

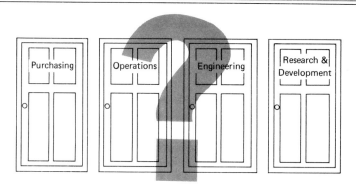

Here is the eternal dilemma of the industrial salesperson. According to the organization chart, the purchasing agent is the first person to see.

"It Ain't Necessarily So"

The organization chart is not always consistent with practice. Competent purchasing agents are indeed open and alert to locate new items and sources. Yet there are purchasing agents who see their function as keeping things out rather than bringing things in. This is a classic reason for the importance of the preapproach.

"We Hear You Have a Widget That Doesn't Wiggle"

Sometimes one of the other departments calls your company directly to request information. Before you make this sales call, it is wise to ascertain whether the purchasing agent is one who objects to direct contact. If so, clear the call with purchasing first.

When you know there will be no repercussions, it is advantageous to make the initial contact with the other department. For example, you might phone the R&D manager and say something such as, "We've developed a widget that doesn't wiggle. Would you like to see samples and technical data?" If your call is off limits, the R&D manager is likely to suggest that you go through channels. The reply might even be that purchasing will be requested to ask you to call.

There is no ironclad rule for this. Technically, you should not even question protocol. However, when your preapproach investigation reveals that you will not alienate purchasing by directly acquainting other departments with new items, you will find it worthwhile to do so. This calls for discernment, tact, and diplomatic skill—important attributes of the professional salesperson.

7. Does the prospect now have a means of satisfying the need or want that your product or service will answer? (This can be the patronage of a competitor, the use of a substitute, or a do-it-yourself approach.)

8. How is your product or service more advantageous to the buyer than the present means he or she has of answering the need or want?

9. What objections or other resistance are you apt to encounter, and how will you handle them?

10. When is the best time to see this prospect and where?

11. What is the best way to get to see the buyer? By appointment or through a cold call? If by appointment, through telephone call or letter? By referral from another buyer, friend, or acquaintance? By delivering a gift, report, plan, or something else of interest to the prospect? By any other idea or device?

Sources of Information   Where do you obtain the information about your prospect? First, there are published sources like professional and trade publications and newspapers. For example, if you sell office supplies, you should read the local publication in this field. If you need information on a particular buyer, the chances are that someone on the staff of one of those publications has it. Other likely sources are people at the prospect's trade or professional associations.

Another source of intelligence is other salespeople who call upon the same buyer. Information swapping by noncompetitive sellers is a common practice. You also can sometimes obtain information about a prospect from other buyers to whom you sell. Your inquiry is even apt to result in an *introduction* to the new prospect.

Use Your Eyes and Ears   Firsthand observation will yield valuable information about a prospect. For instance, a sales representative for a soft-goods line, planning to approach a retail chain, will learn a great deal about the buyer's business by simply visiting one of the chain's stores. A sales representative for a meat packer, before approaching a restaurant buyer, eats a meal at the restaurant and notes the decor, service, menu, prices, and other aspects of the restaurant's personality.

Ask the Buyer   The prospect can indeed be asked for information. An insurance broker says to the prospect, "I'm not here to sell insurance at this time. But I'd appreciate some information to ascertain whether I have an advantage to offer you that is worth your attention." A travel agent asks a recently retired jurist what she and her husband consider the most memorable vacation they ever spent. This will enable the agent to keep the couple informed of similar travel opportunities. Incidentally, a request for information is disarming. When the prospect knows the first purpose of the call is for information, with selling a later consideration, resistance is generally lessened.

"I wonder if you can give me a few facts about your truck fleet operation?" the leasing company representative asks the prospect. "We have some new information on when it pays to lease instead of to buy. The study includes facts, numbers, and dollars. But it doesn't apply in every case. With only a few questions I can tell whether there's any point in taking up your time."

Fill in at the Interview   You can learn much at or before the interview by asking the right questions in the right manner. A husband can supply vital intelligence about his spouse. A secretary or assistant generally knows a lot about the business of the executive you will be seeing. As a matter of fact, it is a good idea to ascertain the accuracy of your advance information by checking it with the prospect early in the interview. For example, an industrial real estate salesperson might open with, ''Am I correct in assuming that you need about thirty thousand square feet?''

Checking facts early in the sales interview precludes the risk of a false start. It also adds to your credibility as a professional salesperson. The buyer will sometimes even take the initiative in supplying information—if the salesperson draws the buyer out. That is why the competent seller tries to make it truly a sales *interview* rather than a selling monologue. Above all, do not make the cardinal error of committing your selling line to a fixed course until you are reasonably sure it is the right course.

In some selling classifications, it generally is advisable to devote one or more calls to learning all about the prospect's business before narrowing your sales presentation to an effort to close. For example, if you are selling a soft-drink bottling franchise to a multiline bottler, there are many variables to be understood and agreed upon by both you and your prospect before a closing can be made. The same would apply to the placement of an exclusive distribution agreement for a brand of office copier or word processor.

It's Easier the Second Time   When it takes more than one call to close the sale or when your product or service is reorderable, thus requiring periodic calls on the same buyer, you can really get to know the buyer and the buying situation. This makes for intelligent selling.

You should note on your prospect or customer card not only the facts on the buyer's needs, wants, special problems, and buying habits but also hobbies, dates like birthdays and anniversaries, names of children, and any other information that might serve a purpose in a continuing relationship. These facts are valuable reminders in linking call to call. For example, your periodic call on a regular customer might start with something like this: ''The last time I was here, Hank, we discussed summer promotions, so I've brought along a pamphlet that I think you'll find interesting.'' Or in a re-call on the purchasing agent of a packaged foods processor who has never bought your ingredient, you might start out, ''Ms. Gould, when I was last here you expressed reservations about how Sparex would affect the acid base of your products. Here's a lab report that I believe will reassure you.''

All the information you have on a customer or prospect should be entered on a 3×5 card, using your own code for ease in recording and retrieval. For important buyers, a more detailed file should be kept. Noting facts in one record makes for easy reference later.

No Two Selling Situations Are Exactly Alike   Selling situations really are *buying* situations in reverse, for it is the way in which the buyer buys and his or her reasons for buying that guide you in how to sell. No two selling situations are

EXHIBIT 7.4
MIX-UPS IN MENSWEAR

identical. The buying motivation and mechanism for the once-in-a-lifetime purchase of a home or a business are entirely different from those for the simple purchase of a pair of gloves. The approach to a prospect who will resell what he or she buys, as in a retail store, is different from the approach to a terminal buyer who will actually use your product. In addition, there are selling situations where the objective is to regain a lost customer or to handle a complaint. In short, selling situations come in all shapes and sizes. Each prospect, each selling situation, must be considered separately. That is why the preapproach to apply selective strategy for the case in question is so important.

How Much Advance Information Should You Seek?   How much information should you seek in the preapproach, and how much should you wait to develop in the sales interview? This depends on the nature of the selling situation. In selling an engineering firm's services to a government for a study of natural resources, advance research might take a year and the time would be well-spent. In selling paper goods to small offices, the advance research would of necessity be very limited or nonexistent.

The amount of preapproach research is normally in proportion to the dollar importance and complexity of the selling situation. How much information is needed and purposeful? Are potentials for sales and profits worth the cost? These are the bottom-line questions. (See Exhibit 7.6.)

EXHIBIT 7.5
SELLING THE SAME SHOE—WHOLESALE AND RETAIL

EXHIBIT 7.6
DEFINING THE BUYING-SELLING SITUATION*

1 What class of buyer buys?	2 What class of goods or service?	3 For what direct purpose?	4 With what demand intensity?	5 In what buying mode?	6 For what satisfaction?	7 Where?	8 When?	9 With what frequency and regularity?
Industrial	Commodity*	Use	Emergency	Impulse	Hunger or thirst	At home	Specific time of day	At *frequent regular* intervals
Institutional (hospitals, schools, etc.)			Necessity		Sex		Specific time of week	*Infrequent regular*
Commercial		Direct resale	Convenience	Routine	Security	Afield	Specific time of month	
Political	Specialty†	Indirect resale	Luxury	Deliberation	Aggression	Buyer's place of business	Specific time of year	*Frequent irregular*
Professional					Elemental sensibility‡		Specific time of life	*Infrequent irregular*
Ultimate consumer					Esthetic sensibility§	Seller's place of business	Any time of day	
							Any time of week	
							Any time of month	
							Any time of year	*Rarely*
							Any time of life	

* A commodity is an item of goods or service that has no special identity or no special feature, hence no special attraction other than price or accessibility (examples: wheat, iron, raw sugar, etc.).
† A specialty is an item of goods or service that has a special identity or a special feature, hence a special attraction other than price (examples: automobiles, golf clubs, magazines, typewriters, etc.).
‡ Satisfaction of elemental sensibility is the urge for pleasurable, uncompounded sensations of sight, smell, taste, touch, or physical comfort.
§ Satisfaction of esthetic sensibility covers the urge for harmonious organization of separate factors into congruous patterns of sound, sight, smell, taste, or touch.

Adapted from Bud Wilson, *Principles of Merchandising—A Key to Profitable Marketing,* Fairchild, New York, 1979.

Planning and Preparation

With the advance phase of your preapproach completed, you can plan your approach to the buyer with a reasonable chance of being on target. To be sure, you may not have been able to obtain all the information you would have liked. Use what you have. It is better than going in blind. You will at least know what you don't know and can fill in the gaps by deft questioning as you talk with the buyer.

Six Planning Points That Will Put You Ahead Now to make capital of the information you have obtained on the prospect's needs, wants, or special problems, prepare your sales call with this six-point procedure.

1. Relate your product or service features to the prospect's needs, wants, or special problems.
2. Rank these pertinent product or service features in order of interest to this prospect as a guide to organizing your presentation. This way you will be sure to present the benefits most important to the prospect. If time runs out, the features you have to skip will be of lesser importance.
3. Plan your approach and sales presentation with every point expressed in terms of the buyer's selfish interests. Know what you will say as you walk through the door.
4. Never forget your objective: to convince the prospect that your product or service is distinctively different from others and superior in answering the buyer's needs, wants, or special problems.
5. Try to anticipate possible objections, and plan on how you will handle them. (This will be covered in detail in Chapter 12.)
6. Review your plan over and over again. The lines and gestures that apply generally to most prospects are worth practicing—the same as an actor rehearsing a part. Your approach and presentation will become better and better with continued practice and use. (This will be discussed in detail in Chapters 9 and 10.)

Preapproach Action

The third phase of the preapproach is the active effort to pave the way to a sales interview. The ideal situation of course, for most kinds of selling, is for an appointment to be set up. In some cases, as in professional buying offices, regular buying days and hours are posted and the door is open to all sellers in order of arrival. At the other end of the spectrum is the field of direct selling to homes, offices, and small shops where advance appointments often may not be practical for either buyer or seller.

Even in direct selling, however, the most successful salespeople plan for orderly area coverage and make appointments wherever possible. Obviously, the interview by appointment carries more weight than one that results from a cold call. However, good door-to-door and office-to-office salespeople try to avoid the implication of hit-or-miss selling. For one thing, they try to learn the prospect's name and use it throughout the sales call. The start might be ''Mrs. Jones?''— with a pause for acknowledgment.

How to Get the Appointment   Appointments are sought and arranged by writing, by phoning, or through a third party.

Writing for the appointment   In many circumstances, a letter, individually addressed to the prospect, is a sound way to bid for an appointment. But it should offer something in exchange. There should be a "hook" in the letter. It should promise something useful to the prospect. An advertising agency offers a survey report. A household insurance company offers a home inventory book. A bank offers a set of personal budget forms. An office-equipment seller offers a startling solution to a common office management problem. The item offered will, of course, be delivered by the sales representative.

In some cases, the letter requests an appointment and encloses a stamped, preaddressed reply card. In others, the letter says you will call on the buyer at a specific time unless you hear to the contrary. In still others, the letter simply states you will be calling "in the near future." A fourth type of letter says you will phone for an appointment.

If the prospect is a business organization, a letter signed by the head of your firm is a logical approach. The better known your company or its head officer, the surer you are of an affirmative reaction.

When you are writing to the prospect personally, a handwritten note is more likely to be effective than a typed letter. The mail that comes in every day is full of typed and printed letters and literature, generally ignored by the buyer. A handwritten letter, by contrast, is personal and inviting. But, of course, be sure longhand is appropriate. If the letter is lengthy or deals with a major business announcement, for example, longhand would be out of place. Legibility and ease of reading must also be considered. In the case of a $60 million bond offering by an investment banker, a handwritten letter would be apt to disturb the confidence of prospects.

There is divided opinion on the usefulness of letters in gaining appointments. The "antis" believe a letter can give advance warning and forestall an interview that otherwise might have taken place. The "pros" take the position that only a bad letter brings this negative result—that a well-composed letter, aimed at the prospect's selfish interests, actually influences the prospect to welcome the sales call.

The obvious caution is to make sure you have something to say that is honestly worth the buyer's interest. If not, save the postage. But if you do have it, headline it. Start with a line that arouses curiosity and interest. An example of this is a letter to pharmacists that begins, "Would you like to hear about a new asthma remedy that relieved symptoms in 72 percent of the patients using it?" Not many factory owners will fail to take notice if the first line of a letter asks, "Would you like to hear about a proven way to cut your power cost by 30 percent?"

Phoning for the appointment   The most widely used method for making appointments is the telephone call. Follow the same cautions as in the letter approach. One way is to promise a benefit the buyer will not be able to resist. For example, "Would you like to hear about a tax-exempt bond that yields 12 percent?"

EXHIBIT 7.7
THE TELEPHONE IS A VALUABLE SELLING
AID (*Source:* Stephen L. Feldman/Photo Re-
searchers.)

Try to avoid revealing too much. Your objective is to make an appointment, not a telephone sale. Another device is to offer to deliver something useful to the buyer, like a recipe book to a restauranteur or a survey of consumers' shoe preferences to a shoe store owner.

Make the call as brief as possible, and get as quickly as possible to the time for the appointment. Heed Elmer Wheeler's time-proven principle: "Don't ask if—ask which."[3] "I can be there at ten or ten-thirty tomorrow, or any time in the afternoon. Which is more convenient for you?"

Seeking the appointment through a third party By far, the most desirable way to gain access to the prospect is, of course, the referral by a friend, acquaintance, or other third party. When someone known to the buyer personally or through reputation phones or writes to make an appointment for you or to arrange for you to call and set the time, the odds of your getting the appointment

---

[3] Sales theorist Elmer Wheeler made many important contributions to the art of selling. You will read more about Wheeler later.

are vastly increased. This method is used effectively for finding prospects as well as getting appointments to see them.

The Odd-Time Appointment   Some salespeople suggest odd times for the appointment, like 9:50 or 10:20. The reasoning is that people usually make dates on the hour or half-hour. They are more apt to be free at ten minutes before the hour or the half-hour. Also, the suggestion of an odd time implies that you are busy and businesslike and might be worth seeing.

PRECALL PREPARATION

Thus far we have discussed the longer-range aspects of the preapproach. Now imagine yourself actually on the firing line, right outside the prospect's door. What immediate precall preparation can significantly raise your odds for success after you go through that door to meet your prospect face to face?

One outstanding successful salesperson said, "I would rather walk the sidewalk outside the prospect's door for two hours before an interview than to approach that prospect without a perfectly clear idea of what I am going to say." This is good advice that has been followed by successful salespeople in many fields.

Think before You Leap

No matter what you sell or to whom, what you do immediately before the sales call is at least as important to a favorable outcome as what you do in the interview. *Think* about it.

A ROOKIE SALESPERSON SELLS AN ABRASIVE

Twenty-two-year-old Craig Lasker stands waiting to see the owner of a machine shop. He represents a well-known manufacturer of abrasives. As he wonders how to approach the owner, Hans Kasmier, he hears Kasmier speaking impatiently to someone.

"Come to the point. I'm a busy man. What's the bottom line?"

Lasker has his line. When it is his turn to see Kasmier, he wastes no time. He quickly identifies himself and his company and lays a piece of his company's literature on Kasmier's desk.

"Quality assured," Lasker says, "delivery guaranteed, and price ten percent less than you're now paying."

Kasmier grins at the young salesperson in amusement. "How soon can you make a delivery?" he asks.

Are you about to call on an investor to sell a bond? Before you cross the threshold, consider the possibilities. What do you think the investor is most interested in? Security? Yield? Maturity date? Tax advantages? Think about it. What kind of a person is he or she? Think about your opening line.

Are you about to visit a government procurement officer to sell airplane parts? a business organization to sell computers? a department store to sell furniture? or

EXHIBIT 7.8

Classics in Selling
THE FATHER OF SALES TRAINING

John H. Patterson, founder of what is now NCR Corporation, was the first business leader to recognize selling as a profession. He sponsored the first training program to help his salespeople improve their productivity as closers.

Yet, for the selling of cash registers, Patterson did not believe in rushing to close. On the contrary, he believed his salespeople should make no effort to close during first calls on a dealer.

"It is one of our fixed principles," he said, "that no talk about buying should be started until the agent knows all about the prospect's business."

NCR sales representatives were completely instructed in how to go into a store and what to look for; to make a purchase and see how it was handled; to watch vigilantly for a mistake that might cause a monetary loss which the NCR cash register would have averted. Patterson wanted his salespeople to understand the merchant's real problems before trying to sell. He believed that NCR representatives should conduct themselves with an aura of professionalism, not as sellers of cash registers but *as experts, able to counsel* merchants on the systems and controls that NCR cash registers could provide.

EXHIBIT 7.9
THINK BEFORE YOU CROSS THE THRESHOLD (*Source:* Photo by Craig Callan.)

a grocery chain to sell olives? Are you about to approach a prospective lamp buyer on the floor of a retail store? or a cosmetic buyer at home? It doesn't matter whether your objective is the sale of a 400,000-square-foot factory building or a raffle ticket. The principle of precall preparation still applies. Sometimes it takes an hour, sometimes but an instant. It pays dividends. Think before you cross the threshold into the prospect's presence.

Precall Preparation for a Major Sales Call

In the case of a major sales call, you will have acquired much essential information in your preapproach research. For example, if you are after the contract to lay the foundations for a major housing development, you will have read the engineering specifications and building code requirements. You also will have visited the architect to learn the design objectives. You will have visited the bankers who are financing the project. You will have discussed the project with media people who are following this important community development. You will have determined from among these people who in the building contractor's organization will make the final decision and what influences will have a bearing on that decision. What you were not able to learn in advance, you will develop by inquiry during the first interview with the prospect's buying representative or committee. As already stated, you will be careful not to commit your presentation to a direct course until you have the facts.

There still is helpful information you can spot on the threshold of the approach, some of it perhaps superficial but revealing of the nuances and characteristics of the people with whom you will be dealing. The reception room, the pictures on the walls, the furnishings, the dress and manner of personnel, the magazines and other literature in the reception room—these and other seemingly minor details may provide valuable clues on how to approach the prospect. For example, if you see a plaque honoring your prospect as former president of the Rotary Club, a friendly comment like, "I see you're active in Rotary," can be a purposeful ice-breaking pleasantry. Conversation with a receptionist or secretary also is apt to bring important information to light.

Preapproach Preparation for a Small Retail Sale

Preapproach observation and thinking also can aid the smallest transaction, even though the looking and thinking are swift and fleeting by comparison. For example, you observe that the woman browsing at the lady's blouse display is quite apt to be partial to blue. Why? She is wearing a completely blue outfit: dress, handbag, hose, shoes. So your opening might be something like, "Have you seen these new blouses by Anton? They just came in." As you speak, you hold up one of the blouses—a blue one—for the customer to examine. Or the man nearing the tie counter seems to be a conservative type. He is short and broad and is wearing a brown tweed suit. "Have you seen our new line of homespun knits from Scotland?" you ask as you hold out a brown knit tie for the buyer to feel.

EXHIBIT 7.10

Classics in Selling
HE MADE "THINK" A MOTTO

One of the greatest salespeople of all time was Thomas John Watson. At the turn of the century he left his job selling organs, pianos, and sewing machines at Painted Post, New York, to join National Cash Register (now NCR Corporation) as a selling agent. In time he became general sales manager and had close contact with John H. Patterson, NCR's founding president.

In 1913 Watson left NCR to become president of a fledgling company that would change its name in 1924 to International Business Machines Corporation (IBM). Sales were running approximately $2 million annually when Watson stepped in. This was barely 4 times what Watson would be earning personally not too many years later.

In leading this giant corporation to multibillion-dollar proportions, Watson liked to be called "Salesman Number 1." Like his mentor, Patterson of NCR, Watson thought of his company as a *sales* company. This was a new breed of business leader at the time, a breed that thought from the buyer back to the company, rather than from the company out to the buyer. All efforts were aimed at finding out the buyer's needs, wants, and problems and answering them.

Watson made the IBM motto one word—*think*. It appears on IBM desks, walls, and intracompany literature throughout the world.

Blind Approach—No Preapproach

The importance of the preapproach and especially precall preparation was vividly dramatized by a real estate salesperson who had a prospect for a summer cottage. The agent showed the prospect a house with a panoramic view from its lofty perch on a ridge high above the shore. The buyer was not interested in this house nor, from then on, any other house this seller would have shown. A simple inquiry about the prospect's family would have revealed that this family could not possibly have been interested in this cottage with its 240-foot stairway to the beach. One of the children was confined to a wheelchair.

> There weren't any ashtrays in the reception room or in the office of the important buyer with whom the young salesman had finally managed to get an appointment.
> "Have a cigar," said the salesman.
> "I don't smoke," was the icy reply.

RECAP

In selling, as in sports, the averages are what count. Behind the score is the telltale law of averages. One key secret of a favorable "batting average" in obtaining sales interviews and converting those interviews into successful closings is a good preapproach.

The elements of the preapproach are research, planning and preparation, and preapproach action. The amount of time and effort that should be spent on each of these depends on the nature and importance of the sales call.

The preapproach means finding out all you can about the prospect, the buying situation, and the problems you may encounter—in advance of the call or in the early stages of the sales interview. It means using this information to advantage, for advance preparation, where possible.

The preapproach also means using the right strategy to obtain an appointment in cases where an advance appointment is advisable.

Finally, the preapproach includes precall preparation on the very threshold of the approach. Seek clues that will further guide you to say and do the right things at the opening and during the interview.

REVIEW QUESTIONS

1. What is the preapproach? Explain its importance.
2. What are the three elements of a sound preapproach?
3. Name at least seven kinds of information your preapproach should seek.
4. What are some sources of preapproach research information?
5. What guides should be used to determine how much advance information to seek?
6. What are the six points of preapproach planning?
7. Name three ways in which you can obtain advance appointments for sales interviews. Comment on the usefulness of each method.
8. What is meant by precall preparation? Why is it so important?
9. What is the precall preparation for a major sales call?
10. How can the principle of precall preparation be applied in retail selling?

DISCUSSION QUESTIONS

1. As southeastern sales representative for the National Steel Desk Company, you have been assigned by your sales manager to sell Ivy-Leonard on becoming National's exclusive dealer for the Jacksonville, Florida, market. Your line of steel desks and related office furniture is of top quality and reasonably priced with a provision for a good gross profit for dealers. It is selling well in many markets, and the company's objective now is to open new markets so that an economically feasible national advertising program can be begun. Your sales manager has told you that Ivy-Leonard is the leading office-supply dealer in Jacksonville but carries no furniture line. This is your first trip to Jacksonville. You had never heard of Ivy-Leonard until you received this assignment.

   (a) How will you go about the research phase of your preapproach to Ivy-Leonard?

(b) Using your imagination to supply details not covered above, describe the case you will present to Ivy-Leonard for taking on your line, based on the findings of your advance investigation.

(c) Using your imagination to supply details not covered above, how will you get an appointment to present National Steel's proposition to Ivy-Leonard?

2. As president of Valhalla College, a small, privately endowed institution, you want to sell the Grant Hemingway Foundation on supporting your college. The special curriculum for which Valhalla is known and respected is a series of courses in the communication arts and sciences. In fact, an alumna has recently become president of Harding Broadcasting Corporation. Your appointment is with Carl Sands, a retired chemical engineer who manages the foundation. Grant Hemingway, owner of a regional chain of movie houses, died twenty years ago, and the foundation was created by his will. You have arrived an hour early for your appointment with Sands to read the foundation's literature and to give thought to precall preparation. Cantor, the receptionist, receives you cordially, and when you tell her why you have arrived early, she gives you three pieces of literature: "The History of Grant Hemingway Foundation," "Objectives of the Grant Hemingway Foundation," and "1983 Report of the Grant Hemingway Foundation."

(a) Using your imagination for contents of the three pieces of literature, what can you learn from them to aid your approach and presentation to Sands?

(b) There is no one else in the reception room and Cantor appears to be a sociable type. What precall clues can conversation with her yield as to Carl Sands and how to deal with him?

(c) What items in the reception room might provide precall clues on Sands and the foundation? Use your imagination and relate the item to its specific clue.

3. Your appointment with John Kennealy, National Food Stores' confectionery buyer, to present your dietetic candy line is set for 10 A.M. It is 9:40 A.M., and you have arrived early for your appointment. You observe from the receptionist's appointment list that another caller waiting to see Kennealy is the Snakko Nut representative. This is your first call on Kennealy.

(a) What precall information can the Snakko salesperson give you?

(b) How can you obtain this information?

LEARNING EXPERIENCES

1. As chairperson of the nominating committee of the United Community Fund (UCF) of Denver, you are waiting to see Harry Clayton, a successful management consultant, to sell him on accepting the presidency of the UCF for the coming year. How many precall clues can you find in Exhibit 7.11, an illustration of Clayton's outer office? What are they? How would you approach Clayton? What would be your opening line?

150

2. You are an account executive with Knowles-Henderson Associates, a medium-sized advertising agency in Chicago. Most of your agency's billings are for packaged-goods accounts. Now, an appointment has been set up for you to make a presentation to a group of executives of the Turner Pharmaceutical Company, a publicly owned manufacturer. Your purpose in making this presentation is to capture the advertising business for Turner's Sun Guard skin oil. You know that the group will include Marie Hardwicke, chairwoman of the board; Scot Allenby, president; Ed Goldstein, vice president—marketing; Sara Turner, general sales manager; Charles Solar, treasurer; and Hal Jodice, product manager for the division that includes Sun Guard skin oil, Turner's biggest-selling product. Your appointment for the presentation was set up by Jim Herrold, a partner in Turner's law firm. You know Herrold well, and he has agreed to lunch with you to tell you all he can about Turner. Prepare a checklist of all points of information you will seek from Herrold to aid you in your sales presentation to the Turner Pharmaceutical Company.

3. You are an insurance representative for Calhoun and Morse. Your specialty is group plans for industry. You read on the business page of the daily newspaper that Jack Lamson has just been named president and chief executive officer of Harrison Chemical Company. You know that Harrison's employee benefits

EXHIBIT 7.11
RECEPTION ROOM

package is behind the times. But you have never been able to sell the idea of updating it—or to sell any insurance for that matter—to the previous president. The change of leadership has opened the door.

(a) Prepare a checklist of the things you would do in your preapproach to make sure that you get an appointment with Lamson and that the meeting will be productive both for you and for Lamson.

(b) Write a letter to Jack Lamson to get an appointment. Use your imagination for any facts to appeal to Lamson's interests as head of Harrison Chemical Company.

4. *Role playing.* Alice Cass, residential real estate representative for Brooks Realtors of Sacramento, California, is meeting in her office with Harvey Clarin. Clarin explains at the outset that his wife will have the final word on what they should buy. He has just been transferred to Sacramento and is living in a hotel. His wife, Hilda, will join him in a couple of weeks, and all he wants now is to become familiar with the Sacramento real estate situation prior to Hilda's arrival.

(a) One person is to play the part of Alice Cass, and another is to take the part of Harvey Clarin. This really is a *preapproach* interview, since the main decision maker, Hilda Clarin, is not present. Cass's purpose is to learn all she can about the prospects Harvey and Hilda Clarin and what kind of house they should, and will want to, buy and also to lay the groundwork for making the sale after Hilda's arrival in Sacramento.

(b) The rest of the group observes the interview and, remembering that this is a *preapproach* interview, offers comments, suggestions, and criticism to the role players.

(c) Now let different people play the roles. Then let the group review the role playing and comment again.

CASES

THE MARLBOROUGH DINING ROOM

Sheldon Astrom has just entered the office of Marianne Littleby, owner of the Marlborough Dining Room, a popular-priced restaurant with an English countryside theme. He is to present his line of restaurant supplies. This is Astrom's first call on the Marlborough, as he is relatively new in the job. Here is what took place in the interview.

ASTROM: Miss Littleby, we have a complete line of restaurant supplies, everything from tableware to paper goods. This is our Hartlin tableware line (*takes samples from sample case and places them on desk*). Serving plate, soup bowl, bread-and-butter plate, salad plate, dessert dish, and cup and saucer. Beautiful, isn't it?

LITTLEBY: I'm *Mrs.* Littleby. I have a big inventory of tableware, specially decorated for our English countryside theme. We don't use salad plates. There are plastic salad bowls at our salad bar. Tableware is the last thing I'd be interested in. Also, you've caught me at a bad time, a half-hour before the luncheon rush, so you'll have to excuse me.

Questions

1. What was missing in Astrom's approach to Littleby?
2. How many errors can you spot that resulted from this omission?
3. Rewrite Astrom's opening statement in a better way.

CAROLINDA LAUNDRY COMPANY

Young Herb Wilson was pleased with himself. He represented M. R. Weiser Associates, accountants and management consultants specializing in route industries. On the way to an appointment in the Bronx, he had found his route going right by Carolinda, one of New York's largest cleaning and laundry companies, with some 300 driver-salespeople on the road. "What can I lose?" he said to himself. "I'm going right by the plant. I may as well try a cold approach."

When he handed his card to the receptionist, she was confused as to whom Wilson should see. At this point a dignified older gentleman, walking through the reception room, asked what the problem was and, looking at Wilson's card, said, "Come into my office." As Wilson followed, he noticed the name on the door. He was about to meet with Harold J. Lane, Carolinda's president! No wonder he was pleased with himself.

"Tell me about your service," said Lane.

"It's a special management consulting service keyed to the problems of route industries like yours," answered Wilson. "Systems, controls, marketing with a training program for supervisors and route salespeople, materials and processing flow, and production engineering."

"Production engineering, eh," said Lane. "That happens to be a special interest of mine. Tell me more about what you might be able to do for us in that area."

Wilson had a green light. Off he went, launching into an enthusiastic description of Weiser's spectacular production engineering department headed by Ray Carlson.

"Carlson's one of the best in the business," he said. "He spent several years with Harley, Jansen, & Moore on productivity improvement through worker incentives, time and motion study, and work simplification. He's really a genius on machine placement and factory layout. In one case he tripled production per worker-hour on flatwork ironers. Incidentally, you know that key-lock identification system introduced by ALM?"

"I'm familiar with it."

"Well, Carlson set up a system for applying it at the Knickerbocker Laundry that eliminated all the guesswork. If an item gets lost, Knickerbocker knows about it and communicates with the customer before the customer even knows it's missing.''

''Mighty interesting. I'd like to meet your Carlson one day.''

Next morning Herb Wilson told Ray Carlson about his call on Lane.

''Whew!'' exclaimed Carlson. ''You know, I'd give a month's pay just to be able to listen to Lane for an hour. Herb, Lane *invented* the ALM Key-Lock Identification System! He collects royalties for his patents on some of the leading machines in the business. The only reason he's at Carolinda is that he owns part of it.''

Questions

1. Should Wilson have made the cold call on Carolinda? Explain your answer.
2. Once in Lane's office, what key selling principle did Wilson violate?
3. If you were in Herb Wilson's place, how would you approach Carolinda and Lane on your next call?
4. If you were in Herb Wilson's place and this sales interview had *not* taken place, how would you approach Carolinda as a potential client?

EIGHT

CHAPTER OBJECTIVES

To emphasize the critical importance of the approach

To explain the psychology behind the prospect's responses to your approach

To acquaint you with the realities affecting the approach: time, place, circumstances, extraneous distractions

To describe proven approach principles and the various techniques through which they are applied

CHAPTER OUTLINE

THE APPROACH

Your first ten words are more important than the next ten thousand.

Elmer Wheeler*

It happens in a flash, your first face-to-face contact with the buyer. In that incredibly short time, maybe ten seconds, you and your prospect will meet and mesh or miss—personally, emotionally, and intellectually. The approach is the springboard that gets your sales interview off to a good start or pushes it off the track. Many a sale is made or broken in these first seconds, for the way in which you open is the first step toward the ultimate closing. It's only a fraction of a minute, but it determines whether you will have a chance to make your sales presentation and also whether you will make it under favorable or unfavorable conditions. A skillful approach is the bridge that links your sales preparation with selling fulfillment. In your closing, you sell goods or services. In your approach, you sell the interview itself.

An effective approach wins the buyer's attention, but even more important, it opens the buyer's mind. This chapter will cover theory and practice on how to accomplish this.

*Elmer Wheeler, *Secrets of Successful Selling,* Prentice-Hall, Englewood Cliffs, N.J., 1956 (Published in paperback by Dell, New York), p. 78.

THREE APPROACHES THAT WORKED

The ways in which you can make your first seconds count in approaching a prospect are many and varied. Here are three examples of how three salespeople in different situations gained the prospect's attention.

A RELEVANT APPROACH THAT STRUCK HOME

"Are you interested in how you can increase your sales through *exception spotting?*" is the opening question put to Stanley Barkman, vice president of Frangold Frozen Food Distributors, by June Aston of Harwood Business Systems as Barkman pauses at the Harwood booth at the Chicago Business Show.

How can Barkman say "no"? That would belie the validity of his position and the reason he came to the show. So there he stands, all ears, waiting to hear June's sales presentation.

This approach was successful because June did four things:

1. She identified a want of most buyers at a business show—how to improve management.
2. She related a feature-benefit of her product to that want in her opening.
3. She presented the appeal tersely—*in terms of her prospect's interest and frame of reference.*
4. She did so with a question that could elicit only a "yes" answer.

A PERSONALIZED APPROACH THAT WON THE BUYER'S EAR

Harold Rodman, president of Rodman Supply Corporation, has asked an accountant to introduce him to his client, Joseph Martindell of the Martindell Development Company. He is after the six-figure order for bathroom fixtures for the new apartment house Martindell is about to build.

"Be brief and get out," is the accountant's advice to Rodman. "Martindell is a no-nonsense man. If you take more than five or ten minutes, you'll lose out."

Yet Rodman spends three hours with Martindell, is invited to have lunch with him, and sets the stage for winning the contract. All because of an opening question that *attracted Martindell's attention, pleased his ego, and got him talking about something that interested him.*

"While waiting for you, Mr. Martindell," he began, "I've been admiring your office furnishings. Isn't that lamp French Lalique?"

Martindell beamed. "Yes," he replied. "You spotted it. Genuine French Lalique glass. You don't see it around much today. That lamp has a story. I found it years ago on a side street in Paris."

A DRAMATIC APPROACH THAT COMMANDED ATTENTION

"Oops!" exclaims the Corning sales representative, dropping a Centura dinner plate on the floor of the buyer's office as though by accident. Sitting up in her chair, the buyer waits for the crash of breaking china. But there is no crash, only a dull thud as the plate hits the floor and stays intact.

"Centuraware won't break. It's backed by a lifetime guarantee," explains the sales representative with a proud smile.

This approach was fast and effective. It moved the prospect's attention directly into the presentation. The reason is showmanship with a capital *S*.

June Aston made her approach effective by stimulating Barkman's curiosity and self-interest. Harold Rodman appealed to Martindell's ego. The Corning sales representative used showmanship—not an empty, bizarre, theatrical display but *purposeful* showmanship that dramatized a product feature and its benefit to the buyer.

These are but three of an almost limitless number of approach techniques. You will become acquainted with many more as this chapter progresses.

REALITIES OF THE APPROACH

You often have to make two sales to win one order. Your first objective is to sell the prospect on *spending time* to hear your presentation. If you cannot make this sale, you never will have a chance to persuade the prospect to *spend money* for your product or service. The degree of ease or difficulty that you encounter in approaching a buyer can vary all the way from an uphill climb to a downhill coast, depending on a variety of circumstances and what you do about them. The professional salesperson accepts the realities and employs strategic devices to deal with them. Let us examine some of the variables you are apt to meet as you make your approach.

The Selling Situation

Is this sales call on a new prospect, a regular customer, or a former customer? Are you visiting a factory, an institution, a home, or an office, a consumer or a distributor? Is it a one-call situation like the approach of a salesperson traveling from town to town with a line of advertising specialties, or is it the beginning of a series of calls to cultivate an important buyer of repeat items? Is it a major selling project in which you will devote several visits to different members of an organization to persuade them to favor your product or service? Is it a *cold* call, or have you an appointment? Different selling situations call for different approaches.

Flowered Path or Fortress?

Ease of access to the buyer is highly variable. It can be a primrose path or a rocky road. For example, a buyer who buys for resale, like a retailer or wholesaler, is on the *lookout* for merchandise; it is that buyer's stock-in-trade. The same applies to an industrial purchasing agent, whose job depends on knowing all sources of supply. These classes of prospects have open doors, usually regularly scheduled buying hours. Selling in a retail store also presents no serious approach problem. The buyer has come to the store voluntarily.

Direct selling of an office specialty like typewriter ribbons or duplicating supplies is quite another story. In this case, the economics make it necessary to do

158

much calling from office to office without appointments. The buyer is not waiting for you and is not usually anxious to use time to interview you. In fact, receptionists and secretaries often serve as sentries and try to keep salespeople out. Obviously, in this setting, mastery of strategic approach techniques is a critical requirement.

In no field of selling is it more difficult to gain entrance than in direct door-to-door selling. This problem has been accentuated in recent years by the rise of crime and the resultant reluctance of householders to open their doors to strangers. For this reason, many companies which sell door to door have modified their tactics. They use the telephone more, both for advance-of-call notification and, in the cases of some products and services, to seek orders. They provide their salespeople with identifying credentials. They give their representatives gifts to deliver as door openers and tell the prospects about it by phone or mail in advance of the call. They also are resorting more and more to *referencing,* which means being referred to a prospect—or even introduced—by someone known to the prospect, even if only a neighbor. Finally, direct sellers have been forced to be aware of, and conform to, telephone privacy acts and other municipal restrictions and regulations.

The Prospect's Natural Interest

Another factor determining how easy or difficult you will find the approach is the prospect's degree of natural interest in your product or service. For example, many women have a natural interest in fashion merchandise but less interest in house paint and perhaps still less in fuel oil. A young single person is quite apt to be naturally interested in automobiles but less interested in dinnerware and still less in fire extinguishers.

EXHIBIT 8.1
THE MOST DIFFICULT APPROACH OF ALL

The Prospect's Special Interest

Special interest in your product or service is quite another thing, varying with the time, the place, and the circumstances. For example, a person whose natural interest in house paint is normally low can become very interested when planning to repaint a house. A normally low interest in fuel oil changes to vital concern when there is a threat of short supply. The young person who has a lukewarm interest in dinnerware can become very interested in it when setting up a house. Fire extinguishers? They may be of only casual interest, except when a neighbor's house has just burned to the ground.

Demand Intensity

There are four degrees of demand intensity: emergency, necessity, convenience, and luxury.[1] The greater the demand intensity, the easier the approach. A torn

[1]Bud Wilson, *Principles of Merchandising—a Key to Profitable Marketing,* Fairchild, New York, 1979, pp. 50–51.

jacket can be an *emergency* for a career woman away from home; she certainly will seek out a tailor to get it repaired or even seek out a seller. Her daughter, living on a budget in another city, has but three jackets. When one wears out, she replaces it; that is *necessity*. Another woman has a closetful of jackets. Occasionally, she replenishes her supply while shopping for other things; this is *convenience*. But when she is in a specialty store and tempted to buy a new brand or style of jacket at twice what she normally pays, this is, of course, a *luxury* purchase.

Timeliness

How timely is your approach? It takes no selling genius to approach people to buy umbrellas in the rain. It is quite another thing to approach someone to buy an umbrella when the sun is shining.

Advance Preparation

The thoroughness of your preapproach, as explained in the last chapter, makes your approach easier. If you know a lot about the prospect from your preapproach research, you will be that much more prepared in your approach. As covered in the chapter on prospecting, there is a vast difference between a *suspect* and a legitimate *prospect*. Choosing fewer but better prospects reduces the number of purposeless calls. Referrals and appointments set up in advance cut the risk of

EXHIBIT 8.2

Classics in Selling:
HE INVENTED WHEELERPOINTS

In 1938 *The New York Times* ran a front-page story on the dissuasion of a would-be suicide. How did the story make the front page? After all, suicides and would-be suicides are reported quite regularly in a metropolis like New York, but not on the front page.

What made this story different was the way the potential victim was dissuaded. He was influenced to come in from the ledge of the hotel by an employee of the Tested Selling Sentence Institute, who accomplished the feat by appealing to the man's psychological responses. This was Elmer Wheeler's small, new firm, destined to make marketing history by developing *tested selling sentences* for marketers all over the world.

"Don't sell the steak—sell the sizzle" was Wheeler's admonition.

When you ordered a milk shake at Walgreen's and the fountain clerk asked, "One egg or two?" that was Wheelerpoint number 4—*"Don't ask if—ask which."* When the Exxon service attendant asked, *"Fill 'er up?"* that was Wheeler again. And so was the Woolworth line: "Have you tried these *square* clothespins? They can't roll away when you drop them."

Elmer Wheeler made a key contribution to the transition of selling from a gregarious art to a professional discipline.

turndowns. Advance information that enables you to plan your opening improves your approach batting average.

APPROACH PRINCIPLES AND TECHNIQUES

Your effectiveness in gaining sales interviews depends on three factors:

1. The personal equation
2. Adherence to sound approach principles
3. Strategic approach techniques

The Personal Equation

There is a subliminal interaction between you and your prospect that often defies logic or reason. Call it personal chemistry, if you will. But if this interaction is favorable, it can be a positive stimulus. If it is unfavorable, it can upset an otherwise perfect approach.

The first thing the prospect sees and hears is not your approach or your sales presentation. What the buyer sees and hears first is *you*. You are unique and exclusive. No matter how many sellers can match your product or service benefits, *no one can duplicate you*. So make the most of your individuality. Be sure the foot you put forward as you approach your prospect—and throughout the interview—is indeed your best. We are talking about personal presence, the essence of the personal equation. Your presence is a composite of many elements: dress and grooming, posture, facial expression, air of confidence, eye contact, attitude, enthusiasm, voice quality composure, and handshake.

Dress and Grooming   What *you* see in your mirror is not important. What *your prospect* sees is what counts. Your clothing is the frame for the picture of you as seen by the buyer. Let it be appropriate for the time and place.

Posture   This is a text on selling, not physical culture. However, the way you sit, stand, and move helps to command respect from others and self-respect from within. Sit straight. Move with grace. Stand and walk tall. It will help you *feel* tall and raise your self-confidence, which is so important to selling effectiveness.

Facial Expression   Make a pleasant smile a habit. But be sure it is real. There is a vast difference between the smile that is contrived, as though the smiler had pressed a smile button, and the sincere smile that comes from within. A genuine love of people and a joy in being alive are important parts of a charisma that has a magnetic effect on the people you meet, including buyers. Recall, if you can, the waiter with the hearty smile who invited you to order as though it was a pleasure to serve you. Contrast him with the sourpuss who impersonally poised pencil over pad and flatly said ''yes?'' Which one would you rather patronize?

''Do you feel all right?'' the sales manager asks a sales representative. ''I feel fine,'' is the reply. ''Well, you should tell your face,'' says the sales manager; ''It'll help your business.''

Air of Confidence   Confidence not only helps you to do better, but it also has a reciprocal effect on the prospect you are approaching. People have confidence in confident people. Think of what you *are*—not what you are not. Work to develop honest skills and other qualities on which inner confidence is built. In a list of points on how to make a speech, the Dale Carnegie Institute gave the following advice to speakers who would develop confidence on the platform: "Know forty times as much about your subject as you can use." This is excellent counsel for anyone who wishes to develop confidence as a salesperson.

Eye Contact   When you're speaking, always look the prospect in the eye and never take your eyes away. When you're listening, look at your prospect's mouth and nod your head slowly. A drifting eye implies a drifting mind, not a compliment to the buyer. Give the other person your rapt attention, and let it be evident from your eye contact that you are hanging on every word.

Attitude   To apologize for taking the buyer's time is beneath the dignity of the selling profession. This, of course, must not be confused with a common-courtesy "thank you." Buying and selling are complementary functions with mutuality of interest. The salesperson who brings the buyer information, products, and services from which the buyer derives benefits does indeed render that buyer a service. Hold your head high and go about your business with dignity. Be proud of your calling as a professional salesperson, a service career which requires training and special skills.

Enthusiasm   There is an adage that says, "Enthusiasm is contagious." In no field of human endeavor is this more worthy of note than in selling. The more enthusiastic you are about the product or service you are bringing to the buyer and about the solid benefits the buyer will obtain from it, the more receptive the buyer will become. Your own enthusiasm inspires credibility in you and your product or service. We are not talking about noisy, rabid enthusiasm. We are talking about something more akin to confidence, a quiet kind of confidence that breeds trust and acceptance. If you know all you should about your product or service and are not enthusiastic about it, think it over. You need either a new product or service or a new profession.

Composure   Your composure is a composite picture that should show you being relaxed and attentive. Much has been written lately about *body language*, the psychological undercurrents expressed unconsciously in body movements. In addition to revealing undercurrents of thought that are contradictory to what is being said, body language reveals your composure. Excess body language can be unattractive and distracting. It is disconcerting to the prospect to be talking with a salesperson who drums on the desk with fingers, shifts restlessly from one side of the chair to the other, runs hand over cheek, rearranges clothing, or evidences any other form of excess body language.

Voice Quality   The tone of your voice is the music that accompanies what you say. While your words are reaching the buyer's mind, the quality of your voice is

EXHIBIT 8.3

AS OLD AS SELLING AND STILL SOUND

The making of a sale under normal circumstances is a four-step procedure. The salesperson must:

1. Attract the prospect's *attention*.
2. Arouse the prospect's *interest*.
3. Stimulate the prospect's *desire* to enjoy the benefits of the product or service.
4. Spur buying *action*.

Attention—Interest—Desire—Action

This acronym is so old that its specific origin is not known. All texts, old and new, offer principles and methods to achieve these four steps: *how* to attract attention; *how* to arouse interest; *how* to build desire; and *how* to spur buying action. But no one has been able to improve on the bedrock structure itself. It is the basis of all selling.

No matter how advanced or complex your involvement with selling becomes, never lose touch with this underlying four-step process as a guide and test of what you are doing.

AIDA

reaching the buyer's emotions. Make sure your prospect's emotional reaction to your approach is as favorable as the rational response to your words and thoughts. Speak slowly and distinctly. Vary your pitch level to avoid sounding monotonous. Pause frequently to make sure you are communicating, not just talking. Intersperse your statements with questions to focus the buyer's attention. Avoid what public speaking authority Richard C. Borden called "word whiskers", the "ers"

EXHIBIT 8.4
WATCH YOUR BODY LANGUAGE . . . . BODY SILENCE CAN BE GOLDEN TOO

and "ahs" and "you knows" with which some people punctuate their speech. A silence between phrases gives you just as much time as a word whisker to frame your next phrase, but instead of distracting, it actually enhances your hold on the listener's attention. The way to underscore verbally is through choice of words, inflection, and rhythm. This is more effective than raising your voice. Loudness is a sure sign of lack of vocabulary, lack of emotional control, or both.

Handshake   Never extend your hand to a new prospect. This is the buyer's option. Some people like to shake hands and some do not. If the buyer does offer you her or his hand, by all means respond with a hearty grasp. To many people, the way you shake hands indicates the kind of person you are.

EXHIBIT 8.5
VOICE VOLUME

Not all selling authorities agree on speaking to the buyer in moderate tones. Some, like sales consultant Walter Horvath, believe voice volume should be varied from prospect to prospect. Here is what Horvath says:

> For a refined man or woman, a low precise tone is most effective, whereas with a rough, uncouth prospect a loud, hearty, full-throated tone will be more influential. A high, penetrating tone with a thick-skinned, surly customer; a smooth, oily, ingratiating tone with a pompous, conceited positive customer.

Adherence to Sound Approach Principles

Adherence to certain proven approach principles will make whatever approach technique you use that much more effective:

1. Use the buyer's name
2. Sell the sentry
3. Don't settle for half a hearing
4. Apply the "yes yardstick"
5. Plan your opening line
6. Use a "ho-hum crasher"

Use the Buyer's Name   Names are a seller's best friend. Dale Carnegie, the great master of the art of human relations, said that a person's name is, to that person, "the sweetest and most important sound in any language." Andrew Carnegie, the steel pioneer, assured the sales of millions of dollars worth of steel rails to the Pennsylvania Railroad when he named his new mill the Edgar Thomson Steel Works. J. Edgar Thomson was president of the "Pennsy."

Professional salespeople respect buyers' names and note them on customer and prospect cards along with names of secretaries, assistants, and other personal information. They use these names over and over again in conversation and written communications. They are very careful to make sure spellings are correct and titles accurate. Using a person's name is a token of respect, a compliment to the person's individuality. Acknowledging a statement by the buyer with a "Yes, Ms. Jones" is far greater evidence of your undivided attention than "Un-huh."

How to remember names   How do you remember names? By *concentration* and *practice*. In recording input, your mind is something like a computer. Every impression to which you have been exposed from the time you were born is recorded in your memory bank. Broadly speaking, we are all equal in *storage* of names. It is in *retrieval,* or recall, that we vary as individuals. Here are a few simple suggestions to help you remember names:

• *Get the name correctly.* When you are introduced to someone, repeat the name with your "How do you do," "Hello," or "Hi." Concentrate.

• *If in doubt, ask.* Ask the person to repeat the name. For example, "Is that McClain?" Or if the name is complicated, it is a compliment to its bearer if you ask to have it spelled. Then repeat it back. Too many introductions are sloppy. For example, "Jane Ter-eh-ne, may I present Jack Gloooo-z-ah." Break through the fog of such introductions forthrightly by asking the person you are meeting to repeat or spell his or her name.

• *Peg the ID.* Most names are lost in introduction. When you meet a buyer, listen carefully for the name and take a good look at the person. Get a *fix* on person, personality, and name. Some authorities recommend you associate the name and person with something else as a recall cue. This is undoubtedly sound for a person trained in the art of memory. However, when you meet Mrs. Reilly at the Hibernian Club picnic and remember her for the Irish association cue, be careful you do not address her as "Mrs. Irish" the next time you meet.

EXHIBIT 8.6
DON'T SETTLE FOR HALF AN INTRODUCTION

• *Write it down.* The best way to remember names is not to depend on your memory. Write it down. If it is a buyer's name, enter it on a customer or prospect card.

Sell the Sentry   The world of selling is full of sentries at the gate—secretaries, receptionists, assistants, and others. One of the first responsibilities of these "buffer" people is to see that a minimum number of callers, even those with valid credentials and purposes, get in to see the boss. They also must be careful not to exclude or offend someone the boss should see. This is reasonable. One executive estimated arithmetically that if she agreed to see everyone who came to her office, her entire day would be taken up and she still would not even be able to see all the callers.

The way to handle the sentry problem is to sell the sentry. Remember what Abraham Lincoln said, "The way to destroy an enemy is to make that enemy a friend." Make a friend of the sentry. Sell the secretary or other sentry on what the boss will gain by seeing you. Change that sentry into your ally and representative.

To accomplish this, use all the rules and cautions for personal conduct covered in this chapter on the approach. Above all, show no sign of impatience. Let your manner indicate that you consider the buffer person important, that you respect the need to screen callers judiciously.

EXHIBIT 8.7
SIDESTEPPING A TURNDOWN

Don't Settle for Half a Hearing   Suppose, when you make your approach, the buyer meets you in the outer office and invites you to make your presentation right there. Or suppose you are in the buyer's office, but the phone keeps ringing and the buyer keeps answering it. You cannot do justice to the prospect's interests or your own in the face of distraction or interruption. It is better to retreat with dignity and bid for another appointment. One way to handle this problem is to say something like this, "Apparently I caught you at a bad time, Miss Sanders. I appreciate your trying to fit me in, but let me come back at a more convenient time for you. How about tomorrow morning at nine-fifty? Or I can be here at any time tomorrow afternoon."

Apply the "Yes Yardstick"   Measure every opening technique against the *yes yardstick*. This means to evaluate every technique in terms of its potential effectiveness in getting the prospect to sit up and take notice in a positive frame of mind, in a mood to think "yes" instead of "no." If your opening achieves a favorable rating on the yes yardstick, all signals are go. You have taken the first step toward making your sale.

EXHIBIT 8.8
OUTER-OFFICE INTERLUDE

Scene: The reception desk of Evergreen Patio and Porch Furniture Co. Molly Dietrich, the receptionist-secretary, is typing. Enter Jack Stonier, sales representative for Creative Printers, Inc.

What they say	What they think
JACK: (*smiling sincerely, but not overdoing it*): Miss _____? (*waits for answer*)	
MOLLY: *Mrs.* Dietrich.	*That should show him I'm strictly business. No boy-girl stuff.*
JACK: (*pleasantly*): Do you spell Dietrich with a C-K or C-H?	
MOLLY: (*all business*): C-H. What can I do for you?	*I'd like to get back to my typing.*
JACK: (*handing over business card*): I have something to show Mr. Summers. Jack Stonier, Creative Printers.	
MOLLY: Uh-huh.	*Another one of those. God must love printers; He made so many of them.*
JACK: Is he in?	
MOLLY: Yes. But he's tied up.	*Seems like a nice guy. Too bad I have to give him the brush-off.*
JACK: Have you seen this? (*hands Molly colorful brochure describing the new condominium development that is a current local conversation piece*)	*This may catch her eye. Obviously, I have to sell her to reach Summers.*
MOLLY: (*looking at brochure and turning cover page*): No, I haven't.	*This is the kind of place Frank and I would like to live in if we could afford it.*
JACK: You see, Mrs. Dietrich, we're *creative* printers. Most any printer can give you paper and ink. Our specialty is *ideas*—ideas to increase your sales. Doesn't that interest you?	
MOLLY: (*pleased with the implied compliment to her status*): Well, yes. Naturally.	*It's nice to have someone talk to me as though I count for something around here.*
JACK: (*confidently, yet modestly*): As a matter of fact, the reason I called on you folks, Mrs. Dietrich, is to show you a survey report on what influences people in buying patio and porch furnishings. The findings are surprising.	*Now to persuade her we really have something Summers will want to see.* *This should make her curious.*
MOLLY: Really? Let me check and see how long Mr. Summers is going to be.	*He really zeros in. Got to hand it to him. Maybe I better let him see the boss after all. If it's good, I don't want to be in the doghouse if Summers hears about it later.*

EXHIBIT 8.9

OPENINGS THAT SCORE HIGH ON THE YES YARDSTICK

- *Automobile salesperson to car prospect:* "Are you interested in gas mileage?"
- *Marketing consultant to company president:* "Have you ever wondered whether you're reaching all your possible markets?"
- *Podiatrist to foot patient:* "Would you like to get rid of that corn for good?"
- *Furniture salesperson to recliner prospect:* "The only complaint we get on this recliner is that people start to read and then fall asleep."

Plan Your Opening Line   Your opening is too critical to the success of your sales call to leave to chance or play by ear. The secret of "spontaneity" is advance preparation. Plan your opening line. Test to find out what opening line gets you in. Try shortening your opener. Refine it with variations. Then retest it. It will become better and better with repeated use and adjustment. Don't stake your effectiveness on only one opener. Try various approaches. Find out which ones work. Have several different approaches for different situations. And never forget, the shorter your opening line, the better. Here are some examples:

- "Do you like a single- or a double-breasted suit?"
- "Your tires seem to be in the danger zone."
- "Don't you think bakery profits are too low?"
- "May I test the internal temperature of your freezer?"
- "Is your insurance arranged to avoid probate?"

Use a "Ho-Hum Crasher"   Richard C. Borden, in his film on how to make a sales presentation, shows us an audience about to hear an after-dinner speaker. Haltingly, the speaker begins:

"Mr. Chairman (*pause*) . . . President Gorman (*pause*) . . . honored guests on the dais (*longer pause*) . . . ladies and gentlemen" Now comes a delay as the speaker takes his notes out of his breast pocket, slowly places them on the lectern, and puts on his spectacles. Then he clears his throat in a loud and clear manner.

"The subject on which I have the honor to address you," he drones on in a monotone, "as you read in the program (*pause*) . . . and as your chairman has so aptly told you (*pause*) . . . when he introduced me to you (*longer pause and a clearing of the throat*) . . . is traffic safety."

Who cares? The camera pans over the audience. One diner is yawning. Another is struggling to keep from dozing off. An air of boredom pervades the room. Here and there, as the camera continues to pan, one listener after another expresses the reaction of all to the speaker's approach. "Ho-hum," they are intoning.

Then Borden's film shows us how another speaker would have approached the same after-dinner opportunity. No placing of notes on the lectern. No throat clearing. As alert as a racehorse at the starting gate, the speaker opens with a salvo that almost shouts *"Listen!"*

"Last night," he says, "the twelve-thirty-four from Milwaukee pulled into our North Station with a macabre load. Caskets! Two hundred and seventy of them! It could have been many fewer if our city had an up-to-date program for traffic safety!"[2]

The camera scans the audience. Not a single ho-hum. All are leaning forward attentively, hanging on every word, waiting for the speaker's message on how to improve traffic safety in their own town. The speaker has crashed through the indifference of the audience, brought each listener to attention, favorable attention, to hear the presentation.

That is the first scale point on the yes yardstick. Your approach must score on this first checkpoint, or the red light is on and your sales interview is off to a poor start, if not aborted altogether. Regardless of which opening technique you use, be sure it is a real ho-hum crasher.

Strategic Approach Techniques

The list of possible strategic approach techniques is limited only by human ingenuity and resourcefulness. Some of them will be described here as a sampling.

Open with a Question   There are many reasons in favor of opening your selling approach with a question. For one thing, a statement can go in one ear and out the other; a question is more apt to get through to the prospect's mind. Second, a question puts you on track toward establishing the facts about the buyer's needs, wants, problems, and motivations. This helps you frame your selling case. Finally, questions designed to bring "yes" answers are safety valves, assurance against early termination of the interview.

Here are some examples of question openings:

• *Selling fluorescent lighting to factory owner:* "Would you be interested in increasing your production per worker-hour while cutting your power bill?"

• *Selling in retail furniture department:* "What type of room will you use the sofa in?"

• *Selling tires to motorist ordering oil change:* "Have you had any tire trouble lately?" The normal answer, if not "yes," is quite certain to be "no, why?" The salesperson then explains that 90 percent of all tire trouble occurs in the last 10 percent of the tire's mileage.

---

[2]Adapted from "How to Make a Sales Presentation Stay Presented," by permission of Dartnell Corporation, Chicago; also, Richard C. Borden, *Public Speaking As Listeners Like It,* Harper & Row, New York, 1963.

170

Catch the Cat with Curiosity   Curiosity opens ears, eyes, and minds. When curiosity is tied to self-interest, it is irresistible, as in the following situation:

> "I visited each of your stores with my wife, ostensibly to shop," says the store-fixtures sales representative to the president of the retail chain. "There were some startling differences between your stores in the way they handled us. Would you like to hear about it?"

You bet the retailer would like to hear about it! One big question in chain retailing is how things are being done in the local units.

> "Here are two portfolios," the securities salesperson tells the investment prospect. "Each one worth one thousand dollars five years ago. What do you think each is worth today?"

Use an Ego Lever   The buyer's ego sometimes gives you an opportunity to pry open the sales interview with the power of a crowbar. Under every thick-skinned exterior there is apt to lie the heart of a prima donna. Ray Kroc, who founded McDonald's, recalls this incident from the days when he was a representative for Lily Tulip Company.

> Kroc kept calling unsuccessfully on a Chicago restaurant ruled by a manager named Bittner. One day he noticed a gleaming Marmon automobile parked at the rear entrance and was admiring it when a man came out of the restaurant and approached him. "Do you like the car?" he asked Kroc. Kroc knew this had to be Frank Powers, who owned the restaurant.
>   "Yes sir!" he replied. "Say, you're Mr. Powers, aren't you?" The man said he was indeed Mr. Powers, and Kroc told him, "Mr. Powers, if I could aspire to own a car like that, you could have the Rock Island and Heaven too." Powers laughed and, after some conversation about cars, asked Kroc if Bittner was giving him any business. "Well, you hang in there and keep trying," he said. "Bittner's a hard man, but he's fair and square, and if you deserve it, he'll give you a chance."
>   A few weeks later Kroc got his first order from Bittner. Not a word about Powers was mentioned by either buyer or seller.[3]

Request Help or Counsel   One way to gain the prospect's favorable attention is to open with a request for help or counsel. No matter how high the prospect's station or status, a request to give an opinion is quite sure to be an appreciated compliment.

As a young member of the Pennsylvania Assembly, Benjamin Franklin was having trouble with a formidable opposition delegate. Later, this same opponent became Franklin's ally and friend. How did Franklin approach him to change? By requesting the loan of a scarce book from the other man's library. Here are some additional examples.

> • *Packaged-food representative to grocery buyer:* "I'm new in the territory and would appreciate the benefit of your experience. Who are the distributors I should go after here to handle our line?"

---

[3]Adapted from Ray A. Kroc, *Grinding It Out*, Henry Regnery Company, Chicago, 1977, p. 28.

EXHIBIT 8.10
RETAIL STORE APPROACHES

Overworked or Bad Approaches

- "Yes?"
- "What can I do for you?"
- "Something in shirts?"
- "Hi."

Good Openings

- "Good morning." (*with a rising inflection and a smile*)
- "Did you see our ad in this morning's paper?"
- "I noticed you're looking at leather handbags. There's one I'd like to show you."
- "Today is the last day for that sale price."

Why Approach?

Why give special attention to retail approaches? After all, the customer has come into the store unsolicited.

The reason for interest in retail approaches is that there is no guarantee the prospect will buy. The purpose of the retail approach is fivefold:

1. To turn lookers into buyers
2. To get the prospect seeing and touching actual merchandise as soon as possible
3. To close the sale
4. Within the bounds of good business and reasonable discretion, to increase the size of the purchase
5. To do everything possible to assure customer satisfaction and a desire to come back

• *Office-equipment salesperson to office manager:* "We're making a survey of typewriters in use. Can you give us a rundown on your machines?"

Look for Personal-Interest Clues   Personal interests can provide an opening bridge to favorable interaction between you and your prospect. For example, on the buyer's desk is a copy of *Yachting* magazine. "Are you a powerboater or a sailor?" you ask.

The morning newspaper on the buyer's table is folded open to a half-finished crossword puzzle. "Did you get thirty-two across?" you ask with a smile.

On the wall behind the buyer's desk is the photograph of a dog. "What a beautiful dog!" you say. "Is that a golden retriever?"

In using personal-interest clues, be careful not to strain. If it is easy and natural, it works. If it seems to be contrived, the prospect is apt to recognize it for what it is, an insincere ploy, and be "turned off." A second caution is not to overdo it. Be sure you have at least some passing acquaintance with the subject of the buyer's interest. To make a reference to contract bridge, for example, when your speed is old maid can lead to embarrassment and a resounding boomerang. Also, don't let the prospect overdo it. Get the conversation back on the business track promptly. One young salesperson opened the approach to a prospect for a checkwriter with a remark indicating an interest in golf. The buyer beamed, launched into a stroke-by-stroke account of the previous day's round, and, before they even got to the sixth hole, was called away and had to terminate the meeting without one word about checkwriters.

Open with a Referral   There is no surer way to get a hearing for your sales presentation than the tried and true "Joe sent me." It is even better if you can get the friend to phone the prospect and recommend listening to your story because of that friend's satisfaction with your product.

Open with a Showstopper   Amazing facts, carefully chosen and dramatically presented, represent another way to open your approach. Here are some examples.

• A linen supply salesperson pours water from a bottle into a drinking glass. "This is water from the last rinse in our laundering process, *after* the linens are washed," he tells the prospect. "It's so pure you can drink it." Then he takes a swallow.

• "Only one out of fifty business establishments started twenty-five years ago is still in business." says the management consultant to the potential client. "Here is a checklist of the reasons why the one firm made it and the others didn't."

• "Good morning, Mrs. Callaby," says the seller of a new plastic table cover to the wholesaler. He spreads a section of his table cover on the desk and continues, "Have you ever seen anything like this?" as he drops some ink from his fountain pen on it and removes it by lightly rubbing a cloth on it.

EXHIBIT 8.11
Classics in Selling
HE BLAZED THE TRAIL FOR DRAMATIC BUSINESS PRESENTATION

Zenn Kaufman is the name most associated with showmanship in the commercial world. There was indeed showmanship before Kaufman arrived on the scene, but he raised its standards. Through his books with collaborator Kenneth M. Goode and his dramatic talks heard by thousands upon thousands of businesspeople, Kaufman called attention to showmanship as a valuable selling implement. He and Goode elevated showmanship to a dignified level. They made a clear distinction between purposeful showmanship and the circus tactics of some practitioners. "Showman-ship—not show-off-manship" was the way Kaufman explained it.

Kaufman continually warned against succumbing to dramatic devices that called attention to the device itself instead of the product or service being sold. Sound showmanship aids communication of the product or service benefits to the prospect. It is never empty of purpose or far removed from the selling objective.

Kaufman and Goode established a whole series of guides for the effective use of showmanship in business. All salespeople should read the books by Kaufman and Goode.

Source: Zenn Kaufman and Kenneth M. Goode, *Showmanship in Business,* Harper, New York, 1936; *Profitable Showmanship,* Harper, New York, 1939.

- "Whom do you represent?" the prospect asked insurance representative Frank Bettger. "I represent *you,*" replied Bettger.[4]

A survey showed a major newspaper to lead in circulation among women from twenty-five to thirty-four. This would be important to department and specialty stores. How could you communicate this selling point to them dramatically? A newspaper sales representative did it with a pie chart. Not the convential drawing—but a real, delicious apple pie with the pie chart in fondant on top of the pie. This was a showstopper.

Bring Something with You   Everyone likes to get something for nothing. We are conditioned that way from an early age. Your prospect is no exception. A delivery by you gives your sales call a purpose. Call it rationalization, if you will. But it opens doors, eyes, and ears.

We mentioned earlier how Fuller Brush opened with the delivery of a free vegetable brush. Consumers appreciated this gift, and it got interviews started. But there are other things besides gifts that you can bring with you to aid your approach. One example is information of value to the prospect. If advance appointments are advisable, a phone call stating you will make the delivery gener-

[4]Frank Bettger, *How I Raised Myself from Failure to Success in Selling,* Prentice-Hall, Englewood Cliffs, N.J., 1949.

ally will gain entrance for you. Here are some examples of approaches with something for the buyer.

- *Food broker to buyer for mass feeding company:* "This pamphlet on cooking with sour cream was prepared by the Culinary Arts Institute of Chicago. It has some unusual formulations."
- *Securities representative to investor:* "Here's a list of stocks selling below thirty-five with P/E ratios of less than four to one. I have detailed information on each one in this report from our research department."

Buy Your Way In with an Idea   Everyone—individuals, families, organizations—wants things and needs things. If you have an idea to answer these desires, why *shouldn't* the prospect listen? Sometimes the prospect is not even aware of the need, want, or problem. It is a double feat of selling skill and a service to the buyer if the seller brings the need to the buyer's attention and satisfies it. This must not be misconstrued as recommending high-pressure selling. One of the first rules of selling is not to try to sell except in answer to a legitimate need, want, or problem of the buyer. Here are some examples of buying the seller's way in with an idea.

- *Plastic cup seller to food-service manager of drug chain:* "How would you like to increase your fountain sales per stool? We have an idea that resulted in a thirty-three percent increase for a chain like yours."
- *Environmental waste corporation representative to food packer:* "How would you like to *sell* the processing residue that you are now throwing away?"
- *Fund-raising organization representative to entrepreneur:* "Here is a list of brand new ideas from a former IRS counselor on how to increase your tax advantages in connection with donations."

Bring News That Concerns the Prospect   News is a time-tested attention getter. But make sure it is news that concerns your prospect. The news of an election in East Africa is of no particular interest to a dress manufacturer. But the news that Dior has just unveiled a new shoulder style is, for the dress manufacturer, a real tidbit. Remember also that the closer the news concerns advantages to the buyer from your own product or service, the more sound is your approach.

- Camera seller to camera store manager: "Our people have come up with a breakthrough in automatic focusing."
- Doughnut mix and machinery seller to doughnut franchise chain president: "We've developed a new system of cryogenics that flash-freezes your doughnuts at one hundred sixty degrees below zero, and they thaw out better than ever before."

The Five-Senses Approach   One of the most effective ways to open your approach is to appeal to one or more of your prospect's senses: seeing, hearing, tasting, smelling, and feeling.

- "Feel how cold it is," says the milk route salesperson as he hands the ice-cold bottle of chocolate drink to the customer on whom he is making his regular collection call. It is a hot, humid day. The cold bottle feels good in the buyer's hand. The interview is off to a good start. No words can equal the attention value of that cold bottle on a hot day.

- "This is our new Mood Indigo fragrance," says the cosmetics representative to the chain buyer as he opens a vial for the prospect to smell.
- "Taste it," says the food seller to the wholesale grocery buyer as he opens a jar of the new ham spread and spoons some on a cracker for the buyer to try.
- "Listen to that tone quality."
- "Just feel the luxury of pure silk."

Try to have something in your hand as you approach your prospect—something the buyer can see, hear, feel, taste, or smell. It adds *substance* to your approach.

The Celebrity Opener   "This is the new Ben Crenshaw putter," the golf equipment seller says to the golf pro; "Crenshaw helped us design it." The pro takes the new club in hand to try a few strokes on the pro shop carpet.

"Andy Granatelli uses STP in his own car," says the service station attendant. "Okay," replies the motorist. "I'll give it a try." Why? Because Granatelli is a famous auto racer and the customer feels his judgment is valuable.

Frank Sinatra's name certainly can help sell recordings, and the endorsement of a well-known professional photographer can inspire the purchase of a camera. The use of a popular name in your approach is a proven attention-getter.

Implied General Professional Endorsement   Another approach device is the use of implied endorsement by an expert. The tennis enthusiast is apt to be reassured by the survey fact that a certain ball is preferred by 60 percent of top-seeded professionals. The attention of the motorist must be favorably attracted to the motor oil that "is used by 2421 mechanics in their own cars." However, an important caution with all testimonials and endorsements is to be sure they are true. This is not only a matter of business ethics but has legal implications as well.

The Service Approach   This is sometimes called the *oil can approach*. If your product is one that is used beyond the time of purchase, like an office machine or an air-conditioning system, a contributed service is a natural approach. "May I look over your machines to make sure they're shipshape?" asks the office-machine salesperson, who carries a kit with an oil can, a type-cleaning brush, a dusting brush, and a polishing cloth. If the machines are well-maintained, the office manager will be pleased to hear it. If one or more machines need attention or replacement, the need is exposed. The seller who provides this kind of service as an approach is in a good position to sell supplies now and replacement machines later. Here are some other examples of the service approach.

- *Fuel oil seller to hotel owner:* "May I survey your boiler and heating system to check it for efficiency of combustion and heat transfer? We'll give you a detailed report on whether you're getting the heat you should for your heating dollar. No charge. It's our investment in goodwill for the future."

- *Workers' compensation insurance seller to factory manager:* "Here's a twenty-seven-point safety-rating checklist prepared by Smithers & Frank, the safety engineering consultants. May we look over your plant and see how you score against the averages? You'll receive a complete report. There's no charge. It's our method of building goodwill for future business."

Reopening Approaches

What about opening approaches on *re*-calls? How about the return effort after a previous unsuccessful approach? What about the opening with a regular customer who purchases your product or service periodically?

In all cases, the repeat, or follow-up, sales call has a singular advantage over the previous approach. *You know the facts.* You know even more about the buyer's needs, wants, or problems than before the last call. You should know which competitor is enjoying the customer's business and why, or whether this prospect is not buying what you sell from any source and why not. You also should be aware of the buyer's personality and the soft spots or strengths in your interaction with the buyer.

In the case of the regular customer, the approach is, of course, easier than when approaching a new prospect. But don't be complacent. Always, before any call, review the situation and plan your call, especially your opening. Always have something to bring the buyer or to tell the buyer. Never approach empty-handed—or, even worse, empty-minded.

Regardless of whether you have sold to the buyer before, be sure to link the approach with the previous visit. If a specific objection cost you the sale last time, meet it head-on in your reapproach. For example:

- *Via Telephone:* "Miss Kraus? This is John Jolliffe of Century Millwork. I talked to our president about your criticism. He shook things up around here, and we've made some changes as a result of your comments. We appreciate your frankness and want to show you the changed version. Can I see you tomorrow morning at ten-fifty? or at any time in the afternoon?"

Another reopening device is to approach from a new angle entirely. For example:

- "Mr. Kelly, since seeing you, some new listings have come in. One of them is only two blocks from the church, which was an important factor for you."
- "When I visited you last week, you told me our transcriber was too large. Here's our mini model. Use it for a few days and see if you don't become enthusiastic."
- (*To secretary*): "Dr. Carroll cut our meeting short last week because he's afraid of the side effects of Bikonselin. I now have a report from our biochemists that will reassure Dr. Carroll on this point. When is the best time for him to set up a half-hour to review this report?"

The repeat approach follows all the principles and methods of the initial approach. This applies to the third, fourth, and fifth approaches as well. The only difference is that each time you approach the same buyer, it is a more knowing approach. You can choose each time from a narrower list of technique options than the time before. On each successive approach, you can zero in closer to your objective.

SOME CAUTIONS ON THE APPROACH

You have been introduced to a variety of approach principles and techniques and reopening approaches. You will have to use your judgment and experience to determine which techniques to use in a given situation, but the following cautions should always be observed.

• *Avoid clichés.* Try not to use openings that have been overworked. There are some formerly valid approaches like, ''Do you want to make more money?'' that originally had appeal but have dropped to cliché status. Strive to be original if you can, but at least be up to date.

• *Seek areas of agreement.* The approach is not too soon to seek areas of agreement. Use questions that prompt the prospect to say ''yes''—but, even more important, to *think* ''yes.''

• *Don't be too clever.* Too clever an opening risks alienating the prospect by making you seem to be a wiseacre.

• *Keep it simple.* Don't be so different that the buyer does not understand you. Express even complicated thoughts simply, in language the prospect is sure to understand.

• *Be wary of humor.* Humor is a powerful implement. But in selling you must be careful about using it, especially in your opening when you do not know how the prospect will react. Different people may react differently to the same jest, sometimes finding it and the person who used it offensive. In addition, you are there for the serious business of showing the prospect how to benefit from your product or service. Your humor is apt to boomerang and damage the dignity and validity of your sales call. Maybe it won't—but why take chances?

The Right Time to Call

Earlier in this chapter we mentioned the importance of timeliness in the product or service you sell, for example, umbrellas in the rain. This is a *merchandising* consideration. Now let us give thought to the *right time* to approach, a quite different consideration from timeliness. This varies greatly from one selling situation to another. The clock, the calendar, and the habits of the business or person can be worse problems than the smartest competitor with a good product. Don't approach a small-business office at morning or afternoon mail time. A rainy day is a good time to visit a prospect who is outside a great deal. Try to see buyers after lunch rather than before—they are more apt to be in good humor. Learn the broad time patterns of the classifications in which you are selling. For example, if you are selling to retail merchant bakers in New York City, you will soon learn that the industry is segmented by ethnic groups, each with its separate time habits.

EXHIBIT 8.12
PICK THE RIGHT TIME TO CALL

RECAP

Selling is a competitive calling—with or without competitors. In no part of the selling process is this more pertinent than in the approach.

The approach is critical to the outcome of the selling effort since it is the bridge that links prospects with performance and potentials with realizations. In the instant it takes to make this opening move, you get on the track favorably, unsteadily, or not at all.

You must choose the right time to approach and the right opening technique to employ. It is a subject of almost limitless variation. This chapter alone covered fourteen approach devices and a host of principles.

An effective approach sets the stage for a positive sales presentation and a potential closing.

This chapter underscored three essentials:

1. Acceptance of the fact that obstacles are quite apt to be encountered in selling, especially in the approach, as in any pursuit in the real world.
2. The way to overcome these obstacles is study and practice to develop special skills in the art of the approach.
3. This skill in approaching prospects, as in every phase of selling, is the reward for meticulous attention to details and nuances that make the difference between the qualified professional and the novice.

REVIEW QUESTIONS

1. Why is the approach important in selling?
2. Name and explain briefly three of the variables that determine how difficult or easy a selling approach can be.
3. What are the three factors on which your effectiveness in approaching buyers depends?
4. What is the personal equation in the selling approach? List six components that make for a favorable personal interaction between seller and buyer.
5. Why is it important to use a prospect's name? How do you remember names?
6. How can you get by the sentry at the gate?
7. What is the yes yardstick?
8. What is a ho-hum crasher? Give an example.
9. Describe five strategic approach techniques.
10. What advantage do you have in a reopening approach to a prospect compared with your first approach?
11. What are the four cautions to remember in your approach?
12. What are some factors to consider in choosing the best time to make your approach?

DISCUSSION QUESTIONS

1. Is the ability to approach successfully a natural skill or one that is acquired? Discuss in depth.
2. From what you have learned so far and the examples you have seen, do you think prospecting, the preapproach, or the approach is most important to a successful selling career? Discuss.
3. What does the selling approach have in common with Broadway or Hollywood? What principles and techniques apply to both?
4. Is it wise to use humor in your approach? What are some of the cautions?

LEARNING EXPERIENCES

1. Visit a local store that has salespeople (not self-service) and observe how at least three different salespeople approach customers. List the differences in the approaches and evaluate them in a report to the class.
2. Role playing: Clay is purchasing agent for General Industrial Caterers, Inc., which has contracts to provide meals for a large number of factory organizations. Simmons represents Cameo Plastics Corporation, which is introducing a new disposable serving plate to mass feeders. This plate, branded as the Cameo 100, has the following features:

   - Its price is lower than disposable serving plates presently on the market.
   - It is superior to other plates in keeping foods warm or cool.
   - It comes from Cameo Plastics Corporation, located only 20 miles from

General Industrial Caterers, Inc.

(a) Have one member of the group play the role of Clay and another that of Simmons. Simmons is to approach Clay, and they are to engage in a dialogue, using their imaginations to supply facts not stated above.

(b) Let Clay analyze for the class why Simmons did or did not win a hearing or obtained a hearing that at the onset was not enthusiastic.

(c) Let Simmons analyze for the group why he or she approached in the manner seen by the group and explain the strategy in detail.

(d) Have an open-floor discussion on the relative merits of the analyses given by Clay and Simmons.

3. The student senate has delegated you to approach the director of athletics to establish soccer as an intramural sport. The college has a soccer team that participates in intercollegiate activity. Field time and space are available for intramural soccer. However, extension of the activity would require faculty supervision and an investment in equipment at a time when the total athletic budget is under a strain.

(a) Using your imagination for facts not stated above, how would you go about the approach to the director of athletics? Outline your strategy and the reasons you chose it.

(b) Compose three possible opening lines for your meeting with the director of athletics. Rank them in order of preference and explain your ranking.

(c) Let each member of the group take another person's answers to questions (a) and (b) and write a critique on them.

CASE

ARDMORE PHOTOCOPIER COMPANY

Dick Gordon, newly appointed Western Division sales manager of the Ardmore Photocopier Company, has just arrived in San Francisco to appoint a distributor. The company's new cold-pressure-fusing copier is making satisfactory distribution progress, but San Francisco, a leading U.S. copier market, is still open. Ardmore's national advertising is reaching San Francisco buyers, but there is no distributor to supply them and no local selling to follow up on the advertising exposure. Gordon's objective is to appoint a key distributor and to hire a factory sales representative. The representative will coordinate the distributor's merchandising and selling with the factory program, train and motivate the distributor's sales force, and call on the important accounts personally to obtain orders for the distributor.

After two weeks in San Francisco, Dick Gordon has located three possible factory representatives. He had a head start on this through classified ads and an employment agency search before he left his Denver office. He has also determined by field investigation in San Francisco that his first choice for the San

Francisco distributorship is Halwell Office Machine Company, a large local distributor. He has learned that although Halwell is the biggest seller of office machines in the area, its copier sales are inconsequential. The big seller is Xerox—through its company branch and local retail stores—and, after Xerox, a lower-priced line handled by Ace Distributors. Gordon has also learned that Sam Halwell, president of Halwell, is a grandson of the founder, a relatively young man who graduated from Stanford with an M.B.A. about fifteen years ago and became president only six months ago. Gordon phones Halwell and is connected with his secretary.

"Mr. Halwell's office," she says.

"Good morning," Gordon says. "I'm Dick Gordon, sales manager of Ardmore Photocopiers. May I ask your name?"

"Nancy Sanborn. Can I help you?"

"Yes, Miss Sanborn. I wonder if I may speak to Mr. Halwell."

"He's in a meeting right now. Can you tell me what it's about?"

"Of course, Miss Sanborn. I've come to San Francisco to offer your firm first refusal on our exclusive distributorship."

"Let me see if I can break into the meeting. Can you hold for a minute?"

Sanborn is soon back on the phone, and Dick Gordon has an appointment to see Sam Halwell the next morning.

Questions

1. Would you have handled the secretary the way Dick Gordon did? Discuss.
2. Dick Gordon told Sanborn he had come to San Francisco to offer Halwell first refusal on the Ardmore distributorship. Would it have been wiser for Gordon to have replied to Sanborn's question: "I have come to San Francisco to appoint an exclusive distributor for our nationally advertised copier, and Halwell is our first choice for a discussion of possible mutual interests." In selling Sanborn, which of these two answers to her question would you prefer? Or can you suggest a third? Explain.
3. Why do you think Gordon did not write or phone Halwell before he left Denver to set up an advance appointment?

Dick Gordon arrived at Halwell's office the next morning and the following dialogue took place.

"Good morning, Mr. Halwell."

"Good morning. Have a seat. I'm afraid you've come to the wrong place. We don't do much copier business."

"That's why I came here first, Mr. Halwell. I understand you sell more office machines than any other distributor in this market. Is that right?"

Smiling proudly, Halwell replies, "That's what they tell me."

"Then you must have more customers than any other distributor. Is that reasonable to assume?"

"Yes. We have the customers. Buy they don't buy copiers."

"Do they *use* copiers, Mr. Halwell?"

"I guess they must. But Xerox has it mostly locked up, and another machine distributor does pretty well with a cheaper line. We've never thought of copiers as a good line for us."

"Why not, Mr. Halwell?"

"Never gave it much thought, to tell you the truth. We're too busy with all our other lines, I guess."

"Have you any idea how much copier business is done in your market, Mr. Halwell? About ninety million dollars a year! And another thirty million on supplies."

"I never realized it was that big."

"Your gross profit on a ten percent share of that market—thirteen million dollars—would be around four and a half million dollars a year."

"That begins to be interesting. But how do I know you've got the line and the price and all the other ingredients to realize this gross profit. It's attractive, but talk is easy. Accomplishing it can be something else again."

''Believe me, Mr. Halwell, we've got the ingredients you want, or I wouldn't have invested money in this trip. Let me present the whole line and distributor support program to you. Come to Los Angeles with me, as our guest, and meet our Los Angeles distributor, who's doing better than ten percent of the market against the same kind of competition you have here. Also, you can see the whole line in the showroom.''

Questions

4. Do you think Dick Gordon will succeed in getting Halwell to come to Los Angeles to listen to his presentation? Explain.
5. Why did Dick address Nancy Sanborn as ''Miss'' and Sam Halwell as ''Mr.''?
6. Give a general commentary and critique—positive or negative—on Dick Gordon's approach to Halwell.

NINE

CHAPTER OBJECTIVES

To analyze the structure of a sales presentation

To explain the various substance options: what to present and how to choose between them

To describe the various options in presentation technique and how to determine which to use

To examine the procedural-psychological anatomy of the sales interview and how to guide it to a favorable conclusion

To show you how to focus the prospect's attention *favorably* and how to advance that attention to interest *quickly*

To show you how to relate your product or service benefits to the prospect's selfish interests *in the prospect's mind*

To show you how to build the prospect's desire to enjoy the benefits of your product or service

CHAPTER OUTLINE

THE SALES INTERVIEW I: PRESENTATION

The measure of a sales presentation's effectiveness is not how well you present, but how well the buyer understands and is motivated to buy.

Anonymous

A successful approach gained you an audience with the prospect. Now you are on stage to make your presentation during your sales interview.[1]

The aim of the presentation is to explain your product or service in a way that prepares the buyer for your closing. The more skillful your presentation, the easier the close. That is why salespeople especially adept in the sales presentation do not encounter the closing problems met by those who are less competent in presentation.

This chapter will cover the principles and methods of sales presentation. All are designed to aid the buyer's understanding of and desire to enjoy the benefits of your product or service. That is the measure of an effective sales presentation.

[1]The terms *sales interview* and *sales call* are used interchangeably in this text. All sales calls are sales interviews. But at various times, the buyer calls on the seller; the seller calls on the buyer; or seller and buyer meet at another location, for example, at a business show or fair.

PLANNING YOUR PRESENTATION

"Your family will really enjoy the extra features of this station wagon," the car salesperson tells the prospect.

"No," replies the buyer. "I have no family. I want a vehicle that will be good for the samples I carry in my business."

Every sales presentation must have a purpose and a plan—whether it is selling a car to a new prospect, following up on a previously unsuccessful call, or visiting a regular customer. Where possible, the objective should be set in advance and the presentation strategy planned to achieve it. In the automobile selling case just mentioned, the salesperson presented a benefit without first ascertaining the purpose of the purchase. An opening that began with, "What will you be using the car for mostly?" would have been more strategic.

Buying and selling are opposite sides of the same coin. It isn't how much is said. It's how much the prospect hears and believes that makes the presentation effective. Exhibit 9.1 shows how Joanne Hall presented a new plastic sheet material to a dealer. The special feature was the indestructible color. The accompanying analysis shows what Hall was thinking about at each step in her presentation.

EXHIBIT 9.1
ANALYSIS OF A SALES PRESENTATION

Dialogue of Presentation	Analysis of Hall's plan
HALL (*handling strip of plastic covering material and a fingernail file to dealer*): Miss Sargent, here's a breakthrough that will put an end to color complaints. Just try to scratch the color off this Permacel sheet with this fingernail file.	Attention gained through use of physical hand-over objects. Contest holds interest. Which will win, the color or the fingernail file?
DEALER (*scratching file on sheet*): H-m-m, that's interesting. We do get color complaints.	Buyer participates in test.
HALL: Well you won't get them any more. The color of Permacel is indestructible because it's *color-backed.*	Product advantage and dealer benefit proved; interest aroused.
DEALER: I can't argue with that.	Interest confirmed.
HALL: You can guarantee the colorfastness of these sheets to your customers, Miss Sargent, because we guarantee it to you. (*shows window streamer*) This window streamer, tied in with our TV advertising, will increase your plastic sheet sales.	Product benefit and program related to buyer's selfish interests. Buyer ready for closing.

STRUCTURE OF THE PRESENTATION: IS YOUR PRESENTATION PRESENTABLE?

To be effective, a sales presentation must satisfy four requirements.

1. *Pattern.* It must follow a sequential step-by-step plan that will guide the prospect's mental and emotional processes toward the purchase.
2. *Substance.* The presentation must be more than words. It must contain substance. Pattern covers the organization and structure of the presentation. Substance is *what* you present.
3. *Demonstration.* Wherever possible, the presentation should include proof of validity. Nothing breeds credibility like a demonstration. It shows the prospect how the product or service works, how it really delivers the benefits promised.
4. *Embellishments.* The substance of your presentation is its body. Embellishments are the implements you use to dress it up. Some of these are visual aids, demonstration techniques, devices to add credibility and proof, choice of language, and showmanship. Embellishments breathe life into the presentation, make it exciting and interesting for the prospect to follow.

THE PRESENTATION PATTERN

There are many theories on how to structure the presentation of a product or service. Indeed, there are many more than those that will be described here.

AIDA

In Chapter 8, we discussed the acronym AIDA briefly. AIDA stands for what is perhaps the oldest reminder on how to guide a buyer through the successive stages of response to a selling presentation: *attention, interest, desire, action.* Some selling theorists add *conviction* between desire and action. They do this to underscore the importance of gaining the buyer's rational conviction of the rightness of the *desire* to make the purchase and enjoy the benefits of the product or service.

Zeroing In

In Chapter 8 we illustrated the zeroing-in technique for the approach. This technique endeavors by deft questioning to narrow an ever-diminishing circle around the buyer's needs, wants, or special problems. The strategy continues in the presentation stage—the objective is increased identification. Once you expose a want, need, or special problem, you quickly relate a benefit of your product or service to it. This zeroing-in technique makes sure the appeal you use is on target before you commit your course. For example, your prospect needs a car. Is it to be an economy car or a luxury car? Answer: an economy car. The model? Answer: a hatchback. Now you know your economy hatchback is the car to present. (See Exhibit 9.2.)

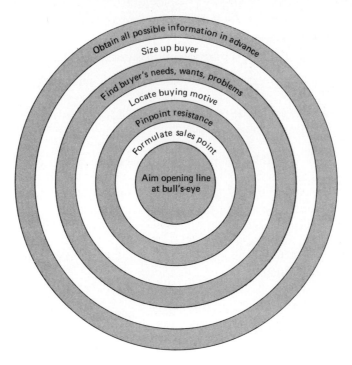

Obtain all possible information in advance
Size up buyer
Find buyer's needs, wants, problems
Locate buying motive
Pinpoint resistance
Formulate sales point
Aim opening line at bull's-eye

EXHIBIT 9.2
TUNING YOUR APPROACH TO BUYER AND BUYING PROFILE: THE ZERO-IN PRINCIPLE

Stimulus Response

In this presentation technique, the salesperson endeavors to trigger an emotional or intellectual response on the part of the buyer that will lead to a purchase. Different buyers are motivated to buy the same product or service for different reasons. If you can determine—in advance of the interview or during the early inquiry stage of the interview—what stimulus is apt to bring a positive response from the buyer, you have your presentation *line*.

Consider the following examples of different stimuli to sell the same product—an automobile—to different buyers.

"This car offers better safety for your family." The stimulus is fear, and the response sought is a purchase motivated by the desire to protect the prospect's family.

"A person in your position *belongs* behind the wheel of a status car like this." The stimulus is aspiration, and the response hoped for is satisfaction of ego.

"With two teenagers ready to enter college, you'll need the extra space of this car to transport them and their friends back and forth." Here the stimulus is practical efficiency, and the desired response is the purchase of this car to avoid inconvenience later.

"We're overstocked on this model and I can get you a very special price." The stimulus is economy, and the response sought is a purchase motivated by the desire to save money.

Four different stimuli are thus seen to spur positive buying responses from four different buyers regarding the same car.

Personal Interaction

Productive interaction with the buyer is the aim of every seller. It covers all aspects of communication and cross-orientation between buyer and seller. We refer here, however, strictly to *personal empathy* between the two. This is the theory that a favorable interaction between prospect and salesperson is the pivotal plank in the sales platform. How well do their personalities mesh?

In the early days of selling, acceptance of this theory and reliance on it were paramount. The advance of professional selling as a science has placed personal empathy between buyer and seller in a more rational perspective. A positive personal interaction is always desirable, and sought, as it is in all fields of human endeavor, but it is to be an advantageous backdrop for your sales interview rather than its prime basis.

Borden's Four-Step Presentation Guide

Probably no better aid to more effective sales presentations exists than the four-step guide developed by Professor Richard C. Borden while at New York University. (See Exhibit 9.3.)

Examine the AIDA formula. What Borden apparently did was to relate each of the four steps—attention, interest, desire, and action—to an everyday expression of listener reaction completely within the prospect's frame of reference.

- ''Ho-hum.''
- ''Why bring that up?''
- ''For instance?''
- ''So what?''

Start with a Ho-Hum *Recrasher* In the chapter on the approach we called attention to the possible, and often probable, indifference of the prospect to what you wish to sell. We described the need for a ho-hum crasher to break through this indifference and capture the prospect's attention.

That ho-hum crasher was to gain an audience. Now, as you begin your sales presentation, you must use a ho-hum *recrasher* as a reinforcing device to sustain the buyer's attention and to heighten interest.

- *Insurance seller to mother of teenager:* An insurance seller has used a pamphlet with information for parents of teenagers to gain an interview. Now she asks the mother of the teenager, ''In three years, how much do you think it will cost for a year at college?'' That is a ho-hum *recrasher*. The mother is all ears.
- *Cosmetics seller to middle-aged woman:* ''This new skin balm will protect you from dry skin,'' the cosmetics salesperson tells the middle-aged woman whose attention she has at the cosmetics counter. ''Does that interest you?''

190

EXHIBIT 9.3

Classics in Selling
PIONEER IN SALES THEORY

Is there a parallel between selling an idea to an audience and selling an idea, a product, or a service to an individual? Richard C. Borden, a professor of English and public speaking at New York University, thought there was. He spent many years in field study with his collaborator, fellow professor Alvin C. Busse, seeking reasonably foolproof principles and techniques to guide the salesperson. These principles and methods proved so sound that Borden was retained by many of America's leading corporations to indoctrinate salespeople in their application.

Borden's books, lectures, and films on such subjects as "How to Make a Sales Presentation" have achieved wide popularity in the marketing field.

If there were a hall of fame in the selling profession, Dr. Borden's contributions to the art-science of dramatic presentation, communications, and dialectics would assure him of a place of honor in it.*

*The Borden references at various points in this text are used by permission of Harper & Row, New York and Dartnell Corporation, Chicago, Ill.

- *Insulation seller to homeowner:* "Did you know that insulating your house will get you a substantial tax deduction?" This question by an insulation seller is an effective ho-hum *recrasher* as he opens his presentation in the prospect's study.

"Why Bring That Up?"   Now what do you do with the buyer's attention before you lose it again? The sequential transition is from ho-hum to another common reaction: "Why bring that up? What does this mean *to me*?"

In answer to the prospect's unspoken "Why bring that up?" you must build a bridge between the point you have made and the prospect's self-interest. You must relate this point and your product or service benefits to the buyer's needs, wants, or special problems. Here is how the three salespeople just mentioned accomplished this.

- *Insurance seller to mother of teenager:* "Do you know that for approximately fifteen dollars a month you can guarantee your son's first year at college, in the event you're not here?"
- *Cosmetics seller to middle-aged woman:* "Are you aware that dry skin is one of the most important things to avoid if you want to prevent wrinkles as you grow older?"
- *Insulation seller to homeowner:* "You'd like to cut your tax bill, wouldn't you?"

"For Instance?"   You have gained your prospect's attention and advanced that attention to preliminary interest. Now the natural response in the prospect's mind, whether stated or not, is the question: "For instance?" This is a call for

EXHIBIT 9.4
BUILD A BRIDGE FROM PRODUCT OR SERVICE BENEFIT TO BUYER'S SELF-INTEREST

proof, credibility of the promise of a benefit from your product or service. "For instance." or "How?" is your cue. Nothing is more persuasive than evidence from real life, tangible proof of the validity of your presentation.

Your "For instance?" brings your presentation down to cases. It takes it from the general to the specific. It convinces. Let us see how the insurance salesperson, the cosmetic salesperson, and the insulation seller did this.

- *Insurance seller to mother of teenager:* "Right here in town, Charles Poletti died suddenly last fall. But, thanks to our tuition insurance plan, Charlie Junior is a freshman at State. He plans to become a lawyer."
- *Cosmetics seller to middle-aged woman:* "Here's a photo of Carla Christian, the movie star, and photos of several other women who have benefited from Dew Fresh Skin Balm. Just look at how soft and smooth their skin appears."
- *Insulation seller to homeowner:* "Here's a copy of the new tax law. And here's a reprint from last week's *Times-Graphic* which tells the whole story. I already have seven orders for insulation right here in your neighborhood. For instance, Mrs. Simonds across the street has scheduled us to do the job next Tuesday. If you'd like to phone her, I'm sure she'll confirm our statements. She's an accountant and she checked us out thoroughly."

"So What?"   When your presentation has progressed to the point where the buyer says, or thinks, "So what?" you could not want a better signal to start your close.

It is perfectly sound to combine sales presentation patterns, to borrow from one while building around another. For instance, while following Borden's four-step guide, you still can, in the course of the sales interview, endeavor to zero in on the prospect's needs and wants. You still can trigger an emotional or intellectual reaction in the direction of a purchase by using the stimulus-response technique.

Order Leads to Orders

The sales presentation should proceed from step to step in logical sequence. The butterfly can flit from one flower to another, but the butterfly is buying, not selling. The salesperson must keep on track.

The first step in the presentation is *fact finding.* Inquire. Establish or verify the facts on the prospect and the buying situation. Ask the prospect questions that will reveal needs, wants, and special problems.

Next comes *exposition.* Present your product or service benefits to match and answer the prospect's needs, wants, or special problems as established in your fact finding.

The final step in the presentation is *conviction.* Buttress your exposition with demonstration, proof, credibility.

Fact finding. Exposition. Conviction. One, two, three. Each step follows the previous step naturally and leads logically to the next. You are ready to close.

THE SUBSTANCE OF THE PRESENTATION: TO REACH THE BUYER'S MIND

Try to plan your sales presentation from the viewpoint of the buyer. Be observant during the sales interview. Try to read your prospect's thoughts and reactions and modify your presentation to stimulate positive reactions. Aim your product feature at the benefit that will mean the most to this particular buyer. Adjust your manner of presentation, even your tone of voice, to what your reading tells you will be most effective.

Selecting the Right Substance Options

All through the selling process, you will arrive at crossroads. Selling forces you to make choices and decisions, often on the spot. The same product or service is bought by different buyers for different reasons and in different ways. Your first decision is selecting the right variety of product or service to present. Then you must select the right light in which to present the product or service to appeal to this prospect.

The Right Product or Service   What is the right product or service for this prospect? For instance, do bonds or stocks fit the portfolio of this securities buyer? What types of bond? Debentures? Convertibles? Quality or more speculative offerings? What type of stock? Common or preferred? Blue chip or speculative or in between? Which specific issues? Answering these kinds of questions perceptively helps you pick the right product or service to present. This is a key secret of successful selling. Carry neither coals to Newcastle nor ice to the Arctic. Pick the glove that fits the buyer's hand.

The Right Price   In entrepreneurial selling (for your own business) or other areas where a salesperson has freedom to set or adjust prices, the seller's skill in quoting the right price is one more key secret of successful selling. Even when firm prices are set by management, you usually will have a choice of products or services at different price levels to select for presentation to a specific prospect. For example, is the right price level for *this* luggage buyer the $100, $50, or $29.95 bag?

The Right Light   The same plane ticket might be a way to get to San Francisco, a trip to the Golden Gate, a time-saver, a bargain, a chance to meet a sweetheart, or an almost endless list of other possible buyer benefits. Which is the right appeal for the prospect in question? How do you present this benefit so that it is under a spotlight, not a gaslight? How do you make sure it comes across to the buyer in the most favorable light, adding substance to the presentation?

The most competent salespeople have the ability to present a product or service in a manner that conjures up in the mind of the prospect the most favorable image of the product or service and its benefits. This is a valuable asset in making a sales presentation. (See Exhibit 9.5.)

EXHIBIT 9.5
THE RIGHT LIGHT

At the bottom of the great economic depression of the nineteen-thirties, Lily Tulip Corporation introduced the first paper cup for serving dressing, ketchup, and similar items in restaurants. Day after day sales representatives reported "no sale." The financially hard-pressed food purveyors were loathe to add a new cost to running an eating place.

Then Fenn K. Doscher, Lily Tulip's sales promotion manager, destined to become company president later in his career, went out with a salesperson. Doscher analyzed and solved the problem almost at the first sales call.

"What? Another paper item?" said the diner operator. "More money to spend! No, thank you,"

"You'll *save* money," replied Doscher. "This gives you *portion control*!"

A paper serving cup costs money. Portion control saves money. It's the same cup—in a different light.

Other Options   In addition to the three options described above, other questions of choice open up in connection with the sales presentation.

There is the option of *quantity*. For example, should you recommend that the distributor buy five or ten cases? Should you recommend the $20,000 or the $30,000 policy to the life insurance prospect?

Another option is *when* to make the presentation. The senior salesperon gives serious thought to the time of day, week, month, season, and other choices in time and timing. For example, one fuel oil salesperson works overtime in the fall when homeowners are thinking of winter heating requirements. Another makes extra calls in the heat of the summer. Although winter is fuel time, summer selling, with little competitive selling, can win contracts or lay the groundwork for contract closings in the fall.

Even the *place* to make the presentation often involves options. For example, is it more advantageous to call on the insurance prospect at home or at the office? Are the odds on selling the machine greater through presenting it at headquarters or at the branch plant where it will be used?

Buyer Receptors

You can reach and motivate buyers only through their external antennae that receive impressions and the internal mechanisms that interpret these impressions.

The buyer's external receptors are the five senses of seeing, hearing, smelling, tasting, and touching. Different people receive impressions with different degrees of sensitivity. Psychologists tell us that 87 percent of our impressions come to us through our eyes; 9 percent through our ears; and 4 percent through our other senses. Nevertheless, some people are more sight impressionable than others, whereas some people are more sound impressionable than others. Likewise, people vary in their sensitivity to smells, tastes, and textures.

Selling is a communicative science. Once you have transmitted an idea through words, pictures, objects, tastes, or smells, the impression received is interpreted by the mind.

The wide variety of ideas you can communicate and the even wider variety of possible buyer reactions are the prime reasons for an individualized treatment of each sales interview. No two buyers are exactly alike, and the most successful salespeople are those who are the most perceptive and analytical in their readings of individual prospects. Have you ever wondered why selling is still necessary even where millions are spent on advertising? The reason is that the *collective* persuasion of advertising cannot custom-tailor the appeal to the needs, wants, or special interests of the individual prospect. It takes personal selling to zero in and make the sale.

Speed and Depth of Buyer Perception

People also vary in their ability to receive and interpret impressions. One person gets things fast. Another thinks more slowly. One prospect can understand the most complex hypothesis, while another requires utter simplicity.

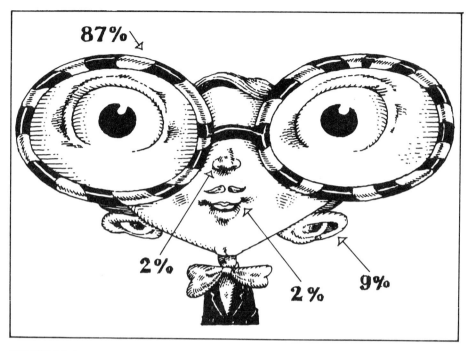

EXHIBIT 9.6
OUR EYES ACCOUNT FOR MOST OF OUR IMPRESSIONS—SEEING IS BELIEVING . . .
AND BUYING

The objective of your sales presentation is to motivate the buyer. No matter how pertinent your selling message is to the buyer or how eloquently you convey it, it is worthless unless the prospect understands it. Otherwise, it is as futile as signaling by flag on a dark night.

The advanced salesperson sizes up the buyer's speed and depth of perception and adjusts the sales presentation to it. Don't hold up the thought processes of a prospect who absorbs things fast, and try not to get ahead of the prospect who gets things more slowly. Follow your prospect's pace, but remember that some of our fastest thinkers do not think well and some of history's greatest thoughts have come from brains that moved slowly. Watch for signs of understanding and readiness for the next idea.

When in doubt, start off slowly and simply, picking up your pace if needed. Your objective is to make a sale, not to win a prize for your presentation.

How to Read Your Prospect

Beyond what you may have learned about your prospect from prospecting and preapproach, there is one best source for information about the buyer as a person. The buyer! Listen to the buyer. Ask questions. Observe reactions. You may be surprised at how much the buyer will tell you about what interests him or her and how he or she likes to buy. Then, when you have established the specifics of the sales opportunity and any problem impeding it, you can sell intelligently.

EXHIBIT 9.7
ADVERTISING REACHES BUYERS COLLECTIVELY . . .
Conditioning them for buying
SELLING REACHES BUYERS INDIVIDUALLY . . .
Customizes the presentation to the buyer's specific interests and makes the sale

197

Selling Is a Qualifying Process

Qualifying means ascertaining the degree to which the buyer needs or wants your product or service, can afford it, and has the authority to buy. The prospect does not always know of this need or want. Indeed, one of the prime functions of the professional salesperson is to identify hidden or latent needs and wants and to make the buyer aware of them.

The qualifying process began in your prospecting and continued right through your preapproach. Face to face with the prospect, you qualify still further, confirming the information you have, becoming more specific as to details.

The whole early part of the sales interview is a process of inquiry—questioning, listening, observation. Gradually, the prospect's needs, wants, or special problems come more and more into view. When the picture has crystallized, you are in a position to match your product or service benefits to the buyer's needs and wants to make an exposition that is comprehensive.

"Sellers must remember that buyers are always the *experts* on their own needs."[2]

When Your Presentation Is Not Presentable

If, after a careful reading of your prospect, you determine that the person to whom you are making the presentation has no legitimate need for what you are selling (in other words, if this person does not qualify as a prospect), stop right there. No self-respecting member of the selling profession tries to sell a product or service that the buyer cannot use to advantage. It is unethical and ill-advised and, indeed, sometimes can boomerang. Take your leave gracefully. If the situation changes and the buyer ever does in fact become a qualified prospect, you will be ahead because of your earlier discretion.

Incidentally, there is another reason to terminate a sales call. This is when your reading of the buyer exposes a need or want that your product or service cannot honestly satisfy. If you continue, you may make the sale. But you are also apt to make an enemy. It is not worth it.

Do not get the idea that a salesperson is accustomed to walking out on interviews. If the product or service you elected to sell was worthy of your choice, you may be sure there are myriads of qualified prospects for every case in which prospect or product does not qualify.

Another reason for forgoing an order occurs when product or service is temporarily off-standard.

> "I know you're having trouble in the kitchen and have hired a new chef," says the club member to the club manager. "I'm taking an important client to lunch Thursday, and he's finicky about food. Can you do me proud?"
>
> "I wouldn't chance it, Tom," replies the club manager. "It'll be another week before we're really back on course."

---

[2]Laura L'Herisson, marketing officer, Crocker National Bank of San Francisco, "Teaching the Sales Force to Fail," *Training and Development Journal,* November 1981, p. 80.

"Thanks for your honesty, Jane," says the member. "I appreciate your saving me a possible embarrassment."

Two months later, the member phones the manager. "I want to congratulate you, Jane. I had dinner in your dining room last night and it was excellent! On March second our Bar Association dinner takes place and I'm making the arrangements. Can you accommodate about three hundred?"

The Art of Questioning

Probably no other implement is as valuable in selling as the question, not only to read the buyer and the buyer's needs, wants, or special problems but as a more effective way to communicate than a positive statement. Questions are preferable to statements on four counts: (1) to avoid a monologue; (2) to gain access to the buyer's mind; (3) to get the prospect talking; and (4) to be sure your presentation is on the right track.

Avoid a Monologue   The perfect sales interview is a two-way street. It is a dialogue in which buyer and seller jointly canvass the buyer's needs, wants, or special problems and the related benefits of the product or service offered. The salesperson is careful to keep the overall tone of the meeting exploratory, not argumentative. Your attitude should be one of seeking to find out, rather than to prove. Prospects are seldom bulldozed into buying. They are informed and led into buying of their own free will. This leading is more easily accomplished with questions than with statements.

Gain Access to the Buyer's Mind   Your presentation is an effort to reach the inner sanctum of the prospect's thought processes. In order to be led to a purchase, the prospect must think, feel, and believe that the benefits of your product or service answer her or his needs, wants or special problems. Exhibit 9.8 charts the comparative effectiveness of the questioning technique as opposed to statements in achieving this goal, and Exhibit 9.9 provides an additional example.

Get the Prospect Talking   One of the first principles of selling is to get the prospect to talk. One-way communication can lead to pontification and possible irritation of the buyer, or even worse, boredom. An invitation to speak is pleasing

EXHIBIT 9.8
QUESTION VERSES STATEMENT IN THE SALES INTERVIEW

Statement	Question
Can "go in one ear and out the other."	Forces attention because of required reply.
Apt to antagonize.	Subtle flattery.
A definite commitment.	Position is retractable.
You make the statement.	Leads prospects to see logic and make statement as own idea.

EXHIBIT 9.9

TAKE A TIP FROM SOCRATES

The Socratic method of inquiry by questioning can serve as a model for any modern-day salesperson.

Socrates used a zeroing-in technique. He would start with a broad question. Then he would query the respondent on the answer just given: question; subquestion; sub-subquestion.

Such questioning, which progressively narrows the area of possible response, is one way to establish a buyer's needs, wants, and preferences. You gradually follow a transitional course from a broad question with no limiting bounds on possible answers, an open question, to a multiple-choice question. After the buyer's answer to the multiple-choice question, your questioning becomes increasingly rhetorical, ending with "Isn't that so?" for example, or—seeking confirmation—"Is my understanding correct?"

SALESPERSON: Where will you be wearing the suit?

BUYER: To business.

SALESPERSON: Oh, a business suit. Fine. Are you in an office?

BUYER: Well, yes, it's an office. But it's in a factory.

SALESPERSON: I see. How formal do you like to be?

BUYER: Not very. I attend meetings in the offices, but I walk through the plant a couple of times a day.

SALESPERSON (*smiling*):   Not exactly a double-breasted pin-stripe situation, eh?

BUYER: You've got it.

SALESPERSON (*taking suit off rack*):   How about this rugged, tweed suit? (*Buyer tries on jacket*) Isn't this about what the situation calls for? Let's try this one for size.

BUYER (*looking in mirror*):   H-m-m. Not bad.

SALESPERSON: It looks good on you, and it will take a lot of wear and tear. How does it feel.

BUYER: Feels pretty good. How much is it?

SALESPERSON: Two hundred forty-five dollars. We have it in your size in gray and brown. Which color do you think would be most suitable for you?

BUYER: I'll take the brown.

to the buyer's ego. It also is protection against a wandering mind. No one enjoys a speech as much as a conversation, with the possible exception of the speaker. The reason for the success of talk shows on radio and television is conversation, and questions are the stuff of which conversations are made.

Be Sure Your Presentation Is on the Right Track   The active part of your sales presentation should not be begun until you have completed the inquiring phase of the interview. When you have enough information on the buyer and the buyer's needs, wants, or special problems to know your presentation will be on

EXHIBIT 9.10
GETTING YOUR PRESENTATION ON THE RIGHT TRACK

Immediate exposition	Inquiry first
Shooting in the dark.	Sets up target.
Feature-benefit may not apply.	Buyer's interests identified in order of priority.
Presentation may be inappropriate.	Indication of how buyer likes to be sold.
May trigger resistance prematurely.	Resistance exposed.
Impression of callowness.	A mature professional air that breeds confidence.

target, that is the time to start. Exhibit 9.10 presents a summary of how your active presentation benefits from exploratory questioning.

More on How to Ask Questions

Questions are supposed to resolve problems, but they often compound them. Every change in inflection changes the meaning of the same question. Consider the simple question, "Do you like raisins?"

- "*Do* you like raisins?" If the *Do* is emphasized, the meaning of the question is "*Do* you or don't you like raisins?"
- "Do *you* like raisins?" If the *You* is emphasized in inflection, the question really is "Do *you* like raisins?" or "Does someone else like them?"
- "Do you *like* raisins?" Here, the meaning is whether you enjoy them, as opposed to "Do you eat them for nutrition?"
- "Do you like *raisins*?" By having the emphasis on *raisins,* the question asks whether there's something else you really prefer; for example, "Do you prefer prunes?"

The caution indicated is to be careful to convey the question you mean. Questioning, like listening, is an often neglected art.

Questioning Style: Open-Ended or Multiple-Choice Questions? When you ask an open-ended question, like "What do you think of the new cars?" you open the gates wide for all possible answers. When you ask a multiple-choice question (sometimes called *forced-choice*), you place a limitation on the possible answers. For example, if you ask "Do you like mustard on your hot dog?" only two possible answers are normally expected: "yes" or "no." In the early stages of the sales interview, when you are feeling your way, your questions are best framed as open-ended questions. Your later questions, when you are endeavoring to boil it down, are more apt to be of the multiple-choice variety.

Four Kinds of Questions Questions are of four types, depending on the motive of the interrogator:

1. *The genuine question*. Seeks information, for example, "Have you been to Mexico?"
2. *The rhetorical question*. Seeks acknowledgment or endorsement of a point that might have been expressed as a statement, for example, "This material is softer, isn't it?"
3. *The superficial question*. Used to express flattery or disapproval, for example, "Has anyone ever told you you're beautiful?"
4. *The stall-for-time question*. Consumes time while you think, for example, "By the way, how many people can the dining room accommodate?"

DEMONSTRATION MEANS PROOF

According to Webster's, to *demonstrate* is to show, to explain, with the help of specimens or by experiment. No words can equal the power of a picture. No picture can equal the persuasiveness of the actual product in action, doing what is claimed for it. To be sure, words can add to the power of the picture or the actual demonstration—but more on that later.

Think of Your Prospect as Eliza Doolittle

"Don't talk of love; show me!" sang Eliza Doolittle to Professor Higgins in *My Fair Lady*. Eliza had grown up in the slums of London. She was street-wise, understood reality, and was suspicious of words. This is not a bad image to have in mind as you plan your sales presentation.

Whenever you can—demonstrate, demonstrate, demonstrate. Back up your words with exhibits and proof. Don't just talk. Show. Don't leave credibility to chance.

Says Barry Glasgow, president and sales manager of Industrial Tool Products, Inc., Rosemont, Illinois, "Air tool selling must be service-oriented. Air tools are carry-show demonstration items. But your salesmen have to be able to demonstrate them. . . . If your customer is grinding, you have to know what kinds of materials he's grinding, what kind of finish he wants and what kinds of grinding wheels will do that for him."[3]

How to Demonstrate

Demonstration is not limited to spinning the eggbeater or brandishing the baton. Demonstration begins the minute you present something tangible as well as words, something your prospect can see, hear, feel, taste, smell, otherwise enjoy, or imagine enjoying.

It can be your actual product or a sample of your product or service. It can be the result of your product or service, a sample benefit, like the aroma of a perfume, the taste of a cake, or a ride on a bicycle. It can be a colorful piece of literature, a

[3]"How to Sell Portable Air Tools," *Industrial Distribution*, February 1982, p. 44.

EXHIBIT 9.11

WHAT INTERESTS PEOPLE?

When Dr. George Gallup was research director of the advertising agency Young & Rubicam, Inc., he ran field investigations to evlauate the relative effectiveness of different kinds of illustrations in advertisements.

First in attention-getting value was the illustration of the buyer enjoying a benefit of the product or service.

Second in rank was the illustration of the buyer using the product or service.

Last was the illustration of the product.

"Can you use this photo of our beautiful modern factory in the advertising campaign?" the company founder asks the advertising agent.

"But I thought you were in the tool and die business," replies the advertising counselor, "not real estate."

swatch of material, a model of your invention, or an architect's rendering of a factory building. These physical things gain attention and focus that attention on the presentation. One thing recommends them. They work. Here are some suggestions on how to demonstrate.

Never Call Empty-Handed   The salesperson who understands buyers and what helps them buy never enters the prospect's domain empty-handed.

• Art Karajan, representing Igloo Bottlers, has a thermometer in his hand as he walks into the Riverside Pavilion.

"What's that for?" asks the proprietor.

"May I take the temperature of your beverage case? Believe it or not, when your box is at exactly the right temperature, you sell more soda."

"What is the right temperature?" asks the proprietor. And this starts a lively discussion of beverage merchandising.

• "This rubber squeegee demonstrates the extra stopping power of our new Supertread," says the tire salesperson to the truck fleet operator. "Here. Try rubbing it on this sheet of glass, wet or dry, and see for yourself."

• "Just feel the luxurious softness of this cashmere," says the department store salesperson, handing a sweater to the buyer.

• Kay Jordan of Century Office Machines carries a small leather case under her arm as she is greeted by office manager Sam Graydon in his office. She places the case on Graydon's desk as reverently as though it contained a crown jewel.

"What's that?" asks the curious buyer.

"Our new C140 calculator," replies Jordan as she takes the glistening machine out of the case and slides it over to Graydon. "Here, try a few numbers with it, and see what a ten-strike our product development people have come up with."

• "Just feel the balance of this racquet," says the sporting goods salesperson to the tennis pro, handing over the tennis racquet.

• "Mr. Carton," says newspaper advertising salesperson Harry Finnegan to the owner of Fashion Fur Salon, "you said you want your advertising to reach upper-income readers. Well we took a thousand consecutive names off our subscription list and photographed their homes. Here's the result, Mr. Carton." Finnegan unreels a strip of film before Carton. "See for yourself. Here are the kinds of homes whose owners can appreciate and afford your fine furs. Hundreds of them."

Use Show-How   It probably is a reasonable conjecture to assume that more sales have been made by show-how than by know-how. To be sure, it takes know-how to be able to show the prospect how to use and benefit from a product or service. But know-how, by itself, is a passive asset. Show-how adds action! Here are some examples of show-how in practice.

• "Sit down at the machine," says the sewing machine salesperson to the prospect, "and I'll show you how to make things you never thought possible."
• Gil Sanders, food broker, is making a sales presentation to a restaurant chef. "Here's a scratch recipe for a superior bleu cheese dressing," he says. "It's easier to make and costs less than your present formulation. Let me make a sample for you."

Show-how has one big thing to commend it. When the prospect sees the product work, uses it personally, feels its weight and construction, and observes its other attributes, what stronger impetus to credibility and conviction could there be?

Use Tests—Make the Prospect the Tester   "I weigh two hundred pounds," says the luggage salesperson to the department store buyer. "Watch." Then he places the suitcase on the floor and jumps on it good and hard. "Do you think this bag is a match for the rigors of the baggage room?" he asks the buyer with a smile.

Convincing? Indeed. But it would have been more convincing if the salesperson had been able to get the buyer to do the jumping.

Prove it with tests. This is a cardinal selling principle. But it always is accompanied by another principle: *Try to make the prospect the tester.*

You have a better chance of selling a fishing rod when you get it into the hands of a fishing enthusiast. The golfer who test-swings the club is more prone to buy than when *you* swing the club.

Mary Jepson is demonstrating a new vegetable-based whipped topping to baker Gunther Schultz. She has just finished whipping a batch in Schultz's mixer, using a formula that combined her product with dairy whipping cream.

Jepson asks the baker to take a taste. "What do you think?" she asks.

"Not bad," replies Schultz. He is a stolid, noncommunicative type. When he says "not bad," Jepson knows he is surprised at how good it tastes.

"Now put some in a bag and see how it handles," suggests Jepson. The baker scoops a quantity of the mix into a decoration bag. He enjoys this because he is proud of his skill as a cake decorator.

As the baker starts to bag out a simple design on top of a cake, Jepson continues, "Handles smoothly, doesn't it? It has a tight, smooth texture that bakers seem to like. You see, Mr. Schultz, Wipso has a smaller air cell than dairy cream." Jepson illustrates this as she talks by making a circle with her thumb and forefinger and then reducing the circle. "The smaller air cell increases stability and eliminates tube spasm." Schultz nods approval, pleased to show his understanding of the technicality.

"Have you a rose tube handy?" asks Jepson. "You know, you can make a fine tube rose with Wipso."

"Really?"

As the baker reaches up to a shelf for a rose tube, Jepson goes on, "The taste and texture are delicate. But you can do almost anything with Wipso that you can do with buttercream. You can comb it, crease it, corrugate it, or almost anything else you can think of."

This salesperson has followed all the rules for a sound demonstration. She talked the baker's language and was familiar with his practices and problems. She showed the baker how to use her product. But the turning point in the sales presentation occurred when she got the baker himself to test the product.

Tests prove. Tests sell. This is especially true when the prospect is the tester.

EMBELLISHMENTS

The embellishments of the sales presentation are the tactical devices that dress it up. Proper embellishments can make the presentation at best irresistibly convincing and at worst not dull.

Some of the embellishments that can add spark and sparkle to your presentation are visual aids, words, and showmanship.

Visual Aids

There are two types of visual aids to help your presentation: the *illustrator* and the *organizer*.

The Illustrator   Illustrators are visual aids that literally illustrate the verbal message in your presentation. Examples are photos, letters, brochures, sound slide films, moving pictures, models, charts, and other graphic devices, numerical tables, and even a part of your product such as a cut-through gear.

The choice of illustrators naturally is guided by the personality of the prospect, the buying-selling situation, and the nature of the product or service being presented. The acid test is whether the illustrator selected helps the communication process.

Creative ingenuity can be brought into play in planning an illustrator as a visual aid. For example, a turf farm representative carries with him a sample of sod in a specially constructed sample case.

Josephine Asche, professional relations salesperson for a drug manufacturer with a new analgesic, sought a way to simplify her presentation to doctors, who

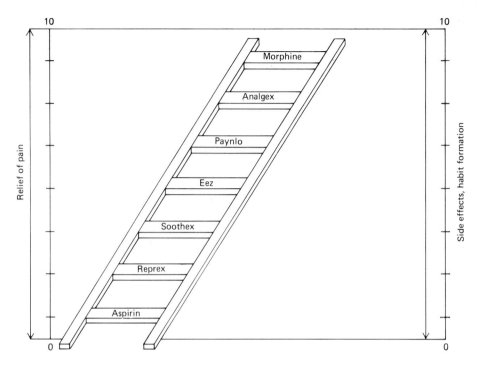

EXHIBIT 9.12
THE ANALGESIC LADDER

write the prescriptions for analgesics. She conceived "The Analgesic Ladder" (Exhibit 9.12), a graphic to show the application of her products. In some cases she would draw the graphic during the sales interview, but she also prepared photocopies for cases where time was limited.

With the help of this visual aid, Asche could quickly depict the scale of relative strengths of the various pain relievers available to the doctor. As she presented it, she explained the exact place of her Analgex in the doctor's repertoire of prescriptions for the relief of pain, along with scales on relative effectiveness, habit formation, and side effects.

The Organizer   This type of visual aid actually organizes the presentation and keeps it on track. The buyer is invited to follow the turning of pages in a manual, portfolio, or flip chart, for example. The salesperson reads aloud, interspersing the reading with questions and comments. Another practice is for buyer and seller to look at a manual or brochure together.

The organizer virtually controls the presentation, with the salesperson monitoring it. The seller is thus relieved of having to think of what comes next. This means freedom to concentrate on the prospect's reactions and on improving interaction.

Both types of visual aid, the illustrator and the organizer, have the same purpose: to add a graphic dimension to the sales presentation.

Words

As stated earlier in this text, selling is a communicating process. In communication there is nothing more elemental than the word. For the word is the wire through which you link your mind with the mind of the buyer.

A doctor carries a bag of medications and instruments. A plumber who forgets to bring tools is the subject of an old joke. One of the most basic tools of the trade in selling is the word.

Advanced salespeople attach great importance to words: how to choose them, how to use them. They are constantly testing and refining word applications, variations, and combinations—ever seeking better and better ways to get across to the buyer.

Words That Paint Pictures   The right words can conjure up the right picture in your prospect's mind. They can stimulate the buyer to visualize, to think, to feel, to want. When this is done exceptionally well, the sales interview often proceeds to a favorable conclusion without any closing mechanism except for the details of ownership transfer. The buyer takes the closing initiative.

Words can convey more than straight meanings alone. There are words and phrases that can transmit color, feeling, tone, shadings. The mastery of these nuances is another significant difference between the salesperson who makes presentations and the salesperson who makes sales as well.

One of the greatest inventions of all time was the alphabet. Only twenty-six letters, yet the possible combinations gave us *Hamlet, War and Peace,* and *The Adventures of Huckleberry Finn.* Twenty-six letters that, depending on who uses them and how they are arranged, can carry us to the moon or put us to sleep.

EXHIBIT 9.13

HOW TO SELL A HAMMER

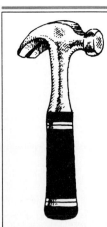

So you thought a hammer was a hammer, with little to choose between one and another. Well, just read how a salesperson in a hardware store presented the highest-priced hammer on the shelf.

This hammer is *full* nickel-plated and has a mahogany finished handle. It's made of crucible cast steel, solid and durable. The faces and claws are tempered just right to pull big spikes without danger of splintering or breaking—yet split to a fine point to pull a tiny nail. Have you ever tried to pull a fine nail and had it slip through the claws? The handle of the hammer head come loose from the handle? This one won't because the handles are put in with iron wedges. Here. Take this hammer in your hand and feel the precise balance. It's designed as carefully as a fine golf club. You'll enjoy using it.

Source: Ivey and Horvath, *Successful Salesmanship,* Prentice-Hall, Englewood Cliffs, N.J., 1953, pp. 109–110.

Every salesperson has access to the same twenty-six letters of the alphabet, the same literature, and the same reference books. The way to improve your choice and usage of words is the same as for developing other skills—study and practice. Harness those twenth-six letters. Strive to become reasonably expert in the limitless possibilities for combining them. Do this, and they are sure to serve you well, in the selling profession and in life.

Semantic Symbols Webster's defines *semantics* as "the meaning of words and other linguistic forms."

The same word can mean different things to different people, based on its association with the listener's past experiences. You can test this out with an old parlor game. Ask subjects to state the first word that comes to mind when another word is mentioned. Don't be surprised if the answers are wide of each other. *Fresh* means *new* to one person, *sassy* to another. *Old* means *outdated, decrepit,* and *familiar* to three separate listeners.

Let us assume you want to present the price of your product or service to a prospect. You can call it *cheap* or *inexpensive* or *economical to use* or *moderately priced* or *reasonable* or *good value* or *an honest value* or *a bargain* or *higher in price because it's better* or *higher in price because it costs more to make.* The list of possibilities could go on and on. Nor is this an idle exercise. There is one best word or phrase to communicate to each individual prospect. Often the choice makes the difference between buying and not buying.

Semantics can mean more than words. The advanced salesperson knows that buyers have individual associations from past experiences that go beyond word symbols. Our past exposures and the resultant subconscious associations that remain make us extremely variable in our individual reactions to nonverbal as well as verbal symbols. Reaction to the same symbol can run all the way from the most affirmative response to the most negative.

Nonverbal symbols cover color, odor, sound, taste, form, shape, and a host of others. An example of contradictory responses is reaction to a train whistle. It fills one person with nostalgia for home. It is a negative emotional stimulus for the person whose father left home during that person's childhood and never returned. (See Exhibit 9.14.)

Speak the Buyer's Language The buyer's language is the jargon of the prospect's occupational or social environment. Use of the buyer's language aids communication. The presentation that relates to the prospect's frame of reference is easiest for the prospect to comprehend. This is essential to an effective presentation.

But be careful to avoid any overly technical jargon of your own industry that may be in your frame of reference, but not the buyer's. For example, listen to this exchange between a computer sales representative and a medical director in a hospital.

SALES REP: What you need is a CPU that has a sixty-four thousand byte capacity with a CRT and a hard-copy output.

EXHIBIT 9.14

ARE YOU A MORNING PERSON?

You feel ebullient in the morning, glad to be alive. It's a wonderful world, and as you spring out of bed, you are happy to be part of it. You relish your breakfast and are full of energetic, joyous anticipation as you leave home for your work.

Think back. Pleasant things probably happened to you in the morning when you were a tot. Perhaps it was the security and joy of a family breakfast with your loving, smiling parents, your brothers and sisters—and the sun streaming through the windows causing your puppy lying in the corner to blink his eyes and wag his tail, thump-thump on the floor, when he sensed you had noticed him.

Or do you awaken in a negative frame of mind and spirit, feel grouchy before your second cup of coffee, and only come around as the morning stretches toward noon?

You quite probably have a subconscious association with unpleasant mornings as a child. Perhaps your father communicated with you only to berate you for such things as not recapping the toothpaste. Your mother might have pushed you impatiently on table manners before you were advanced enough to hold a fork easily. There was little overt parental love, only complaints, criticism, and gloom.

No wonder you are not a morning person.

MEDICAL DIRECTOR: Yeah, yeah, but can it record my diagnoses, medications, LOSs, CBCs, and other lab findings, and run discharge summaries?[4]

By using the jargon of the seller's industry to a fault, this seller started a game of one-upmanship to see which party could confuse the other, instead of an intelligent exchange of information that could lead to a sale.

Communicate to an accountant with figures, to a chef with recipes and flavors, to parents with references to their children, and to a member of the clergy with references to the Bible. To the best of your ability, speak the language of your prospect. Familiar words make the buyer feel comfortable and prevent misunderstanding. Here are some examples of salespeople using the buyer's language.

• Years ago, when farming was largely a family industry, a life insurance seller called on a farmer.

"That's a fine brood of chickens you have there," he said. "I guess you get a lot of eggs."

"Oh, about a hundred and fifty a day."

"What price do you get for your eggs?"

"I sell 'em for thirty cents a dozen."

"For about four eggs a day I can get you a thousand-dollar policy. For thirty-six eggs a day I can get you a ten-thousand-dollar policy."

Without hesitation, the farmer replied, "I think I'll take a five-thousand-dollar policy."

[4]Adapted from L'Herisson, loc. cit.

EXHIBIT 9.15

COMMUNICATIONS THAT CLICK

Advertising counselor Samm S. Baker tripled the sales of a mail-order nursery with the following word changes.

- Strawberry plants: From *giant-size* to *plum-size*
- Gladiolus: From *large-size* to *man-high gladiolus*
- Raspberry plants: From *everbearing* to *three-season raspberries*

Source: Samm S. Baker, *Your Key to Creative Thinking,* Harper & Row, New York, 1962, pp. 215–216.

When the salesperson returned to deliver the policy, the farmer said, "Me and my wife have been thinking over this insurance, and I think we'll take one of them thirty-six-egg ones."[5]

- "The bristles have been coming out of this brush you sold me," complains the buyer.

"You're in the shoe business," replies the salesperson. "I know your quality is tops, but did you ever have a less-than-perfect shoe get out of your plant?"

Buy Words   Here are a few suggestions and cautions on choosing words that lead to sales.

- *Use as few words as possible.* What you don't say sometimes is more conducive to the sale than what you say.
- *Use rifle words.* They penetrate fast because of the preciseness of their meaning to the buyer. Examples include *fast, sharp, cheap, complete, cold,* and *hot.*
- *Use simple words.* One syllable is better than two; two syllables are better than three. Your communication is only as good as the prospect's comprehension of it.
- *Use picture words.* They transmit images and help the buyer to visualize. Examples include *knee action* (automotive), *high-rise building,* and *greenbacks.*
- *Use soundlike words. Gurgling brook* sounds like what it means—so do *splash* and *rat-a-tat-tat.*
- *Use the buyer's words.* Reach into the buyer's frame of reference, and you'll be sure to be understood.
- *Avoid tired words.* These are the words that have been so overworked that they no longer carry a thought effectively. To some prospects they actually are a grating distraction. An example of a tired word is the currently overworked *super.*
- *Use pointed words.* Choose words specific enough to mean something. For example, steer clear of meaningless comparatives like *better, cleaner,* and *softer.*

[5]Ivey and Horvath, *Successful Salesmanship,* Prentice-Hall, Englewood Cliffs, N.J., 1953, p. 17.

EXHIBIT 9.16
KEEP IT SIMPLE AND DIRECT

Albert Lasker, advertising tycoon, is frustrated. Some of America's biggest advertisers are clients of his Lord & Thomas (now Foote, Cone and Belding). But he cannot get little Fischer Corporation to budge. He expects Fischer to grow and become a prize advertising account, and he wants Lord & Thomas to have a hand in the success story. In spite of the modesty of the account, the prospective client is not awed by the overtures of a big-time advertising agency.

Lasker has submitted plans, ideas, prospectuses. He has unleashed the talent of John E. Kennedy, the world's highest-paid copywriter. No luck. And now Lasker has sent Claude Hopkins to try his hand.

The door opens. Hopkins enters and drops a letter of intent from Fischer on Lasker's desk.

"How in the name of heaven did you do it?" Lasker asks.

"Very simple," replies Hopkins, "I merely said, 'Fischer, let me write your advertising and you'll get rich!'"

Words That Work   Here—from Elmer Wheeler's word clinics—are some combinations actually proved on the firing line of sales. They work because they are working words. They were developed by salespeople in practice.

- "Have you arranged the investment of your daughter's life insurance?" (insurance)
- "These peas are garden fresh." (frozen foods)
- "You'll increase the value of your home by ten percent with this planting." (landscaping service)
- "This color looks good on you." (clothing)
- "When is your wife's birthday?" (flowers)
- "Fireproof buildings don't burn, but their contents do." (fireproof files)
- "Are your salespeople calling on poor credit risks?" (credit service)
- "Do your press photos look like you—*now*?" (photography)
- "Here is a necktie that was made for your shirt." (menswear)
- "Which roses do you like best—the red or the yellow?" (flowers)
- "Only one woman can own this gown." (ladies apparel)
- "May I check your watch for correct time?" (watches)

Showmanship

The sample dialogue between salesperson and prospect that you are about to read exemplifies many of the classic principles that contribute to an effective sales presentation. It especially illustrates the use of showmanship. The case is

EXHIBIT 9.17
WORDS WORK FOR DENTISTS TOO

"You have a young mouth," says the dentist as he examines the teeth of an elderly woman.

"Really?" exclaims the patient. She beams. She is sixty years old and her face is wrinkled. How wonderful to learn that her gums and teeth are "young."

You may be sure this patient will pay her bill with pleasure and will be right on time for the next visit.

the introduction of a new bubble packaging service to a marketer of photographic supplies.

PROSPECT: But our developer is a liquid and we ship it in bottles. I'm afraid of breakage.

SELLER: In other words, you're afraid of a bottle breaking in shipping and fragments of glass flying out of the bubble package?

PROSPECT: Exactly.

SELLER: If I understand you correctly, the only thing holding you up, then, is the danger of breakage. If not for that, you'd switch to bubble packaging? Is that right?

PROSPECT: Probably.

SELLER: (*Lifting from sample case a bottle of water enclosed in a bubble package*): Would you say this simulates your product in a bubble package?

PROSPECT: Yes.

SELLER: All right. Here. Throw this package against that brick wall as hard as you can. (*Seller hands package to buyer. Buyer throws package against brick wall. The glass bottle breaks into smithereens, but not a speck of glass or liquid escapes from the outer bubble package.*)

Let us take this sales presentation apart for analysis.

1. The salesperson localized the prospect's reason for reluctance to buy, and repeated the objection even more forcibly than the buyer stated it.
2. The salesperson obtained the prospect's acknowledgment that this was the only point in question.
3. The salesperson obtained an implied commitment to buy if this objection could be overcome.
4. The salesperson introduced a demonstration to prove by test that the bubble package would contain all splinters of glass and flow of liquid in the event of breakage.
5. The seller involved the buyer in the test. The prospect did the testing.

But something even more dynamic brought this sales interview to a happy conclusion. Pervading the entire selling sequence, and enhancing the effectiveness of each selling principle, was the most persuasive of presentation embellishments—*showmanship*. Nothing dresses up and fortifies a presentation like clever staging. As discussed in the chapter on the approach, the use of dramatic stagecraft in business was widely misunderstood until Zenn Kaufman and Kenneth M. Goode placed it in proper perspective. The showmanship employed by the salesperson in the above example was pertinent and purposeful. It was in good taste. It strengthened the selling communication.

RECAP

The presentation is the guts of the sales interview. The approach gains your prospect's attention. The presentation develops the buyer's *interest* and *desire* to enjoy the benefits of your product or service. Without interest and desire, there can be no buying action.

This chapter covered various aspects of the sales presentation: how to structure it; how to be sure the substance of the presentation is valid for the prospect; how to prove the advantages of your product or service by demonstrations; and how to use embellishments to dramatize these feature-benefits and to assure the prospect's understanding of them.

Chapter 10 will enlarge on the presentation, and the interview of which it is a part, by acquainting you with a list of suggestions and cautions.

REVIEW QUESTIONS

1. What are the four components of a sales presentation? Explain each.
2. What is meant by each of the following: AIDA, zeroing in, stimulus response, and personal interaction.
3. Describe Borden's four-step presentation guide.
4. What is meant by the *substance* of a sales presentation? How do you attain it?
5. In what ways do buyers differ as receivers of selling communications? How should the salesperson deal with these differences in the sales presentation?
6. What is the first thing to be accomplished in the sales presentation?
7. If the prospect does not have a need for your product or service, or if your product or service cannot answer the prospect's need, what should you do? Explain.
8. Which are preferable in selling: questions or positive statements? Explain your answer.
9. Sales authorities recommend fact finding in the sales presentation before commitment to a presentation line. Why?

10. What is the difference between an open-ended question and a multiple-choice question? When should each be used?
11. There are four different reasons for which people ask questions. What are they? Give an example of each.
12. What is a demonstration? What is its purpose in the sales presentation? Elaborate.
13. What is show-how? Give an example of show-how.
14. What are visual aids? Give two examples.
15. What is meant by the expression, "Speak the buyer's language"?
16. What is showmanship?

DISCUSSION QUESTIONS

1. You have just entered the office of Harold Madden, proprietor of the Sunshine Super Drugstore, located in the West Farms Mall near Hartford, Connecticut, to present a new aerosol shave cream, *Sof-Soke*. This new shave cream penetrates the beard more readily than other shave creams. It is smoother because of a smaller air cell than competitive products. It costs the dealer $21.75 per case of twenty-four, $1.75 over the general price level for shave creams in the most popular size, 12 ounces. Sof-Soke will be advertised in the *Hartford Courant* and in a saturation schedule of spot commercials over TV channel 3 and AM radio station WTIC. A colorful point-of-purchase rack sign is available.
   (a) What will be your presentation plan?
   (b) Assuming you are successful in selling Madden on stocking Sof-Soke and he asks what you think the size of his initial order should be, should you recommend a quantity that is small, medium, or large?
2. Your presentation of the stereo combination has reached the preclose stage. The prospect has been listening attentively and occasionally nodding affirmatively. "Do you think your son will be impressed by the midrange transducer, Mrs. Kelly?" you ask the prospect. This was a feature you stressed in your demonstration of the speakers. "I'm afraid I don't know what a transducer is," replies the prospect.
   (a) What shortcoming in the sales presentation is indicated by Mrs. Kelly's reply? Elaborate.
   (b) What should you do and say now?
3. You are a member of the student senate at a university. The senate is meeting to discuss what its position should be on the question of on-campus political activism by students. You are opposed to the conservative view just expressed by another senate member. "It's gone too far," she had said, "Almost every time there's a new headline, there's a protest march. We're students. Isn't it time we started leaving politics to the politicians?"
   How do you present your opposition view to sell it to the senate?
4. You are anxious to get the summer job waiting on tables at the Mountain View Resort Hotel. "We have only one spot left," says the campus recruiter. "It's

between you and Marianne Kraus. Tell me why we should hire you instead of her.''

How will you present your case to sell your services?

LEARNING EXPERIENCES

1. You are a partner in Jewelson & Cramer (J & C), management consultants. Your senior partner, Sam Jewelson, has asked you to prepare a proposal for the Johnson-Woodward Corporation, whom he would like to obtain as a client for J & C. Creighton Woodward and Jewelson belong to the same country club, and Woodward has invited the proposal. Johnson-Woodward is a family corporation that was founded by Woodward's father. On his father's death, twenty-five years ago, Woodward became chief executive officer. He is now sixty-three and, with no children to succeed him, is concerned with continuity of management. Woodward is in reasonably good health, but he would like to be able to let up, to take longer vacations, and not to have to worry about the management of the business. All the stock is owned by him and his brother and sister, neither of whom ever has been active in the company. All three principals are directors, along with the family lawyer, the president of the company's main bank, and a partner in its accounting firm. But the board rarely meets and then mainly to rubber-stamp Woodward's corporate decisions. Johnson-Woodward manufactures the J-W blender, a respected kitchen appliance, and markets it through department stores. Although the firm is in sound financial condition, with an excellent balance sheet and no debt, earnings have declined in recent years, and last year Johnson-Woodward sustained its first operating loss in over half a century.

   Prepare a proposal to sell Johnson-Woodward on retaining Jewelson & Cramer to make a study of its business, recommending a course for its future. Draw on your imagination for any facts not covered in the description just given.

2. Get a job for a Saturday, selling in a store. Write a memo summarizing what you learned from the experience.

CASE

THE ROYAL FLUSH

Ray St. George owns and manages the Royal Flush, a bath furnishings and accessories shop at Glen Lochen, a shopping mall at Glastonbury, Connecticut. So complete and original is Ray St. George's merchandise selection that people come from long distances to buy at the Royal Flush.

St. George also happens to be a top-notch salesperson. Listen to him in action on a busy Saturday afternoon.

CUSTOMER A: Where are the guest towels?

ST. GEORGE: Right over there. Make yourself at home and call me if you want help.

CUSTOMER B: What can you suggest for a Mother's Day gift?

ST. GEORGE (*smiling*):   Whose mother?

CUSTOMER B (*laughing*):   My kid's.

ST. GEORGE: Does she like breakfast in bed?

CUSTOMER B: How'd you guess? It's a ritual every Mother's Day morning. My boys bring it in.

ST. GEORGE: My house too. How about this Ronel Deluxe bed tray? (*hands it to customer*) The tray is removable, transforming into a book rest. The center is adjustable. (*changes adjustment to different angle*) The side handles make it easy for even a tot to carry safely. And the side pockets are great for a book or the morning newspaper.

CUSTOMER B: Great! How much?

(*Later, St. George saunters over to the side of a customer standing before one of the fully equipped designer-decorated model bathrooms.*)

ST. GEORGE: What do you think of it?

CUSTOMER C: I must say it's different.

ST. GEORGE: Designer-decorated. The newest idea in bath furnishings. Comfortable. Have you ever used a bath towel that's warmed?

CUSTOMER C: As a matter of fact, I haven't.

ST. GEORGE: That towel rack is electrified. By the way, are you looking for something in particular?

CUSTOMER C: No. Just browsing. We just moved into a new house, and I'm looking for ideas.

ST. GEORGE: Good for you, Mrs. _____?

CUSTOMER C: Simpson.

ST. GEORGE: Thanks for coming to visit us, Mrs. Simpson. I'm Ray St. George. This shop is my business—and my hobby. By the way, where is your new home?

CUSTOMER C: Pleasant Lane, near the corner of Arlen.

ST. GEORGE: A lovely neighborhood. Many of your neighbors shop here.

CUSTOMER C: We expect to be very happy there. Once we get past the awful job of getting settled.

ST. GEORGE: The only thing we can help you with is bath furnishings. Let me . . . (*And St. George goes over each piece in the bathroom set on display and gives facts on each.*)

CUSTOMER C: What does this set come to—complete?

ST. GEORGE: If you buy it by the piece, it totals two hundred and fifty-seven dollars. You can get it as a set for one hundred and ninety-eight dollars.

CUSTOMER C: I'll talk to my husband about it.

ST. GEORGE: Excellent! Incidentally, how many bathrooms do you have?

CUSTOMER C: Three and a half. Why?

ST. GEORGE: Oh, just a thought. Can you make the decision yourself, if you want to?

CUSTOMER C: Well, Mr. Simpson and I generally like to share things like this. But I suppose I could.

ST. GEORGE: You seem to like this particular set so much—and my compliments to you on your taste—why not go ahead on this one now and select the others later with Mr. Simpson?

CUSTOMER C: Can I use my credit card?

Questions

1. What is the secret of St. George's success as a salesperson?
2. Why do you suppose St. George left customer A to fend for herself?
3. What special selling principle made the sale to customer B?
4. Analyze in detail the strategy used in selling to Mrs. Simpson (customer C).

TEN

CHAPTER OBJECTIVES

To provide you with guidelines regarding length of the interview, control of the interview, and comparative merits of hard sell and soft sell

To review product or service knowledge from the viewpoint of how to use it to advantage

To aid your understanding of prospects as human beings in addition to their being buyers

To examine the many aspects of interview strategy

To review specific interview principles and techniques

To familiarize you with the standardized presentation and the extemporaneous presentation and where, how, and to what degree to use each

To acquaint you with the different motivations of different categories of buyer

To prepare you for multiple-party interviews, both joint presentations and presentations to groups

CHAPTER OUTLINE

THE SALES INTERVIEW II: SUGGESTIONS AND CAUTIONS

> Be genuine, be simple, be brief; talk to people in language that
> they understand; and finally and most of all, be persistent.
> Bruce Barton*

A salesperson's special area of expertise is persuasion. Persuasion is
the direct opposite of pressure. It is enlightening the prospect through
intelligent communication to want to enjoy the benefits of your product
or service. When this is done well, the closing becomes almost automatic. One big secret of closing a sale is a well-conducted sales interview.

Chapter 9 described the mechanics of the sales interview with special emphasis on the sales presentation, what to do and how to do it.
Bruce Barton's admonition to be genuine, simple, brief, and understandable does indeed provide a good foundation for your presentation.
But what about extra-tough prospects? Do they cause special problems
or require extra tricks of the trade? This chapter will deal with some of
the broader aspects of the sales interview. It will cover questions, answers, and cautions on strategy, presentation philosophy, and subjects
of controversy. It also will go into special topics like selling to resellers
and multiple-party sales interviews. Chapters 9 and 10 together will
familiarize you with the best thinking and field practice on how to conduct all types of sales interviews.

*Statesman, author, and cofounder of the advertising agency Batten, Barton, Durstine & Osborn,
Inc.

GENERAL GUIDES FOR THE SALES INTERVIEW

Selling is an inexact science. It has no foolproof discipline to guarantee uniform results from a uniform methodology. Because of its extreme dependence on the human factor, 1 and 1 do not always make 2. For this reason selling abounds in controversial subjects.

Length of the Presentation

Dr. George Gallup, when research director of Young & Rubicam, the advertising agency, once sent a bulletin to the Young & Rubicam staff on the length of advertisements. Gallup's summary, the result of field surveys, showed that the length of ads bore no relationship to the reading indexes they attained.

In selling, as in advertising, it is the buyer who determines how long your presentation should be. This depends on how long an attention span your presentation merits, or in other words, how *interesting* your presentation is. There is no such thing as an uninterested prospect—only an uninteresting presentation.

Take all the time you need, but not more than you need. Then *make sure your presentation is worth the prospect's time.* One of the advantages of advance preparation, whether through a standardized presentation (discussed later in this chapter) or any of its modifications or variations, is the saving of words. You polish and prune to squeeze out the water. One commentator on selling believes the time taken for the average sales presentation can be cut in half and actually become more effective in the process. It is surprising how much can be said in a short time when it is planned. Lincoln's Gettysburg address contains only 268 words; he had prepared it in advance.

Controlling the Sales Interview

No one really controls the sales interview. But as a competent salesperson, you can guide the progress of the interview through the stages of attention, interest, desire, and action. You can achieve this through comprehensive questioning, listening, and subtle suggestion. A show of personality force isn't needed. In fact, some of the most outstanding salespeople are not assertive. On the contrary, they are often characterized by humility and patience. But they are smart people, especially proficient in the arts of communication and diplomacy. Under the influence of such a seller, the prospect is led, not pushed or pulled. The buyer feels like the dominant person in the interview while going along as planned by the salesperson.

Soft Sell or Hard Sell?

Selling can be highly aggressive or very low key or somewhere between the two. The buyer's personality and the nature of the selling situation determine which technique is appropriate. Except in cases of unusual buyer personalities, the guidelines are the degree of reorderability of product or service and the nature of the potential transaction. *One-call* selling situations, such as the direct selling of a

EXHIBIT 10.1
"GET TO THE POINT"

Martin D. Shafiroff of Lehman Brothers Kuhn Loeb, Incorporated, who has earned as much as a million and a half dollars in commissions in a single year of selling securities, says:

> Every presentation is divided into three parts . . . the introduction, the middle and the end. . . . Most people concentrate on the middle. . . . I start with a request that a transaction be made with a particular company, and if the individual is contemplating that investment, I immediately flash images of why the investment is an outstanding one. I interweave these reasons with the request for an order. . . . If the individual hesitates, I say "John, do you know of any other company selling at four and a half times this year's earnings which has a 16.7 percent return on equity? The company has a couple of hundred million dollars in working capital, and its book value is substantially higher than the market value. Could we duplicate this company at two or three times its present market price? The answer is *no!*" In other words, *get to the point.*

Source: Robert L. Shook, *The Ten Greatest Salespersons: What They Say about Selling,* Harper & Row, New York, 1978, pp. 146–147.

low-price office-supply specialty from office to office, are more apt to call for hard sell. On the other hand, where the goal is to obtain a *customer,* rather than just an order, such as in the case of a lawn care service, soft sell generally is more effective.

When a degree of hard sell is indicated, the most advanced salespeople are able to raise the buying urgency without raising their voices or waving their arms. They utilize the force of logic or emotional appeal, often with persistent questioning rather than overt dynamism. In this way they avoid the risk of alienating the prospect or of a boomerang termination of the interview.

"This camera has an *automatic exposure control!*" the camera salesperson states loudly as he slaps his hand down on the counter with a thump for emphasis. "Think of it—no more spoiled pictures, too light or too dark! Any other camera is now behind the times!"

"Well, I'm a little old-fashioned," replies the prospect. "I feel comfortable with the camera I have."

Now see how another salesperson made the same point—the same hard sell, but softly executed.

SALESPERSON: Are you interested in the automatic exposure control on this camera?
PROSPECT: Not really.
SALESPERSON: Have you ever had a picture come out too light or too dark?
PROSPECT: Yes, come to think of it, I have.
SALESPERSON: Let me show you how it works.

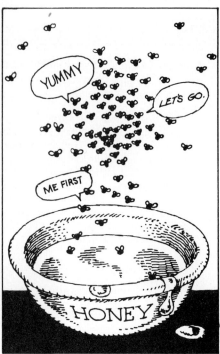

EXHIBIT 10.2
HONEY WORKS BETTER

Sometimes It Is Better to *Under*whelm

On the wall of the office of Kenneth Collins, advertising great, was a framed motto: "Avoid superlatives—They Lead to Exaggeration."

Exaggeration weakens credibility. Understatement strengthens credibility. Sometimes it pays to *under*whelm your prospect.

> "This is the second-best moving service in the area," says the salesperson.
> "*Second* best?" asks the prospect incredulously.
> "Yes. Each of our competitors is the best."

One of the surest ways to win the buyer's confidence is to make an under-promise and an overdelivery. Charles Schwab, the steel master, once was asked by an important buyer if a delivery could be made in six months. "We need eight months," replied Schwab. Then he inspired his production people to outdo themselves to deliver in six months. The buyer was delighted.

Julius Rosenwald, whose talents put Sears, Roebuck on the road to becoming the world's largest retailer, once said, "If Sears had a counter, I would stand on both sides of that counter." In your imagination, place yourself in your prospect's shoes. See how you would react to your own selling. Nothing could bring home more poignantly the shortsightedness of overstatements, superlatives, and exaggeration.

Take that truly tired word, *quality*. The buyer knows the literal definition of *quality*. But hasn't it been so overworked that, in the buyer's gut feeling, it may have lost conviction? Today's buyer, made increasingly wary by constant exposure to every seller's claims of quality and service, is more apt to be interested in *why* quality and *how* service.

Product Knowledge—Boon or Bogey?

"Product knowledge is essential in selling, but it alone does not guarantee success. What seems to contribute most to successful selling is the . . . sales skill of the seller."[1]

Two sales representatives of the Old Town Corporation's New York branch were talking things over. Here's how the conversation went.

> "Tell me, Charlie," said one; "How do you do it? You're a newcomer to inked business machine ribbons. I've been at it for years. I know it from A to Z. You're smart, but you don't know much about our products yet. How do you explain the fact that I'm not doing well and you're taking home fat commission checks every month?"
>
> "Quite simple, George," was the reply; "Out of every hundred prospects, how many would you say know anything about inked ribbons?"
>
> "Maybe two."
>
> "There's your answer. You're selling those two. I'm selling the other ninety-eight."

George suffered from what someone has called *technosis*. He was clouding his sales presentation with product knowledge with the result that both he and his prospects were losing sight of the purpose of the interview. George was impressing buyers. Charlie was selling them.

The salesperson should acquire all the product or service knowledge available. This makes for self-confidence and provides answers to questions the prospect might raise. However, the amount of this knowledge that is conveyed to the prospect should be limited to the requirements of the sales interview.

EXHIBIT 10.3
TECHNOSIS

Understanding the Prospect

Overestimate rather than underestimate the human side of your prospect. Nothing is as inscrutable as the human riddle you must puzzle out each time you make a sales call. The greatest salesperson on earth, presenting the most marvelous product at the lowest price, is dependent upon the decision of the prospect who has the power to buy or not buy. So the wise salesperson plays it safe by taking every precaution not to offend and hopes to please the prospect during the presentation. Here are a few rules to remember.

[1]Laura L'Herisson, "Teaching the Sales Force to Fail," *Training and Development Journal*, November 1981, p. 78.

• *Avoid fact gaps.* The missing link in the presentation sequence can lose the prospect's understanding and the sale.

• *Keep it simple.* Never underestimate your prospect's intelligence or overestimate your prospect's knowledge. Fortunate is that seller who has the ability to make complicated things clear and difficult things simple.

• *Use humor cautiously.* Humor has a place in selling when it is used discreetly. It can lessen tension, make a point by parable, break the ice in a cold situation, or please the buyer's ego. But be careful. If someone is to be the butt of a joke, make sure it is you and not the prospect. One type of humor that is safe is the jest that compliments the buyer; for example, to a hobby golfer: "I hear you can't find anyone to play with since you beat your handicap by eight strokes at the stationer's outing." If you elect to use humor in your selling, give thought to the reaction of the prospect to humor itself, not just to the specific joke. To some prospects, this makes light of your selling mission. Be careful not to overdo it. When in doubt, don't use humor at all.

• *Use plural personal pronouns. We* is more conducive to confidence and credibility than *I.* "We can save you four thousand dollars a year." *We* says, in effect, that the entire team will back up delivery of the benefit you are promising.

• *Sell the way the prospect likes to be sold.* If the buyer likes hearts and flowers, sell with hearts and flowers. If the buyer likes numbers, sell with facts and figures. Remember how young Craig Lasker sold the abrasive to Kasmier who owned the machine shop? He sensed that Kasmier was a no-nonsense, bottom-line buyer

EXHIBIT 10.4
SELL THE WAY THE PROSPECT LIKES TO BE SOLD

who loved brevity, so he approached him with only twelve words and made the sale. Lasker sold Kasmier the way Kasmier liked to buy.

• *Make the buyer the star.* Don't be too clever. You may appear like a wiseacre. Even worse, the prospect may feel inferior and show who is boss by not buying. Don't appear too superior. Be humble—not obsequious like Uriah Heep but sincerely modest. Make the buyer feel superior. Play yourself down, your product or service up. The buyer's ego, once crossed, can kill a sale more quickly and surely than the most powerful competition.

• *Cultivate empathy.* Show interest in your prospect—sincere interest. Make the buyer feel important. No one is too big to enjoy this and to appreciate it. You must like people. That's the beginning of honest empathy toward others. If you don't like people, selling is not the profession for you.

• *Appeal to the buyer's third personality.* Your prospect really is three persons in one: (1) the person he or she really is, (2) the person she or he would like to be, and (3) the person he or she would like others to think he or she is.

The experienced salesperson understands this and appeals to the *buyer's third personality,* the image the buyer would like others to see. Give the prospect a reputation to uphold. In other words, make a liar think you consider him honest; make a dullard think you consider her reasonably clever; make a cad think you consider him a philanthropist; and a sharp opportunist, a person worthy of trust. It is likely that the buyer will enjoy the unmerited reputation and try to live up to it, at least in dealing with you. Here are a few examples.

> "A solid person like you always pays your bills," you tell the deadbeat. "Is anything wrong?"
> "No," the debtor replies, "I've just been busy. Here. I'll write you a check."

This slow payer is used to receiving brickbats from creditors. He enjoys being told he is solid, more so than if he actually were solid. You get paid while other creditors wait.

> "Show Mrs. Kent the best material," the fabric store owner tells his clerk. "That's the only kind she buys."

If Mrs. Kent wanted to economize by trying a cheaper grade, you may bet she did not. It's nice to have a reputation for buying only the best.

STRATEGIES FOR THE SALES INTERVIEW

An inexact science like selling is constantly presenting options in choice of tactics. There are many principles to guide the salesperson in choosing among them.

To Appeal to the Buyer's Mind or Emotions? Fact versus Fancy

Should you present *reasons* to buy or should you appeal to the prospect's emotions? There is no pat answer to this question. The most tough-minded purchasing agent in an iron foundry is still a human being. That seemingly flighty beauty in the slit skirt at the cosmetic counter happens to be a partner in a Wall Street investment banking firm, an arbitrage expert, and a director of four corporations. Everyone buys on the basis of both reason and emotion, sometimes in the most amazing contradiction of what one might expect.

The wise seller plays to reason or emotion as indicated to be appropriate for the prospect in question but never loses sight of the buyer's other side. When you sell to emotion, don't forget reason. When you appeal to reason, don't overlook the possible influence of emotion.

Facts generally are the major consideration in buying decisions where large expenditures or complex propositions are involved. Emotions are more apt to dominate the purchase of a personal item like a dress or a gift item. These generalities must be modified, however, because of the personal characteristics of the buyer. For instance, a purchasing agent or a technical person is very apt to buy a perfume on the basis of reason. Another point to note is that, by and large, reasoned buying decisions are more apt to withstand the effects of time and counterinfluences than decisions based on emotion.

Let the Button Sell the Blazer

The specific proves the general. Smart salespeople make capital of this principle. Their presentations contain plenty of "for instances."

The hearth helps to sell the house. The click helps to sell the camera. The ice-cube maker can turn the tide in the sale of a refrigerator.

Establish Progressive Areas of Agreement

As your presentation progresses, try to gain the prospect's agreement on successive points. This gets the buyer into a "yes" frame of mind. It sets the stage for agreement on major points, including the decision to buy.

The less consequential these points are, the better. For if the approval is not forthcoming, a minor point can be conceded or passed over lightly without jeopardizing the sale. If, on the other hand, you venture too early for agreement on a major point and do not obtain it, the rest of the interview can become an uphill climb.

POLITICAL CANDIDATE: Would you like to see your taxes lowered?
VOTER: Naturally.
CANDIDATE: Well, in the last four years they've gone up, haven't they?
VOTER: And how!
CANDIDATE: And the reason your taxes have gone up is the rising cost of government, isn't that so?
VOTER: I agree.
CANDIDATE: Now why does government cost so much? Would you agree it's *waste?*

VOTER: Yes.

CANDIDATE: Then vote for me. My platform is to *cut waste in government!* Here's a list of the things I'll do.

Modify to Make the Sale

When, in the course of the interview, you find you are on the wrong track, change. Your goal is a sale, not a perfect interview. Perfection only exists in an imperfect mind. The winners are willing to recognize reality and to change course when they find they are wrong.

- "I wouldn't wear that to a dogfight," says the buyer.
"I'm sorry," replies the salesperson. "I thought you were interested in leather. What material do you prefer?"
- "This policy is for investment," says the insurance prospect. "I consider insurance for investment unwise. The only insurance I believe in is for protection. And I want the cheapest I can get."
"That's interesting," replies the salesperson. "You have company in that opinion. And we have a special plan to accommodate it—split-dollar insurance."

The Preclose

The *preclose*, also called the *trial close*, is the testing of the prospect's readiness for closing. It can start taking place any time in the sales interview, from the moment the salesperson and prospect meet. That is why we consider it part of the sales presentation rather than the close itself.

The purpose of the presentation is to prepare the buyer for closing. Once the prospect is ready, no matter when, close! Sometimes this happens very early in the interview. Continuing the presentation beyond that point can lose the sale. (See Exhibit 10.5.)

By utilizing preclose techniques throughout the sales interview, you will know when the prospect is ready for the closing. This is the high point of your ascension of the successive steps in the sales presentation—from attention to interest to desire to conviction. Conviction is the climax. Anything following it will be anticlimactic. So move while the door is open the widest. To continue to sell is to work against a naturally descending interest. This principle is described graphically in Exhibit 10.6.

As your sales presentation progresses, watch for signs of the prospect's disposition to buy. An affirmative nod of the head, for example, is a body sign that the buyer is coming your way. An agreement with something you have said is another signal. It can be as casual as an up-inflecting "yes" or "uh-huh."

Now and then pose a test question to measure your prospect's acceptance level. This can be as simple as a rhetorical "Don't you think?" or "Isn't that so?" at the end of a statement. If you really are confident you are almost "home" and

EXHIBIT 10.5

A RAIN OF WORDS COOLS MARK TWAIN'S ENTHUSIASM

Mark Twain (Samuel Clemens) once walked by a vacant store where a man was declaiming from a makeshift rostrum on behalf of a charitable cause.

Twain went into the store and listened a few minutes.

Thinking the appeal valid, he determined to donate a hundred dollars.

But the speaker drones on and on. Twain's initial enthusiasm gradually dampened.

When the speaker finally had finished, Twain went up to him, handed him five dollars, and informed him he had talked himself out of ninety-five dollars.

can risk the possibility of a negative response, a technique normally to be avoided, you might come right out and ask, "What do you think?"

Another preclosing strategy is to recapitulate the point or points that seemed to register favorably with the prospect. One way to do this is to restate the point and ask the buyer to confirm its acceptance. For example, "Now the headroom on this model was something that interested you, wasn't it, Mrs. Altman?"

Elmer Wheeler's dictum, "Don't ask if; ask which," can be employed as a preclose device. For example, "Which do you think your wife will prefer, Mr. Carlatti, the blend or the hundred percent cotton?"

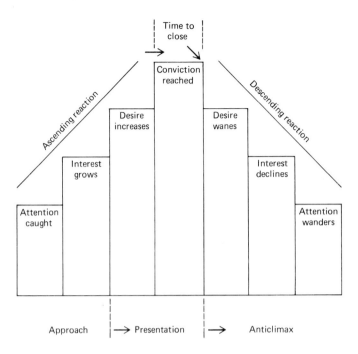

EXHIBIT 10.6
THE SALES PRESENTATION STAIRWAY

Emphasize Product or Service Differences

Why should the prospect buy your product or service instead of another? Why purchase from you instead of from another seller? There are only three possible reasons: (1) your offering is better in terms of value, reliability, or service; (2) it is more accessible; or (3) the buyer has a personal preference either for your brand, its source, or for you.

Throughout the sales presentation, be sure to underscore the points of difference between your product or service and competitive offerings and why yours is superior. Your aim is to convey the conviction that what you sell is uniquely advantageous for the buyer and comes from a source that is also highly advantageous.

The Pause That Revitalizes: Stop Today—Come Back Tomorrow

Some sales take more time to gel than others. It is sometimes worthwhile to invest in more than one sales call. In fact, there are many classifications where multiple-call selling is the rule rather than the exception. Related to the slow-gelling sale is the sales interview where your realistic appraisal tells you that the odds for a successful closing are unfavorable.

In cases like these, why not forgo trying to close? You may even put the buyer at ease by saying you are not there to sell at the time. A statement such as, "My purpose is to become acquainted with your requirements and preferences so that we can develop an intelligent proposal for you,'' can go a long way toward establishing a good rapport.

TYPES OF SALES PRESENTATIONS

There are three different types of sales presentations. The choice of which to use depends on circumstances, such as the purpose of the sales interview, the experience and personal style of the salesperson, the product or service category, the type of buyer, and similar factors. At one end of the spectrum is the standardized sales presentation, the extreme of which is the so-called canned sales talk. At the other end is the extemporaneous presentation. Somewhere between these two is the eclectic presentation, which draws the best features from each.

The Standardized Presentation

There is considerable latitude in determining what is technically a standardized presentation. In the narrowest sense it is a canned talk, prepared for the salesperson by the management, to be memorized, rehearsed, and delivered verbatim. In the broadest sense it is a planned, structured outline approach to make sure the salesperson will keep to a standard in a logical, complete, factual delivery.

The canned talk is commonly used, and often quite effectively, for repetitious kinds of selling. Examples are the selling of sets of books direct to homes and demonstration selling to passersby at fairs or on the street floor of department stores.

The Perennial Controversy   There always has been divided opinion among sales theorists over the standardized presentation. The arguments pro and con follow.

Those in favor of the standardized sales presentation have stated the following:

1. Nothing is left out.
2. Selling points are presented in logical order.
3. The most effective thoughts, words, demonstration devices, and even the manner of delivery by the salesperson are controlled through preparation by experts.
4. Buyer resistance can be anticipated and forestalled or overcome before it is expressed.
5. It saves time for both buyer and seller, since advance preparation squeezes out all superfluous words.
6. Not having to search for words, the salesperson can concentrate on the delivery itself and on studying the prospect's reactions.
7. Mastery of the set presentation builds the salesperson's confidence. It eliminates options, questions, and doubts.
8. Inexperienced salespeople are able to tell the sales story to prospects more accurately.

Those against the standardized sales presentation have stated:

1. The presentation is apt to become parrotlike, stilted, and singsong.
2. Repetition can become monotonous—zestless for the salesperson and with a negative effect on the listener.
3. Some people become self-conscious speaking a piece.
4. The standardized presentation is apt to be wide of the mark. No two buyers or sales situations are identical.
5. With a set presentation to follow, the salesperson is deprived of the chance to develop and exercise an important aspect of expertise: that is, the talent for ascertaining the prospect's individual needs, wants, or special problems before commitment to a selling line.

The Extemporaneous Presentation

The extemporaneous presentation is a free-flow, off-the-cuff type that allows the salesperson complete flexibility in what to say. Spontaneity rather than verbatim delivery is the objective in this type of presentation.

However, the most effective extemporaneous presentations are still planned. Yes, that's right. The salesperson making an extemporaneous presentation uses lines and devices that have proved to be effective in communicating the selling message and in responding to buyer responses. It may sound extemporaneous. But it is not. Indeed, the secret of much apparent spontaneity is careful preparation. A famous politician was approached by reporters one day with a critical question loaded with possible repercussions. "Come back in a couple of hours," said he, "and I'll give you a smart extemporaneous answer."

The Eclectic Presentation

The eclectic presentation maximizes the strengths and minimizes the weaknesses of both the standardized and extemporaneous presentations. The general direction of the presentation is planned, and the prospect's questions and objections are anticipated. The salesperson has many memorized lines and nonverbal communicators to draw upon to explain succinctly product or service features and the benefits the buyer will receive. However, these lines may be modified to fit circumstances.

The eclectic presentation combines the thoroughness of the standardized presentation and the flexibility of the extemporaneous presentation. The extreme canned sales talk is intended to avoid thinking under fire, embarrassing pauses and gaps, and the omitting of important sales points. The eclectic presentation is thinking in advance. It is preparation.

At the top level of the selling profession is the advanced salesperson who is given only *information* and personally develops methods of presentation. But it should come as no surprise that these superior salespeople are the very ones who study, plan, and practice the most. They do indeed plan their lines.

There is much to be said on behalf of the eclectic presentation, the compromise between two extremes. Such a presentation is not a straitjacketed, one-way

EXHIBIT 10.7
FINDING THE "LINE" IN INDUSTRIAL SELLING

Cy Grenfel, seller of industrial food ingredients, had tried many ways to present the uniformity protection feature of his synthetic sour cream base. Then he found a line that rang the bell almost every time with chemically oriented product development managers. So he standardized on it.

"Dr. Smith," Grenfel would say, "would you be interested in assurance of a constant acid base in your finished product? Krinx has a fixed pH of 4.1 to 4.3 that will buffer acidity development in your formulation."

Was this a sudden brainstorm? An accident? Nonsense. Grenfel thought about his prospects, their problems, and their frames of reference. Then with infinite patience, he tried line after line until he found one that worked. Then he worked on that line testing it, refining it, and practicing his presentation.

monologue or a blind charge with no consideration of the variables in different situations. It is, in fact, an exciting and purposeful presentation that follows all the rules of good selling with the added benefits of diligent preparation and planning.

No matter what your product or service is, there are certain words, phrases, gestures, and collateral devices that boil out the superfluous and express the essence of your offer in the most succinct, telling presentation of what the prospect wants to hear. Whether you are presenting a $1 million insurance policy or a $2 gadget, the great salespeople attach maximum importance to these words, phrases, and nonverbal communicators and spend untold effort to seek them out. Selling is constant research, an endless quest for a better way to make the presentation. (See Exhibit 10.7.)

DIFFERENCES IN BUYING PURPOSE

Buyers buy for one of three purposes:

1. For personal use or consumption, as in the case of shoes bought by a consumer who will wear them
2. For resale, as in the case of a wholesaler or retailer who buys shoes for inventory
3. For use in a business organization, as in the case of the shoe manufacturer who buys leather to fabricate into shoes

Each classification of buyer seeks different benefits from the seller's product. The consumer might be interested in the shoes for style, comfort, durability, and value. The reseller is usually interested in such things as trade discounts, turnover rates, promotional support, and credit terms. The manufacturer customarily considers such things as price, a guaranteed standard of quality, service, and credit terms.

In planning the sales presentation, a salesperson should recognize these differ-ences. The wearer of shoes might consider style in terms of ego satisfaction or approval from others. The reseller of shoes, on the other hand, might measure style as a spur to increased turnover.

"It has to be a two-way street," says George H. Nusloch of Olin Corporation's chemical group. "When a buyer and a salesman finish talking, they must swap hats. When they go back to their companies, each must know enough about the other's position to represent him."[2]

MULTIPLE-PARTY SALES INTERVIEWS

The sales interview is not always a one-on-one presentation. There is a great deal of selling to groups of two or more people, with or without committee status. Even a call on two business partners or a married couple is a group presentation. The major buying decisions of retail chains today are tending to be more and more under the authority of buying committees, at least on policy and often on new items. In the industrial selling field, the buying decision often is a joint responsi-bility shared by purchasing, technical, operating, and financial personnel.

Group Presentations

In selling to a group, all the principles and methods described in these pages apply, as in the one-on-one presentation. However, a few modifying cautions are in order.

• *Don't react too soon.* Wait till you can sense the degrees of dominance of the different group participants and how they interact, both with each other and with the group.

• *Address the group rather than any one individual.* The exception is when one individual is the dominant decision maker and is so accepted by the others. Move your eyes from one participant to the other. Question each on what seems to be his or her special province or interest. But address answers to the group. Your objective is to cultivate a favorable interaction between yourself and the group and between the separate members of the group. Take care not to make any comment or gesture that suggests your presentation favors one member of the group over the others, even though this actually may be the case and you are indirectly focusing on the key decision maker.

• *Get the names and the functions of each person present.* Use these names frequently. This is even more important in a group presentation than in a one-on-one effort.

• *Watch for disagreement between the buyers.* If the disagreement is minor, try to stay on the sidelines, remaining silent while the buyers resolve it. But, if the disagreement is important and the group members do not seem to be able to

---

[2]Somersby Dowst, "Buyers and Sellers Have to Swap Hats," *Purchasing,* April 15, 1982, p. 29.

EXHIBIT 10.8
GROUP PRESENTATIONS CALL FOR SPECIAL DIPLOMACY (*Source:* Burlington Industries, Inc.)

resolve it, try to offer a proposal that compromises the divergent positions without demeaning the dignity of any one party. For example, if a wife and husband disagree on whether to take the lawn chairs in green or white, stand back and wait—or, if possible, continue the presentation without the color decision. However, the following case is sharply different and serious to the outcome of the presentation.

You are presenting a pump-dehydration-sanitation system to the buying committee of a food processing company.

CHAIRPERSON: The Harring Company believes its system will solve our problem of too much residual fat disposal for the capacity of our septic tanks. Mr. You is here to answer our questions.

YOU: Thank you, Mrs. Kastner. You've all probably read over the literature and drawings we submitted along with the quotation.

HALLEY: I have—and I think eighty-seven thousand dollars is a lot of money for that purpose. I'm opposed to the installation on principle.

CARNEY: What principle?

HALLEY: We'll be moving to larger facilities some day, and when we do, we can't take that installation with us. I can think of lots of better places to put our money.

CARNEY: But we're spending money all the time to pump out excess waste and to sink new tanks because our septic tanks are getting more than they can take.

HALLEY: Not eighty-seven thousand dollars.

CHAIRPERSON: Our cash flow is running slower than it used to run—and for a company of our size, eighty-seven thousand dollars is an expenditure to give us pause. On the other hand, having clogged tanks is not a good idea for a food processor.

After the argument has continued for a few minutes, you conclude that it is apt to cost you the sale and you had better try to help resolve it.

YOU: Mrs. Kastner, I meet this problem all the time, and I've seen companies settle it one way or the other. Perhaps I can be constructive here. Mr. Halley is completely in order in suggesting caution on a long-term capital investment to replace short-range expenditures. However, as a point of information, what do you do when your tanks are overloaded?

CARNEY: We call a service that pumps them out and trucks the sediment away, and from time to time we have to sink extra tanks.

YOU: What does that cost you?

CARNEY: Three hundred dollars a load for the disposal plus twelve hundred dollars for a new tank.

YOU: How many loads have you had to dispose of in the last year?

CARNEY: About twenty.

YOU: That's six thousand dollars. How many new tanks?

CARNEY: Seven.

YOU: That's another eight thousand four hundred dollars, bringing it to about fourteen thousand dollars a year. And I'm sure the Board of Health would prefer a more scientific sanitation system. But I wonder if you've considered something else.

CHAIRPERSON: What's that?

YOU: Your building foundations. If you're sinking seven new tanks a year and pumping out twenty overflowed tanks, I'd suggest you have an engineering examination of the strength of your building base.

CHAIRPERSON: That's an important consideration we hadn't thought of. We'll do it. I think it's clear we *must* look into the Harring proposal. It's a big outlay for us—but the alternatives are serious.

• *Aid the buying decision.* Observe whether any member of the group starts to take the lead toward a decision. If not, try to coordinate the group's position. Try to act as the alter ego chairperson to summarize the facts for a decision. The expert can accomplish this as a service, without appearing overly presumptuous.

Joint Presentations

The counterpart of group selling is joint selling, a sales presentation by a team of more than one seller.

There are various types of joint selling efforts. It might be a presentation by a consulting firm with several specialists on the presentation team. It might be an industrial sales call with an engineer, a chemist, or other specialist accompanying the salesperson. It might be a call in which a company executive accompanies the salesperson. It might even be a joint presentation to a group, for example, when the key people of a consulting firm meet with the key officers of a prospective client company. There are, of course, many variations of the joint sales call.

Some things to remember beyond the standard selling principles in a joint selling presentation are these:

1. In advance of the call, establish clearly what the objective is to be and the strategy that will be employed to attain it.
2. Establish agreement as to what part each participant will play in the presentation.
3. Determine which participant will be the leader, and let that person lead.

Sometimes a joint sales effort occurs in separate segments. For example, a prospective client of an advertising agency might want to talk with each person who will render service on the account, copywriters, art directors, media specialists, merchandising counselors, and others. Here it is critical that each person meeting with the prospective client know all the facts and be posted on the meetings that have already taken place. It is imperative that no contradiction or other lapse occur.

RECAP

Chapter 9 concentrated on the step-by-step process of the sales interview, while Chapter 10 provided a broader perspective of the sales interview: presentation philosophy, subjects of controversy, and questions and answers on strategy. It gave you principles to guide you in your sales interviews and techniques through which to apply these principles. It covered the various types of sales presentation: standardized, extemporaneous, or eclectic in style; one-on-one or multiple presentations of different kinds.

Dominating the spirit of the sales presentation, as described in this chapter, is the importance of getting and holding the prospect's attention and interest. That is what it takes to redirect the prospective buyer's thought process to your message. This idea may be original, clever, or dramatic. But above all, it must relate to the prospect's self-interest.

REVIEW QUESTIONS

1. Describe the three types of sales presentation.
2. How much time should a sales presentation take? Explain.
3. Should the sales presentation appeal to the prospect's mind or emotions? Elaborate.
4. What is technosis?
5. What is the preclose? Give an example of a preclose.
6. What are some cautions for group sales presentations?
7. What are some cautions for joint sales presentations?
8. What are the three different purposes for which buyers buy?
9. What are the separate interests of a consumer patronizing a retail store, a manufacturer buying a raw material, and a retailer buying for resale?

DISCUSSION QUESTIONS[3]

1. You represent A.M. Claussen Co., machinery manufacturers. Your company has a new machine that washes and peels potatoes, which are dropped into a hopper in bulk, and removes any stones that might have been picked up in the harvesting. The features of Pot-A-Peel are its speed of operation (10,000 pounds per hour with only one operator required, compared with 50 pounds per hour per operator by hand) and its closer peeling tolerances (80 percent potato yield, compared with only 70 percent in the hand operation). You are presenting the machine to Charles Harding, president of the Farm-Fresh Salad Corporation.
    (a) The machine weighs 3 tons. Obviously, it cannot be taken to the prospect's factory. Yet the claims are so great and the machine so new that some proof is necessary. Why is proof necessary?
    (b) How can you provide proof and credibility for the prospect?
    (c) How can you demonstrate Pot-A-Peel?
2. In selling the following products and services, how might you employ showmanship in your sales presentation?
    (a) The Pot-A-Peel machine, described in Discussion Question 1
    (b) An instant-developing color camera
    (c) A landscaping service
    (d) A sewing machine
    (e) A mutual fund
    (f) A sofa-to-bed convertible

LEARNING EXPERIENCES

1. *Role playing.* Let one person take the role of a sports equipment salesperson making a presentation to a group consisting of a college's athletic director, coach, and treasurer. Others play the roles of the college representatives. The sport or sports are to be chosen by the person making the presentation.
2. Interview five consumers and question them on their preferences about summer vacations. Write a brief report on your findings and indicate how your research could help a travel agent in planning sales presentations.
3. Assume at a sales meeting you are debating the merits of different selling strategies. One member of your group can speak for the affirmative (*for* the strategy), another for the negative (*against* the strategy). Allow five minutes for each exposition and one minute for each rebuttal. Open floor discussion after the speakers have finished.
    Subject 1: The standardized sales presentation is more effective than the extemporaneous presentation.
    Subject 2: Soft sell is more effective than hard sell.
    Subject 3: The prospect's mind is more important than the prospect's emotions as an object of selling appeals.

[3]The Discussion Questions relate to material presented in Chapters 9 and 10.

CASES

COPYCRAFT COPIERS

Sid Hallowell is demonstrating the Copycraft electrostatic photocopy machine to a prospect who is equipping a small office for a new business venture. He has just finished showing the C-300 economy model.

"I like it," says the prospect. She takes a closer look at the sample copy just run off. "How much is it?"

"Three thousand dollars," replies Hallowell. "It's a great little copier. But I want you to see the Ultra 400 too. It has many additional features."

After the demonstration of the Ultra 400, the prospect looks at it wistfully. "Yes," she says, "it does have more to offer. But it's five hundred dollars more."

"Because it's at least five hundred dollars better," says Hallowell. "In the long run you'll be ahead by taking the better machine."

"I don't know," answers the buyer. "I can't seem to make up my mind. I'll think it over and come back. May I have the literature on both machines?"

Questions

1. What selling principles did Hallowell violate in losing the sale?
2. How would you have made the presentation to this prospect?

GUNDY ORCHESTRAS, INC.

As the business manager of Gundy Orchestras, Inc., you are making a group presentation to the entertainment committee of the Rotary Club of Denver. You have explained that you can provide whatever kind of music the committee wants for its annual dance since Gundy has twenty-seven orchestras ranging in style all the way from conservative ballroom music to the most avant-garde varieties of rock and jazz. You demonstrate examples on a cassette player. The chairman of the committee, a mature type, punctuates each recorded playback with a statement of his preference for the great dance music played by the big bands of the forties and fifties. By the looks on their faces, the other members of the committee—all younger than the chairman—have different tastes from his. But the chairman seems to dominate the meeting and does not even seem to assume there could possibly be any disagreement with his choice of music for the dance.

Questions

1. How do you handle this presentation problem to give the committee majority what it wants without offending the chairman—and without losing the sale?
2. How would you have handled the presentation if different members of the committee did indeed speak up and you found there was no unanimity of preference? One wanted hard rock. One wanted jazz. One was strong for country rock.

ELEVEN

CHAPTER OBJECTIVES

To present buyer resistance as a technical
  problem to be solved, not a monster to be
  feared
To explain the psychological and economic
  origins of buyer resistance
To examine the seven general resistance
  categories
To define the specific kinds of objection
To state and explain the general principles
  for handling buyer resistance
To describe techniques for helping the
  prospect overcome objections

CHAPTER OUTLINE

BUYER RESISTANCE I: FUNDAMENTALS

Selling begins when the prospect says "no."

Anonymous

Challenges breed opportunities. If there were no sickness, there would be no need for doctors. If there were no buildings to be built, there would be no need for architects.

Selling begins when the prospect says "no." If there were no buyer resistance, there would be no need and opportunity for salespeople. Overcoming buyer resistance is the salesperson's business.

The new salesperson is apt to be apprehensive about objections. The senior seller welcomes them as indications of interest, seeks them out as evidence of progress in the buyer's reaction to the sales presentation and as a guide to strategy.

When you have completed this chapter you will understand buyer resistance. You will anticipate objections as a natural phase of the interview, to be expected on the road to the closing. You will know how to handle them constructively.

ELEMENTS OF BUYER RESISTANCE

Buyer resistance is reluctance to buy. *A buyer objection* is the specific reason, stated or unstated, for not wanting to buy. In actual practice the terms are used interchangeably. When there is no objection, there is no resistance.

There are three degrees of negative buyer reaction: buyer indifference, buyer inertia, and active buyer resistance. *Buyer indifference* represents a total lack of interest in your product or service. *Buyer inertia* is the case where your prospect is not necessarily uninterested, but does not feel impelled to act on whatever degree of interest exists. *Active buyer resistance* occurs when the prospect has an objection to making the purchase, whether the prospect is aware of it or not. The objection might be overt or hidden and based on reason or emotion.

It is an innate human instinct to resist change, and effecting change is what selling is all about. The salesperson's economic function is to bring about change—change in habits, practices, viewpoints. The objection is the buyer's defense: to cling to the old and the familiar, to resist the new and the unfamiliar, and to protect set habits from the nuisance of learning new habits. There is security in habit—in the old brand of breakfast cereal, in the store where we have always shopped, in the car we drive, in the seashore vacation spot we have visited for years. It is easier to continue these habits without change. For this reason many a prospect takes the offensive in expressing objection to a purchase. Real or contrived, this objection is the prospect's defense against buying. Its purpose is to place the salesperson on the defensive.

Another reason for buyer resistance is that buying is for most people a highly selective process. One cannot buy every product or service that is for sale. So a purchase must go through progressive stages of questioning in the prospect's mind: "Do I want it?" "Do I need it?" "Do I need it now?" "Is there an alternative?" "Is it worth the price?" "Is it worth the expenditure, or could I use the money to better advantage elsewhere?" From this standpoint of selectivity, buying resistance is a series of negatives to test the positive.

The human aversion to change and the selection process are formidable challenges to the sales representative. They are the reasons why buyer resistance is an ever-present reality in the world of selling. To repeat, if there were no resistance, no hurdles to clear, only a downhill coast to the order, there would be no need for selling or salespeople.

The leaders in the selling profession respect the validity of buyer resistance and its importance. They have learned how to deal with it. That is one reason why they are leaders. Expertise in handling objections is a prime mark of selling excellence.

The Psychology of Buyer Resistance

What was just explained, the *mechanism* of buyer resistance, is only the surface. It tells you what resistance literally is and how the prospect resists. Underneath this surface lies a deep well of subconscious motivation. The more you understand this resistance psychology, the more effective you will be in handling buyer resistance.

EXHIBIT 11.1
BUYING IS A SELECTIVE PROCESS

As explained in Chapter 4, every human being has what Freud called the *id,* the *ego,* and the *superego.* Additionally, each of us has an *ego ideal.* This is the image to which we aspire.

Take a close look at that prospect who is saying "no." The psychology behind that *no* is the net effect of an id that wants, an ego ideal that aspires, a superego that strives to preserve a socially acceptable balance between id and ego ideal, and an ego that is the buyer's real self.

As expressed in nontechnical terms in an earlier chapter, the buyer's resistance beyond the id influence is based on (1) what the buyer is; (2) what the buyer would like to be; and (3) what the buyer would like others to think she or he is.

The Riddle of Resistance

The prospect's underlying personality pattern leads to many resistance riddles. For example, you are presenting a rider lawn mower and snow remover. It is a top-brand product. Your prospect has a large lawn and plenty of money. Why, you reason, should such a person push around an old-fashioned, mechanical lawn mower and remove snow with a shovel? Why indeed! There can be a wide variety of reasons for the prospect's reluctance to purchase, reasons that have nothing

EXHIBIT 11.2
REMOVING OBJECTIONS IS WHAT MAKES SALES

whatever to do with the product, its price, or the prospect's ability to pay for it. Let us look behind the voiced objections and into this buyer's mind and emotions, as shown in Exhibit 11.3.

Objections as voiced by the prospect may sound reasoned and logical. But behind them are apt to be emotional resistance points that are unrelated to the voiced objection. Some of these undercover points of resistance have to do with

EXHIBIT 11.3
LOOKING BEHIND OBJECTIONS

What the buyer says	What the buyer may think or feel
"That's a nice machine, but the price seems high."	"I want it."
"Isn't it dangerous for my 12-year-old son to use?"	"Will it spoil my son? I had to work as a kid."
"It's a bit fancy for me."	"The neighbors might think I'm showing off my money."
"It has a lot of moving parts. If it conks out, I'll be stuck."	"I'm on easy street compared with the way my parents work back at the farm. But why should I feel guilty?"
"What about service? I live a long way from your store."	"Another mark of affluence to set me up for charity collectors."

ego, self-esteem, status, guilt feelings, prejudice, habit, background and personal orientation, self-pity, defeatism, compensation (the so-called defense mechanism), and escape from reality via rationalization or projection of shortcomings and inner feelings to others.

The human psyche is complex. One must take nothing for granted. The hidden resistance is often the real resistance. How to uncover it will be discussed in the next chapter.

The Positive Implication of Resistance

Buyer resistance is evidence of interest in your product or service. Once the prospect expresses an objection to the purchase, you know you do not have to overcome indifference or inertia. It is strictly a question of handling the objection.

If there is no objection, overt or hidden, or if the objection is removed, a favorable closing may be expected. For this reason, advanced salespeople not only welcome objections but actually seek them. If the buyer won't buy, the obvious tactic is to try to find out why. You can't conquer an unseen enemy. Once you uncover the objection, you can direct your efforts to overcoming it. Only then can you move toward a closing.

SALESPERSON KUNTSLER COOLS A FIRE

"There is your roofing cement going up in flames!" exclaimed building supply wholesaler Smithers to salesperson Adam Kuntsler.

Kuntsler had said his roofing cement was fireproof. Smithers had said "Oh yeah?" as he spread some of the sample on a pine board and lit a match to it. It had burst into flames.

Calm and collected, Kuntsler said, "Very interesting, Mr. Smithers. However, when you lit the cement roofing, you didn't ignite the compound itself. You set fire to the benzene which is added to the compound to keep it in a liquid state for easy application to a wood surface. Once it is applied, the benzene evaporates and the roofing cement is left in one solid piece that is nailproof, holeproof, windproof, waterproof, and *fire*proof."[1]

CHANGING ASPECTS OF BUYER RESISTANCE

Buying has undergone significant changes in recent years and may be expected to keep changing in the future. Buyer resistance, a component of buying, likewise has changed and will continue to change.

The main changes in buying that have affected buyer resistance are:

1. More buying options
2. More emphasis on specialty considerations
3. Less emphasis on price
4. More sophisticated buying

[1] Adapted from *Secrets of Successful Selling*, copyright 1956 by Prentice-Hall, Inc., Englewood Cliffs, N.J., pp. 159–161.

More Buying Options

Yesterday's buyer had fewer choices than the buyer of today. There has been a veritable explosion in the quantity and variety of things to buy in both products and services. This applies to every type of buying—for government, business and industry, home and family or individual. The service industries, hardly in existence at the turn of the century, now employ over half the workers in the United States.

As one example of this product and service explosion, consider the food store. The average food retailer of 1975 stocked 5000 to 6000 items. By 1980 the number had risen to over 10,000 in the traditional supermarket. Both the consumers of today and the wholesalers who buy for inventory and resale must reject more offerings than in earlier times.

"Retailers are also resisting the glut of products competing for scarce shelf space," according to Bill Abrams of the *Wall Street Journal*. "Sloan's Supermarkets in New York," Abrams continues, "says it has a choice of 22 laundry soaps, each in six sizes ranging from seven ounces to 211 ounces. Of that field of 132, Sloan's carries 51. When recently offered four sizes of Pert, a new Procter & Gamble shampoo, the chain took two."[2]

The increased diversity of buying options today has heightened the competitive bidding for the buyer's dollar. This has reached staggering proportions and has resulted in necessary changes in buyer resistance. (See Exhibit 11.4.)

More Emphasis on Specialty Considerations

Long ago we began to emerge from a commodity merchandising era to a specialty era.[3] Human ingenuity and resourcefulness have brought forth a veritable cornucopia of products and services that our ancestors could not have imagined possible. Each raw commodity is being fabricated into more and more specialties for human satisfaction, facility, and convenience.

It is only natural that buying decisions in a specialty merchandising era, and the buying resistance inherent in them, would change. This has indeed taken place. These buying decisions are becoming more influenced by specialty appeals than by questions of accessibility, convenience, or price, as in commodity transactions.

Less Emphasis on Price

As a result of all the products and services now available to buyers, the importance of price as a buying objection has been declining.

[2]Bill Abrams, "Food Chains Pressure Suppliers, Altering Industry Power Balance," *Wall Street Journal,* Aug. 21, 1982, p. 25.

[3]A *specialty* is a product or service bought for some motivation other than price. A *commodity,* by contrast, is like every other competitor's product, making price, service, and accessibility the basis of buying decisions. Raw sugar is an example of a commodity. A Daimler-Benz Mercedes is an example of a specialty.

EXHIBIT 11.4
THE MERCHANDISE EXPLOSION

The small hardware store of 1975 stocked 7000 items. By 1980 the figure had increased to more than 9000 items.

The so-called home center is a relatively recent development. It stocks hardware, electric goods, plumbing supplies, lumber, all kinds of do-it-yourself goods, and many other classes of merchandise. In five years, through 1980, the number of items stocked in the home center rose from around 11,000 to over 18,000.

The superdrugstore, handling many items that never would have been found in a drugstore in earlier times, stocked from 15,000 to 20,000 items in 1980, compared with 10,000 to 12,000 items five years earlier.

The marketplace of today is full of classes of outlets that did not exist a decade ago. If they did exist, they have changed almost beyond recognition. But both the new types of retail outlets and the more orthodox types are teeming with merchandise and services in greater and greater variety, forcing the average buyer to buy more selectively and to object more readily.

Do not be misled by those newspapers and other media full of price advertisements. Most of these are *retail* ads, using price as a *merchandising hook* to spur buying action and to outdraw retail competition. Generally speaking, the specialty appeals and decision to buy come first. The price shown in the ad influences where and when to make the purchase. In this context, price does come up, but as a question of *value* and *ability to pay*, rather than as a reason to buy.

Most consumers, for example, must choose whether to buy a new car or to overhaul the old car, to buy or to lease equipment, to opt for a new stereo or a vacation, to invest through a corporate security or shares in a mutual fund, to purchase a coat or a suit, or to buy beef or poultry.

This question of whether and what to buy that precedes price consideration has been underscored because of two critical variants in disposable income. The first is the inflation of our currency. The second is the rising portion of income—for both organizations and individuals—that goes for taxes. These have placed additional restrictions on buying freedom and have increased buying resistance. It took approximately $2.95 in April 1983 to equal the buying power of a dollar in 1967. Someone earning $10,000 per year in 1967 needed to earn $29,500 per year to live in the same style in 1983.

More Sophisticated Buying

All told, it is abundantly clear that the modern buyer has been forced to selective discretion. The buyer, professional and household consumer alike, is learning how to buy. This means increased, sharper, and more sophisticated resistance. It means more hidden resistance. It also means increased rewards for the salesperson who masters the principles and techniques for handling buyer objections.

GENERAL RESISTANCE CATEGORIES: WHY BUYERS SAY "NO"

The first cardinal rule for handling buying objections is to *classify them*, to study each one intensively, and to develop an answer for it. For example, Frank Ruoff, vice president of Eureka Vacuum Cleaner Company, told the following story of an Iowa farm lad who had come to Chicago and joined Eureka's selling staff.

HOW DO YOU HANDLE THIS ONE?

When we hired him we had misgivings. He had trouble learning the prepared sales talk. But he kept at it. Then he went out to sell. We didn't hear from him for several days. We were sure he had quit.

Then one afternoon he appeared and asked me, "How do you answer this one? She said the cleaner she had was doing just fine."

When I gave Charlie the answer to this objection, he wrote it down on a 3 × 5 index card. Then he left.

We didn't see him for another few days. When he showed up, I saw no sign of defeat. I asked him how he liked selling, to give him a chance to get some discouragement off his chest. All he said was, "Shucks, I can see you ain't never worked on a farm." Then he asked, "How do you answer this one?" And again he wrote the answer down on a card.

Charlie went out religiously every day for almost a month, and still no sale. Only every once in a while he would ask, "How do you handle this one?" and—you guessed it—he'd write the answer on a card.

Then one day Charlie made a sale. And the next day another sale. And a few days later, two sales. Pretty soon he was ringing the bell with amazing regularity. I decided to see what he was doing. Flushed with success, he was glad to have me accompany him.

It took very little time to see why Charlie was destined to become our star sales representative. What this raw recruit from the Iowa cornfields was doing was in the finest tradition of scientific selling. He had located and classified each buying objection he encountered. When a prospect expressed an objection, he would pull out the card and *read* the answer. Later he developed a totally new strategy. "Mrs. Jones," he would say, as he fanned out his 3 × 5 cards like a bridge hand, "here are the fourteen reasons I've found for not believing you should buy this vacuum cleaner. Look 'em over. I've got a ten-dollar bill for anyone who can show me a new one."[4]

One of America's leading life insurance representatives makes a practice of calling on small-policy prospects, even though his main business is writing major policies. He has the following explanation:

I lose money on this, but it is very profitable in the long run. You see, these small prospects are constantly raising objections. This gives me clues as to the hidden resistance in the minds of big prospects. The prospect for a six-figure policy often asks few questions and offers few objections in the early stages of the interview. But these questions and objections are in the buyer's mind nevertheless. They have to be brought to light and answered satisfactorily for a successful closing.

[4]As related to author Bud Wilson.

We will now examine the seven broad categories of buyer resistance and many kinds of specific objections. Later in this chapter we will cover general principles for dealing with resistance, and Chapter 12 will include specific techniques for handling specific objections.

Genuine Objections: The Honest "No"

All buying resistance separates into two main categories. The objection is either *genuine* or *spurious*.

Regardless of whether it is valid or without merit, the *genuine* objection is sincere. Even if it is based on misinformation or motivated by illogical emotion, the prospect truly means it, and it must be dealt with respectfully and intelligently.

"We are overstocked," says the women's apparel buyer in the specialty store. "My open-to-buy is zero." The salesperson has just come off the selling floor. Rack after rack was loaded with dresses, suits, coats, blouses, and skirts. The salesperson may have an opening for an odd specialty item or a fill-in. But she has seen the inventory with her own eyes. The buyer's objection is obviously a genuine objection.

EXHIBIT 11.5
WHAT REAL OBJECTION IS THE SMOKESCREEN COVERING?

Spurious Objections: The Phoney "No"

The spurious objection is neither valid nor sincere. Its purpose is to delay, complicate, or otherwise defeat the potential closing. It may even be a psychological exercise by the prospect to satisfy some inner need. Nevertheless, the spurious objection must be dealt with, although the strategy will be different from that used to handle a genuine objection.

"You're wasting your time," the maintenance manager at the factory tells the plumbing supply sales representative. "We've got enough fittings to last for a year." The truth is that this maintenance manager buys all his plumbing supplies from his brother-in-law, who represents a competitor.

Whether genuine or spurious, an objection is an objection, and a sale cannot be made till it is removed or circumvented.

Overt Objections: The Open "No"

"I can get four hundred more on the trade-in from another dealer," says the car prospect. This may or may not be the truth. It may be genuine or it may be spurious. But it is voiced. It is an overt objection.

An overt objection provides a starting point. Further questioning and observation may reveal whether it is genuine or spurious. For example, if the prospect is willing to name the dealer who allegedly has offered the "four hundred more," the objection is more apt to be genuine than if the prospect prefers not to say. If all buyer's objections were overt and genuine, selling would be a much simpler profession.

Hidden Objections: The "No" You Don't Know

The hidden objection is more difficult for the salesperson to handle. Here the prospect answers your questions and voices an objection. But the objection is superficial, a smoke screen to cover up the real resistance.

In some cases the hidden objection is consciously *controlled* by the prospect. The prospect deliberately sets up a blind to hide the real objection. The purpose of this ploy might be, for example, to preserve self-esteem by hiding inability to afford the purchase. It also might be to guard against betraying an obligation to another seller.

The hidden resistance also may be *uncontrolled*. In this case the buyer makes a genuine, sincere objection, unaware that it resulted from subconscious motivation. For example, a prospect for a new house says, "It's nice, but I don't want a house with an old-fashioned kitchen." The real underlying roadblock to the purchase—of which the buyer is not conscious—is the fact that the buyer does not feel comfortable with the predominant ethnic group in the neighborhood.

Silent Objections: The Unstated "No"

Even more complex than ordinary hidden resistance is the objection that is not only hidden but also silent. In this case, the prospect listens, sometimes with respectful attention, to the sales presentation. But not a word, not a telltale body movement or change in facial expression, to indicate any positive or negative reaction.

You assume that the prospect had some preliminary interest since he or she agreed to see you. But your preclose test questions elicit only vague, noncommittal responses, giving you neither encouragement nor enlightenment.

How to smoke out hidden resistance and how to probe the puzzle of silent resistance will be covered later in this chapter.

Reason-Based Objections: The "No" the Buyer Knows

The discussion of controlled and uncontrolled hidden objections made the distinction between reason and emotion as the source of the objection. But the incidence of reason or emotion as a resistance origin is broader than that. All buyer resistance, genuine or spurious, overt or hidden, voiced or silent, originates in the prospect's conscious or subconscious mind.

A reason-based objection is one that comes from intellectual consideration of cause and effect. Here are some objections that exemplify this:

- "The benefits of the system are not worth the outlay."
- "The other car gives more miles per gallon."
- "Sorry. My brother is in the business."

Emotion-Based Objections: The "No" the Buyer Doesn't Know

An emotion-based objection is grounded in human feelings, human will, and other expressions of the buyer's emotional responses. It can be deliberate, but more generally an emotion-based objection is a subconscious reflex mechanism. Here are some examples:

- "Sorry. I'm too busy." (Emotional origin: *"I don't like you."*)
- "Unless you can give me blue, cancel the order." (Emotional origin: *This buyer unknowingly associates blue with a childhood blanket that meant comfort and security.*)
- "I can't afford that car. I want something less pretentious." (Emotional origin: *The buyer can afford the high-priced car, but she grew up in poverty and has a subconscious apprehension about expenditures.*)

Reason-based resistance is handled one way, emotion-based objections another way, as you will see.

SPECIFIC RESISTANCE CATEGORIES: THE NUB OF THE "NO"

Thus far we have examined the skeleton of buyer resistance, the broad categories of objection, classified in terms of motivation, expression, and diversionary tactics. Now let us take a look at the specific categories, the grass-roots types of objection you actually will meet in the marketplace. A complete list would be almost endless, so we have selected some representative examples.

EXHIBIT 11.6
THE DOUBLE HELIX OF BUYER RESISTANCE

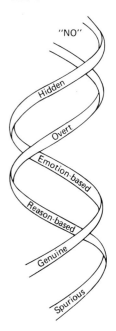

"NO"

Hidden

Overt

Emotion-based

Reason-based

Genuine

Spurious

Nothing will be said here about resistance to the sales interview itself. This was covered in the chapter on the approach. Neither will we say much here about the genuine objection, for which there is no sound answer. However, this excludes only a fraction of a percent of immediate sales potential. The senior salesperson considers the loss of one sale under these circumstances a worthwhile trade-off for goodwill that may later lead to many sales. Only objections that may arise during the interview as obstacles to the closing will be discussed.

Left-Field Objections: The Meaningless "No"

We use the slang term *left field* for its connotation of objections that are of minimally true importance. Often the buyer voices these left-field objections idly, carelessly, or for personal amusement.

There are four kinds of left-field objections: (1) trivial, (2) petty, (3) farfetched, and (4) irrelevant. Here are examples:

- "If I buy the umbrella and the rain stops, I'll have to carry it with me." (*trivial*)
- "It's a good buy in a used car. But with that color I'll have to wash it a lot." (*petty*)
- "Suppose I buy it and the price goes down later?" (*farfetched*)
- "My sister in Peoria will be jealous." (*irrelevant*)

Buyer-Oriented Objections

This class of resistance relates directly to the buyer's needs, wants, or special problems. Some examples are:

- "I have all the insurance I need."
- "Our textbooks are still in good condition."
- "Your electronic security system sounds good, but our plant has done without it for twenty years without a break-in. So I think we'll pass."
- "When we added your sequestering agent to our mix in the test we got a high viscosity that slowed the flow through our processing machinery."

Examples of buyer-oriented objections met by the salesperson calling on retailers are:

- "We've had no call for your brand."
- "We have no space for another item."
- "Our customers just won't buy a three-hundred-dollar suit."
- "I don't think it will sell."

Product- or Service-Oriented Objections

This class of buyer objection relates to alleged product or service shortcomings. It also covers misgivings as to credit terms, service standards, or guarantees. Examples are:

- "It's too light. Flimsy."
- "Your credentials just don't warrant my investing with you."
- "It's too heavy."
- "We prefer to own our equipment. Your lease plan will cost us more."
- "Only guaranteed for ninety days?"
- "I hear you're slow on claim investigation."
- "I'm used to the other keyboard. I'd have to learn all over again."
- "The trunk on this car is too small for my needs."

Decision-Oriented Objections

This class of objection occurs perhaps more frequently than any other. You have won your prospect over to the value of your product or service as a fitting answer to a need, want, or special problem, but the prospect is having difficulty coming to a decision to buy. This is apt to be a question of excuse, rather than reason. The common expressions that describe it are stall, brush-off, or dodge.

Here are some examples of decision-oriented objections:

- "I'll have to take this up with the finance committee."
- "Come back after Labor Day."
- "We're over our budget."
- "I'll have to think about it."
- "I just can't make up my mind."
- "I'll have to talk with my boss."
- "The samples have gone to marketing, and we'll have to wait for their approval."
- "My partner will have to be in on this."

Price-Oriented Objections: The "No" That Often Means "Yes"

Price-oriented objections often are concerned with more than the price tag. There are many things that alter the final sale price to the buyer: terms, cash, or trade discounts, introductory and special offers, combination deals, advertising and promotional allowances to resellers, spiffs to salespeople,[5] alterations, installations, continuing service, guarantees, prepayment or nonpayment for delivery, selling support and personnel training for distributors, and so on. There are many, many variables.

Typical price objections by buyers are of three varieties: "It's too high," "It's not worth it," and "I can't afford it." The objection, "I can buy it for less elsewhere," is really a competition-oriented objection and will be covered under that class of resistance.

The same objection expressed by several prospects may not always mean the same thing. For example, "I can't afford it" might mean that the prospect literally does not have enough money to pay the price. It also can mean that the prospect does not consider the purchase a wise one at the price, even though funds are

---

[5]*Spiffs* are special incentives in cash, merchandise, or other valuable considerations to motivate a reseller's salespeople.

available. Or it might mean that the prospect considers the price fair and the purchase prudent but is unable or unwilling to lay out the cash at this time. The first two cases have to do with the price level. The third has to do with cash flow. Inability to pay the price, unwillingness to do so, and inability or unwillingness to lay out the cash are three different matters.

Price is generally overemphasized. There is a strong rationale in support of the thesis that price is not the main reason for which prospects buy or do not buy. Price may be the determining element in *when* and *where* the buyer buys. That explains its dominance in retail advertising. But the decision to buy a new car, a refrigerator, a house, or a vacation cruise is usually more related to the buyer's net assets and his or her cash flow and ability to finance the purchase than to the price of the product or service itself.

Consider, for example, the purchase of equipment for one's hobby or special interest. A person of even very modest means is apt to buy the highest-priced gear for skiing, tennis, photography, classical music, or whatever else is the big interest in that person's life. Just show an avid golfer a putter that might cut a few strokes, and he or she will not quibble over the price. Nor will the fishing enthusiast hesitate to pay dearly for a fly that might catch a trout. Many people who economize on necessities will go into debt for hobbies.

An excessive concern over price resistance can be a problem for salespeople. It is not uncommon for a new salesperson's apprehensions about price resistance to transfer to the mind of the buyer who had not been concerned with price—and to make that buyer price-conscious. (See Exhibit 11.7.)

EXHIBIT 11.7

THE GREAT HOUDINI IS HUMBLED

When magician Harry Houdini died, he took with him his secrets on how to open locks.

"If the world knew what I do," he said, "no lock would be impenetrable. No vault would be secure."

Yet here he was on a hot summer's afternoon in a ramshackle shire jail in the Midlands of England and about to be embarrassed before audience and press. He had met his master. The lock on the cell gate in the country jail would not yield.

Houdini had been bound in chains and thrown into New York's East River, and he emerged in seconds. He had been locked in vaults of famous banks, and he walked out quickly. But he could not unravel the secret of this, one of the flimsiest locks he ever had encountered.

Finally, incredulous and frustrated, Houdini conceded defeat and, in his utter fatigue, leaned against the cell gate.

The gate flew open under the weight of the magician's body. It had not been locked.

Think about that. How much buyer resistance originates with the buyer? How much originates with the salesperson and is unwittingly *suggested* to the buyer?

When you size up a prospect's price-range capacity, be careful not to assume your prospect is able to spend what you can spend, as in the following example.

Macy's of New York once gave ten professional shoppers $100 each with instructions to enter a Macy's department to buy merchandise without mentioning price. The shopper was to buy whatever was offered by the salesperson—up to the $100. Not one of the shoppers was able to get rid of more than $35. For example, when one shopper asked about lady's hats, the salesperson brought out a hat within her own price range—$15; the buyer could have bought a $100 hat.

A price-oriented objection is indeed a "no" that often means "yes." The prospect who tells you the price is too high is telling you indirectly that she or he wants to buy.

Competition-Oriented Objections

"What a line!" exclaimed the not too smart salesperson to the other clown in the old-time burlesque skit.
　　"What are you selling?"
　　"Mosquitos."
　　"Mosquitos! Who wants to buy mosquitos?"
　　"That's just the point. No competition!"

As long as there is selling, there will be competition. Brand competes with brand, company with company, product with product, service with service, industry with industry. The seller of shoes competes with other sellers of shoes. But the shoe seller also competes with sellers of coats, television receivers, medical services, insurance, typewriters, and an almost endless multiplicity of other products and services. All are vying for a share of the same buyer's dollar, shrunken from inflation and guarded with increasing caution and selective discretion in determing what to buy.

Here are some examples of competition-oriented objections.

- "Their price is only twenty-nine fifty."
- "The other lamp base is cast. It won't dent."
- "Acme Exterminating Service has taken care of us for fifteen years. We would not consider a change."
- "Their sour cream is cultured."
- "Their sour cream is acidulated."
- "The reason I'm considering the other car is because your service wasn't all that good."
- "Jack Kander of Unifrax and I are lodge brothers."

Source- or Salesperson-Oriented Objections

Product, service, and proposition may be exactly to the prospect's liking, but the sale is blocked because the buyer objects to the company offering it or the salesperson representing it.

Most buyers will not tell a salesperson that his or her personality, approach, or any other personal characteristic stands in the way of a sale. It has to be sensed. But prospects can be very outspoken about objections to the company you represent. These objections can be based on reasonable business considerations or on just not liking the source. Here are some examples of both types.

- ''The Stanley plant is right here in town. We like to patronize local business.''
- ''Your snow-removal service is well-recommended. But our present source is down the street. We don't have to worry about their getting here.''
- ''We don't like those political speeches your boss is making.''

Prejudice-Based Objections

Another kind of buyer resistance is the objection that is based on conscious or unconscious prejudice. Anyone who has viewed Archie Bunker on television has seen a perfect example of prejudice. Archie is bigoted, stubborn, and unshakable in his convictions, most of which are based on prejudice, generalizations, or stereotypes. Archie's convictions cover every situation and color every day in his

EXHIBIT 11.8
THE BIGGEST COMPETITOR

calendar. Moreover, Archie is just as surprised at the shock his prejudice renders to others as they are shocked at his prejudice.

A salesperson is apt to encounter prejudice against people, institutions, or things. There are the obvious prejudices against sex, race, creed, color, religious affiliation, and ethnic and nationality groups. There also are prejudices against products, services, and companies. Here are some examples of prejudice-based objections.

- "I only buy American products."
- "The West German products are engineered better."
- "I only invest in blue chips."
- "I hate dictating machines."
- "I can't stand their representative. As long as he calls on us I won't buy."

CATEGORIES OF RESISTANCE WITH ULTERIOR MEANINGS

The categories of resistance discussed thus far are major categories. However, they do not exhaust the list by any means. Sometimes a buyer objection means something other than what seems to be the case.

There are four main types of objections with ulterior meanings:

1. Test objections
2. Devil's advocate objections
3. Objections as calls for help
4. Objections as buying signals

Test Objections

Bryan Houston, advertising agency vice president, has been listening patiently as a magazine advertising representative presents an analysis of why his agency's client, Gulf Oil, should advertise in this magazine. Suddenly Houston breaks into the presentation: "Halverson, you don't know what you're talking about!" he snaps at the advertising representative.

Houston does not really mean this. What he is doing is *testing* Halverson. If Halverson caves in or becomes flustered, it may raise suspicion as to the validity of his case. If, on the other hand, Halverson comes back strong, the indication is that the case is valid, as far as the salesperson knows.

Devil's Advocate Objections

The devil's advocate objection often has little to do with the product, service, or proposition. There are some people who just enjoy taking the opposite side of anything. If you say "sweet," this self-appointed devil's advocate says "sour." If you present your office machine as a means of saving time, this prospect feels impelled to disprove your claim. Since devil's advocate objections, rather than being serious, are exercises for people who enjoy being contrary, you should try to uncover what the real objection, if any, is.

Objections as Calls for Help

A salesperson has been presenting an electric organ with a numbered diagram attached to the keyboard as a guide for learning to play without formal instruction. "I'm afraid I could never master it," says the prospect dolefully.

This objection is really a call for help. The buyer wants the organ but needs reassurance that she can really learn to play without taking lessons from a music teacher. It is an indirect request for more information about the learning method to show how simple it is. The prospect is looking for credibility.

Objections as Buying Signals: The "No" That Means "Maybe"

Some buyer objections are really signals for you to start closing. The interview has progressed to the point where the prospect *wants* your product or service, but she or he needs help in rationalizing the purchase. So the buyer sets up a *dummy objection*. This spurious objection says, in effect, "I want it. Show me how unsound this objection is to reinforce my conviction or to remove any qualm of conscience that is giving me pause."

The car prospect who says, "I don't know if the rest of the family will like it," reveals a desire to buy the car and a desire for you to convince him or her of the advantages to the rest of the family.

GENERAL PRINCIPLES FOR HANDLING RESISTANCE

There is a vast difference between how the run-of-the-mill salesperson and the superior salesperson deal with buyer resistance. The superior salesperson does not overcome objections. He or she helps the buyer to overcome the objection.

That is the philosophy of contemporary selling—not to overcome but to help the prospect overcome, not argument but objective exploration and educational persuasion.

Overcoming means winning. If someone wins, someone else must lose. No one likes to lose. You may win the argument but lose the sale. In overcoming the objection, you may become personally objectionable.

No, argument is not the way to win in selling. Argument may work in a court of law where a third party decides or in an election where the voters decide. But it won't work in winning a customer.

The only way to win an argument is to avoid it. Consider the Japanese, so polite and conciliatory in business and social intercourse. Their motto is worthy of note by anyone aspiring to a professional selling career: "It is easier to win agreement that an argument."

There is only one way to deal with resistance: persuasion. (See Exhibit 11.9.)

There are, of course, techniques for forestalling objections before they arise. There are also ways to circumvent an objection. And there are some objections you do not answer at all. These will be covered in the next chapter.

Regardless of what the resistance is, three rules will guide you in helping the buyer to overcome it:

1. Adopt a persuasive posture.
2. Identify the objection.
3. Lead the prospect to recognition of the true objection.

Adopt a Persuasive Posture

In the spirit of helping rather than overcoming, the contemporary salesperson displays a persuasive attitude.

The persuasive posture is disarming. It is a constant reassurance to the prospect that you are both on the same side, not opponents. The implied message it conveys is, "I am here to serve your interest, not to force a sale in my interest." The persuasive posture makes the buyer feel comfortable.

To achieve the persuasive posture, one must observe certain elementary rules of conduct: listen, listen respectfully, be professional in manner, and use the language of diplomacy.

Listen   It may come as a surprise to you to hear that some of our most successful salespeople are better listeners than talkers. This does not mean they cannot

EXHIBIT 11.9
WINNING THE ARGUMENT AND LOSING THE SALE
Help the buyer to overcome objections by explanation and persuasion.

EXHIBIT 11.10
WISDOM FROM WAY BACK

A Quaker friend informed me I was not content with being in the right when discussing any point, but had to be insolent and overbearing about it—of which he convinced me by mentioning several instances. Endeavoring to cure myself of this fault, which I now realized had lost me many an argument, I made the following rule: to forbear all direct contradictions of the sentiments of others and all over-positive assertions of my own. Thereafter, when another asserted something I thought an error, I denied myself the pleasure of contradicting him abruptly, and of showing immediately some absurdity in his proposition. Instead, I began by observing that in certain cases of circumstances his opinion would be right, but in the present case there *appeared* or *seemed* to me some difference, etc.

I soon found the advantage of this change in my manner. The conversations I engaged in went on more pleasantly. The modest way in which I proposed my opinions procured them a readier reception and less contradiction. I had less mortification when I was found to be in the wrong, and I more easily prevailed upon others to give up their mistakes and join with me when I happened to be right. To my new tactics I think it principally owing that I had early such weight with my fellow citizens when I proposed new institutions, or alterations of old, and so much influence in public councils when I became a member. For I was a bad speaker, never eloquent, subject to much hesitation and my choice of words hardly correct in language—*and yet I carried my points.*

Source: From *The Autobiography of Benjamin Franklin*, Pocket Books, New York.

express themselves effectively. It means they are listeners first and talkers second. Indeed, there are many competent salespeople who are not spectacularly eloquent. But a successful salesperson who is not a good listener is a rarity. (See Exhibit 11.11.)

Listen Respectfully   No matter how ridiculous an objection may seem to you, it is a serious matter to the prospect, perhaps the most formidable obstacle to your closing. Any and every objection deserves your attentive listening and your respect. It is offered by the prospect in time he or she is expending for the interview with you. It is volunteered information that will aid the ultimate closing.

Just as important as your sincere respect for the buyer's objection is making sure the buyer is aware of this respect. Look as though you are hanging on the buyer's words with rapt interest, not as though you can hardly wait to answer. Heed the admonition of Dick Borden not to "listen faster than your customer talks."[6] (See Exhibit 11.12.)

[6]Richard C. Borden, *Overcoming Objections*, Dartnell Corporation, Chicago, Ill., 1976, p. 51.

EXHIBIT 11.11
LISTENING VERSUS TALKING IN HANDLING OBJECTIONS

Talking	Listening
Prospect's attention may wander.	Prospect's attention assured.
Prospect's interest may wane.	Prospect's interest can grow.
Unexpressed objections become magnified.	Expressed objections stay in perspective, sometimes diminish.
Enforced silence may cause personal irritation. The circumscribed objection may expand into resistance to product, company, and salesperson.	Prospect has a chance to express resistance. Interaction between prospect and salesperson improves.

Be Professional in Manner   What is the professional manner? First, to be a professional, you must have the expertise of a specialist. It takes know-how to be able to earn a living as a professional in selling as in law or medicine.

Second, the professional manner is a consultative manner that examines every problem objectively and cooly. It seeks answers through scientific inquiry—fact finding rather than trying to prove things.

Third, the professional manner accomplishes goals by gentle induction rather than force, by skillful leading rather than by overpowering.

Use the Language of Diplomacy   Some wag once observed that the reason nations have difficulty understanding each other is that they speak different languages. This jocular oversimplification becomes serious when one conceives of language as the symbol for all communication, verbal or otherwise. The language of diplomacy includes the music as well as the words, every gesture and every nuance of meaning.

The job of the diplomat is to gain objectives by improving understanding. In no instance does this apply more aptly than in the handling of buyer resistance. If the seller has a valid answer to a need, want, or problem of a prospect, the prospect's objection must be the result of misunderstanding. Clear up the misunderstanding, and the objection is removed.

If you would aspire to a position of leadership and fulfillment in selling, learn the language of diplomacy. It is a first essential.

Be modest   In both manner and speech, be modest. When your prospect has made an objection to your product or service that is ill-founded or absurd, don't gloat over it. Find a rationale for the buyer's thinking. For example, you might say, "I understand your reasoning, Ms. Simmers. However, have you ever thought of it this way?"

It is important to the outcome of the sales interview that you help to protect the prospect's self-esteem. You must be careful not to appear superior. If anyone is to feel superior, let it be the buyer. You can lose out for being wrong, but you also can lose out from being too right.

EXHIBIT 11.12
TWO WAYS OF HANDLING THE SAME OBJECTION

What they say	What they think
Method A	
BUYER: I think we'll continue to use Kreelex.	*There's not that much difference between Kreelex and Trolon.*
SALESPERSON: You're buying a perishable item from a source 2000 miles away with a 4-week lead time requirement.	*He's stupid!*
BUYER: Well, that's the way we've done it for years—without trouble. I don't see why we should change. Good day.	*What gall! Who does she think she is? What does she know about our business?*
Method B	
BUYER: I think we'll continue to use Kreelex.	*There's not that much difference between Kreelex and Trolon.*
SALESPERSON: Well, you have a reputation as a sound purchasing manager, Mr. Connerly. So I'm sure you have good reasons for anything you do. Am I off-base in asking the reason for your decision?	*To identify the objection, I'll ask Connerly directly why he won't consider another source.*
BUYER: No. As a matter of fact it's just that we've done business with Kreeco for 12 years and we've never had a problem.	*It's nice to have a good reputation. She seems pretty smart. Her question is intelligent and reasonable.*
SALESPERSON: Customer loyalty is a great thing. I wish we had more customers like you. Kreeco is a good company and clean competition. By the way, Mr. Connerly, have you ever considered the advantage of having an alternative source for comparison purposes or for emergencies due to "acts of God?"	*My problem is force of habit and his loyalty to Kreeco.*
BUYER: Actually, we have, but never got around to doing anything about it. Tell you what. Send in some fresh samples, and we'll look into it.	*She's not afraid to say something good about a competitor. I like that. They must be pretty sure of themselves. She does have a good point about emergencies. We do have two sources on almost everything else. Maybe we're wide open on this one. If we ever got caught in an emergency, I'd be in the doghouse. Better do something about it.*

Be tactful Be not only polite but also comprehensively considerate of the buyer's reactions. For example, "Don't you think?" is more tactful than, "I think." "May I suggest you consider it from another angle," is more tactful and less apt to grate than, "Look at it this way."

Don't sound too positive In fact, avoid positive statements. They are apt to create an impression of arrogance or even belligerence. Use questions, or make the statement a rhetorical question by adding, "Don't you think so?" "Isn't it?" or "Don't you agree?" Another device to avoid headlong positive statements is to preface them with, "It would seem that," "We've been told that," or some similar phrase. This will soften the potential sharpness of the statement.

Seek areas of agreement Search for things on which you can go along with the buyer's objection. If you can accept the prospect's objection on a point that will not impede the closing, concede the point. The more important the agreement, the better. But if you have to dig deep into the barrel, even agree on the weather.

There are two main reasons for seeking areas of agreement. First, by setting up points of compatibility between you and your prospect, you can create an atmosphere of positive interaction. This is the most salutary direction for the interview to take. Second, by finding something on which you and buyer are in agreement, even conceding minor objections, you prove your honesty and objectivity. This will earn the buyer's consideration of your major points later.

Stay away from controversial subjects Politics, religion, sex, or any other subject on which people might differ in their views should obviously be avoided in the interest of selling diplomacy. There are enough possible counts on which the prospect may object, without risking extraneous differences.

Identify the Objection

"Joe," says Judge Elbert Gary, head of U.S. Steel Corporation, to real estate salesperson Joseph Day, "I think the Steel Corporation should have its own building. We want our present view of the Hudson River or an overlook of New York Harbor. Keep your eye on possibilities."

Day spends weeks studying possibilities, making charts, maps, estimates. But none of these are used. Instead, he sells Gary a building with two questions and five minutes of silence.

From the start, one of the possibilities has been the very building in which Steel is already located, the old Empire Building itself. From nowhere else is Gary's beloved view more inspiring. But Gary seems to favor a more modern building next door, and some of his fellow officers, he has told Day, definitely want to buy it.

Day suggests to Gary that U.S. Steel stay where it is and buy the Empire Building. He points out that the view from the building next door will soon be cut off by a new structure; but in the Empire Building Gary's outlook over the river will be safe for years to come.

The steelmaster objects strenuously—too strenuously, it occurs to Day, but he does not oppose his prospect's objection. He listens and thinks.

Gary seems dead set against the Empire Building, and he is proving his case, like the lawyer he is. But the objections he is making—such as the old-fashioned woodwork, for example—seem specious. The real resistance, Day begins to suspect, is hidden. By the prospect's eloquent exposition, the true nature of the puzzle begins to unravel. Gary wants the Empire Building, Day concludes. The real desire to move is coming from U.S. Steel's younger officials.

Both men sit for a moment, looking out the window at the view Gary loves so well.

Without turning his eyes from this view, Day says very quietly, "Judge, where was your office when you first came to New York?"

Gary thinks a bit and answers, "Why, it was in this building."

Day waits a minute. Then he asks, "Judge, where was the steel corporation formed?"

There is another thoughtful pause before Gary speaks. "Right here," he says, "in this very building where you and I are sitting now."

"The judge spoke very slowly," said Day, as he recounted the story years later, "and I said nothing more. Not a word! For five minutes—and they seemed like fifteen—we sat there in absolute silence, gazing out of the window. Finally, with a half-defiant note in his voice, Gary said, 'Almost every one of my junior officers wants to leave this building, but it's our home. We were born here; we've grown up here; and here's where we're going to stay!' " Within half an hour the deal was closed.[7]

Root the Reason Out of Resistance   The buyer objection may be overt, or it may be hidden—even emotion-based and uncontrolled as in the Day-Gary case above. If the reason for the resistance is not openly expressed or if you suspect it is spurious, root it out. One of the areas in which contemporary selling has made strides over yesteryear is in recognition of the importance of identifying the objection and in applying principles and techniques to expose it.

"What you have to do is get inside the guy's mind," advises Jerry Whitlock, owner of AAA Seals & Packing in suburban Atlanta. "I try to break down why he's buying from somebody else, then I show what I can do and how I can help him."[8]

Get the Buyer's Help   As explained earlier, the first step in identifying the objection is to listen. As in every aspect of selling, listening and watching are the keys. Seasoned salespeople are in general agreement that in more cases than not the prospect, given a chance, will voluntarily reveal the objection. (See Exhibit 11.13.)

Ask   Why not? When you want to find something out, isn't it logical to ask the person who knows? Many a great brain has wallowed in conjectures and speculative hypotheses in an ivory tower while a lesser brain might have obtained the solution simply by going directly to the source and asking.

---

[7]Adapted from Ewing T. Webb and John J. B. Morgan, *Strategy in Handling People.*
[8]"How to Sell Packings, Gaskets, O-Rings and Seals," *Industrial Distribution,* January 1982, p. 79.

EXHIBIT 11.13
NAÏVETÉ PAYS OFF

Sometimes one can be too sophisticated. Naïveté can bring rewards.

Rose Kaye worked in a dress factory on Seventh Avenue in New York's garment district. She was young and full of ambition. "Please, Mr. Shuster," she said to her boss, "please give me a chance to go out and sell."

"Why not?" replied Shuster. "What can we lose? If you don't make it, come back to the cutting room."

Kaye was given some samples and nothing else, not even instructions on where to go. She was too naive to realize that Shuster's motive was to get the selling urge out of her system and to get her back in the cutting room.

Off she went to Saks Fifth Avenue, one of the leading fashion stores in the United States, where she brashly and enthusiastically went to the office of Clarence Overton, vice president and fashion merchandising manager. Overton took a look at the line and, with a straight face, said, "This stuff belongs on Division Street." His reference was to the bargain shopping area on Manhattan's lower east side.

A year later Kaye bounced into Overton's office and smilingly placed a bottle of champagne on his desk.

"Mr. Overton," she said, "Your suggestion made me. Last year I made a pile of money selling my dresses on Division Street!"

Kaye told this story about her early selling efforts years later when she was a successful manufacturer.

For example, when the buyer says, "Sorry, I'm not interested" or "I guess I'll wait," isn't it the most natural thing in the world for you to say, "May I ask why?" You might be surprised at how much you will learn.

"We've decided to sign up with Gotham," says the prospect.

"I'm naturally disappointed," says the salesperson. "Yours is a very desirable account. Am I out of order in asking the reason for your decision?"

"Not at all. Their pickup schedule happens to coincide with our accumulation and assembly timing."

Use the double why   Remember the wisdom of Socrates: question sub-question, sub-subquestion. Narrow the circle around the possibilities as you zero in, coming ever closer to the answer.

Your second *why* is even more important than your first:

"You took no delivery last month," the food broker says to the food-service distributor. "Is everything all right?"

"Well, as a matter of fact, our co-op has introduced a house brand. We had to try it."

"Is this a change or just a trial?"

"It's a trial. But naturally we try to buy all we can from our own co-op. If we get no complaints, we'll stick with it."

"Can you tell me how we compare on price and quality?"

"I'll know more about quality when our salespeople get some feedback from our customers. If they don't complain, that's all that matters to us."

"How about price?"

"The co-op price is a little lower than yours."

This may not be encouraging information. But it is better than shooting in the dark. At least you know what the resistance is and can plan a way to deal with it.

Try the clay-pigeon test   The clay-pigeon test is an exploratory technique. In effect, you send up a clay pigeon, as in skeet shooting, and give the prospect a shot at it to try to learn what is on the buyer's mind. You state a suspected or possible objection in a rhetorical question.

"Tell me, Miss Flannery," asks the architectural supplies salesperson, "Is it price that is holding you back from giving us the contract?"

"No, Harry," replies the construction company president. "Quite frankly, we're waiting for a report on some stress tests we're having made on your product and some others."

EXHIBIT 11.14
THE CLAY PIGEON STRATEGY
(1.) Adopt a persuasive attitude; (2.) identify the objection; (3.) lead the prospect to recognition of the true objection; (4.) close.

Another rhetorical question might be as follows:

"Is it that you hesitate to buy from a small, young company?" asks the salesperson of the resident buyer.

"As long as you said it, Mr. Amber, yes. Get a bit of a track record and then come back."

Be a Doubting Thomas   Many an objection is indeed spurious. Many others are hidden. To accept an objection totally is to risk being led off the track. Don't hesitate to be a doubting Thomas. When the prospect says, "My taste runs to smaller cars," is this factual or is the real resistance based on price considerations? When the buyer says, "I've decided to wait till next year," is the truth really, "I'm not going to buy it; I'd better get rid of this salesperson?"

Lead the Prospect to Recognition of the True Objection

As long as the prospect's objection is hidden, you cannot make an intelligent bid to close. If, in addition to being hidden, it is uncontrolled or emotion-based—the problem is compounded.

In such a circumstance, the superior salesperson takes steps to help the buyer see what the real resistance is. As in psychoanalysis, when the real underlying resistance is exposed to the light of day under up-to-date conditions, it may cease to be an objection. The prospect, seeing the objection for what it is, often changes tack. It is in the buyer's interest as well as yours for the true objection to be exposed.

RECAP

If there were no buyer resistance, there would be no need for selling. Selling begins when the prospect says "no." A prospect who objects is still a prospect.

Buyer resistance is divided into seven broad categories of objections: genuine, spurious, overt, hidden, silent, reason-based, and emotion-based. Specific kinds of objection orientation vary from buyer to buyer. You need to determine the nub of the "no" to deal effectively with the objection. To help the prospect overcome objections you should adopt a persuasive posture, identify the objection, and lead the prospect to recognition of the true objection. The general principles for following these three guides were explained.

Mastery of this chapter is essential background for the specific strategies and techniques in handling grass-roots objections, which will be covered in Chapter 12.

REVIEW QUESTIONS

1. Why does buyer resistance exist?
2. What is the psychological basis of buyer resistance?

3. What is the positive implication of buyer resistance?
4. How has buying changed in recent years?
5. What is behind these changes?
6. What is the first cardinal rule in handling buying objections?
7. What are the seven main categories of buyer resistance?
8. What is meant by silent resistance?
9. What are the two types of hidden objections?
10. The text described many kinds of specific objection categories. Name and briefly explain five of these.
11. What are four possible meanings of price-oriented objections?
12. What is meant by resistance with ulterior meanings? Name four categories of objections with ulterior meanings, and briefly describe each.
13. What is wrong with the expression, *Overcome the buyer's objection?*
14. Name three guides to effective handling of buyer resistance.
15. How can a salesperson protect the buyer's ego?
16. What is meant by the professional manner?
17. What is meant by the language of diplomacy? Name some diplomatic cautions for the salesperson.
18. What are five ways to identify the buyer's objection?

DISCUSSION QUESTIONS

1. As a floor salesperson at the London Shop, you are presenting a men's suit to a portly middle-aged customer of apparent conservative tastes. You have just brought out a single-breasted three-piece Harris tweed suit, and the customer is trying on the jacket before the three-way mirror.

   "Don't you think it looks well on you?" you ask. The customer nods but does not answer.

   "How much is it?" he asks.

   "$199.50, reduced from $249.50."

   "Why is it reduced? Is there anything wrong with it?"

   "No. The suit is reduced for inventory reasons, along with many other items in the department."

   (a) Of the seven general resistance categories, which might be holding up this sale?

   (b) Which classes of specific objection might apply in this case?

   (c) Select any one of the possible classes of objections you named in your answer to (b), and describe how you would handle that objection.

2. As manager of the Minorville branch of the South Side Bank & Trust Co., Nancy Hausman has the personal checking accounts and savings accounts of Norman and Marcia Grant. Grant owns the Grantmoor Furniture Mart, and Hausman would like to get Grantmoor's account for her bank. At present this business is enjoyed by the Denver National Bank. Since Hausman knows

Grant, it was easy to arrange to call on him at his office. Among the objections raised by Norman Grant were the following:

- "This move could not be made without the approval of Jim Barr, treasurer of Grantmoor,"
- "We've been doing business with our present bank for seventeen years,"
- "Barr drives to Denver every day to lunch at the Harvest Club; the bank is next door to the club,"
- "All our corporate papers, legal documents, deeds, securities, etc., are in a safe-deposit box in the vault of the Denver National Bank,"
- "We have established our credit with Denver for short-term working-capital loans, critical for us during certain seasons; right now we are on their books for a substantial loan."

(a) Discuss your analysis of the buyer resistance faced by bank manager Hausman in winning the business of the Grantmoor Furniture Mart.

(b) What do you recommend to Hausman as strategy for getting by this resistance? Use your imagination to supply facts not included in the story.

3. As president of the Nashville Chamber of Commerce, you are anxious for the Tennessee State Teacher's Association to hold its annual three-day conference in Nashville. The objections offered by Alice Torrance, the association president and conference committee chairperson, are these:

- "Last year we met in Memphis and everyone liked it,"
- "I especially like it because I live in Memphis,"
- "We have already run our meeting in the Memphis Civic Center and know it to be excellent for our purpose,"
- "The conference committee meets next month to finalize all details, and it has been almost taken for granted that we would go to Memphis again."

(a) Discuss your analysis of the resistance you face in moving the conference to Nashville.

(b) How would you handle each of the four specific objections expressed by Torrance? Use your imagination for unlisted facts. For example, what could the Nashville Chamber of Commerce offer the association to help it change its decision in favor of Nashville?

LEARNING EXPERIENCES

1. Write a short report describing the changes that have been taking place in consumer buying, the effect of these changes on buying resistance, and what you anticipate as changes in buying and buying resistance to occur in the next ten years.

2. Select any advertisement appearing in a magazine. List all the objections you can imagine for not buying the product or service advertised.

270

==

CASE

==

BUILDING PROTECTION, INC.

Jack Aron, sales representative for Building Protection, Inc., is presenting his company's plant security system to Jarvis Nelson, president of Harbison Systems Corporation, assemblers and marketers of custom stereo systems. Harbison has just moved into a new building. After the presentation of Aron's cross-beam electronic detection plan, the following dialogue takes place:

NELSON: You say that the instant anyone walks through one of these electric fields an alarm bell will be activated and the local police signaled?

ARON: Exactly.

NELSON: How about daytime when we're all here?

ARON: The system is only switched on when you close.

NELSON: Won't the alarm bell scare off the burglars before the police get here?

ARON: Perhaps, Mr. Nelson. But isn't the object to save your expensive components rather than to catch the thieves?

NELSON: I suppose so. But I'd like to do both. Incidentally, what would this cost us?

ARON: It figures out to eight hundred dollars a month.

NELSON: Wow! That's an expense we haven't anticipated. Ninety-six hundred dollars a year!

ARON: Do you have a night guard, Mr. Nelson?

NELSON: No. Our plant is too small for that luxury.

ARON: Well, if you had a bigger plant, you'd probably have a night guard. That would be the ultimate security, wouldn't it?

NELSON: Sure. But if my aunt shaved, she'd be my uncle. We're *not* big enough for a night guard.

ARON: How much would a night guard cost you, Mr. Nelson?

NELSON: Forget it, Aron. We're not now spending that money for a guard. Your ninety-six hundred a year is increased expense.

ARON: Correct, Mr. Nelson. However, you have easy-to-carry expensive units here. What percent of your inventory would ninety-six hundred dollars represent?

NELSON: A small percentage. I'll grant that.

ARON: Did you know you can get a reduction on your insurance premium if you have an approved automatic signal security system?

NELSON: Really? How much?

ARON: You'll have to ask your insurance carrier. It's variable.

NELSON: Look, Aron. What really are the chances of our having a break-in? I haven't heard of one around here in the year and a half we've been here.

ARON: They don't always get into the newspapers, Mr. Nelson. There have been three in this industrial complex in the past year.

Questions

1. Comment on Nelson's objection about the alarm scaring off the burglars before the arrival of the police.
2. Why did Aron ask Nelson if he had a night guard when he knew he did not?
3. What was Aron's strategy in questioning Nelson about the size of his inventory?
4. Do you think Aron did a good job of handling Nelson's objections? Why or why not? Explain in detail.

TWELVE

CHAPTER OBJECTIVES

To stress the importance of trying to anticipate objections

To explain how to receive objections

To explain how to remove objections without becoming objectionable

To describe specific strategies for handling
some of the most common classes of objections

To acquaint you with some classic techniques used by successful salespeople to
deal with objections

To provide some special overall cautions to
guide you in handling objections

CHAPTER OUTLINE

BUYER RESISTANCE II: SUGGESTIONS AND CAUTIONS

> The essence of all selling is helping the buyer to overcome objections.
>
> Anonymous

Buyer resistance is a challenge that can be as exciting as a chess game. The challenge lies in persuading the prospect away from an objection that may be valid or may be based on wrong information, wrong thinking, a preconceived mind-set, or even emotion.

Chapter 11 introduced the subject of buyer resistance—what it is, categories of objection, and the broad principles for dealing with it. Chapter 12 will bring the subject down to cases. It will cover strategies and techniques for applying the principles introduced in Chapter 11. It will list specific objections, like price, for example, and tell you how to handle them. It also will acquaint you with cautions to observe as you help your prospect overcome an objection.

MORE ON GENERAL STRATEGIES FOR DEALING WITH RESISTANCE

Chapter 11 presented three basic principles to help the buyer overcome an objection: adopt a persuasive posture; identify the objection; and lead the prospect to recognition of the true objection.

Here are three corollary rules to remember in applying these principles:

1. Try to anticipate the objection.
2. Receive objections resiliently.
3. Remove objections both tactfully and tactically.

WEBER FORESTALLS A BUYER OBJECTION

Claudette Weber had a problem. She had won her appointment as a sales engineer with the Bronson Machine Corporation. Now she had been on the job for two months and had not seen even a glimmer of prospective business. She knew that technical industrial selling is normally a process of cultivation rather than immediate orders. But she still was worried.

Tomorrow Weber was to call on Chester Scanlon, purchasing agent for Hathaway & Holmes, a major user of this class of machinery. In her preapproach research, Weber had talked with Ty Sanders, who was doing a lot of business with Scanlon on wire.

"Scanlon can't buy anything technical without a go-ahead from Sam Maltbie, the director of engineering," Sanders had said. "But he's sensitive about it and won't let on. So he'll make phony objections to avoid getting to a decision—to hide his lack of authority. These objections are meaningless. What's more, if you go straight to Sam, Scanlon will be madder than a wet hen and you'll never sell him."

Weber thought and thought and finally came up with an idea. She discussed it with Henry Coan, Bronson's director of research and development, who agreed to cooperate.

The next day, when Weber arrived at Scanlon's office, she was not alone.

"Mr. Scanlon," she said, "I'd like you to meet Henry Coan, our director of R&D. When he heard where I was going, he asked to come along, to try out a couple of engineering ideas on you."

"Well actually," interposed Coan, "I'm experimenting with alternative base materials to give our machines more durability under long stress periods. I can go in various directions, and I'd appreciate an opinion from someone who sees this kind of machinery under practical operating conditions. I hope this isn't an imposition."

"Not at all," replied Scanlon. He might have been able to hide a sales objection. But he could not hide his pleasure at being consulted for his opinion. "However, why don't you let me introduce you to Sam Maltbie, our director of engineering? He works with these machines and sets their specs when we buy. I have a feeling he could be helpful. After I introduce you and Sam, I'll talk with Claudette. I want to know more about your company's products and service."

Try to Anticipate the Objection

If you know in advance, either from previous sales calls or from your preapproach investigation, what the prospect's objection is apt to be, you are way ahead. Your approach and presentation can in fact forestall the objection, or circumvent it, before it is even expressed by the buyer.

Claudette Weber forestalled objections in her approach to Hathaway & Holmes. She learned from Ty Sanders that purchasing agent Scanlon did not have the necessary buying authority and would hide this because of a sensitive ego on the subject. So she played to his ego, making it unnecessary for him to defend it. This removed the true resistance, an emotional matter, and gained access to Maltbie, the real decision maker. (See Exhibit 12.1.)

Receive Objections Resiliently

The resilience of a spring, when compressed, determines how effectively it recoils.

In a tennis volley, the way in which you get set to make the return is critical to the return you make.

The return of a buyer objection in a sales interview is no different. The way in which the salesperson receives the objection vitally influences the effectiveness of the response. Here are five checkpoints to guide you in receiving objections.

Be Receptive   The first rule on receiving objections is to do so graciously. Show no sign of resentment, annoyance, or antagonism.

Be Relaxed   Move *with* the objection, not against it. If your tone of voice, your facial expression, or even a body movement betrays any sign of impatience, the prospect will sense it.

Be Attentive   Never forget the first rule of selling: *listen*. As the prospect voices the objection, look the person in the eye to indicate you are indeed listening. This does not mean just to *appear* attentive. It is really to listen for some clue that will help you close the sale.

EXHIBIT 12.1
HOW TO GET A TIGHTWAD TO MAKE A CHARITABLE CONTRIBUTION

"Mr. Holden at the bank suggested I call on you, Mr. Excelbess. The only people we ask to help are people of affluence, position in the community, and with an interest in aiding the less fortunate."

This opening line by a charitable-fund raiser is designed to anticipate and forestall resistance. The seller has learned in advance that the prospective donor rarely gives to charity. But it also was learned that the prospect is nouveau riche and has been unable to gain admittance to membership in a country club of which banker Holden just coincidentally happens to be president.

In fact, the social service salesperson making the sales call was given the prospect's name and other information by banker Holden himself in a list of potential donors.

Excelbess contributed.

Pause before Replying   The reflective pause implies serious consideration of the objection. Overeagerness, by contrast, can convey an impression of lack of confidence in the credibility of your case. It also can suggest overaggressiveness, which may antagonize the buyer. Incidentally, the pause gives you a little extra lead time to plan your answer.

Restate the Objection   This assures the buyer you understood it, precluding later repetition of the same objection. It also adds still more lead time to plan your response.

Even better than restating the objection back to the prospect is restating it in different, or your own words. This may help the buyer see the objection in a different light that makes it appear less valid. And still better is phrasing your restatement as a question.

> "Your line looks good," the menswear retailer tells the representative of a sportswear house who has proposed the installation of a floor display unit to introduce a new line of sweaters. "But, as you can see for yourself, we're cramped for space. I wouldn't know where to put it."
>
> "In other words, Mr. Stiles," replies the seller, "you can't find four feet by six feet that can yield you a gross profit of about forty dollars a month per square foot? That's what our specialty store customers are averaging."
>
> "Well, suppose you help me find the spot. Come on."

EXHIBIT 12.2
CHANGE OF MIND?
By repeating the prospect's objection in different words, the salesperson leads the prospect to see questions in a different light—here, changing the objection from *whether* to buy to *when* to buy.

Remove Objections Tactfully and Tactically

Once you have received an objection, how can you help your prospect get past that objection to the purchase? How does a senior salesperson remove a buyer objection?

Here are four checkpoints to guide you in removing objections both tactfully and tactically:

1. Avoid the acute angle.
2. Tell it tersely.
3. Build bridges to favorable interaction.
4. Time your response.

Avoid the Acute Angle This is perhaps one of the most important admonitions in the entire literature of human relations. It has special significance for the salesperson faced with a buyer objection. The source is Dale Carnegie's *How to Win Friends and Influence People*. "The only way to get the best of an argument is to avoid it," wrote Carnegie. "Nine times out of ten, an argument ends with each of the contestants being more firmly convinced than ever that he is absolutely right."[1]

No matter how strong the objection, the smart salesperson never lets it become an argument. The strategy is to *blunt* the objection with gentle handling—to cushion any possible "acute angle" sharpness in the situation, as a car's shock absorbers soften the impact of a bump in the road. There are many ways to accomplish this. One of the simplest is to agree, with qualifications, before replying. This is the so-called yes-but technique. We prefer *however* to *but* as more in keeping with the nonargumentative spirit of contemporary selling. For example, "You're very perceptive, Mrs. Granby," the real estate seller tells the condominium prospect. "However, have you ever thought of it this way?"

Here are some more examples of how to avoid the acute angle.

STEREO CUSTOMER: That tone grates. It's awful!
SALESPERSON: If you don't like it, let's listen to another. You're the one who's paying for it, and you're entitled to what you want.
FACTORY PURCHASING AGENT: I'll be frank. Your machine is below our specs.
SALESPERSON: I'm naturally unhappy to hear that, Mr. Carton. Can you tell me where we fall short?
RETAIL BUYER: Your scarves are doorknobs! We're still sitting on your last shipment! I want to return it!
SALESPERSON: I'm sorry to hear that, Ms. Arlen. If you can't sell, we can't sell. However, before you and I quit, can we explore what's happening at the point of sale?

In each of these cases, the buyer expressed an extremely negative objection, almost cruelly abusive. The natural instinct of a salesperson would be to become

---

[1] Dale Carnegie, *How to Win Friends and Influence People*, Pocket Books, New York, 1977, p. 112.

defensive. This would have magnified the objection, created an almost insurmountable acute angle. But in each case the salesperson *blunted* the objection, kept it down to size as though it were an informative response instead of a blatant challenge.

Tell It Tersely   Answer an objection as briefly as possible. Neither belittle it nor exaggerate it by the amount of attention you give it. However, the less time it takes to satisfy this requirement, the sooner you will get back on the track of your presentation aimed at closing. While you must do the objection justice, try not to let it interfere with the orderly progress of your presentation.

Build Bridges to Favorable Interaction   A favorable interaction between buyer and seller is an important essential to closing. The competent salesperson sets up bridges to link common interests and is careful to avoid anything that might disturb this interaction.

> "That's a fine rate of interest," says the bank prospect to the bank officer. "But I have to leave the money on deposit for four years. That's a long time if I need cash for an emergency."
> "You have a good point," replies the banker. "But there's a way around it. Any time you need cash—and I hope you never have an emergency—you can just walk into the bank and get *instant cash* on a passbook loan."
> "My wife is leaning toward the other car," says the automobile prospect, "because it has more dash and style than your car."
> "I'm glad you brought that up," answers the car salesperson. "You're quite right. Their *forte* is style. Ours is engineering. You'll have fewer repair bills with our car and a *bigger trade-in value.* Here's the evidence right in the book. If you had bought the other car and our model two years ago, here's what the book value would be today on their car, and here it is for our car. Quite a difference. The more extreme the style, the sooner it goes out of style."

"Thanks for reminding me," "You're quite right in your assumption," "You raise a good point," and similar introductions to your response are good examples of the application of psychology in contemporary selling. They show respect for the buyer's perception and encourage a fair-minded judgment of your response to the objection, unimpeded by emotional complications.

Time Your Response   You can answer an objection *immediately, later,* or *never.* Much depends on the nature of the objection, the credibility of your answer, the circumstances of the interview, and the prospect's personality.

A serious objection that can be critical to the buying decision should normally be answered immediately. To delay may give the prospect misgivings as to your ability to answer it and cast an aura of doubt over the entire sales interview. To step in promptly and confidently implies that you have a convincing answer to the objection. It engenders credibility even before you give the answer.

At the opposite pole is the inconsequential objection. An example would be the left-field objection, described in Chapter 11. This may be ignored entirely, unless the prospect seems intent on having it answered. It also is a logical possibility for a strategic concession, a subject that will be discussed later in this chapter.

A second case in which you should try to avoid answering an objection is when it is unanswerable. You can sense whether the omission seriously impairs your chance of closing. In minutes you will know whether the issue is a passing matter or whether it is indeed a stumbling block. If the latter is the case, above all, don't double-talk. Any effort to beat the truth is a losing game. We will have more to say about handling unanswerable objections later in this chapter.

In between the immediate answer and not answering at all is the delayed answer. Reasons for deferring your response to an objection can be:

1. To avoid interfering with the continuity of your sales presentation
2. To stall for time when you do not have enough information to make a convincing response
3. When the objection is inconsequential and you hope to avoid answering it
4. When the importance of the objection to the total sales interview is not yet clear and you want to see how it fits as the presentation progresses
5. When you feel that if you hold off, the importance of the objection will decline in the buyer's mind or the buyer may answer the objection for you

How do you defer your answer to an objection? This is accomplished by acknowledging the objection and promising to get back to it. For instance . . .

- "That's a good question and I'll get to it in a bit."
- "Of course. I'll cover that later in this presentation."
- "You're right. However, if you'll bear with me, that's covered later in this demonstration."

STRATEGIES FOR SOME SPECIFIC OBJECTIONS

Buyer resistance is of various types. Especially common are objections on competition, price, or prejudice and attachments to relatives or friends. There are strategies for dealing with each category.

How to Handle Competition-Oriented Objections

There are only two reasons for which a sale can fail to materialize. The prospect does not buy or buys from someone else.

Surprising as it may seem to a person new to selling, most senior salespeople would rather run up against a competition-oriented objection than resistance to the generic product or service itself. Generally speaking, changing a habit is the most uphill of selling assignments. It is easier to sell an automobile to a motorist than to a nondriver.

The vigorous competition between passenger airlines today is not nearly as frustrating as the resistance of half a century ago when people were apprehensive about flying itself. Selling computers for use in the home today is more difficult

EXHIBIT 12.3

COMPETITIVE BRAND VERSUS INGRAINED HABIT

A drug manufacturer is discussing the introduction of a new product with an advertising counselor. The new product is a dentifrice, neither a paste nor a powder but superior to both.

"How much can you appropriate for the campaign?" asks the advertising agent.

"A million dollars."

"It's not enough. Save your money."

"You mean you can't get this breakthrough product off the ground with a million dollars to spend?"

"That's right. We can change a brand with even less than a million. But to change a habit takes much more."

than selling a particular brand of television, refrigerator, or air conditioner against competitive brands. (See Exhibit 12.3.)

Helping the buyer overcome a competition-oriented objection to the purchase requires special know-how and special application.

Know Your Competition   First, you must know your competition. When your prospect says, "I've always been satisfied with Brangold" or "I can buy it for less" or "The Saraband copier gives sharper copies," you must know what your prospect is talking about. You must be thoroughly acquainted with each product or service that competes with yours. You must know which is better, your product or service or the competitive brand—and why it is better—in terms of intrinsic quality, benefits, economy, convenience, and answering the prospect's needs, wants, or problems.

How do you become thoroughly knowledgeable about your competition? By listening to what is said by customers and prospects; by paying attention to competitive advertising and studying competitive literature; by visiting competitive places of business; or even sometimes by direct inquiry—through others if your identity presents a problem.

The value of knowing your competition is well-illustrated in the case of the car buyer who said, "I can buy this model for six hundred less from another dealer."

"Grab it quick!" replied the salesperson. "And make sure you're getting all the options covered in my quotation. They pay the same as we do to the factory, and what they've quoted you is below their cost."

If the prospect was bluffing, the salesperson called the bluff without questioning the prospect's honesty. If the buyer was speaking truthfully, you may be sure that list of options would be checked meticulously. In the latter case, if the buyer found the competitor had masked a lower bid under a shortened list of options, the prospect would be pretty apt to buy from the salesperson who had not tried to gain a competitive advantage unethically.

Evaluate the Objection: Is the "No" a "No-No"? Knowing your competition enables you to assess the validity of your prospect's objection. If it is not valid (that is, based on misinformation or misrepresentation), you can set the facts straight for the buyer. If the buyer's objection is in fact a valid objection, you can deal with it.

The very question, "How does your product compare with Carver's?" is a competition-oriented question, even if it is not a literal objection. Knowing your competition enables you to answer this question to your advantage.

Should you discuss a competitor? To what extent should the salesperson acknowledge the competition to which the prospect refers in the objection? Indeed, should you ever mention competition in your presentation and, if so, to what extent?

There are conflicting opinions on this, and a great deal depends on circumstances. For example, some sellers believe in making outright comparisons, calling competitive products or services by their actual brand names. Others believe with equal conviction that reference to a competing brand increases the prospect's awareness of that brand, possibly stimulating a desire to know more about it.

Both schools of thought are in agreement, however, that when the buyer brings up the name of a competitor, it must be acknowledged. To dodge it would imply lack of confidence in the merits of your own product or proposition. To accept the buyer's reference to a competitor with dignity and respect shows the prospect that you have a good answer.

One-on-One and Multibrand Comparisons In recent years there has been a trend, both in advertising and selling, to make one-on-one or multibrand comparisons.

"Let's compare all three," says the salesperson, virtually removing kid gloves and exposing bare knuckles; "Let's start with price," Point by point the exposition continues, obviously in an endeavor to set up wooden soldiers and to knock them down one at a time.

Sometimes this is very purposeful, especially when your brand is a poor third in buyer recognition and acceptance, perhaps a relative newcomer, while the other two brands are old and well-established. Burry Biscuit Corporation, now a division of Quaker Oats, used this technique when it was breaking into the biscuit market. At the time the campaign began, Nabisco and Sunshine, between them, enjoyed approximately 70 percent of U.S. biscuit sales. Burry's sales amounted to only 3 percent of the total.

When biscuit buyers in the food chains were exposed to the compare-all-three approach, they listened attentively. Many of them had never thought of a triple choice. The Burry salesperson then showed them that whichever of the other two they stocked, there were advantages in adding Burry, with a different kind of appeal for consumers who might pass up Nabisco or Sunshine on their shelves.

Negative Selling Above all, when a competition-oriented objection arises (one that cannot be ignored), do not speak disparagingly of the competitor. Don't be foolishly guilty of what Shakespeare meant when he wrote, "The lady doth protest too much, methinks."[2]

A mild compliment for the competitor is even sometimes wise. Especially when the prospect says something like, "Cardell gives a six-month guarantee," and you are able to reply, "I'm glad you appreciate the importance of guarantees; ours is for two years."

The show of respect for the competition-oriented objection is pleasing to the buyer's ego. An opposite attitude is apt to place the buyer on the defensive.

"Knocking competitors" is of course shortsighted. Negative selling shrinks total markets, diminishes acceptance of the generic product or service, both yours and that of the competitor. Read the following dialogue between an office copier salesperson and an office manager.

PROSPECT: Thanks for calling, but we've decided to get the Hammond.
SALESPERSON: Hammond? Lots of fancy attachments, but I know someone who bought one, and it was constantly breaking down.
PROSPECT: Very interesting. How about your machine?
SALESPERSON: Our copier never fails. You can depend on it.
PROSPECT: I appreciate your reminding me about operating interruptions. We need our copier every minute. Come to think of it, our present copier, though not the latest, works all the time. I think I'll wait awhile.

Knocking a competitor and planting a seed of doubt by stating a positive feature of your product or service with no reference to the competitor are not the same thing.

For example, you know that the linen supply competitor, has a record of poor service. It is not negative selling but actually smart selling to say to the prospect, "Our Clock-Set delivery system means you can almost set your watch by the promptness of our delivery and pickup."

Or suppose you are a fuel oil salesperson. You know that during last winter's blizzard this prospect was without oil for a day. You say, "Mrs. Callahan, one thing you will like about Paragon is our Tank Patrol Service. You don't call us for an order. We deliver automatically. We keep a record of your requirements, based on the amount of oil you consume. A computer correlates this information with the number of degree-days of weather to signal us when you need fuel."

When a Competitor "Knocks" You   Suppose your product or service is on the receiving end of a competitor's negative selling. There is only one way to deal with rumor: facts.

Counteract misinformation with true information. The antidote is education.

The factual response to a deprecating rumor is even stronger if you can support it with proof. For example, if the rumor implies that your dairy standards are not satisfactory, you might reply, "That's mighty surprising, Ms. Snow. We are

[2]*Hamlet*, act 5, scene 2.

EXHIBIT 12.4
ONE WAY TO HANDLE AN OBJECTION

The board of directors of Walgreen Drug was in session to consider the election of Justin Dart to the presidency.

Thomas E. Dewey, former New York district attorney and later governor of New York, represented a group that opposed Dart's election.

Attorney Dewey was eloquent and intensely serious as he enumerated reason after reason why Dart was unfit for the job.

When Dewey had finished, the chairman of the board asked Dart for his response.

"It's much worse that that," Dart smiled. "I could have given Mr. Dewey much more for his list if he had only asked me."

Dewey remained serious, but everyone else present laughed. Dart was elected and went on to steward Walgreen so outstandingly that its name was later changed to Dart Industries. In 1980, Dart Industries merged with Kraft, Inc., and Justin Dart became chairman of the executive committee of this giant food, drug, and plastic manufacturing firm.

checked regularly by the Board of Health, and we serve most of the hospitals in this area."

How to Handle Price-Oriented Objections

Price resistance always has been a mental stumbling block for the least accomplished salesperson; a challenge to the more competent salesperson; and something to be taken in stride for the most competent salesperson.

Let us bring the price-oriented objection down to size. Let's thaw the ice out of price.

Value Is in the Mind of the Beholder Your price is as high or low as the prospect *thinks* it is.

Examine Exhibit 12.5. The blocks symbolize value points. The more solidly you build these blocks into your sales presentation and the more convincingly you convey them to the buyer, the greater support you provide to justify your price.

Price is a static thing. But the value is a variable, depending on what the prospect believes your product or service to be worth. It is evaluation, not just value.

For a modern view of attitude on price from the buyer's side, read what Jack Carmody, general manager of Peachtree Doors, Inc., St. Joseph, Missouri, has to say: "Value analysis as a functional approach should always be in the mind of a purchasing manager or buyer. Cost reduction isn't just beating suppliers over the head. It's working with suppliers to find better materials and better methods.

284

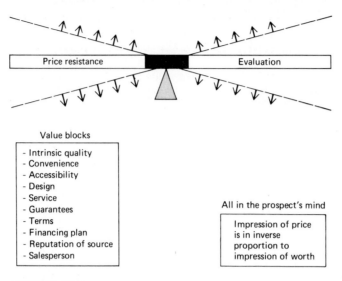

EXHIBIT 12.5
VALUE IS BASED ON EVALUATION

Maybe the lowest price isn't the best. Quality and on-time delivery have a relation to total cost."[3]

The buyer's impression of whether your price is high or low or in between is in inverse proportion to the buyer's impression of how good your product or service is. This is of course influenced by the quality of your sales presentation.

The buyer's impression also is influenced not a little by what you think yourself. When you walk into the presence of the prospect with an air that says, "I have the best," some of it has to get across to the buyer. Enthusiasm, confidence, assurance, and positive thinking are contagious.

Don't be sensitive about what your product or service costs. Be proud of what it's worth.

What Will It Cost Not to Buy?   "You must have a mountainous phone bill," the sales representative remarked to the Boston egg broker. The quaint little old man was seated at a rolltop desk, a headphone attached to his ear, talking to Omaha as though it were a local call. "Cheaper 'n going there," he replied.

In selling to industrial buyers especially, but not limited to these classifications, the seller must realize that the buyer's motivation is profits, or savings in cost from the purchase of the product or service.

- "This hot-water return system will cost you eighteen thousand dollars to install. But it will save you about six thousand dollars a year on your oil bills."

---

[3]Somersby Dowst, "Management Adopts A New Yardstick to Rate Buying," *Purchasing*, June 11, 1982, p. 14.

- "Your franchise fee is eight thousand dollars. Your start-up costs will run about ten thousand dollars. Based on the average sales and profits of other franchises in markets of your size and type, you should earn twenty thousand dollars your first year. You're in business for free at the beginning of your second year."

- "Yes, Mrs. Slocum, our Styli-jean does cost more. Because it's *better!* Look at the seams and the needlework. Note the cut and the detail. And the Styli-jean will be advertised starting in February in your local newspapers and on TV. The newspaper ads will list the stores that carry Styli-jeans. You pay ten dollars more for the jean, but you'll sell it for fourteen dollars more and you'll gross more than on run-of-the-mill jeans. Also, the promotional support will give you a faster turnover. The higher quality assures customer satisfaction and an absence of complaints."

What will it cost *not* to buy? That is the real question, especially when you are selling to industrial buyers.

No one quibbles with a surgeon over price—before the operation. (See Exhibit 12.6).

Magnify the Value Image   Since value is in the mind of the beholder, you can increase a prospect's evaluation of your product or service to equal or exceed its price by dramatizing what it can do for the buyer.

"It's a lot of money for a golf club," says the club member to the golf pro.
"But is it a lot of money for an extra twenty yards from the tee?" replies the pro.
"Here, try swinging a metal driver and see what it feels like."

Shrink the Price Image   Every yardstick measurement is bidimensional: what it actually is and what it appears to be to the observer. A hundred is high or low, depending on who is considering it. A coin that is of small moment to an adult is a substantial consideration for a small child.

The price that is high for one prospect is low for another. The same product or service presented to the same prospect by one salesperson can seem overpriced, fairly priced, or underpriced by comparison with how another salesperson presents it.

This provides room for creative imagination in quoting prices. The same dollar is ten dimes, four quarters, twenty nickels, or a hundred pennies. The doughnuts are 20 cents apiece, six for $1.20, or a dozen for $2.40.

EXHIBIT 12.6
WHAT WILL IT COST *NOT TO BUY?*

Choking on a fishbone, a man rushed into a doctor's office. His face was red. He was perspiring profusely. He was gasping for breath.

The doctor quickly and expertly removed the fishbone. The patient sat back in a chair and breathed easily again, glad to be alive.

"What do I owe you, doctor?"

"Just give me what you figured it was worth when you were choking to death."

You can quote your price on the silver service by the piece, by the setting, or for a twelve-place chest.

You also can compare the price to a yardstick within the prospect's frame of reference—like the price of a newspaper.

In using these various devices, your aim is to shrink the price image by comparison or division. Some examples of shrinking by *comparison* follow;

- ''Over the next few years you will spend many times as much for film as the price of this camera. It will pay you to get a good one.''
- ''The price of this encyclopedia is less than you spend for movies in a year. Which will do your children more good?''
- ''You have a sizable investment in good furniture. This humidifier will keep the wood from drying out and cracking.''

Some examples of shrinking price image by *division* are given below:

- ''The difference between the top quality and the cheapest for a full year is less than you spend for your daily newspaper.''
- ''Only ten cents a day.''
- ''What you spend for a bus ride.''

EXHIBIT 12.7
PRICE ISN'T EVERYTHING

EXHIBIT 12.8

VALUE IS IN THE MIND OF THE BEHOLDER

Professor Seton left his teaching post in the midwest after twelve years to accept a seat on the faculty of New York University.

He and his family liked the town of Great Neck, Long Island, and rented an apartment there. Then Seton visited a real estate office to start house hunting.

"What price range are you interested in?" asked the real estate salesperson.

"Oh, about thirty thousand dollars," replied the professor.

"That's a tough bill to fill," said the seller. "We'll keep our eyes open and call you if we spot anything."

The same type of dialogue took place in three other real estate offices. Nothing happened.

Then one day, Mary Otis, head of one of the offices, asked one of her salespeople, "What happend with Professor Seton?"

"He's no prospect," was the reply. "I couldn't find him a doghouse for what he wants to pay."

"Do you mind if I handle him?" asked Otis.

"Be my guest."

Otis called Dr. Seton and asked if he would like to take a ride around Great Neck with her.

"We haven't been able to find anything for you yet," she told him as they started out. "But I'd like to show you some properties and, in so doing, become more familiar with your needs and wants."

Within an hour Otis learned that Professor Seton's buying power was well able to handle a transaction in Great Neck. She also learned that Seton's ideas on house prices were gleaned from his last buying experience when he had bought a house for twenty thousand dollars in Joliet, Illinois, in 1968!

A few days later Otis closed on a house with Professor Seton, a house with which he, his wife, and his children were truly enchanted. The price was one hundred thousand dollars.

Show the prospect who raises a price-oriented objection the advantages of your product or service through a telescope—the cost through a microscope.

Answer Price Objections Promptly   The time to start helping the prospect overcome a price-oriented objection is the minute it arises. There are good reasons for this:

1. Failing to get this resistance out of the way quickly may cause it to remain in the prospect's mind as a shadow, blocking receptivity to the sales presentation.
2. Hesitating to answer the price objection promptly may imply fear of it and lead the prospect to assume that the price objection is indeed valid.

3. Procrastinating in answering the price objection may cause it to grow in importance in the mind of the buyer—it is wiser to nip it in the bud.
4. It is in your interest to get the price objection out of the way so as not to disturb the continuity of your presentation—get it over with and get on with it.

The only exception to answering a price objection promptly is when it arises so early in the sales interview that the buyer has not yet had a chance to develop any value concept regarding the offering. But, by and large, it is wiser to avoid letting price become an anticlimax later.

How to Handle "Uncle" Competition

One of the stickiest classes of competition-oriented resistance is the case where the buyer is doing business with a relative or friend. As difficult as it is, though, it is not always the end of the road to selling the prospect in question.

Granted, it may not be a prudent investment of time to try to sell your product or service to someone whose aged and cherished father collects a commission on the prospect's purchases. This is especially so when the item bought can be obtained from many sources, like a car, an appliance, or a security. However, here are a few checkpoints for considering whether to invest your time and how to make the most of it.

Is There a Nick in the Nepotism? Not all relationships are as close as parent and child. In some cases the buyer patronizes the friend or relative without much enthusiasm and would like a valid reason to stop doing so. The prospect will never reveal this, but you never can tell.

Be Next in Line Parents die. Relatives move. Friends sometimes have a falling out. If the stakes are worth the effort, go ahead with your sales presentation, even though you know Uncle Charlie will get the order. Be at the head of the favored list after Uncle Charlie.

Avoid Placing the Prospect on the Defensive Be gracious. If the buyer admits that the objection is based on patronage of a friend or relative, appear understanding. A prospect on the defensive presents a double obstacle. "Naturally you prefer to buy from your sorority sister, Miss Carroll, but I'd like to tell you the facts on our service anyhow—just in case."

Make Sure "Uncle" Is Delivering Being charitable about the buyer's nepotism does not mean to refrain from competing with it. You can be the devil's advocate. Make sure the friend or relative is giving the buyer the best value obtainable. Anything short of that may open the door. Sellers are sometimes careless about how they deal with captive buyers. We all know the old saying, "With that kind of friend, who needs any enemies?"

"Naturally you want to buy from your friend," you say to the office manager to whom you would like to sell your inked ribbons, carbon paper, and duplicating supplies.

"Acme is a good house. That wax-back Solon Brand carbon paper they brought out last year was a breakthrough. It gave us plenty of trouble till we were able to duplicate it."

"Solon Brand?"

"Yes. Solon. The carbon we had to develop to match it sells for three-fifty a box, and it's just as good as our seven-dollar brand."

"Is that so? Funny, Joan never mentioned it. I'm still using Acme's seven-dollar box."

You may rest assured that you have planted a doubt in that office manager's mind. If you don't get his business now, you may very well get it later. Or you may get part of it. This buyer now recognizes that one sometimes pays a premium for friendship. Two sources (including you) could be a check for value, one on the other.

What Do You Have That "Uncle" Doesn't?   Not all product or service features are available from all sources. One specialty feature you have to offer is *yourself*. You are an exclusive feature. There is only one you. Your exclusive personality—your expertise in the knowledge of what you sell and how to get the most out of the purchase—is yours alone. So is your special talent for understanding the prospect's needs, wants, or problems and how to answer them. All these are areas in which you can differ in the extreme from another salesperson selling the same brand of vacuum cleaner or automobile. "Uncle" may suffer by comparison. He may continue to get the buyer's orders. But if the buyer would prefer to give them to you—even though this is not possible at present—it is a good start.

How to Handle Prejudice-Oriented Objections

Prejudice-oriented objections are among the most difficult to handle. The clue as to how to help the prospect overcome such an objection lies in the word itself. A prejudice is a prejudgment. The antidote with the best chance of success is a postjudgment suggestion. Lest we be accused of misrepresentation, this is not guaranteed to work. But it is the only device that has a chance.

Prejudice is learned at the gut level, usually without much reasoning. Most prejudices are of long standing. Helping the prospect see the object of the prejudice in the light of a later time makes a change possible.

The first thing to do when you are faced with a prejudice-oriented objection is to avoid any show of disparagement for it, regardless of what your personal sentiments may be. This keeps the door open.

Then, in restating the objection, try to reword it in such a way as to show it from a different perspective. Your aim is to suggest a postjudgment that will alter the prejudgment.

A good way to lead your prospect past a prejudice-based objection is to suggest that this prejudice is not compatible with the prospect's other opinions and beliefs, as in the following situation.

Sam Kraus, a newspaper sales representative, was told by a druggist he would not advertise in Kraus's paper because of its politics (Independent Republican). This was obviously a prejudiced objection.

Said Kraus, "I appreciate your frankness and I understand your point. However, Mr. Harris, since you are making politics an issue in your advertising—and you have every right to do so—do you check the politics of your customers?"

"What are you getting at?"

"Well, you obviously don't mind *selling* to people with different politics from yours. Right?"

"Yes. But what are you driving at?"

"There are about 200,000 Independent Republicans who might like to buy your cut-rate drugs. But they don't know your products because they don't see your ads in the paper that they read."

Sam Kraus won an advertising contract by helping the prospect overcome a prejudice-oriented objection. He accomplished this by showing the druggist that his attitude in not using an Independent Republican newspaper for his advertising was inconsistent with his practice of selling to Independent Republican voters. Kraus suggested a postjudgment to the prospect and the prospect made this postjudgment.

SOME CLASSIC TECHNIQUES FOR HANDLING OBJECTIONS

There are some classic methods for handling objections which may prove valuable:

1. The direct denial
2. The sidestep
3. The counterquestion
4. Making the objection for the prospect
5. Conceding minor points

The Direct Denial

When the objection is a serious one and there is a convincing response, it is in the interest of the entire interview to get it out of the way promptly through direct denial, as in this example:

An industrial purchasing agent says to a seller of packaging machines, "I'm sorry. I don't care how good your machines are. Your plant is in Michigan. We've had trouble on other machines with parts and service, and we're not going to go through that all over again."

The salesperson answers, "You're right to be concerned with service, Ms. Johnson. However, did you know that we have a fully stocked warehouse and three service engineers right across the river in Englewood?"

The Sidestep

Sometimes the prospect makes a reasonable objection for which you have no solid answer. But the objection is not major enough to interfere with a closing. In this case, sidestep the objection. Either change its orientation or counter with other features that will outweigh the objection. Here are two examples of changing the objection's orientation:

> The wholesaler prospect says, "We'd only realize a gross of fifteen percent on your crackers. The other lines show us twenty-five percent."
>
> "That's true, Mr. Chalkley," replies the salesperson. "However, do you pay your bills with percentages or with dollars?"
>
> "Yes, with dollars. So what?"
>
> "Well, Rinks is the fastest *turnover* item in the biscuit industry. Here are the numbers from several chains. Three times the turnover of the cracker average from the same dollar investment and the same shelf space."

> "Your tubing is not as flexibly resilient as Jarco's."
>
> "That's right, Ms. Harlan. However, let's compare the two on tensile strength, wearing quality, and—price."

In this case the salesperson acknowledged the buyer's objection because of another brand's greater resiliency but countered with other features on which his product was superior—in an effort to outweigh the resiliency feature of the competitive brand.

The Counterquestion

When there is a head wind, the sailor tacks—the crew uses the sails to reverse the force of the wind and propel the craft forward against the wind. The counterquestion does the same thing with the buyer's objection: reverses it with a question that makes the actual objection a reason to buy. This technique also has been called *closing on the objection*. Here's the use of a counterquestion in handling a retailer's objection.

> PROSPECT: I'm overstocked.
> SALESPERSON: Overstocked on all sizes and colors? After all, Pyramid is the fastest selling line in the industry. Your customers call for it every day. Can you afford to be without a full assortment?

Some price objections can be handled with a counterquestion too.

> PROSPECT: I don't think we could sell a lathe at such a high price.
> SALESPERSON: I naturally respect your opinion on what sells and doesn't sell in your own stores, Mr. Jarret. However, I'd appreciate it if you would explain for my understanding why you don't think your customers will go for a premium-quality lathe.

Making the Objection for the Prospect

A flour company representative approached a retail grocer in this way:

> "I know you'd rather not take time to talk about flour. The only reason you're doing it is because you're a nice guy. You'd be better off if you didn't have to carry a stock and could keep your investment down."

The grocer stared in openmouthed amazement.

"But you have to carry a certain stock," the salesperson continued, "so you should make a profit in some other way from selling flour."

Then the salesperson explained a related merchandising display plan which would help the grocer sell more butter, eggs, table syrup, and baking powder.

This approach surprised the grocer. But also it stole his thunder. Had he raised the objection to flour merchandising, he would have felt impelled to defend it. When the representative did it for him, there was nothing for him to object to.

Such reverse psychology—stating the prospect's case—can work in buying as well as selling. A clever woman wanted to rent a summer cottage. She and her husband found just the cottage they wanted. However, the price was more than they felt they could pay. Read how she got the rental at her price by using reverse psychology.

"It's just what we've been looking for," she told the owner of the cottage. "We've been all over, and this is the first place that suits us. Just look, George," she said in an aside to her husband. "A modern kitchen in a beach house!"

She walked into the living room, the owner behind her.

"What a spot! Right on the beach. We can watch the kids from the veranda. Don't tell me! A beautiful Italian fireplace for a cool day. Wonderful!"

Then she went from room to room, husband and owner following her. At each point she noticed something special, discovered a new goodie to make the cottage more desirable. Her husband could not have looked more disgusted. She was throwing the game.

Finally, she turned to the owner and said, "Just perfect! I'm heartbroken that we have to pass it up. It's five hundred more than we can afford to pay."

The owner opened his mouth, but no words came. His cue was to play up the features of the house to justify the higher price. But there was nothing left to say. The prospect, in this case a masterful salesperson, had said it all.

Sheepishly, the owner said, "Well, okay. You're nice people and will take good care of the place. You've got a deal."

Conceding Minor Points

When your prospect raises an objection, ask yourself how important this objection is to the ultimate outcome of the sales interview. The more you can concede along the way, the easier it will be for you to get the buyer to concede on buying your product or service.

This is the *law of minor concessions*. Answer only the objections you have to. Yield and agree as much as you can.

By conceding a point, you impress the prospect with your open-minded honesty. This will add credibility to your positive expositions. You stamp yourself as one who seeks the truth rather than to win arguments. You help make the interview truly a means by which you and the prospect jointly explore the prospect's needs, wants, or problems and how your product or service might answer them.

John Hays Hammond, after graduation from Yale University and three years at the university in Freiburg, Germany, is seeking his first job as a mining engineer. His prospect for employment is Senator Hearst, one of the leading mine owners in the West.

Hammond knew that Hearst was little enamored with what he called "collar-and-cuff theoretical mining engineers."

"The only objection I have to you," the brusque senator tells Hammond, "is that you've been in Freiburg and have your head filled with a lot of fool theories. I don't want any kid-glove engineers."

Hammond then concedes a point and makes the sale—that is, gets the job.

"If I tell you something," he says to the older man, "will you promise not to tell my father?"

"Of course."

"I didn't learn a single thing in Germany!"

"Come around and start work tomorrow."[4]

SPECIAL CAUTIONS

As we near the end of the two chapters on buyer resistance, here are a few cautions to keep in mind.

Protect the Buyer's Ego—Don't Lose by Winning Too Well

Reference has already been made to the importance of a modest attitude in handling objections and also protecting the buyer's ego when the objection is removed. The competent salesperson is careful to express answers to buyer objections in a manner that precludes resentment on the part of the buyer. When the prospect accepts the answer to an objection, the salesperson must take care that the buyer considers this as an aid to a sound buying decision, a victory for his or her judgment, not a reflection on his or her intelligence.

Listen to how Sophie Erdlitz protects the buyer's ego as she helps a food chain buyer overcome resistance to her line of imported cheeses.

"I see," says the prospect. "At today's exchange rate we're a little better off. I guess I'm a bit rusty on import arithmetic."

"To tell you the truth, Mr. Simmons, it's *very* complex. I have trouble keeping up with it myself, and I have to make a living with it. I wish they'd quote in dollars instead of kroner."

When There Is No Resistance: Don't Tilt at Windmills

Sometimes there are no buyer objections, no resistance, and a clear field to the closing. Make sure you give this a chance to become evident.

---

[4]Ewing T. Webb and John J. B. Morgan, *Strategy in Handling People*, Boulton, Pierce, and Company, Chicago, 1931.

• A young salesperson was enthusiastically hailing the features of his auto fleet leasing service when the prospect broke in and said, "That's not necessary, Jason. We decided to sign with your firm before you got here."

• "If I may interrupt," says the office manager to the metal file salesperson, "I'd like to place an order."

Sometimes Silence Is the Best Answer

There are instances where a prospect will answer his or her own objection, or abandon it, if allowed to talk it out. The weaker the objection, the more effective it is to let the buyer keep the floor. Silence can be very eloquent.

Under normal circumstances, avoid answering a stupid objection or an irrelevant objection that is sometimes intended to throw you off the track. Give the prospect a chance to talk about it. Go along with it for a while. Be patient. It will pay you dividends in successful closings.

If your ignoring of the objection causes it to slip out of the buyer's consciousness, it could not have been important, and you will have gained by not answering it.

Use the Buyer's Language

Harold Sadd had taken a shine to Wanda Will. Here they were at a mutual friend's home watching slides.

"Now's my chance," thought Harold. "I'll wink at her. That's how to flirt." He winked while the room lights were still out.

In selling, as in romance, what you have in mind does not count. It's only what you are able to communicate to the other party that matters. A wink won't work in a dark room.

In the last chapter we discussed the language of diplomacy. Selling is a kindred field. The superior salesperson gets communications across by using the buyer's language, by striving to reach into the prospect's frame of reference. You would not try to communicate to a monolingual Frenchman in Spanish or to a senorita in Madrid in French.

Use the buyer's language, or at least use language the buyer can understand. Penetrate the semantic barrier.

• "It fizzes in your stomach like soda in a glass," says the drug salesperson.
• "Here. Swing this racquet yourself."
• "Just smell this aroma."
• "Take a taste."

Compare the new with the old. Proceed from the known to the unknown, from the familiar to the unfamiliar.

When a musician makes an objection, your answer has its best chance of being understood if you are able to use a musical analogy. Technical facts get through to an engineer. Talk figures with an accountant and people with a personnel director.

EXHIBIT 12.9
RASPUTIN OBJECTS—LUBIN ANSWERS

David Lubin, who founded the International Institute of Agriculture, now the Food and Agriculture Organization of the United Nations, was meeting with Rasputin in Moscow to urge Russia's attendance at the opening conference in Rome.

"What could Russia possibly gain by joining the Institute?" was Rasputin's objections.

"Do you realize, Excellency," replied Lubin, "that your Czar is involved in an international pinochle game? But although his chips are on the table, he is *under* the table and can't see what is going on. Membership in the institute will give Russia a place at the table to protect her interests."

The Russians showed up at Rome.

Source: As related to Bud Wilson by Benjamin Salinger, Lubin's grandson.

Don't Answer the Unanswerable

How do you handle an objection that is valid and logically unanswerable? Neither avoid nor evade. Concede the point. To argue with the truth is a losing game. Do not try to answer the unanswerable. It will only magnify the importance of the objection.

A closing generally does not result from one feature. Neither does it generally fail for one objection. By conceding the point readily and sincerely, you show your honesty.

Then get on with it as quickly as possible. Your strategy must be to get by the point on which you lost and to win on other points sufficiently to outweigh the lost point on balance.

There are only two alternatives open to you when you face an objection that is legitimately unanswerable: You can modify your proposition or modify your presentation.

Modifying Your Proposition If at all possible, remove the reason for the objection. The easiest, most direct way to remove an objection is to make it unnecessary. Always try to offer the buyer what the buyer wants—in product, service, price, terms, guarantees, or any other part of your proposition. When this is possible, selling is a simple process. For example, suppose you are presenting a power cruiser to a prospect and this prospect likes your boat more than any other on the market. However, you establish that although this prospect has a good income, he is short of ready cash to meet the down payment your company requires, whereas a competitor is willing to take the order with no cash down. A modification of your proposition might be to offer a no-cash-down lease-purchase plan or to suggest—delicately, of course—obtaining a loan from a bank, credit company, or other source.

Naturally, one cannot always modify the selling proposition. Some are flexible, with freedom of movement for the salesperson. Others are ironbound and unchangeable. In that case, you have no choice but to modify your presentation.

Modifying Your Presentation   Your product or service, your prospect's needs, wants, problems, and personality—as well as the proposition itself—each has more than one aspect. Remember that the same glass of water is half full or half empty, depending on how one views it, which, in turn, can be influenced by how you present it.

Modifying your presentation means *diversifying* it. Reexamine your proposition. What other features that it offers compensate for the point objected to and may be strong enough to counterbalance it? Now change your presentation to stress that feature or features. Try to switch the reason for the buying decision from an objectionable one to a desirable one.

For example, as a wholesale floor lamp salesperson, you have observed that most floor lamps on display in the lamp department of Ronson's Department Store have cast-metal bases. By questioning other wholesale salespeople, you have learned that Sylvia Sitchell, the buyer, has an unshakable objection to spun-metal lamp bases. As far as you are concerned, this is indeed an unanswerable objection; every lamp in your line has a spun-metal base.

Obviously, you cannot change your company's line of lamps from spun to cast-metal bases. It is impossible for you to modify your proposition. However, you can modify your presentation. What other features of your lamp line can be stressed to diversify your presentation away from the decision point on lamp bases?

In the first place, your lamps are selling well in other stores right in Sitchell's market, stores that carry both cast- and spun-metal lamps from which the consumer can choose. Second, spun-base lamps cost less, making possible lower prices for Sitchell's low-end customers. Third, your lamp styling is designed to fit the latest trends in room decoration. Finally, your firm is offering an advertising allowance to help Sitchell promote the line. Yes, Sitchell's objection to spun-metal lamp bases is unshakable and unanswerable. But that does not mean you will fail to sell to her.

STANDARDIZED RESPONSES

Earlier in this text we discussed standardized sales presentations. The same device can be used to help a prospect get by an objection.

No matter what product or service you sell, you will not be at it long before you find the same or similar objections occurring in a great number of your calls. This was discussed earlier.

Analyze these common objections, plan comprehensive answers, test the answers, refine them, and practice them.

A standard variety of resistance gives the salesperson a chance to have high-quality standardized responses ready.

EXHIBIT 12.10

TRICKS OF THE TRADE: HOW TO LIGHTEN THE STING OF A SETBACK

Rufus Choate, the great trial lawyer, was once trying a case when a witness unexpectedly gave evidence most detrimental to Choate's side. Choate proved what Knute Rockne, legendary football coach, meant when he said, "The true test of a team is how it acts in adversity."

Choate had the witness repeat the testimony slowly while he, pencil in hand, wrote out every word of it. Phrase by phrase, as he had written it, he faced the jury and read it aloud as though to make sure each juror had heard the testimony.

This surprise move complimented each juror's ego. It also consumed time, which cushioned the shock of the evidence.

The testimony stood in the record. But Choate had lightened its sting, which is especially important in a jury trial.

RECAP

This chapter completes the two-part treatment of the subject of buyer resistance. It covered practical techniques for handling the various categories of resistance described in Chapter 11, as well as specific classes of objection met in the field.

We close this two-chapter coverage of buyer resistance and how to deal with it with a summary table (Exhibit 12.11) and a reminder of three statements of fact:

- The essence of all selling is helping the buyer overcome objections.
- If there were no resistance, there would be no need for selling.
- Selling begins when the prospect says "no."

REVIEW QUESTIONS

1. What are the two things you can do when you anticipate an objection? Explain.
2. What are the five checkpoints for receiving objections resiliently?
3. What is meant by "avoid the acute angle"?
4. What is the Yes-however technique?
5. What is the first rule for handling competition-oriented objections?
6. What is meant by negative selling?
7. What determines the value of a product or service?
8. What are two things you can do to improve the prospect's value image of your product or service?
9. When is the proper time to answer a price objection?
10. What is "uncle" competition?
11. Name at least three considerations for the salesperson faced with "uncle" competition.

EXHIBIT 12.11

GRASS-ROOTS OBJECTIONS SALESPEOPLE MEET AND HOW TO HANDLE THEM

Kinds of objections	How to handle
Competition	• Evaluate the objection—how important is it? • Counteract misinformation with facts. • Know your competition—strengths and weaknesses. • Lead from your strength. • Don't knock competitors.
Price	• Don't be sensitive about your price—be proud of what your product or service is worth. • Magnify the value image. • Shrink the price image. • Emphasize what it will cost *not* to buy. • Answer price objections promptly, except very early in the interview.
"Uncle"	• Don't place buyer on the defensive. • Be next in line. • Seek a nick in the nepotism. • Make sure "uncle" is delivering. • What can you offer that "uncle" cannot?
Prejudice	• Avoid any show of disparagement. • Restate objection in different words. • Suggest incompatibility between the objection and the prospect's other opinions.
Left-field objections	• If not important to closing—concede. • Sidestep.
Buyer-oriented objections	• Probe for the basis of the objection. • If factually based, don't dodge it. • If correctible—correct. • If objection is not factually based, use a counterquestion to show it from different perspective. • Try to provide proof.
Product- or service-oriented objections	• Verify the facts. • Correct misunderstandings and misinformation with true facts. • Try to provide proof. • If appropriate, use the direct denial technique.
Decision-oriented objections	• Make sure it's genuine, not a brush-off. • Provide a reason to decide—favorably. • Show disadvantages of putting off decision.
Source- or salesperson-oriented objections	• Verify the facts. • Correct misunderstandings and misinformation with facts. • Try to provide proof. • Use direct denial technique, if appropriate.
Test objections	• Meet the test head-on with confidence.
Devil's advocate objections	• Probe for the real objection, if any exists.
Calls for help	• Reassure prospect with more information. • Reassure prospect through examples of others. • Try to provide proof. • Demonstrate. • Help.

12. How can you handle buyer objections based on prejudice?
13. What are some classic techniques for handling objections? Explain each briefly.
14. In overcoming an objection, how can you lose by winning too well?
15. What is meant by the admonishment to salespeople that "sometimes silence is the best answer"?
16. How do you handle an objection that is valid and logically unanswerable?
17. What is meant by a standardized response to an objection?

DISCUSSION QUESTIONS

1. As a travel agent, you are reviewing your proposed itinerary for a month-long European trip with Mr. and Mrs. Atwood. Mr. Atwood retired last month from his position as office manager of the Garrison Novelty Company. Since the trip will take place in April, your recommendation is for the Atwoods to fly to Paris for a week; travel by rented car to and from the Loire Valley for another week; go by train from Paris to Brussels for three days and then on to Amsterdam for three days; and spend a final week in London before flying home. Mrs. Atwood is enthusiastic. But Mr. Atwood expresses many reservations. Among these objections are, "Isn't a week a long time for Paris?" "Without speaking French, won't I have trouble driving through the Loire Valley?" "Brussels doesn't excite me," "I hear the prices in London are exorbitant," and "Belgium and Holland are so much alike, maybe we should skip one of them and cut the trip down a bit." Mrs. Atwood remains silent as Mr. Atwood continues to offer objections to the itinerary.
   (a) Analyze the objections expressed by Mr. Atwood.
   (b) How do you explain Mrs. Atwood's silence?
   (c) By what strategy can you identify your closing problem?
   (d) How will you bring about a successful closing? Use your imagination for details not stated in the hypothesis.
2. "Four dollars and seventy-five cents to clean a suit? That's much higher than I paid in Freeport. I think I'll get prices from some other cleaners." The prospect has come into your cleaning establishment with a number of garments. She is new in the neighborhood.
   (a) What are the possible meanings of price resistance in this case? How can you determine which is the key one?
   (b) How would you go about handling this objection? Explain each part of the strategy you would employ.

LEARNING EXPERIENCES

1. Seminar: "How to Thaw the Ice out of Price." Let one member of the group be the chairperson. The rest of the group will participate as sales executives. The object of the seminar is to discuss all aspects of price resistance and how to

deal with it, arriving ultimately at a series of points to guide your salespeople in dealing with price objections.

2. Write a brief memo on psychological considerations in handling buyer objections.

3. You represent a commercial car-leasing company, and you are about to call upon the general manager of a company to bid for the contract to lease cars for seventy-seven salespeople.

   (a) List every possible objection that may come up.

   (b) Select any three of these objections and explain how you would handle them.

CASES

CLARENDON GROWTH FUND

Marion Kraus, representing the Clarendon Growth Fund, a mutual investment fund, is calling on Howard Elie, operations vice president of Sanders & Co. Elie had sent a magazine clipping to Clarendon, requesting information. Kraus has made her sales presentation, and Elie has been studiously attentive, asking a question now and then on a detail. Finally, Kraus—having received a "go" response to a preclose test question—asks Elie if he would like to participate in the Clarendon mutual fund. To her surprise, his answer is negative. Here is the dialogue that followed.

KRAUS: It's your decision, of course, Mr. Elie. If I'm not out of order, may I ask why?

ELIE: Oh, your fund sounds good. But I have other places to invest my money.

KRAUS (*Smiling*): Let me in on it, will you? Maybe that's what I should be selling instead of Clarendon.

ELIE: No. There's a market for everything. I just think I'm better off to go straight to a broker and buy stocks on my own.

KRAUS: In other words, Mr. Elie, you have more confidence in your ability to pick a stock than our portfolio committee.

ELIE: Oh, I wouldn't go so far as to say that. But when I pick a stock, I get leverage by buying that stock alone. In your mutual fund, the good selections are diluted by the bad ones.

KRAUS: That's very interesting, Mr. Elie. I respect you for having the courage of your convictions. However, would you mind taking a look at our average for all selections last year? Here's the sheet. A twenty-one percent overall gain.

ELIE: That's an impressive record. How about the year before?

KRAUS: Here's the record for the last five years. If you had placed a thousand dollars with Clarendon on January 15, 1979, and reinvested your dividends, today it would be worth two thousand four hundred and eighty-eight dollars.

ELIE: I'll think about it, and maybe later I'll go in.

KRAUS: Mr. Elie, you acknowledge the Clarendon record in picking growth stocks. Has your broker done better?

ELIE: No. But he's an old friend, and I've given him my business for some fifteen years.

KRAUS: I admire your loyalty. However, whom does your broker really represent?

ELIE: Why, me, of course.

KRAUS: He certainly should. However, has it occurred to you that in a *mutual* fund like Clarendon, the people who make the portfolio decisions get nothing from the transaction? Their income depends on how well the fund does.

ELIE: That's an interesting point.

KRAUS: I'm glad you recognize that, Mr. Elie. You also seem to respect our investment record. Is that right?

ELIE: Yes.

KRAUS: How much time do you devote to studying the market and the individual issues?

ELIE: Not enough. I admit it.

KRAUS: Wouldn't it be nice not to have to? You have enough to do watching your own business. We watch the market for you and report to you regularly. You always know what's going on.

ELIE: Tell you what. I'll start a small program with you and see how it works out.

Questions

1. How did Kraus know Elie had a preliminary interest in Clarendon?
2. Give your analysis of why Elie initially objected to participating in the Clarendon Growth Fund.
3. What unexpected objection was exposed?
4. Comment on Kraus's conduct of the sales interview, with special reference to her handling of Elie's objections. Explain her strategy and her overall personal conduct.

RAMPAL TIRE SERVICE

The following dialogue took place between Gil Harte, Rampal Tire Service salesperson, and Harry Simkins, motorist. Simkins is waiting in the office while a slow leak in one of his tires is being repaired.

HARTE: How long have you driven these tires, Mr. Simkins?

SIMKINS (*Chuckling*):   They don't owe me anything.

HARTE: Well, they're smooth, and I think you're making a mistake in not changing them now.

SIMKINS (*Laughing*):   You talk just like a tire dealer.

HARTE: (*Seriously*):   Well, I represent a tire dealer, and it's my job to see that our customers are driving on safe tires.

SIMKINS: Safe?

HARTE: Yes sir! Safe is what I said. With the tires you have on your car now, you're looking for trouble.

SIMKINS (*Sarcastically*):   Thanks. You know, I've been driving for thirty years and I've never had an accident.

HARTE: Well you're lucky. Those tires are dangerous.

SIMKINS: Okay. Thanks for your concern. I'll remember that when I need new tires.

Questions

1. Criticize Harte's general handling of Simkin's resistance.
2. What principle for handling objections did Harte violate?
3. Rewrite the dialogue to illustrate how Harte should have handled the resistance. Use your imagination for facts not known from the original dialogue.

SUNBELT PROPERTIES

Marcia Gordon had just finished showing the Bradleys the vacation sites being offered by Sunbelt Properties. Mr. Bradley was a man of approximately sixty and Mrs. Bradley seemed to be about the same age. The following dialogue took place.

MR. BRADLEY: Very nice. But I think we'll wait.

GORDON: Well, thanks for looking anyhow. I assume you're favorably inclined, so the visit wasn't wasted.

MR. BRADLEY: Not at all.

GORDON: Does that mean you may buy a lot some time in the future, Mr. Bradley?

MRS. BRADLEY: It's entirely possible.

GORDON: In other words, you like what we have to offer, but our timing is off. Is that right?

MR. BRADLEY: Exactly.

GORDON (*Smiling*):   If you won't consider me nosy, may I ask what's wrong with our timing?

MR. BRADLEY: I'll be frank. Both Mrs. Bradley and I work. We're both scheduled to retire in four years. That's when we'll want to pull up stakes and get into a vacation area.

GORDON: That makes sense. I understand now why our timing is off. How-ever, in the interest of the time when you will be ready, may I ask you a few questions?

MR. BRADLEY: Go ahead.

GORDON: Do you both like this area?

MRS. BRADLEY: It's lovely.

MR. BRADLEY: When we're ready to go, this is just what we'll be looking for.

GORDON: Have you considered that when you're ready, these lots may be gone?

MR. BRADLEY: There'll be others.

GORDON: I'm sure there will be. But you and Mrs. Bradley seem to really like this spot, and, frankly, you're the kind of people we think will be right for this community.

MRS. BRADLEY: Maybe we should think about this some more, George.

MR. BRADLEY: Mary, we'd be tying up money and losing interest on it long before we use the land.

GORDON: In other words, Mr. Bradley, although you seem to be people of substance, even a millionaire doesn't like to tie up funds that could be produc-ing income. That's businesslike judgment—and I respect it. However, if you could find an equally good business reason for owning this land now, might you reconsider?

MR. BRADLEY: What good business reason could there be for tying up funds in something we won't need for four or five years?

GORDON: Do you think your dollar will be worth as much in five years as it is today?

MR. BRADLEY: I know. Inflation.

GORDON: This land will be priced at far more in five years than you can buy it for today. Land is a hedge against inflation, and the improvement of this country property and promoting it will increase its value way over the inflation loss in the dollar.

MR. BRADLEY: That's a point.

GORDON: When will you *build* your dream house here, Mr. and Mrs. Brad-ley? Or order one of our prefab models?

MR. BRADLEY: When we retire.

GORDON: Good. You can gain a financial advantage by building now. Would you like to know why?

MR. BRADLEY (*Grinning*):   I think I know what you're going to say. But say it anyway.

GORDON: You're way ahead of me. You know you can swing it for lots less now. Building costs have been rising year after year, and there's no end in sight. In addition, the financial service charges are tax deductible. If you are like most people, your taxes are higher now than they'll be when you retire.

MR. BRADLEY: Yes. We'll admit that.

GORDON: But above all, you seem to be taken with that lot on the lakefront. You can enjoy it while you're using it as an inflation hedge and a tax advantage. You live only a hundred miles from here. You can come here for weekends and vacations long before you retire. You can fish and sail in the lake. In another year our golf course will be ready. Free vacations. What will that save you in a four-year period? And you'll begin to make new friends in your new community, which will ease your transition into retirement.

MRS. BRADLEY: George, I'd like to have a private talk with you.

Questions

1. It looks as if Gordon is going to sell that lot and maybe a house along with it. Give your analysis of her handling of the objection.
2. Give your opinion on how Gordon applied diplomacy and psychology in dealing with the objection of the Bradleys. Explain in detail.

3. Mrs. Bradley had very little to say during this part of the sales interview. But apparently Gordon considered her an important participant. How did Gordon utilize the influence of Mrs. Bradley to help the Bradleys overcome their resistance?

4. Since Mr. Bradley's main objection to buying the lot now was his unwillingness to tie up money that could be earning income, why did Gordon raise the amount to be tied up by adding the investment in a house?

5. In a sense, Gordon was handling a price objection, not because of the prospect's concept of the value of the lot but because of the financial outlay. Explain in detail Gordon's strategy in dealing with this objection.

6. What added benefit did Gordon introduce that was related directly to purchase at this time?

THIRTEEN

CHAPTER OBJECTIVES

To give you an appreciation of the importance of timing in your closing effort

To develop your ability to pick the right time to close

To give you an understanding of basic closing principles

To acquaint you with specific closing techniques

CHAPTER OUTLINE

CLOSING THE SALE

Napoleon, on being asked what troops he considered the best,
replied: "Those which are victorious."

Anonymous

The goal of selling is to close sales. That is what selling is all about. If
there is no close, there is no sale.

The closing is the climax of the sales interview. It is the point at
which all that has gone before—prospecting, preapproach, approach,
presentation, and handling of buyer resistance—are tested against reality. Either the prospect buys or does not buy. Anything else is extraneous.

A skillful closing can vary all the way from a dramatic pro-con summary to absolute silence, depending on what the specific situation calls
for.

This chapter will guide you in picking the right closing strategy and
applying it expertly, skills generally agreed to be the most important in
the technology of contemporary selling. Proficiency in closing is what
makes your selling efforts count. It is the critical ingredient that trans-
forms buyer interest into buying motion.

308

PRINCIPLES AND GUIDELINES FOR CLOSING

As in every other aspect of the selling process, there are principles to guide you. These principles cover timing, tactics, and cautions. They are distilled from the experiences of thousands of salespeople winning and losing in millions of closing efforts.

JOHN MISSES . . . MARY HITS

"Will you want financing on your new car?" John Sibley asks his showroom prospect as he places a credit application form on the desk before him.

"You're way ahead of me," replies the prospect as he rises to leave. "I think I'd better think the whole thing over some more."

"Will you want financing?" Mary Calderone asks her showroom car prospect. She is relaxed against the back of her chair and her hands are on her lap under the desk.

"I suppose I will," answers the prospect, and Mary knows she is about to close.

There is much more to these seemingly parallel trial closings than one might think. When you have finished this chapter, you will know why John missed and Mary hit.

When to Close

There is no pat time to move for a closing. The right time to close is *when the prospect is ready to buy.* This can occur before a word is exchanged between seller and buyer. It can come about at any time during the approach, the presentation, the appearance of an objection, or later. Again: The right time to close is when the prospect is ready.

How do you know when a prospect is ready to buy? E. H. Boullioun, who sells billions of dollars worth of airplanes for Boeing says, "Quite often, when the last item is settled, they just smile."[1]

Indeed, the effort to close begins at the very beginning of the sales call. It rises and relaxes strategically throughout the sales interview, but it is always there. That is why we placed the subject of the preclose under the sales interview rather than in this chapter on the closing. We wanted to underscore the fact that the selling process is not a random number of disjointed steps but a series of interrelated progressions, all unified under the one objective, to effect a favorable closing.

Transition into the Closing You really have been closing throughout your sales presentation. You have been gaining the prospect's acceptance of your proposition progressively as you offered buying point after buying point. There is a *natural* time to close. It is easy and transitional and flows right into place when the prospect is in fact ready. The seasoned salesperson can sense it.

The better the approach and sales presentation, the easier will be the removal of resistance and the transition into the closing. If you have gained favorable *attention* at the outset and have created sufficient *interest and desire* as the

---

[1] Eric Pace, "He Sells the New Boeings," *The New York Times,* Mar. 29, 1981, p. F6.

EXHIBIT 13.1
TRYING TO CLOSE TOO SOON

interview moved along, when the time comes for action, the prospect will be ready to buy.

Don't *Oversell* When the Prospect Is "Sold"   Close at the climax. To delay beyond the point at which the buyer is ready can dampen the promise of a successful closing. Once the high point in the buyer's interest level has been reached, it begins to recede. The longer you wait beyond this point, the more difficult will be your closing. Like a piece of fruit, the prospect's disposition to buy ripens. If it is not plucked from the tree when ripe, it is apt to become overripe and rot. When the buyer is ready, stop selling and close.

It also can be disastrous to try to close too soon.

Too Hard Too Soon   Although the closing can be initiated at any part of the sales call, from "hello" to "goodbye," doing so prematurely can be disastrous. Many a sale is lost because the salesperson moves to close too hard, too soon.

The prospect must indeed be ready. This might have been the case even before you began your sales presentation. However, under more usual circumstances, you have to *earn the right to close*. To move before the prospect has been sold—that is, before his or her desire to enjoy the benefits of your product or service has crystallized—is to risk defeat.

> "Which of these pups do you think your kids will like?" asks the pet store salesperson of the woman standing by the cage.
>
> "I really don't know," replies the prospect. "I think I'll come back another time. Good day."

Sounds ridiculous, doesn't it? There must have been some preliminary interest for the prospect to have entered the store. What the seller did not know was that this woman had a hidden objection to buying a dog at all. She had come to the store to humor her husband, who believed their children should have a pet. But underneath there lurked a fear that she, and not her young children, would become "nursemaid to a puppy."

Until this objection is exposed and the prospect helped to overcome it, any closing effort is premature and doomed to failure. By making the closing move too soon, the salesperson brought the buyer to the brink of action before she was ready and forced a confrontation from which the prospect escaped by terminating the sales interview.

Had the salesperson tested the level of the prospect's interest and found it far from ready, the interview could have been kept alive for a later closing effort with a better chance of success. For instance, the salesperson might have asked, "Which breed do you like best yourself, Mrs. Coulter?" The response to this preclose test question would have revealed that Mrs. Coulter was not ready, but the test question would not have terminated the interview. The prospect might have deliberately cloaked her resistance by saying something evasive like, "Oh, I like them all." On the other hand, she might have provided the seller with a clue. For instance, she might have said, "To tell you the truth, I don't care much for dogs. They're nice, but they're a lot of trouble."

The minute the prospect said "trouble," the seller would have had a clue to the resistance and what it might be. He or she could have said, "Yes, Mrs. Coulter, a dog does have to be taken care of. But don't you think it's worth it for your children? For the fun they'll have with a dog and also for the experience they'll get in taking on some responsibility?" By relating this question to the interests of the prospect's children, the seller would have struck a safe chord, sure to be echoed by the prospect, even if with reservations. Now, with the buyer's area of possible resistance narrowed, the circle around the nub of the problem would have become smaller. The prospect might even have countered with "Yes, but who do you think will wind up taking that responsibility?"

"Well, I can tell you how one of our customers with two kids of six and eight handled it, Mrs. Coulter, and it worked."

Now the resistance would have been out in the open, because the seller did not rush in too soon but waited for the prospect to express a reaction. The seller could have dealt with the resistance, knowing that once the prospect was helped over this hurdle, closing time would have arrived.

In closing, try to be *on time*, neither too late nor too soon.

Buying Signals That Say "Close Now"   The prospect may unintentionally reveal when he or she is ready for the closing. Here are some direct giveaways.

Changing from broad questions to more specific questions   A fuel oil prospect's "Do you think we'll be having a cold winter?" is a broad question. But when the prospect asks, "How long does it take you to deliver when we call in an order?" it is a definite signal to start closing. So are questions like these:

EXHIBIT 13.2
TIME TO CLOSE
Learn to recognize the signals that say it's time to close. Not too soon—not too late.

- "What is your trade discount schedule?"
- "How much lead time do you need on orders?"
- "How soon can you ship?"
- "Do you have it in brown?"
- "What about replacement parts?"
- "How long a warranty do you give?"
- "Can you put in a stock on consignment?"
- "What about service?"
- "What is the size of the can?"
- "What days do you pick up and deliver?"

Of course, you must use judgment in interpreting the meaning of a specific question. For example, a request for price information in a later stage of the sales interview is an obvious buying signal. But when the prospect asks the price at the outset of the interview, before he or she is sold or even knows much about the proposition, try to defer answering the question.

Last-ditch objections   When the buyer's objections become obviously contrived rather than reasonable, it's time to close. "I can't afford it" is a good example. The prospect has betrayed a desire to have the product or service and is following a natural human instinct in setting up a last defense.

- "Our business is different."
- "It's a fine piano, but I live in a twelfth-floor apartment. We couldn't get it in."
- "It would be great if I were twenty years younger."
- "Your service sounds good, but it's such a nuisance to go through a changeover."
- "Our clerical people are used to the other system."

Nonverbal signs   A buying signal does not have to be a question or an objection. It can be as simple as a change in the inflection of the prospect's voice, a nod of the head suggesting affirmation or agreement, a change in facial expression like the wrinkling of the brow indicating concentration, or a grin implying favorable reaction. It can even be a pause—or a second look—in examining product or literature.

The buying signal can be overtly physical. Watch for telltale body language signs like scratching of the head, wiping of the chin, brushing of the cheek, leaning forward and listening, or watching more intently. These, and others like them, are buying signals telling you that the interest level is high and it is time to close.

Increased attention to demonstration paraphernalia is another sign favorable for a closing. Other signs are trying on a jacket for a second time and going to the mirror to examine the reflection admiringly or taking the blouse to the window to see it in daylight. Watch for those buying signals, verbal and physical, that say, "Close now." Being alert to recognize them is another mark of a salesperson who makes sales.

Test Questions to Determine When the Prospect Is Ready   All authorities are agreed that the effort to close begins at the very beginning of the sales interview and continues throughout. You should be posing test questions throughout the sales interview, watching for a response that indicates the prospect is ready for closing. Test questions help you check the progress of your presentation as you go along, measuring the prospect's acceptance of what you have been presenting. Examples of test questions are:

- "Do you see how this will simplify your payroll preparation?"
- "Which do you prefer, the long sleeve or the short one?"
- "Would your bank finance the purchase or would you like to hear about our credit-installment plan?"
- "For a family of your size, how many sets would you need?"
- "You came in today, Tuesday, at four for the presentation. Is Tuesday at four a good time for you?"

When the Prospect Does Not Reach the Ready Point   Should you try to close even though you are unable to bring the prospect's interest and desire to the point of readiness for a closing? If you are selling a one-call product or service, like a stock advertising campaign to local bankers and dry cleaners on a town-by-town selling trip, you have little choice but to try to close. Indeed, many products and services are marketed under economic factors that limit selling to a one-call limit. Generally, the experience of these marketers has shown a low return and a prohibitive cost on follow-up calls. A famous insurance agent was astounded, on checking his selling records, to learn that for a full year *70 percent of his sales had been closed on the first call!* He found that 23 percent of his sales had been closed on the second call and 7 percent on all others. We would not rush to conclude from this agent's experience that insurance selling is a one-call process. This agent happened to be *a top-notch prospector* and had a rare talent for quickly bringing prospects to the ready stage. Above all, he was a masterful closer.

There are some business classifications where selling results come slowly. These are the fields where the buying decisions are critical, large, infrequent, or for long-range commitment. In these cases, the selling also is long-range in strategy, often involving long multicall periods of information assembly, contact cultivation, and slow education. This is very common, for example, in industrial and high-technology classifications. One large industrial marketer made a two-year study of reports turned in by its sales force. It showed that 75 percent of this company's sales came from orders obtained *after the fifth interview.* Even more startling was the revelation that 83 percent of the company's least successful salespeople had stopped calling on prospects they were unable to sell *before the fifth interview.*

If you can close, close—always. But if you cannot close, or the selling category is one where multicall strategy is in order, close the interview. Don't overstay or oversell. Again: If you cannot close the sale, close the interview in a manner that leaves the door open for the next call. We call this the *billiard strategy.* Watch a champion billiard player in action. That player makes every shot for maximum score—but also plays position, that is, sets up the table for the next shot.

EXHIBIT 13.3
WATCH FOR THOSE TELLTALE SIGNS THAT INDICATE YOUR PROSPECT IS READY TO BUY

Cleats in the Closing? Yes and No

The aggressive closer pins down each buying point as it scores so it cannot get away. This kind of salesperson builds a step-by-step case for buying that virtually puts cleats in the closing, a bid for the order that is difficult to oppose. In fields where competition is heavy and prospects shop several offerings before deciding, like automobiles and typewriters, for example, this aggressive closing strategy is the time-proven way to make sales. However, the advanced salesperson employs this technique in a way that does so without seeming to be high pressure. That is the mark of the expert, the ability to put cleats in the closing *without cutting*. It is accomplished by a superb knowledge of human nature, an air of confidence that does not grate, a talent for human relations, and the ability to be forceful without shouting. In fact, in the personal makeup of a salesperson, perhaps nothing is more valuable than the ability to speak authoritatively in a quiet voice.

Then there is the *soft close*. This is the exact opposite of the cleat close. It is an easy transition, as described in an earlier page, in which the close flows naturally out of a well-cultivated conviction and desire related to your product or service. Here is a defense of the soft-closing technique by a salesperson who opened up 600 new accounts the first year, introducing a new ingredient to merchant bakers.

> When your demonstration has been well executed, the actual closing comes about quite naturally. As simple a test question as "About how much whipped topping do you use in a week?" tells you by the ease of the baker's reply that he is ready. There are all sorts of clever closing devices. I never needed them. I found that with a good presentation and demonstration behind me, a straightforward "Would you like to take a trial can?" almost never failed to get the order. I emphasized the word *trial*. If the baker asked "What do you mean by trial can?" I answered "Your money back if Moj isn't everything we claim."

Emotion and Reason in Closing Appeals

Earlier in this text we discussed buyer motivation and its two components, reason and emotion. Sales are closed by comprehending and appealing to the prospect's reason or emotions or both, the degree of relative emphasis depending on the case. Yes, both reason and emotion. The most tough-minded buying decision cannot escape emotional influences, for—as stated earlier—every buying decision is made or influenced by humans, subject to all their positive and negative emotional tendencies. Every one of us acts out a front-stage role. But this role is directed by urges and instincts working behind the scenes, some of them conscious and some of them subconscious. (See Exhibit 13.4.)

The advanced salesperson never underestimates the impact of emotions on a buying decision. Note the emotion-directed overtones in the following closing appeals.

- "Won't this be an exciting surprise for your husband?"
- "You'll sleep better, knowing your premises are protected, won't you?"

- "Just wait till your friends see it."
- "The designer of this dress must have had you in mind."
- "You'll *feel* as young as you look."

Whether your closing appeal is directed at a whimsical young person or a hardheaded executive, a pleasure-bent honeymooner, or a facts and figures purchasing agent, always remember this: Reason can be rationalization to answer an emotional need. No buying decision is devoid of emotional influences, no matter

EXHIBIT 13.4

A WEEKDAY CAR FOR REASON—A WEEKEND CAR FOR EMOTION

J. Carver Cranston is vice president of Atlantis Industrial Corporation. He drives a conservative, gray Oldsmobile '98. This is in keeping with his position in the prestigious old New England firm. It also suits his pre-sixty age bracket.

The Cranstons, J. C. and his wife Monica, were in the showroom of the local Olds dealer to buy a new car for Monica.

"What kind of a car did you have in mind?" Olds salesperson Marion Hartley asked Mrs. Cranston.

"Oh, something not too big, not too small. In dark blue," replied Mrs. Cranston as Mr. Cranston stood by in silence.

"You mean an intermediate like our Cutlass," said Hartley. "Let me show you the Cutlass Salon."

As they were examining this four-door model, Mr. Cranston asked, "What's that car over there?"

He was pointing to a white sports car with bucket seats suggestive of airplane seating, a glass top, a manual shift, and oversized tires. It was the last car in the world you would have selected for the wife of J. Carver Cranston—dignified, distinguished, and somewhat of a stuffed shirt.

"That's a special Hurst package," said Hartley.

"What's the price with all the options I see there?"

"Eighteen thousand three hundred twenty-six dollars."

Mrs. Cranston appeared surprised. "That's a bit sporty for me, Jackson, don't you think?" she interposed. "Flashy. More for a youngster."

"Nonsense, Monica, don't be so old fashioned," said Cranston. "I think that could be just the car for you."

After a road test, Cranston placed the order.

"I'm flabbergasted," said Hartley later to her boss. "That second car is in such contrast to the other Cranston car."

"Maybe you shouldn't be," was the reply. "You see, I happen to know J. C. well. He *has* to be conservative in the way he dresses and the car he drives *to business*—in keeping with his position. But you can bet Monica will get *his* car on weekends, while he drives the sporty job to his golf club for his cronies to see. Underneath, J. C. would like to be youthful, dashing, debonair—like a racing driver in the movies. That's what the Hurst model will do for him. I'm not as stunned as you by his choice."

EXHIBIT 13.5
SO YOU THINK YOU THINK?
Closing Appeals That Aim at Emotion as Well as Reason

Appeal to reason	Underlying appeal to emotion
"Buy the Moxilator and you'll save your company twenty thousand dollars next year."	"A smart buy like this could prove your brains and ability to your boss."
"This car has everything. It was designed especially for people like you who have made the grade."	"You don't have to feel guilty over such luxury. You've earned it!"
"The choice cut does cost more, Mrs. Morey. It's the best you can buy."	"Why not go all out and show those in-laws when they come to dinner Sunday?"
"Yes, this cruise costs more because it's a *luxury* cruise. Your mother will never forget it."	"Go ahead. Be a hero to your mother. Let the relatives see how well her daughter has done."

how reasoned it seems. Emotion often is even the more dominant factor. (See Exhibit 13.5.)

The "What If" Psychology

Sometimes you are more apt to close by stressing the consequences of not having your product or service than by posing the positive advantages of buying.

"Our security coverage will get you a reduction on your insurance premium," says the salesperson to the factory owner.

"That's interesting," is the reply. "I'll consider it."

"Did you hear about the break-in at Jobson's last week?" continues the salesperson. "They had our electronic beam surveillance, which signaled the precinct house, and the police were there in minutes. They caught the crooks in the act. With what you have invested here, isn't three hundred a month worth it for peace of mind?"

"If you prepare the food for the party yourself, you'll have the work, the confusion, and the mess," says the caterer. "If we do it, you can actually have as much fun as your guests."

"I recommend you replace these tires now," the tire dealer tells the motorist. "Your wife drives your kids in this car, doesn't she? Well, these tires look pretty smooth to me. I don't want to worry you, but I owe it to you as a customer to call your attention to the dangerous condition of your tires."

Point-by-Point Agreements: Building Blocks for the Close

The entire sales interview is a buildup for the close. The agreements you gain, point by point along the way, are the building blocks on which your ultimate closing depends. The more "yes" answers you can obtain as you make your presentation, the surer you are of a "yes" on the final buying decision.

The bid for each component "yes" has a twofold purpose. First, of course, it seeks the prospect's understanding and acceptance of each point as a building block for the close. But second, each question is a preclose test. Each successive "yes" answer is monitoring your progress, telling you when to move in for the close. These building blocks are the *keys* that unlock the door to a meaningful closing effort.

Three Keys to Closing

The three keys to sound closing strategy follow.

Count Off the Keys In as few words as possible, recapitulate the points on which you have obtained the buyer's agreement, the building-block keys to closing. Ask for the prospect's acknowledgment, for example, with an "Isn't that so?" If the buyer does not say, "I'll take it," suggest the purchase with a simple "Would you like to try it?" or some other low-pressure suggestion to buy.

Key In on the Keys That Count The fewer points you make in your closing, the more effective each will be. The prospect may have one predominant need,

EXHIBIT 13.6
KEEP IT SIMPLE. KEY IN ON WHAT COUNTS

want, or special problem. If so, concentrate your closing appeal on this opening. When the prospect has many needs, wants, or problems, selecting the key points to stress is not so easy. You must evaluate the relative priorities in the prospect's interests and aim at the ones that seem to count the most. Above all, remember that the fewer points you present to the buyer in your closing rationale, the easier you make the buying decision. Key in on the keys that count.

Skip the Keys That Don't Count It is exciting to have a nice, juicy sales point. But the smart salesperson gains from passing the point up if it does not really count with the prospect of the moment. Skipping the keys that don't count is the other side of the coin from "Key in on the keys that count." It is expressed both ways for emphasis, because this is a major point in selling strategy.

The late Joe Kirkwood's golf exhibitions thrilled millions. He hit the ball while blindfolded, or with a rubber hose in place of the rigid shaft, and displayed other amazing feats of control in directing the golf ball to the green. "How is it that Kirkwood doesn't win all the tournaments?" a golf professional was asked. "Kirkwood has so many shots that he doesn't know which one to use," was the reply.

Don't try to close on too many points. Narrow the number of choices and decisions for the prospect to make. Don't present your whole line to the buyer. Select those items that count with this prospect and concentrate on them.

The Sales Point in Reserve: Your Sunday Punch

Smart salespeople do not exhaust all their ammunition in the sales presentation. They hold some in reserve as a "Sunday punch" in case they need it for the closing as in the following example, where the prospect is almost sold and the closing has begun.

"It sounds good," says the buyer, "but I think I'll wait."

"I almost forgot to tell you," says the salesperson, "there's a merchandising offer of one free with a dozen that ends tomorrow night."

"Frankly, I'm having trouble deciding between your service and Allied's," says the prospective cable television subscriber.

"Did I tell you we're on tap twenty-four hours a day?" answers the salesperson. "Oh, by the way—if I forgot to mention it—we're adding three more channels to our CATV service next month. You'll be able to take your choice between the Red Sox, the Yankees, and the Mets."

Don't say it all too soon. Save something for the closing. Have a Sunday punch in case you have to call on it at the close.

The Merchandising Hook: Antidote to Delay

Here are examples of what is perhaps one of the biggest obstacles to the closing, the reason there are more sales interviews than sales.

- "See me your next time around."
- "I'll have to think it over."
- "I want to visit some other stores before I decide."
- "I'll have to talk it over with my partner."
- "I can't decide till I'm sure of the numbers."
- "I'm in no hurry. I'll wait."

Your prospect is sold, but not sold enough to buy today. What do you do? What is the antidote?

One antidote to delay is the *merchandising hook*. It is used effectively by seasoned salespeople. It is the reason they take "not today" resistance in stride and overcome it.

The merchandising hook has been used by department stores and other retailers almost since their origin. The retail ad offers special price inducements with a time limit; personal appearances by authors, beauty experts, and fashion designers; and attractive combinations such as a tie with the shirt, a scarf with the sweater, a lipstick with the perfume.

What are some merchandising hooks that a salesperson can employ to get the order now instead of next week, next month, or never? Here are some examples.

- "You like it in red? Let me call the warehouse to see if we have it in stock. Red has been selling like wildfire."
- "Why don't you place a deposit on the house? That will protect you if someone else shows up and wants it before you see your bank."
- "If you order today, I can protect you at the present price."
- "We have a pooled trailer leaving San Francisco tomorrow. If you give me your order now, I can phone it in and get your shipment aboard."
- "The special offer terminates tomorrow night."
- "We're already installing the air conditioning at Salter's. It's a hot month, and I don't think you want to let your competitor get ahead of you. Say the word now, and I can get our service crew in tomorrow."
- "You look pretty healthy, and I have no doubt we can get you past the medical requirement for the insurance. However, why not take the test when you're sure to pass it? I'm no pessimist and I hope you live to be a hundred, but life is funny. Say the word, and I can get our doctor to examine you tomorrow, right here in your office."

Whatever product or service you sell, merchandising hooks can help the buyer overcome an allergy to action. Find them. Study your proposition to make sure you have them on tap when you need them. If you cannot find these merchandising hooks to help you close, discuss this with your management or source. It is just as important to them as it is to you to score well on closings.

Closing the Retail Sale

Retail closings are generally not as complex as some others are apt to be, though no less critical. The prospect has come to the store, which in itself is evidence of at least preliminary interest. Nevertheless, it is surprising to note how many retail sales are lost because of weakness in closing. Here are some typical retail sale closing lines:

- "May I write this up for you?"
- "Will this be cash or charge?"
- "Are you planning to take this with you, or do you prefer to have it delivered?"
- "This is the last suit we expect to have at this low price."
- "Our annual storewide sale ends this evening."
- "As soon as these are gone, there will be an increase in price."[2]

SEVENTEEN CLOSING STRATEGIES

Thus far in this chapter we have dealt broadly with the subject of closing the sale. The emphasis has been on principles, philosophy, and fundamentals. Now we will describe practical devices and techniques for applying those broad fundamentals, as used by today's most successful salespeople. Each sales situation is unique and calls for a matching closing technique. Your objective is to become knowledgeable at choosing the right closing method for a particular selling situation and at employing it skillfully. We present seventeen of these closing techniques. Some of them may seem to overlap with others, but they are indeed different. You will see this clearly when you are engaged in actual closing efforts in the field.

Selling is a highly mobile and evolving profession. While we are listing seventeen closing strategies below, a salesperson in Albuquerque probably has developed an eighteenth and is polishing it in practice.

Closing on an Objection

If the objection offered by a prospect is the reason for not buying, it would seem to follow that removing that objection would result in a closing. This is closing on the objection.

> "I like the storm coat," the prospect tells the salesperson. "But I'm afraid it won't be warm enough. The material is synthetic."
>
> "It certainly is synthetic," replies the salesperson, "one hundred percent Orlon acrylic pile. It will keep you warmer than animal fibers because it holds air space static. Same way you insulate a house. Just like a Thermopane window."
>
> "I'll take it."

This strategy also has been called *closing on the final objection* to emphasize that it is most applicable for an objection of critical importance. Here is how it is used by a prepared salad representative calling on the proprietor of a fine restaurant.

> BUYER: We make our shrimp and chicken salads from scratch. We couldn't get away with commercial quality like a supermarket.

---

[2]Robert F. Spohn and Robert Y. Allen, *Retailing,* Reston Publishing Company, Reston, Va., 1977, p. 248.

REPRESENTATIVE: I know your reputation, Mrs. Crandon, and understand your policy. What you are saying is that you can't give your customers anything less than top quality. Is that right?

BUYER: That's it.

REPRESENTATIVE: Less mayonnaise and a chunkier look?

BUYER: You've got the idea.

REPRESENTATIVE: In other words, if you could get that quality in a prepared salad, would you consider it?

BUYER: Yes, there are advantages to buying it prepared. But we understand each other on why I can't use it here.

REPRESENTATIVE: Mrs. Crandon, are you familiar with the Oak Tavern?

BUYER: A fine restaurant. They make things from scratch like us.

REPRESENTATIVE: Here is a sample of our shrimp salad. The Oak has been buying it for over a year.

BUYER: The Oak? Let's see your samples.

The Assumptive Close

The assumptive close assumes the prospect is going to buy. The word *will* is used in preference to *would, when* to *if.* The seller's posture is one of confidence, yet it is modest. It assumes the buying decision has been made and it is just a question of variety selection, credit establishment, and wrap-up details. An excellent model for the salesperson using the assumptive technique in closing is George Gershwin when he was an aspiring young composer. A friend said of him, "He was self-assured but not overbearing. He went about Tin Pan Alley with a quiet confidence in the importance of what he was doing." Let your confidence show through quietly—without seeming to usurp the buyer's authority over the buying decision. When you employ the assumptive close, try not to look like the cat who has just eaten a bird.

Let's examine an assumptive close as used in an interview between a real estate agent and a house prospect.

REPRESENTATIVE: Perhaps we can help you crystallize your thinking, Mrs. Sherman. You seem to like the house on Huckleberry Lane. What do you especially like about it?

BUYER: Oh, the grounds and the trees—and the staggered room between the first and second levels would be good so we could hear our baby from the living room.

REPRESENTATIVE: That's a perceptive analysis. Now how about the house on Peachtree Drive? What do you like about that?

BUYER: That *beautiful* kitchen and dining alcove!

REPRESENTATIVE: That's interesting, Mrs. Sherman. It seems you have to decide which means more to you, spacious grounds and a staggered floor or a beautiful kitchen and dining alcove.

BUYER: That puts it rather neatly, doesn't it? Of course, we can ultimately modernize the kitchen on Huckleberry Lane and include a breakfast bar. But we could never duplicate the grounds.

REPRESENTATIVE (*smiling*): I think that way down deep you're voting for Huckleberry Lane. Perhaps you should place a deposit in case someone else gets the same idea before Mr. Sherman has a chance to see it.

Here are some more examples of assumptive closing lines:

- "When can we get your logo for the package design?"
- "Do we bill Charter Corporation or the Carrington Division?"
- "Our truck passes here Thursday. Shall we put your order aboard?"

There are some reorderable product classifications of selling where both seller and buyer assume the close. A food broker checks a distributor's inventory and makes out the order before talking to the distributor. A factory representative for a hosiery manufacturer uses a fill-in form to list sizes and shades that are low in inventory on the selling floor. The representative shows this to the buyer at the start of the sales call.

With the increased use of computer processing for ordering and inventory control, many food-service distributors provide their salespeople with a computer-related order form.[3] The salesperson checks the customer's inventory and fills in the recommended quantities of each item to be reordered. The numbers of the items are codes in the computer programming system. After the buyer approves the order, the salesperson uses his or her assigned computer-code designation and the code for the account in phoning in the order. Each salesperson has a set time to phone, and the line is clear at that time. The reason for phoning is to allow the sales call to be made on the last day before delivery in the interest of sharper inventory control. Buyers appreciate this as a service "plus."

There are many variations of the assumptive close. Three of them are the *physical action close*, the *binder close*, and the *order blank close*.

The Physical Action Close   An office furniture salesperson is presenting a metal filing cabinet to a prospect. The seller pulls out a file drawer and slams it shut with a bang.

"See," says the salesperson to the buyer, "this file can take anything!" This is the physical action variation of the assumptive close.

If the prospect seems at all disturbed by the abuse of the cabinet, it means that at the subconscious level this buyer already considers it to be his or her property. The sale may be assumed to be closed except for the wrap-up details. "How soon will you want this file cabinet?" the seller asks confidently.

Sometimes what you do is more effective than what you say. It also is safer, because it avoids an overt commitment to confrontation and possible rejection.

When the menswear seller picks up the jacket and calls for the alterations tailor, this salesperson is implying the assumption that the sale is closed—without saying so. If this is not the case, it is not too difficult to backtrack and show other garments.

---

[3]Food service distributors are suppliers to restaurants, hospitals, schools, airlines, caterers, institutions, and other quantity buyers.

EXHIBIT 13.7
THE ASSUMPTIVE CLOSE

The Binder Close   "I'll phone the office if I may use your phone," says the accident insurance representative, "and you'll be covered right now. Then you'll receive a confirming binder. That's as good as the policy certificate you'll receive later."

You may be sure that when this insurance prospect consents to let the insurance representative use the phone to "bind" the insurance coverage, the sale has been closed. Of course, there is an outside chance that the buyer will not honor the invoice when it comes in and the sale will be lost. But this is not common.

The Order Blank Close   This is still another variation of the assumptive close. The salesperson, while talking or listening to the prospect, casually places an order blank on the desk or table. "How do you spell your name, Mr. Androselli?" asks the seller. (Caution: For goodness sake, don't do this if the buyer's name is Jones—an inquiry about street address will do as well.)

If the buyer answers without seeming to object to the presence of the order form, this obviously is an indication of intent to buy. The salesperson continues, filling in the name and address of the buyer and the details of the model selected, and finally hands the form to the prospect for signature.

If the prospect showed any displeasure over the introduction of the order form, the salesperson would have recognized this as a sign that the prospect was not "ready." In that case, the salesperson might have swung into another closing strategy such as the honest inquiry technique.

The Honest Inquiry Close

"I assumed you had made up your mind, Mr. Androselli," says the salesperson to the buyer who showed annoyance at the sight of the order blank. "Apparently I was mistaken. May I ask what your reservations are?"

This is the *honest inquiry close*. It is characterized by forthrightness and candor, inviting a similar attitude on the part of the prospect. The implication is "I thought you were ready to buy—but you're not. Well, what is the obstacle? Either I'll be able to answer it to your satisfaction or I'll make my exit."

A direct question is very apt to bring to light some unsuspected obstacle to the closing. You can get to the town hall by walking two blocks left, three blocks right, and taking the fourth right; or you can get there by walking straight through this park. Asking the prospect directly is not a bad idea. Moreover, it is surprising and sometimes refreshing to a buyer to receive a frank question as to what stands in the way of the decision to buy.

Closing on a Minor Point

The truly professional seller tries to avoid placing a mountain before the buyer approaching the buying decision. A molehill is much easier to cross.

That is the essence of the so-called minor-point closing technique. Let the bolt sell the battleship. The smallest decision is the shortest distance to the closing. *Minimize the decision* which the buyer must make. Close on a minor point. The order will be just as large as if you had gotten it through a major decision on the part of the prospect. The minor-point closing is also helpful when it is necessary to save the buyer's face. Perhaps you led the prospect to the ready point with some difficulty, having had to help this buyer overcome many objections along the way. Now the prospect is convinced, ready to buy. But, to some prospects, this is embarrassing. It is an about face, an admission of defeat. The stronger the objections that had to be overcome, the more the prospect is apt to shy away from acknowledging a change in thinking.

So you submit a molehill for decision, steering clear of the mountain. You give the prospect a chance to *close on a detail* to save yourself and the prospect the possible complication of confrontation with an ego or an ego ideal.

Here are some examples of minor-point closings, expressed as questions to ease any conflict with the prospect's psyche.

- "How much do you think you can sell a month?"
- "Will you keep it in the living room or the sun porch?"
- "Do you want the large model or the smaller one?"
- "You can either lease or buy this machine. Which is best for you?"

Closing on a Note of Silence

Do you remember how Joseph Day sold the Empire Building to Elbert Gary with two questions and five minutes of silence? The silence was just as important to the closing as the two questions. The questions stimulated Gary's thinking. The silence gave him time to think. The decision to buy the Empire Building against the wishes of Gary's junior officers had to be made in the mind of the prospect, not in Day's mind. To have broken that silence would have interfered with Gary's thinking and deciding.

Sometimes it pays to ask a question or to make a point and then just sit. Used at the right time, silence can be more effective than anything you might say.

A pause gives a point a chance to sink in. The apex of dramatic presentation is knowing what to leave out. This often is more penetrating than what you include.

The SRO Method

Standing room only, or SRO, is the sign of a hit play on Broadway. It also has a place in closing psychology.

The apple at the top of the tree is the juiciest. Forbidden fruit is sweetest. These old saws express the human preference for what is least attainable.

When a prospect is "sold," but having difficulty in *buying,* the SRO technique can help.

- "It's the last one on the floor."
- "This is one of the last two lots in the development. It's only fair to tell you that I have dates with other people to show them today and tomorrow."
- "We're going to give this franchise to only one person in each market. Someone is going to make a lot of money with it. If you want it, I suggest you act before someone else does."

When you use the SRO technique, be sure it really is an SRO situation. There must be a legitimate scarcity to support your premise. Misrepresentation is a shortsighted selling policy, avoided by self-respecting salespeople for selfish as well as ethical reasons.

The Try It Out Close

"Leave one of your ties and let us clean it with our compliments. See for yourself."

Thus does the cleaner with the new special tie-cleaning process set the stage for obtaining the prospect's regular cleaning business. But the try out does not have to be free.

- "Take in a *trial* shipment of our handbags. If they don't sell, we'll take them back for full credit."
- "We'll *lend* you one of our Zetex electric writing machines. Let your secretary use it for a month. Then, we'll either take it back or bill you, whichever you tell us to do."
- "Here's what we'll do," says the packaging machinery salesperson to the food processor. "You don't know whether a portion pack will sell? Let's find out. We'll deliver and install the machine on memo billing. We'll sell you a limited quantity of portion cups. Offer them to your customers. In ninety days we'll both know what happened. At that time we'll either send the invoice or lease contract or take back the machine."

There are some negative considerations in connection with trial orders, particularly merchandise for resale. One cannot be sure that trial merchandise will get a fair trial. After all, a trial order is tantamount to a consignment shipment. What the reseller pays for and owns is going to be merchandised. What can be returned for full credit may be neglected and fail to sell even though it is highly salable. The caution for the salesperson selling a returnable trial shipment is first to make sure there is enough stock in the shipment to avoid its getting lost. Next, there should be a definite understanding between buyer and seller that the buyer will give the item normal merchandising support. Finally, the salesperson should follow up and know that the buyer is indeed giving the goods a fair trial.

The Proof-by-Example Close

One way to close is to show the prospect the case of another buyer in similar circumstances who derived satisfaction from your product or service.

> "The Imperial Hardware Store took our line on a year ago," the drill and bit salesperson tells the hardware retailer. "They're in a market like yours, and they've shown a remarkable increase in sales since putting in Brandco. I'd be pleased if you'd call Mr. Hansen and confirm what I say. Here's his phone number. We can call him right now."

The Instruction Close

Ask the prospect if he or she would like to know how to use the article—then start giving the instructions. For example, "Let me show you how to put the cartridge in and start the machine." If the prospect says "Okay," get out your order book.

The "How Would You Like?" Close

This closing technique is designed to project the prospect mentally and emotionally into imagined enjoyment of what your product or service promises. The idea is to give the buyer an imaginary taste of the benefits of the purchase you are endeavoring to close. Here are some examples.

- "How would you like to be out of this cold, lying on a tropical beach?"
- "Can you see the looks on the faces of your friends when you show up in this luxurious mink?"
- "How would you like to be your own boss, to come and go as you please, and to be able to tell others what to do?"
- "Can't you just see yourself as the department manager? This course will help you get there."

Asking for the Order Directly

All courses on selling stress asking for the order. Some advise asking for the order at the very beginning of the call and continuing to ask for the order throughout the interview. Others are less extreme in this recommendation. Still a third group of authorities believes you should not ask for the order until you have earned it. This last school believes that, if the approach, presentation, and handling of objections have been properly carried out, the prospect will almost do the closing for you.

EXHIBIT 13.8
MORE SALES ARE LOST BY FAILING TO ASK FOR THE ORDER THAN BY ASKING FOR IT

How persistently and aggressively to ask for the order depends on what, where, and how you are selling. In one-call selling, for example, the aggressive approach often applies. In contrast, it would indeed be ill-advised to open a meeting to present a building construction service to a board of directors by asking for an order for a building. Between these two contrasting situations are the less extreme cases. Here, although you insert preclose test questions to make sure the closing time does not slip by, the direct request for the order is not made until you are reasonably convinced that the prospect is sold. However, it should be noted that more sales are lost by failing to ask for the order than by asking for it.

Not to ask for the order at the high point of the prospect's interest is to risk losing it altogether. Interest can cool, or something may occur to change the buyer's mind.

The Alternative Decisions Close

This closing style became famous as a ''Wheelerpoint,'' the selling strategy of the author of the selling classic *Sizzlemanship*.[4]

[4]Elmer Wheeler, *Sizzlemanship*, Prentice-Hall, Englewood Cliffs, N.J., 1946.

"Don't ask if—ask which." The strategy is to lift the prospect over the hurdle of whether or not to buy. The alternative options posed to the prospect can be major or minor. Here are some examples.

- "One egg or two in your malted?"
- "Do you prefer the blue or the yellow?"
- "Will you start redecoration in the living room or the bedrooms?"
- "Will you handle the financing yourself or do you want us to handle it for you?"
- "Do you prefer to buy or lease?"

The Service Close

The service close is another variation of the assumptive close. The salesperson acts as though the buyer has made a favorable decision regarding the purchase.

- "Here," says the by-the-day lessor of automobiles, "let me call someone to dust off this car before you take it out."(*The prospect normally will not let such a service be rendered if the decision to rent the car has not been made.*)
- Says the kennel owner to the dog prospect, "I'll give you a couple of pounds of the dog food he's used to, so you'll be covered till you have a chance to get some on your own."
- "Let's try on the other shoe. Walk around a bit to make sure they're exactly what you will be comfortable in."
- "Let me adjust that belt to your size. It may need another hole."

The Toy Soldier Technique

Under this strategy, you obtain the prospect's agreement that if a special feature can be added, the sale will be closed. It is like a game of toy soldiers. You set them up and knock them down. Some examples are:

- "If I can get you those terms, do we have a deal?"
- "If I can get you a written guarantee of exclusivity, will you take on the line?"
- "If I can get my company to go along with the indemnification guarantee you want, can I ship you the machine?"
- "I'm going to write the order with the price schedule exactly as you want it. Let's see if I can get the office to accept it."

The Credit Clearance Close

The necessity for clearing credit, one of the realities of modern business, also provides an opportunity to close a sale.

A representative for a house with a leading line of blank books for the office and stationery trade has presented the company's line to an office supply dealer. The salesperson believes the prospect is ready for the closing. Here is how the closing was accomplished.

"Mr. Mergeson, I'd like to set up a line of credit for you. Here's the credit application form. With your help I'll fill it out." After the credit form was completed, the seller asked, "Do you want to send in a trial order with this credit application?"

328

The Pro-Con Close

This is sometimes called the balance sheet closing. On a sheet of paper or verbally, depending on the circumstances, you review the merits and also the demerits of the product or service offered, being careful to express each point in terms of the prospect's interests. Point by point, you list each plus and minus. The inclusion of negatives as well as positives, insofar as this prospect's particular interests are concerned, conveys a note of honesty and credibility.

The spirit of this type of close is to appear to be making the list to help the prospect come to a valid decision. It is apt to be especially pertinent in technical, systems, and industrial selling. If the case is one-sided in favor of your product or service, little has to be said at the conclusion. If, on the other hand, the case happens to involve comparison with a competitive offering and is not one-sided, you make a summary comparison, such as the following.

> "Well, Mrs. Cartwright, that's the way it seems to stack up. On parts delivery service, there is little to choose between Glaco and us. On price, you can save a few cents with them. On the other hand, the length-of-life record of our machine is so superior that it will more than make up for the small initial cost difference. Power costs are comparable. From this comparison, Mrs. Cartwright, I would suggest to you that the big thing in our favor is our engineering service department. We're only about fifty miles from here and our engineers are on the ready to help you with any problem from machine location and general plant layout to creative ideas that can help you increase your production per worker-hour and per machine-hour."

The Spotlight Close

During your presentation the prospect seemed particularly impressed with one feature of your product, service, or proposition. It could have been, for example, a design feature, ease of operator training, parts replacement, or service. Your product, service, or proposition also might have one feature with a hands-down advantage over competition or one that is singularly applicable to the interest of the prospect.

EXHIBIT 13.9
CONCENTRATE
ON WHAT
COUNTS

In your close, put the spotlight on this feature. Use it as a key to closing, as covered earlier in this chapter. For example, listen to how a retail menswear salesperson closes on a sport jacket sale.

SALESPERSON: You seem to favor this one for the material, don't you?
BUYER: Yes. I like its rugged look and feel.
SALESPERSON: Well, that happens to be a Donegal tweed from Ireland. You can wear it in rain or shine, and it will outlive you and me. Looks good on you, too. Shall I call the tailor?

Here are some other spotlight closings:

- "You're right. The Tri-Wal is stronger. For protecting your appliances from vertical stress, there isn't another corrugated that can match it. Would you like me to have our engineering department test your actual products in this casing under actual shipping conditions?''

• ''Our minimum deposit policy seems to fit your present requirement like a glove. Maximum protection for minimum outlay. If I may use your phone, I can make a date to have your medical taken care of right here in your office''

THE WRAP-UP: BUSINESS DETAILS IN CLOSING

Beyond study of the principles and methods of closing, you should give consideration to a few peripheral aspects of the closing.

Contracts—Boon or Bogey

There are some selling categories in which contracts are customarily verbal. For example, a food processor orders a carload of an ingredient by telephone. The order is shipped without question, as long as the buyer's credit standing is known and acceptable. In some cases the order is confirmed by a written purchase order; in other cases there is no confirmation. Strangers to this field are amazed. ''What if the buyer refuses to accept the shipment or to pay for it or to honor the price agreed upon during the phone conversation?'' they ask. The answer is that when speed is essential—and in many instances it is not even a question of speed, just habit and custom—the parties to the transaction take each other's word. To break this word would end the buyer's ability to buy in this way in the future. Verbal agreements of this type have been a custom for almost 200 years in the United States.

By contrast, there are industries where contracts full of fine-print clauses are necessary. When the closing on the sale of a major New York office building took place, seventy-five lawyers were stationed at various points and coordinated by a complex system of electronic communication in order to complete the transaction.

In between the fields where written contracts are critical and the fields where contracts are verbal, there is a vast area where written contracts are employed and usually signed without benefit of legal counsel. They are not taken seriously by either buyer or seller—*until something goes wrong* on either side. Then a written contract takes on significance.

Few people read the fine print in their insurance certificates or the bill of sale for the car, the vacuum cleaner, and the many other products and services they buy.

If you sell in a field where written contracts are involved, make sure your customer understands the terms. Go over the critical clauses and explain them. The buyer who knows exactly what to expect from the seller and what the seller expects from the buyer is less likely to be a problem later. This often-neglected phase of the closing, explaining the contract to the buyer, is an indication of responsibility and a spirit of service. Most customers appreciate it.

A long, tortuous contract can be awesome and sometimes even frightening to the buyer. Your explanation simplifies it and eases the buyer's apprehensions. Be sure to emphasize, with illustrations, that the contract protects buyer as well as seller.

Get It in Writing

Unless the custom of the industry in which you sell is contrary, always get the prospect to give you a signed order or to sign your order form. In closing by telephone with buyers who have formal ordering procedures, the common practice is to get an order number. This means that your order is entered in the serially numbered purchase order register.

When you ask the buyer to sign your order form, it is a good idea to have an order pad with plenty of used carbon copies. This is a subtle communication to the buyer that others have been buying too.

Payment with an Order

There are selling classifications in which credit is normally extended, but in which the first order from a buyer must be accompanied by a payment (until credit and a credit line for the account have been established).

How do you ask for money?

The first thing to remember if you must ask for payment with the order is not to be sensitive or timid about it. Buyers know that sellers have to follow protective credit practices. If they are in business, they do so themselves. No good credit risk is offended by a request for payment. If the buyer is offended, beware. This is one classic sign of the deadbeat. Moreover, if you have to ask for payment, you may be sure that this is not a novel experience for this buyer.

However, there are many ways to request payment. It is just as important for you to know the right and wrong way to request payment as the right and wrong way to ask for an order. One down-to-earth entrepreneur says, "It's not a sale till there's an order and an order is no good till it's paid for." Here are some examples of how you can ask for payment graciously and effectively.

• "In order to set up a credit line for you, Ms. Sands, I'll need some information to send in to the plant. In the meantime, to avoid delay, would you like to give me a check to send in with the order?"

• "If you'll give me your check for nine hundred dollars, I'll send it right in with this order." (*This is said while the salesperson is writing the order.*)

• Or, quite directly, as you begin writing the order, you say to the prospect whose credit rating you are not sure of, "This comes to nine hundred fifty dollars. Please make your check out to Brothers Manufacturing Co., Inc., and I'll send it in with your order. If you want to set up a credit line for your future convenience, I'll be glad to fill out a form for our credit department right now."

Thanks and Goodbye

Once the closing is completed, be on your way without delay. Don't wait around for the buyer to have second thoughts.

RECAP

The hottest prospect is still only a prospect until a sale is closed. Mastery of closing is critical to a successful selling career. This chapter reviewed the many ways in which prospects are converted into buyers. It emphasized the ideal of a selling attitude that focuses on closing as the goal and the yardstick for measuring selling accomplishment. It suggested that the activation of buying by effective closing serves the interests of buyer and seller alike.

Selling today is even more conscious of the importance of closing than was selling in the past, and it tends to be even more scientific in going about it. More thought is given to why and how the buyer buys and how to work with the prospect's motivation and habit. In closing, as in every other aspect of selling, today's selling discipline underscores service, understanding the buyer's needs, wants, and special problems and answering them for long-range mutual benefit rather than for short-range sales accomplishments. The long-range sales accomplishments and the accompanying rewards come from this service approach.

REVIEW QUESTIONS

1. What are some buying signals to watch for to know when to start closing?
2. What is the "what if" psychology in closing?
3. What are the building blocks for the close? How can you use them to help your closing?
4. What are the three keys to closing? Explain.
5. What is meant by closing on the final objection?
6. What is the assumptive close?
7. What is the minor-point close?
8. Explain the honest inquiry technique.
9. Describe two ways to get payment with the initial order on closing.

DISCUSSION QUESTIONS

1. Reread the example "John Misses . . . Mary Hits" in the beginning of this chapter. In it we wrote, "When you have finished this chapter, you will know why John missed and Mary hit." Now give your opinion as to why John missed and Mary hit in closing a car sale.
2. Give your views on timing of the close.
3. Discuss the various factors involved in whether to try to close on the first call or not.

4. Discuss the question of aggressive versus soft closing. Which would you prefer to use? When might the other be more appropriate?

5. Which is more important in closing appeals, emotion or reason? Explain your opinion fully.

6. As a representative of Apex Air-Conditioning Service, which offers a year-round on-call service to business establishments, you have called three times on the Hanes & Kline shoe store. They have a centrally controlled air-conditioning system and no service contract. Mr. Hanes seems favorably inclined toward Apex, but in each of the previous calls, when you thought you had it wrapped up, he found a reason to put you off. He is always courteous and you know he will greet you cordially when you arrive tomorrow, but it is already April and the close is long overdue. How will you avoid Hanes' delaying tactics when you call tomorrow?

7. The sales profession is thought by some people to be high pressure—especially in its closing methods. Give your views on this criticism. As a salesperson, how can you avoid this negative image?

8. Of the different schools of thought on when and how persistently to ask for the order, which do you favor? Explain.

9. Give your views on contracts in sales transactions. Are they advisable? If so, how formally should they be applied? Discuss the effect of contract practices in buyer relations.

LEARNING EXPERIENCES

Role playing: The scene is at the ski equipment and clothing section of Hall's Sporting Goods Store. The characters are to be played by members of the group and include Aaron Strait, a middle-aged, athletic type; Janet Strait, Aaron's daughter, à student at Fairmont College, home for the Christmas recess; and Hank Gilman, a salesperson. The situation is this: Janet has been invited to the Dartmouth Winter Carnival and has never been on skis; the visit to the store is being made to acquire ski equipment for her. The scene begins when Hank tries to close the sale, with each character using imagination to supply facts essential to the story and not stated above. After completing the exercise, answer the following questions:

1. Let Aaron and Janet, separately, give their reaction to Hank's closing, explaining why they bought or did not buy.

2. Let Hank explain to the group the principles followed and the strategy employed in the closing.

3. Let three other members of the group take the same three parts, repeat the action, and answer Learning Experiences 1 and 2.

4. Let the entire group, in open discussion, give views on the closings of each of the two Hanks, noting differences between them, expressing preferences, and commenting generally.

CASE

SUNNYDALE TRAVEL COUNSELORS

Charles Danforth is in top spirits. His wife, Mary, has a three-week vacation coming in March and, unknown to her, Charles has arranged to vacation at the same time. He plans to surprise her by booking reservations for a cruise to the Bahamas. That is why he is in the office of Marlene Kroll at Sunnydale Travel Counselors. The only problem is that cruise prices have risen substantially since Danforth last looked into it seven years ago, and he is forced to wonder whether he should go ahead with the planned surprise at all.

"And you dock back in New York on the seventeenth," Kroll said as she finished her presentation of an itinerary—"tanned and relaxed," she added with a smile.

"The tan is what gives me pause," replied Danforth seriously. "Have you read about sun causing skin cancer?"

"Not recommended reading for travel agents," said Kroll good humoredly.

"That's one reason I'm not sure about a cruise. What's a cruise if you don't bask in the tropical sun?" As Danforth said this, Kroll thought his laugh was a bit forced.

"Would you like another suggestion?" she asked.

"Why not?"

"I heard you say you were an enthusiastic golfer. Is that right?"

"Yes, not very good, but enthusiastic—yes."

"Does Mrs. Danforth play?"

"Yes, she plays, but she's not as enthusiastic as I am."

"Well, I only mention it because at that time of the year I can get you some beautiful golf vacation packages—Pinehurst, Doral, even Bermuda—at very attractive prices. And, although it's a golf vacation package, golf is only one part of the package. The price tag, of course, is much less than the cruise."

"Oh, I don't mind the price," protested Danforth. "I just began to wonder whether a cruise was the right thing for us."

"Naturally, Mr. Danforth. Another possibility is Las Vegas. Would that interest you?"

"Never thought of it, to tell you the truth."

"Well, what I'm trying to do is to think of something that would appeal to you and Mrs. Danforth. You said you want to surprise her. Is that right?"

"Exactly."

"Well, I've named three possibilities: a Carribean cruise, a golf package in the Carolinas, Puerto Rico, or Bermuda, and Las Vegas. Which do you think would be the most exciting surprise for her?"

"That's easy. The cruise would win in a walk."

"Then I hope I'm not overstepping the bounds of good taste in asking, Mr. Danforth, but is it only the sun that's holding you up? If it's something else, maybe I can help."

"Quite frankly, Miss Kroll, I had no idea a cruise would cost that much. With inflation on everything these days, I wonder if I hadn't better skip the vacation idea."

Kroll smiled understandingly. "You're so right. We're all feeling the pinch. However, would you be interested in a booking on just as luxurious a cruise to the Bahamas if I could get you and Mrs. Danforth aboard for about two-thirds of the price I quoted you?"

Danforth brightened. "How?"

"By making it a ten-day cruise on the Rotterdam instead of two weeks on the other boat. Everything else is comparable," answered Kroll, as she dropped a booking pad on her desk.

Questions

1. Did Kroll close the cruise sale?
2. Explain Kroll's strategy in closing. What principles covered in this chapter did she follow?
3. To Kroll, what was the significance of Danforth's apprehension of the sun?
4. Why do you think Kroll suggested other vacation possibilities to Danforth?
5. Kroll employed more than one closing technique. Name and explain as many as you can. Which do you think was most effective?

FOURTEEN

CHAPTER OBJECTIVES

To examine the characteristics and opportunities in selling to the consumer

To acquaint you with the relative size of the real estate, insurance, and retailing industries

To examine unique characteristics of these industries

To review the usual qualifications, selling process, and special challenges for real estate

To familiarize you with the usual qualifications, selling process, and special challenges for insurance

To familiarize you with the selling process and opportunities in retailing

CHAPTER OUTLINE

336

SELLING TO CONSUMERS: REAL ESTATE, INSURANCE, AND RETAIL

> Good selling means a house becomes "my home"; insurance becomes "peace of mind"; perfume becomes "a road to romance."
>
> Anonymous

There's a lot of money in consumer selling. If you think about it, each day each of us is involved in some type of consumer sales. Whether it's food or fads, stereos or sundries, carriages or credit cards, skis or shoes, houses or horseradish, we buy or we sell.

There are many job opportunities and much money to be made in consumer selling. Real estate, insurance, and retailing are considered in this chapter because of the sales volume of these industries, the large number of sales opportunities which currently exist and are projected for the next decade, and the uniqueness of selling within each of these industries. The general principles of selling which we have discussed in the preceding chapters apply, as is evident from the many examples we have used from each industry. However, there are unique characteristics of each which often result in special selling situations.

OPPORTUNITIES ABOUND

The real estate, insurance, and retailing industries are large and are expected to continue to increase during the next decade. All three industries employ a substantial number of salespeople. The National Association of Realtors estimates that the real estate industry currently employs 555,000 active salespeople, and this number is expected to increase.

The National Association of Real Estate License Law Offices estimates that more than 2 million people were licensed in 1978. Even though the high interest rates in the early 1980s slowed down home sales, the prospects for future employment are excellent and are expected to rise faster than the average for all occupations in the 1980s.

The favorable outlook for employment in this field is due to increased demand for housing, particularly condominiums and rental units. The high birthrates in the 1950s and the 1960s have caused a shift in the age distribution of the population, resulting in a large number of young adults with careers starting and family responsibilities. See Exhibit 14.1. Young adults are characteristically the most geographically mobile group in our society and the group that makes the bulk of housing purchases and rentals. As the income of this group increases, its members can be expected to move up to larger homes and properties.

The insurance industry currently employs more than 500,000 salespeople (called agents and brokers). About half of the agents and brokers specialize in life and health insurance, the others in some type of property-liability insurance. A growing number of agents, called *multiline agents,* offer both life and property-liability policies to their customers.

Retail sales account for over 50 percent of disposable personal income. Currently, there are approximately 3 million salespeople employed in retail businesses. They work in stores ranging from small drug or grocery stores employing perhaps one employee to the giant department store chains that employ thousands of salespeople. They also work for door-to-door sales organizations and for mail-order companies. The largest employers of retail salespeople are department stores and stores selling general merchandise, apparel and accessories, and food.

UNIQUE CHARACTERISTICS OF THESE INDUSTRIES

Each of these industries has characteristics that make it unique. This places special demands on the selling process and may result in some modifications of the selling process.

Real Estate

Real estate is unique in several ways. First, the salesperson has two major functions: to obtain listings for real property and then to sell these listings. In most selling situations, you are provided with the product, and your job is to sell it successfully. But as a real estate salesperson, you must obtain the product (the

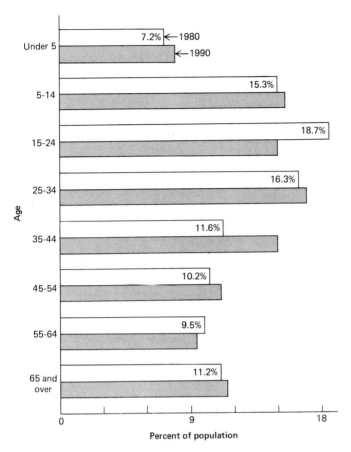

EXHIBIT 14.1
THE BABY BOOM COMES OF AGE: 25–44 YEARS OLD, POPULATION BY AGE GROUPS

listing) as well as sell it. The real estate salesperson's income is derived from commissions paid both for the listing and for the sale. For example, a typical commission from the sale of a property is 6 percent. (This percent prevails in most markets but is not fixed by law. It may vary.) If a house sells for $100,000, the commission is $6000. The salesperson who obtained the listing for the house, that is, got the owner to list it for sale—will get a listing fee. The percentage allocated as the listing fee varies from firm to firm but usually ranges from 10 to 20 percent of the commission. In the above example, let's assume it is 15 percent. Multiply 15 times the $6000 (the total commission dollars available) and you have a $900 listing fee.

A second major difference in real estate sales is that you must take the prospect to the product (the land, the house or condominium, the commercial property, etc.). This requires considerably more time than the usual consumer selling situation in which you can assemble the entire product line in one location and then present it to the prospect.

EXHIBIT 14.2
ONE OF THE MOST IMPORTANT STEPS IN THE REAL ESTATE SALES PROCESS IS
PRESENTING THE PROPERTY   (*Source:* Electronic Realty Associates, Inc.)

A third major difference (which is related to the previous difference) is the
relatively large amount of time involved in the presentation. This, of course,
results from the physical distance usually involved between properties, as well as
the complexity and time needed to show each property.

A final difference centers around the magnitude of the decision that you must
guide the prospect into making. Purchasing real property is normally the most
costly decision the prospect has made or will ever make. You must have knowledge of property values, knowledge of real estate finance, and skill in building
feelings of trust and confidence.

Insurance

Insurance is unique in several ways. One of its unique challenges is that the
product is intangible. Essentially, as an insurance salesperson you are asking the
prospect to purchase a *promise* that at some future time the company will pay a
benefit if certain conditions exist. Selling a promise involves an enormous amount
of trust and confidence. By and large, these are characteristics that must be very
clearly evident in the salesperson, who is the main tangible the prospect can deal
with.

EXHIBIT 14.3
MANY AGENTS HANDLE SEVERAL LINES OF INSURANCE AND FINANCIAL
SERVICES   (*Source:* Bob Combs/Photo Researchers.)

A second characteristic of insurance is that the product is highly complex and diversified. There is the difference between the stock company and the mutual company which you must understand so that you can communicate it to the prospect.[1] There are a highly divergent number of product lines from individual life policies, of which there are many variations, to homeowners' and apartment dwellers' policies, to group policies and commercial lines.

A third characteristic of insurance sales is the emotional nature of the product. Most people would rather not think about death, accidents and illnesses, fires, and thefts. It's something we'd rather put off for another day. But you must skillfully and tactfully raise the prospect's consciousness about the risks facing him or her if a sale is going to be successfully closed.

Retail Selling

Retail selling is distinctive in several ways. In retail selling, the prospect usually comes to you. This is particularly true if the retail establishment advertises well. The fact that the prospect comes to you allows you to make a positive assumption of interest or readiness to buy. Obviously, this isn't always the case, but a good number of times it is a valid assumption.

---

[1]Stock companies are owned by the public (stockholders), mutual companies by the policyholders.

EXHIBIT 14.4
THE FACT THAT THE PROSPECT COMES TO THE SALESPERSON ALLOWS YOU TO
MAKE A POSITIVE ASSUMPTION OF INTEREST AND READINESS TO BUY

Another characteristic of retail selling, at least in-store selling, is that prospects select themselves; that is, as a retail salesperson you do not select or prescreen. This may necessitate a more general initial approach to customers until their ability to purchase becomes clearer.

SELLING REAL ESTATE

Housing, whether a single-family dwelling, a condominium, or an apartment, is the single most expensive item in most people's budgets. Therefore, these people usually willfully seek the help and advice of a competent real estate agent or broker when trying to meet their housing needs.[2] This is because professional real estate salespersons have a thorough knowledge of the housing market in their community. They know which neighborhoods will best fit their prospects' life-

[2]*Agent* and *broker* are terms used to define real estate salespeople. An agent must be licensed and affiliated with a broker. A broker, who also must be licensed, can work independently.

styles and budgets. They know local zoning laws, tax laws related to real estate, and where to obtain financing.

The major activities of a real estate salesperson are as follows.

1. To obtain properties to sell or rent (listings)
2. To develop lists of people interested in buying or renting property
3. To serve as a mediator in price negotiations between buyer and seller
4. To sell the specific properties which best meet the needs of the prospects

To successfully sell real estate, you need to be able to price property accurately, to be imaginative in the sales and advertising methods employed (in most firms, the salesperson writes the ads for his or her own listings), and to be particularly capable in dealing with the wide range of sellers and prospective buyers because of the length of time involved in this sales process.

Product knowledge is critical to your continued success as a real estate salesperson. This is due in part to the quasi-legal nature of the salesperson's relationships with both the owner-seller and prospect and in part to the fact that both parties to the sale use the real estate agent as a personal consultant. You should have a keen knowledge of the region, town, and neighborhood you serve; the taxes; the school system; the municipal services; and the effect of location on property values. To sell a home, you must know it extremely well: the architecture, the structural characteristics, its strengths and weaknesses, the annual heating expense, and other costs.

Real Estate Licensing

Real estate agents and brokers must be licensed in every state and in the District of Columbia, which require prospective agents to be high school graduates, to be at least eighteen years old, and to pass a written examination. Most states require prerequisite course work which is usually available at local colleges. For the general sales agent's license, a minimum of thirty hours' classroom instruction is usually required. For the more difficult broker's license, a minimum of ninety hours' instruction, as well as a specified period of time as a sales agent (generally one to three years), is usually required. The trend across the country is to increase the requirements for prerequisite course work. Some states are considering college degrees as minimum requirements. In addition, as real estate transactions become more complex, many large firms are requiring a college degree for a sales position.

Personal traits are also important in selling real estate. Brokers look for applicants with such characteristics as good personality, honesty, maturity, and favorable appearance. Tact and enthusiasm for the job are also important to motivate the buyers in this highly competitive field. Also, agents do better if they possess a good memory for names and faces.

Many firms offer excellent training programs for new agents. In addition, many colleges and universities have developed a major in real estate, which would provide a good foundation for those interested in pursuing this field.

The Process

As we've already said, *prospecting* in real estate takes place on two fronts: obtaining listings and getting prospective buyers. Both lists of prospects, the properties and the buyers, can be developed by following most of the suggestions in Chapter 6. In addition, being actively and closely involved in the community and neighborhood is very important. Essentially, you want to know what is happening when it happens: who is thinking of moving, who is being transferred, who have just had another child (bigger house), who have had their last child move out (smaller house), etc. Maintaining an active liason with the personnel officers of local companies will also provide useful leads, both for potential listings and for potential buyers.

The presentation can successfully employ many of the techniques we've discussed in Chapters 9 and 10. But again, it is a special situation. In selling property, you usually first meet with the potential buyers to get a feel for the type of property the buyers would like and can afford. Then, you usually take the client or clients to a number of properties that appear to meet their needs and income. Because real estate is so expensive, you may meet with clients many times and, if there is interest, may have to present the property several times before the client is ready to close.

In answering questions and *handling objections,* you must present the property in terms of the client's needs. To a young family, you might emphasize the convenience of the floor plan, the convenience and reputation of the neighboring schools, etc. Often in real estate, houses within the pocketbook of the average buyer will have some shortcomings. It is important for you to skillfully point out that compromises usually have to be made, especially with first homes. In these cases, the trade-in value of the house should be emphasized. You should point out that with equity buildup, the client could move to a better house in several years.[3]

Because of the large dollar amount of real estate transactions, costs are often the basis of objections. An agent who is skilled in finance, in income tax laws, and in the positive effects of inflation on equity should be well-equipped to counter these types of objections with logic. For example, a typical objection is to the high interest rate for mortgages and the resultant high monthly payments. This objection can be met by explaining that the monthly payment is largely interest for only the first several years. (Exhibit 14.5 shows a typical amortization table for the first five years of a thirty-year mortgage with interest at 14 percent. Notice how much of the monthly payment is interest.) It should also be explained that the interest is an income tax deduction. Let's assume that the prospective buyer is in a 35 percent incremental tax bracket. This means two things. One is that the buyer's monthly payments are subsidized by 35 percent. This effectively reduces them in the first year from $592.44 to $279.00. This subsidy makes the effective interest rate not 14 percent but 10.1 percent. Sounds much more palatable, doesn't it?

The *close* in real estate transactions is also somewhat different. This is because in most cases the close is conditional upon the buyer's obtaining adequate

[3]*Equity* is roughly the difference between the outstanding mortgage and the market value of the property.

EXHIBIT 14.5
AMORTIZATION OF A $50,000 MORTGAGE

LOAN AMT	:	$50,000
INT RATE	:	14.00
LOAN YRS	:	30

* PYMNTS/YR	:	12
* PYMNTS 1ST YR	:	12
PYMNT AMT	:	$592.44

PAYMENT	PRINCIPAL	INTEREST	BALANCE	PAYMENT	PRINCIPAL	INTEREST	BALANCE
1	9.11	583.33	49,990.89	37	13.83	578.61	49,581.62
2	9.21	583.23	49,981.68	38	13.99	578.45	49,567.63
3	9.32	583.12	49,972.36	39	14.15	578.29	49,553.48
4	9.43	583.01	49,962.93	40	14.32	578.12	49,539.16
5	9.54	582.90	49,953.39	41	14.48	577.96	49,524.68
6	9.65	582.79	49,943.74	42	14.65	577.79	49,510.03
7	9.76	582.68	49,933.98	43	14.82	577.62	49,495.21
8	9.88	582.56	49,924.10	44	15.00	577.44	49,480.21
9	9.99	582.45	49,914.11	45	15.17	577.27	49,465.04
10	10.11	582.33	49,904.00	46	15.35	577.09	49,449.69
11	10.23	582.21	49,893.77	47	15.53	576.91	49,434.16
12	10.35	582.09	49,883.42	48	15.71	576.73	49,418.45
ANN TOT	116.58	6,992.70		ANN TOT	177.00	6,932.28	
13	10.47	581.97	49,872.95	49	15.89	576.55	49,402.56
14	10.59	581.85	49,862.36	50	16.08	576.36	49,386.48
15	10.71	581.73	49,851.65	51	16.26	576.18	49,370.22
16	10.84	581.60	49,840.81	52	16.45	575.99	49,353.77
17	10.96	581.48	49,829.85	53	16.65	575.79	49,337.12
18	11.09	581.35	49,818.76	54	16.84	575.60	49,320.28
19	11.22	581.22	49,807.54	55	17.04	575.40	49,303.24
20	11.35	581.09	49,796.19	56	17.24	575.20	49,286.00
21	11.48	580.96	49,784.71	57	17.44	575.00	49,268.56
22	11.62	580.82	49,773.09	58	17.64	574.80	49,250.92
23	11.75	580.69	49,761.34	59	17.85	574.59	49,233.07
24	11.89	580.55	49,749.45	60	18.05	574.39	49,215.02
ANN TOT	133.97	6,975.31		ANN TOT	203.43	6,905.85	
25	12.03	580.41	49,737.42				
26	12.17	580.27	49,725.25				
27	12.31	580.13	49,712.94				
28	12.46	579.98	49,700.48				
29	12.60	579.84	49,687.88				
30	12.75	579.69	49,675.13				
31	12.90	579.54	49,662.23				
32	13.05	579.39	49,649.18				
33	13.20	579.24	49,635.98				
34	13.35	579.09	49,622.63				
35	13.51	578.93	49,609.12				
36	13.67	578.77	49,595.45				
ANN TOT	154.00	6,955.28					

financing. In many cases there are other contingencies, such as an engineer's report, a termite inspector's report, and the like. These contingencies can actually make the closing process *easier,* because they remove some of the psychological fear of making one of life's largest commitments on the spot. If the buyer feels there is some escape clause, he or she will more readily sign. Of course, you should make certain that these clauses are comprehensive so that the buyer doesn't use them as an excuse to back out of the sale.

Special Challenges

Two special challenges in selling real estate are selling to the wary buyer in a tight market and, at the other end of the spectrum, selling luxury property to the high end of the market.

Selling in a Tight Market   Your prospect may be disheartened, convinced that there is no way he or she can afford a house. Or the prospect may be just plain cautious—determined to sit things out until the market improves, interest rates come down, prices fall, etc. Fortunately, there are creative ways to meet these challenges.

Build confidence   Your first task is to build confidence, and one way to do this is to provide clear, accurate answers to the prospect's questions. One company provides a home finance answer line. This is a phone service maintained to provide answers to the many questions about how to finance a home purchase. Although the service is designed to create goodwill and locate prospects, no selling is permitted over the phone. It is felt that selling at this point would erode confidence in the intentions of the company.

Another way to build confidence is to employ third-party endorsements. People are more likely to believe a neutral third party than a person who is trying to sell to them. Third-party endorsements can come from satisfied buyers in the form of letters or personal face-to-face testimony. Reprints of articles which suggest that now is a good time to buy, from sources such as the *Wall Street Journal* or *The Kiplinger Letter,* can be very effective.

A third way to build confidence is by educating the prospects. Several companies have successfully offered home-buying seminars which are free to the public.

Create a "buy now" attitude   Creating a "buy now" attitude can be done in several ways. Some realtors are in a position to guarantee that a home can be refinanced when interest rates drop.[4] This takes the objection out of high interest rates.

Another way to create a buy now mood is to make inflation your ally by focusing on the costs of inflation versus the costs of *not* buying. Exhibit 14.6 shows the cost of waiting to buy a $60,000 house for one year, given a 10 percent

[4]*Housing,* May 1980, p. 58.

EXHIBIT 14.6
COST OF WAITING TO PURCHASE A $60,000 HOME
(ASSUMING A 10 PERCENT RATE OF INFLATION)

	Today	Next year*	Next year†
Price of home	$60,000	$66,000	$66,000
Down payment	12,000	13,200	13,200
Balance to finance	$48,000	$52,800	$52,800
Interest rate	12%	11%	12%
Monthly payment (principal and interest)	493.77	502.87	543.13
Additional payments over life of mortgage	0	16,019	30,521
Additional down payment	0	1,200	1,200
Cost of waiting	None	$17,219	$31,721

Source: Adapted from *Housing*, August 1981, p. 43.
*If you wait and interest rates drop 1%.
†If you wait and interest does not drop.

rate of inflation. Note that the cost of waiting is $17,219 if interest rates *drop* a percentage point (from 12 to 11 percent). The cost is $31,721 over the life of the mortgage if rates do not drop.

Display finance facts If the finance facts are well-displayed in the form of diagrams, charts, and graphs, the prospect usually has a clearer understanding and becomes more confident. Some finance facts that will encourage buyers include a table showing effective aftertax interest rates, an inflation graph showing anticipated appreciation of a $70,000 home over the next ten years at various rates of inflation (see Exhibit 14.7), an explanation of renegotiable mortgages, and an explanation of shared-appreciation mortgages.

Prospect creatively Several successful real estate companies have put together packages that companies can hand out to relocated employees. They include information about points of interest, facts about financing, and descriptions of typical listings.

Another company maps neighborhoods and marks areas from which recent sellers have moved. This often uncovers prime areas to prospect for listings, such as a subdivision with assumable mortgages.

Selling to the Affluent Market Not to be overlooked is the high end of the market, the one that is least affected by interest rate fluctuations. Whether times are good or bad, there will always be a market for luxury housing. It may be small in total numbers, but it represents a substantial amount in dollar sales. (The commission on one $500,000 property equals the commissions on *ten* $50,000 properties.)

EXHIBIT 14.7
APPRECIATION OF A $70,000 HOUSE IN 10 YEARS AT 10%, 12%, AND 15% INFLATION
RATES

What do luxury buyers want? First of all, they want a top location, one where similar properties will be found. They also want a specific location and site that enhances the architecture of the house and, for example, embraces or enhances a one-of-a-kind view. They are also looking for a sense of graciousness, ranging from the scale of the rooms to well-handled details.

In addition to graciousness, they often want a feeling of spaciousness, space that is well-proportioned and is enhanced by volume, light, and openness. A real

EXHIBIT 14.8
IN GOOD TIMES AND IN BAD, THERE IS ALWAYS A MARKET FOR LUXURY HOUSING
The compensation is good: The commission on one $500,000 house is equal to that on *ten* $50,000 houses.

sense of luxury is given by extra space in bathrooms and dressing rooms, for example. Also, public areas, such as entry halls, should be spacious.

Upper-end buyers are also turned on by extras that allow them to state "We've made it." It might be an unusually large living room with an unusual imported marble fireplace, or it might be an enclosed swimming pool. Lavish use of wood often creates the desired impression, as do exceptionally well landscaped grounds.

SELLING INSURANCE

Salespeople who sell insurance are referred to as *agents* or *brokers*. A broker differs from an agent in that he or she is not under exclusive contract with any particular company. A broker can place a client's business with any company which best meets the client's needs and interests. Otherwise, agents and brokers do similar work and perform much the same selling function. Essentially, agents and brokers sell policies that protect individuals or businesses against future financial losses. They help the client develop an insurance or income program to meet the needs of a family; they advise about insurance protection for an automobile, a home, a business, or any other property; they may help a client settle an insurance claim.

Agents and brokers usually deal with one or more of three basic types of insurance coverage: life, property-liability (casualty), and health. Life insurance agents, sometimes called *life underwriters,* offer policies which will provide survivors with financial protection and security in the event that the policyholder dies. Life policies can additionally be designed to provide for retirement income, educational benefits, and several other benefits.

Life insurance agents may also sell health policies. Health insurance policies offer protection against the costs of hospital and medical care and the loss of income resulting from accidents and illnesses. Some agents also offer additional financial services, such as mutual fund shares and variable annuities.

Casualty insurance agents sell policies that offer financial protection against damage or loss to property: automobile accidents, fires and thefts, and other risks. They also offer the owner of the property protection against the liability that such property ownership entails, such as being sued by a neighbor who falls on your front steps. They also sell industrial and commercial lines: workers' compensation, product liability, medical malpractice, and others.

Insurance Selling as a Profession

A professional insurance salesperson must be well-versed in product knowledge and often has specialized training in the field.

Jim Trotta has just come from a meeting with his regional sales supervisor. Jim has been selling for Aetna Insurance for two years and is doing quite well. He graduated from Central State with a bachelor's degree in business and chose to remain in the area—the same area where he grew up. "Why not," he said. "I like it here as well as anywhere and, besides, I have lots of friends and contacts who have been very helpful in selling insurance."

His concern now is about a suggestion his boss made. "You're doing well—right on target for a new agent," Mr. Moynahan had said. "But I don't think you're reaching your potential. I'd like you to take course work to prepare for the CLU examinations.[5] I want you to become a professional."

Jim was a bit surprised. He had always figured that a college degree was more than adequate to be a professional insurance salesperson.

Insurance agents and brokers are required to hold a license in the state where they sell insurance. In most states, licenses are issued only to applicants who pass written examinations. These exams cover the fundamentals of insurance, company operations, and state laws governing insurance. Most of the better-known insurance companies prefer college graduates for agents. The insurance companies provide extensive training programs in their home offices and major field locations.

Agents and brokers can broaden their knowledge of the insurance industry by attending conferences, seminars, and programs sponsored by insurance organizations. The Life Underwriter Training Council (LUTC) awards a diploma in life insurance marketing to agents who successfully complete the council's two-year course. They also offer a course in health insurance. As agents and brokers gain experience, they can qualify for the *chartered life underwriter* (CLU) designation by passing a series of examinations given in locations throughout the country by the American College of Bryn Mawr, Pennsylvania. A number of colleges and universities offer courses to help the agent prepare for these examinations.

In a similar fashion, a property-liability agent or broker can qualify for the *chartered property casualty underwriter* (CPCU) designation by passing a series of several examinations given by the American Institute for Property and Liability Underwriters. The CLU and CPCU designations are widely recognized and prestigious marks of distinction in their respective fields.

Personal traits are also important in selling all forms of insurance. To be a successful insurance salesperson, you should be intelligent, enthusiastic, self-confident, and able to communicate effectively. Initiative and independence are important because as an agent you usually work with very little supervision.

The Process

As an insurance agent you must use initiative in *prospecting*. Few can survive through normal business and social contacts; the field is simply too competitive. To identify prospects, many agents follow newspaper reports to learn of newcomers to the community, births of children, and business promotions. Some agents specialize in certain occupational groups, selling to doctors, farmers, or small business owners. Most agents use telephone or mail solicitation. All agents rely on satisfied clients to provide leads for future sales.

---

[5]CLU is the professional designation for chartered life underwriter.

The *presentation* of a life insurance plan usually takes place in the prospect's home or office. The presentation of a property-liability plan may also take place there but often takes place in the agent's insurance office or, with commercial lines, in the prospect's place of business. In either case, you would generally open by explaining your services, after the usual social amenities. Following the sound sales techniques we have previously discussed, your presentation must be adapted to the particular insurance needs that each client faces. An older person, for example, may be interested in the provisions relating to retirement. New parents may wish to insure for their children's college education.

During the presentation, with the agreement of the client, you develop an appropriate insurance plan. In some cases, this will involve a single policy. In other cases, you will consider the client's complete financial position and develop a comprehensive program covering death benefits, payment of balance on the mortgage in the event of death, a retirement fund, property coverage, and protection against personal liability. To best satisfy the client's needs, you have to draw upon a variety of the insurance alternatives available.

With experience, you learn how to best handle the *objections* and questions raised by insurance prospects. You must be able to describe the coverage a company is offering in clear, nontechnical language. This is difficult, given the complexity and legal nature of the insurance business. Objections usually center around the client's inability to understand the coverage and concern over the promissory nature of the contract, that is, whether the company will be able to meet its future obligations. Be prepared to answer these objections with facts.

Closing the sale is the climax and perhaps the most difficult part of the process. At this point, the client must decide whether to buy the recommended plan, ask for a modified version of it, or do without the coverage. Assuming that the client decides to buy, you typically must obtain a completed insurance application and the first premium and send them along with other supporting papers to the insurance company. The company then decides whether to accept or reject the applicant. If accepted, the sale is complete and a policy is issued.

Special Challenges

Selling insurance creates special challenges which you should be familiar with. One results from the fact that insurance is intangible. Another challenge results from the multiple-line nature of the product.

Selling an Intangible   Intangible products like insurance cannot be tried out, inspected, or tested in advance. Prospects therefore are generally forced to rely on the word or testimony of someone else to evaluate what it is they will get. Prospects for intangibles can only be sure of what they have bought after buying it. This is unlike tangibles which can usually be experienced—seen, touched, smelled, felt, and tested—in advance of the buying decision.

Insurance, to be saleable, must be "tangibilized" in some ways, and most often this is done through image building. The companies themselves help presell the prospect by providing a visual "picture" of their promise: "a piece of the rock," an "umbrella" of protection, or "you're in good hands." It is you as the salesperson, however, who is the embodiment of the promise. You are the flesh and blood connection with the promise. Therefore, your total impression and appearance become extraordinarily important. So does the continuing relationship you provide to customers, through servicing the account after it has been sold.

We saw in Chapter 3 that people use appearance to make judgments. Consider for a moment that you are interested in a life insurance program. You call two agents to present their policies to you. Agent A arrives in a slightly unkempt car. She's casually dressed and carrying a thin folder which contains three or four policies. After a quick introduction and the usual social amenities, she explains her newest $100,000 policy to you. She says it will meet all your needs, both now and in the future. She wants your decision now so she can fill out an application for the company.

Agent B arrives in a clean car and is neatly groomed and appropriately dressed. She is carrying an attaché case with several brochures, sample policies, and questionnaires. During the introduction she hands you a clean business card which indicates a CLU designation. She spends an appropriate amount of time on social amenities and gracefully works them into a line of questioning about you and your needs. This includes questions about your occupation, your age, your income needs, etc. She asks if you would like to fill out a complete insurance-needs assessment questionnaire and explains that the results of this questionnaire will be entered into the company computer so that an insurance plan can be specifically programmed to meet your special needs. Her interest, she explains, is to sell you enough, but not too much, insurance. From which agent would you buy?

The continuing relationship you provide also helps "tangibilize" the intangible insurance policy. To keep customers satisfied so they won't drop the policy, and also so they will call you as they have additional needs, you should remind them from time to time of what they are getting. Silence and lack of attention can be death to the relationship. Without being reminded, most customers cannot recall for long the kind of insurance package they bought, and they often forget the name of the agent and the company. To combat this, one company has its agents send one-page notices to its policyholders. They explain that the coverage remains intact, provide an update of any changes, and provide a brief review of recent tax rulings affecting insurance and financial planning.

Selling Multiple Lines Many agents specialize in certain lines of insurance. The most usual distinctions are between life and casualty-property lines or between personal and commercial lines. But this can be a costly mistake. One very successful agent explains, "Doing a good job in the life business depends upon prospecting, and nearly all of my life insurance prospects come from the casualty business."

When someone comes into your agency to purchase automobile or homeowners' insurance, be sure to let them know you also sell other forms of insurance such as commercial lines and life insurance. If they work for a business or are in business for themselves (or know someone who is), they are good prospects for commercial insurance.

As a casualty agent you are in an excellent position to identify prospects for life insurance. You are one of the first to know when prospects reach sixteen years of age and get a driver's license, because they will be added to an existing policy or purchase one of their own. Record their names and birthdays so you can get back to them in two or three years. When a young person gets married, you are also the first to know because their auto premiums usually drop if they are under twenty-five and married. Married prospects offer all kinds of possibilities for many lines of insurance over the years: life, accident, health, apartment dwellers' and later homeowners', auto, and eventually endowment and annuity policies.

RETAIL SELLING

Self-service and self-selection have become customary in many retail stores, particularly variety-store and discount chains.[6] These stores don't stress selling. Instead, the employees—often called *salesclerks*—are expected to help the customer find the merchandise and ring up the sale. However, many specialty stores, such a those selling apparel, cameras, furniture, appliances, and jewelry, want people who can actively sell the merchandise. Likewise, most departments in department stores require salespeople who can sell. Good retail salespeople are needed and rewarded by many retailers.

"The biggest problem is to develop capable selling personnel" states Milton Penn, owner of the Puritan Clothing Stores on Cape Cod. "What do we do? We try to get the best people we can and keep training them."[7]

Many retail sales positions are staffed by part-time salespeople or by full-time people who see it as a job offering a pleasant environment and relatively good security. However, retail selling also offers opportunities for career-minded individuals.

Retail selling skills are particularly important to those who operate their own stores, want a retail selling career, or are in a training program.

For Your Own Store

The dream of many people is to have a business of their own, and, because of relatively easy entry, a store is often the answer. It may be a camera store, an apparel store, or some other kind. You'll need to pay attention to all kinds of things—bookkeeping, displays, window cleaning, buying, and selling. Regardless of how well you do everything else, if you can't sell the merchandise, forget it! The merchandise may not sell because nobody's coming into the store, because the location is bad, or because you're not advertising effectively. It may not sell

---

[6]Steve Weiner, "Find It Yourself," *Wall Street Journal*, Mar. 16, 1981, p. 3.
[7]Isadore Barmash, "New Men's Store Sales Drive," *The New York Times*, Apr. 17, 1981, p. 31.

because you're not buying the right kind of merchandise for your market. What we're concerned about here is merchandise that you're not selling because you don't know how to sell.

As a Career

The people selling apparel at Saks Fifth Avenue know fashion and like money. The people selling gems at Harry Winston's know jewelry and like money. The people selling appliances at Sears know appliances and like money. Retail selling is their career. At many of the established specialty and department stores you'll find dozens of salespeople who have been in their territories for decades. The difference between their territories and those of other kinds of salespeople is size. Rather than covering a city, or a state, or a region, they operate in an area of a few hundred square feet.

The difference between a job and a career in retail selling is the concern one has for using sound selling techniques.

As Training

The merchandising division is generally responsible for buying and selling in larger stores and chains. People called buyers are responsible for buying specified merchandise classifications such as housewares, furniture, and menswear.

Stores often require their buyers to spend some time selling so they understand customers' needs and salespeople's problems. The buyer must be able to help salespeople by pointing out special merchandise features and the kinds of objections that might be raised by customers. By understanding selling principles, the buyer can show salespeople how to present merchandise and how to handle objections.

In addition to selling during their training program, most buyers continue to do some selling throughout their career. They sell during peak periods and at other times to get a "feel" of what's happening out on the floor. (See Exhibit 14.9.)

The Process

As stated earlier, the main difference between retail selling and other kinds of selling is that the prospect comes to you rather than the other way around. Unlike the other types of selling we've discussed, retail salespeople rely on advertising, window displays, and other types of services to attract prospects into the store. Some people entering the store are real prospects. They come in with a need to fill, the authority to buy, and cash or a credit card to pay. Others are really just looking. They may come in to do some comparison shopping, to get warm on a cold day, or to get cool on a warm day.

Your approach may give you your first clue about whether the shopper is a prospect. Many people don't want to be approached. Sometimes even those who intend to buy want to be left alone until they are ready to deal with you. Often, the customer approaches you and says, "I'm interested in seeing your size-forty sports jackets." This is the best possible situation. Take advantage of it by taking the customer to the sports jackets and looking at them with the customer. This gives you the opportunity to do some fact finding and make a sales presentation.

Retail Approaches   You can initiate several kinds or combinations of approaches. The most traditional and perhaps the safest is the greeting approach, but the service or merchandise approaches are also typical.

The greeting approach   Simply say "Good morning" or "Hello." If you know the person's name, use it in the greeting. People like to hear their names spoken. A customer who is greeted does not get the frustrated feeling that he or she will be ignored when help is needed.

The service approach   This approach stresses the willingness of the salesperson to help the customer. This is the most difficult—the stereotyped "May I help you?" "No, I'm just looking" scenario. You may avoid this scenario by saying (after the greeting), "Let me know if I can help you" or "Let me know if I can explain anything." The response may be an immediate request for help or a "Thank you, I will." Or try: "Do you want some help, or would you like to look around first?" This is a forced-choice question that assumes you'll be helping either now or later.

The merchandise approach   The merchandise approach is effective when you notice that the customer has some interest in a particular item. The customer may spend considerable time observing the item, reading its label, or feeling its texture. You can respond to this apparent interest by making an explanatory remark such as "It's one hundred percent virgin wool," "It's only two pounds but will withstand the weight of an elephant," or "It is guaranteed for life." The secret for the successful use of this approach is that you state facts, not opinions, and that you do not comment indiscriminately on everything the customer notices.

Once you have made a successful approach, you can use the techniques discussed earlier in the book for conducting the sales presentation, handling objections, and effecting the close. However, you should be aware of some other aspects of retail selling, covered below, that are somewhat different from other selling situations.

Demonstration   In other kinds of selling the salesperson often has a sales manual that describes the product or perhaps a sample, but usually the actual product to be sold is back at the factory or in the warehouse. In retail selling the merchandise is right there for the customer to see, touch, and, where applicable, try. You can demonstrate a product's quality and operation. You can encourage the customer to try on the dress, look through the telescope, feel the smoothness of the fabric, hear the sound quality, or try operating the calculator. Get the customer involved with the merchandise.

Buyer procrastination Many consumer purchases are more postponable than most purchases made by those who buy for resale or for use in a business. The buyer for a store must buy now from some vendor so that there's merchandise to sell on the shelves. The buyer for a factory must buy machine oil to keep the factory humming. However, a consumer can more easily postpone the purchase of a bathing suit, sofa, camera, and so forth without drastically affecting his or her lifestyle.

If the consumer needs the product or service, or wants it badly, and can afford

EXHIBIT 14.9
RETAIL STORE CHARACTERS

it, you'll be doing a favor if you help make the decision with an effective close. "Will this be cash or charge? Do you want to take the chair with you or have us send it?" These are traditional and effective retail closes. Buyer procrastination is often caused by not wanting to part with the money or by a lack of confidence in making the decision. A statement such as "As soon as these lawn mowers are sold out, there will be a price increase" or "Our anniversary sale ends this evening, Mrs. Brooks" often help the customer overcome his or her hesitancy. Obviously, such statements can be made only if they are true.

If you can't recognize any of the following characters, you've *never* been in a store.

• *Steve straightener.* He straightens the shelves while the customer waits and fumes. He usually straightens his way right out of his job. Reason: Shelves stay straightened because no one ever returns to the store to unstraighten them. *Advice:* Pay attention to customer now; straighten later.

• *Pete the pusher.* He sells what he has, not what the customer needs. You need a size-40 jacket and all he has is size 42. He sells the size 42 jacket and a bulky sweater and extols the stylishness of the layered look. *Advice:* Order the right size or recommend another store.

• *Mathematical Marge.* She's quick with her simplistic answers. You ask her the difference between the $650 stereo and the $500 one and her answer is $150. She usually leaves selling because she dislikes dealing with stupid customers who don't understand simple arithmetic. *Advice:* Learn value as well as price. Get product knowledge.

• *Oblivious Olive.* She may or may not know you're there. Regardless, she keeps it a secret by not recognizing your presence. She usually leads the pack in "walk-outs" but is unaware that she's the leader. *Advice:* Acknowledge the customer's presence by saying "Hello" or "I'll be right with you" or with a smile.

• *Hovering Harry.* He's like a noose around your neck. You can't look at anything without a pitch from him. He says that everything is the best, is just right for you, or was made for you. He's a nuisance. *Advice:* Be perceptive. Give the customer space by standing in the background watching for your cue to assist.

EXHIBIT 14.10
IN RETAIL SELLING, THE MERCHANDISE IS RIGHT THERE FOR THE CUSTOMER TO TRY
ON   (*Source:* Rohn Engh/Photo Researchers.)

More than One Customer   Retail selling is unique in that you must often deal
with more than one customer at a time. Sometimes you'll feel as if you're engaged
in a juggling act. The main thing to remember is to acknowledge the presence of
all customers. Let them know that you'll be with them shortly. The first customer,
who is deciding on which color to get, will probably not mind if you excuse
yourself for a minute or two to help another customer.

Suggestion Selling   This is selling a complementary product to the customer—a tie with a shirt, an extra chain with the chain saw, film and flashcubes
with the camera. You've already made a sale; the customer is in a "yes" mood. In
many cases the sale just made to satisfy a need automatically creates the need for
another product. For example, the camera without film is inoperative. By making
the suggestion sale you are assuring that the camera can be used by the customer
and thus assuring that the customer will get pictures, which is what is really
wanted.

RECAP

Many selling opportunities are available in the real estate, insurance, and retailing industries, each of which has some unique selling characteristics.

The professional real estate salesperson must list and sell properties, know the area, and be well-versed in financial matters. The closing is different and difficult due to the legal and financial details and the size of the investment and cash outlay. There are special challenges and opportunities in selling to the many buyers and, especially, in selling to the upper end of the market.

Insurance salespeople are required to hold a license in the state in which they sell. As agents and brokers gain experience, they can qualify for the professional designations CLU and CPCU. Some agents specialize in life and health insurance, while others specialize in casualty-property lines. A growing number sell all lines, using information from one to provide prospects for the other.

Retail selling is a major area of consumer selling. Retail selling skills are important to those who operate their own store, want a retail selling career, or are in training programs. There are several aspects that make retail selling different from other selling situations: the demonstration, handling buyer procrastination, handling more than one customer at one time, and suggestion selling.

REVIEW QUESTIONS

1. About how many salespeople are employed in the real estate industry? in insurance? in retailing?
2. What are the two major functions of a real estate salesperson?
3. How is selling real estate unique as compared with selling other products and services?
4. In what ways is selling insurance unique?
5. How does retail selling differ from other types of selling?
6. What is the single most expensive item that most consumers ever purchase?
7. What are the major activities of the real estate salesperson?
8. What are the usual qualifications to become a real estate salesperson?
9. How do life insurance agents and casualty insurance agents usually differ?
10. What is a CLU? a CPCU?
11. Name several approaches in retail selling.
12. What is suggestion selling?

DISCUSSION QUESTIONS

1. What population characteristics do you think will affect the job market for real estate and insurance? Do the characteristics of your state coincide with the national projections?
2. Call the real estate commission in your state and find out what the requirements are for a salesperson's license. Why do they have minimum requirements? Do you think that these minimum requirements should be stiffened or lessened?
3. A characteristic of the insurance industry is that continuing training and education is prevalent. Agents may acquire several designations: CLU and

CPCU are two. Do you think these designations help the consumer or simply provide for prestige within the profession?

LEARNING EXPERIENCES

1. Visit a prominent real estate office in your area. Find out what the salespeople see as their most difficult task in selling properties (i.e., getting listings, arranging for financing, etc.). Compare your finding with the findings of others in a group discussion.
2. Obtain a copy of a life insurance policy. Use you own, if you have one, or borrow a blank one from your local insurance agent. Read only the first two introductory paragraphs. Now try to rewrite or itemize the points in everyday language as if you were presenting them to a prospect.

CASE

WHICH HOUSE SHALL IT BE?

Sheila was faced with the kind of problem that most real estate agents love to face: her clients, Dick and Maria Black, had narrowed their choice down to two houses. But they were having trouble deciding which one they wanted—each had its drawbacks. In fact, they were beginning to wonder if they shouldn't go out and look at other listings. Perhaps the house of their dreams was still out there somewhere.

Sheila knew her market well and felt sure that there was nothing else available that would suit the Black's needs as well as the two properties under consideration. She had already shown them twenty-one listings over the past four weekends.

The Black's were good clients. They were realistic—but, like most people, wanted to be very sure they were getting the best house for their needs and money. This was by far the largest financial commitment they would ever make. Sheila had listed in her mind their objections for each property.

The Collins Street property, a five-room ranch with a nice yard and a one-car garage, met their needs. It was in a clean, young neighborhood with comparable well-cared-for houses. It was fairly priced at $70,000 but required a 20 percent down payment. Since the Blacks had only $8000, they would have to borrow the difference. The house was in move-in condition.

The Elm Street house was a five-room Cape style and also had a nice yard, but no garage. It was in a neighborhood of somewhat better houses, all of which were well-cared-for. Its asking price was also $70,000, and only 10 percent was required as a down payment. The house had better basic architecture than the

Collins Street property, but the exterior needed painting. Sheila also estimated that it would need a new roof within the next five years.

It was clear to Sheila that she should nudge the Blacks toward one of the properties.

Questions

1. Do you agree that Sheila should push them toward one of the properties?
2. On what basis should she present the choice?
3. How should she attempt to close this sale?

FIFTEEN

CHAPTER OBJECTIVES

To explain the nature of the industrial market

To categorize industrial goods

To identify the decision makers

To distinguish the differences between different kinds of industrial selling situations

To emphasize the particular importance of looking beyond the industrial sale

To point out the potential barrier reciprocity might present

To introduce bidding as a means for getting industrial sales

To show the role of the salesperson in relation to the distribution process

CHAPTER OUTLINE

SELLING TO INDUSTRY

The business of America is business.

Calvin Coolidge

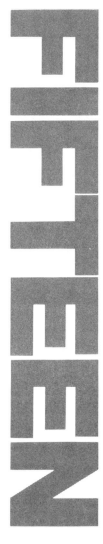

The person who just bought a new Chevrolet was involved in a rather simple (but quite expensive) transaction—one person sold and one person bought. However, there were many complex sales transactions taking place behind the scene. At General Motors thousands of people were responsible for buying products and services from 50,000 vendors to make that car. The people doing the selling were industrial sellers; the people doing the buying were industrial buyers. In this chapter we look at how sales are made to this industrial market.

THE INDUSTRIAL MARKET

In the broadest sense, the industrial market includes all those businesses, organizations, and institutions that buy the goods and services used directly or indirectly in producing their goods and services. Manufacturers, hospitals, schools, government agencies, and professional practitioners are all part of this vast market. Retailers are part of this market (as we have defined it) only when they buy something for use in the business—a cash register, shelving, window-cleaning service—not when they buy merchandise for resale. Selling to retailers for resale is covered in the next chapter.

The way to approach the industrial market depends considerably on the type of product or service being sold and on the specific segment of the industrial market being dealt with. Most aspects of the selling strategy and the selling process must vary accordingly.

CATEGORIES OF INDUSTRIAL GOODS

Industrial goods range from the common paper clip sold to virtually every business and organization to a $300 million generator sold to a utility company. There are all kinds of industrial goods that are bought for various reasons by the industrial user. It is important to categorize the product you sell because many aspects of the selling situation vary with the type of product. In this section we describe the major categories of industrial products and assess the selling implications of each. You will be introduced to terms and principles new to you and will have a chance to see the applications of previously learned material to this significant selling arena.

Major Equipment

Every business has a primary mission—to produce a product or service. Most businesses need major, and usually relatively expensive, equipment to produce that product or service. The utility company needs a generator; the manufacturer needs a plant and production machinery; the hotel operator needs a building; the airline needs airplanes. Generators, plants and machinery, buildings, airplanes, and other major equipment needed by a firm are called *fixed assets*. New firms must buy new equipment, and existing firms must replace and update major equipment. Because of the expense involved, these purchases must be planned for, or budgeted. Purchases of fixed assets are called *capital expenditures*. Products and services cannot be produced without them.

You do not normally sell products that are capital expenditures on the first sales call. The negotiation period might take months or years and involve several sales support people and several people from the buyer's organization. Price is not usually the major consideration. Design capabilities and the ability to deliver when promised are primary concerns of the customer.

It is unlikely that you will be engaged in this kind of selling early in your career. Most sales involving capital expenditures are made by senior salespeople or sales executives—sometimes even company presidents. They usually have an engineering background and many years of experience. You may, however, find yourself selling certain kinds of machinery considered to be major equipment by smaller manufacturers.

Accessory Equipment

This equipment is not used in producing the product or service but is needed to run the business. Trucks, typewriters, cash registers, and computers are typical examples. The market for these products is widespread. Accessory equipment often is seen by the buyer as a nonproducing capital expenditure that ties up money and adds to the expense of operating the business. The buyer can see the benefits of producing capital expenditures, but the benefits of nonproducing accessory equipment are not always obvious. Thus the buyer is generally not thrilled about making this kind of purchase.

You have to look for ways that your product will improve your prospect's customer service, reduce other operating expenses, improve the company's image, or offer some other benefits. A cash register, for example, provides benefits beyond being a depository for money and a printer of receipts. It can be used for inventory control that may save the prospect many more dollars than the cost of the register. Sell inventory control and your prospect will reap all kinds of benefits: increased sales, better customer service, and reduced inventory costs.

The prospect doesn't want to tie up a lot of money or spend time worrying about accessory equipment. Low prices or a reasonable leasing arrangement and trouble-free operation of the equipment are of key importance to the buyer.

Raw Materials

Raw materials are unprocessed products such as wheat, timber, iron ore, and oil. They are sold to companies that process them for use in making other products. Wheat is converted to flour, which in turn may become part of a loaf of bread. Timber may be converted to lumber, which in turn may become a wooden toy. Iron ore is converted to steel, which in turn may become a fender of an automobile. Oil may be converted to polyethylene, which in turn may become a garbage bag.

Most raw materials are sold to large buyers on a contractual basis. The buyer is concerned with uniform quality and a guaranteed supply. The success of the buyer's own business depends on having the proper grade and the right amount of material always available. In terms of opportunities, raw materials are similar to major equipment: There are fewer opportunities for inexperienced salespeople than there are in other industrial products categories.

Component Materials and Parts

When the government announces that it has awarded a contract to General Dynamics Corporation to build submarines or to United Technologies Corporation

EXHIBIT 15-1
THE HOTTEST ACCESSORY EQUIPMENT AROUND   (*Source:* Apple Computer, Inc.)

to build aircraft, dozens of companies place help-wanted ads in the newspapers. Why? These companies supply materials and parts that go into the building of the submarines and aircraft. Tire sales are down because automobile sales are down. Semiconductor sales are up because watch sales and electronic games sales are up. Why? Because tires are component parts of automobiles and semiconductors are component parts of many kinds of watches and of electronic games.

Most companies buy all or a portion of the materials and parts used in the production of their finished products. They assemble parts supplied by other manufacturers. In fact, automobile manufacturers call their production facilities assembly plants. Almost every company is buying materials and parts from somebody. Even the manufacturer of component parts usually buys processed materials and (ready for this?) parts for the parts. As consumers, we usually are concerned only with the finished product. Often, we can't even see all the parts that make up the whole. For every company producing (or assembling) finished products, there are dozens behind the scenes producing and selling the components.

Companies have to decide whether to make the parts themselves or buy them. Your selling situation might involve convincing a prospect to buy a part from you rather than make it. How difficult your task will be depends a lot on whether the part is standard or specially designed. Standard parts such as bearings, switches, and springs are mass-produced for use in many kinds of products and usually can be purchased more cheaply than they can be made by the prospect. Often, a part made to a prospect's own specifications can also be produced more efficiently by a manufacturer who may have lower overhead costs and superior engineering expertise.

MRO Supplies

This category consists of maintenance (M), repair (R), and operating (O) supplies. MRO supplies typically purchased by organizations include office supplies such as paper clips, stationery, and forms; machine lubricants; cleaning solvents; and a host of other expense items. What distinguishes these items from other industrial goods is that they are clearly and wholly expenses in running the organization. They do not go into the finished product as materials and parts do, and they do not have the long life of major and accessory equipment.

Most supplies are purchased routinely. The purchasing agent issues a purchase order when the various supply items reach prescribed order levels. When the initial decision to choose a supplier is made, the users of the supplies are often consulted before a supplier is chosen. The office manager provides input for office supplies, plant line supervisors for production supplies, and maintenance people for maintenance supplies.

Such a wide range of products falls into the MRO category that it's difficult to generalize about what is most important to the buyer. However, we can say that service is more important for production supplies than it is for office supplies. To a factory, immediate delivery of a belt or oil for a machine is more critical than delivery of typing paper. That's why industrial distributors with nearby, well-stocked warehouses often have a competitive advantage for many MRO items.

Services

Services are a significant expense item for most organizations. Typical examples of services are communications, advertising, data processing, consulting, and maintenance. The buyer has three kinds of decisions concerning a particular service. (See Exhibit 15.2.)

1. To have it or not have it or, if already existing, to upgrade it or live with it
2. To perform the service within the company or to contract an outside firm to perform it
3. To choose a supplier for the service or for the items needed to perform the service itself

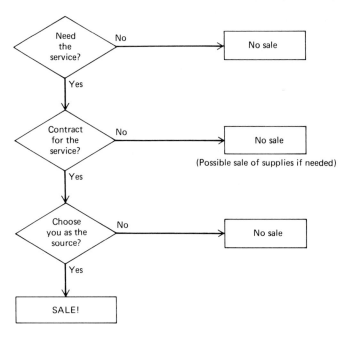

EXHIBIT 15.2
THE SERVICE DECISION

Advertising and consulting are two services that a firm may elect to either have or not have. You have to point out the benefits of having them and show how your company is best qualified for providing these services. Data processing and maintenance are necessary activities in any organization. It's just a matter of who is going to process the data or do maintenance and repairs around the place. It is similar to a make-or-buy decision for component materials and parts. There are numerous service bureaus for processing data for firms that don't have the capability or inclination to process their own data, and there are industrial maintenance services for cleaning office buildings and factories. As a salesperson for one of these service firms you would stress the advantages to the customer in having specialists handle these peripheral tasks so that the company's personnel can concentrate on those activities that are more directly pertinent to the business.

THE BUYING DECISION

In most industrial selling there is more than one person directly or indirectly involved in the buying decision. Notice the concerns and inputs given by the purchasing agent, chief engineer, and plant manager in this scenario.

"Warwick doesn't service what it sells. Automatic Manufacturing should be renamed Semiautomatic. Exeter's prices are higher than a kite. Sample Controls is not dry behind the ears. The need will no longer exist when Feriton delivers." These remarks were made at a meeting attended by the purchasing agent, chief engineer, and plant manager of the Chemtron Company.

"What's most important to you, Charles?" the purchasing agent asked the chief engineer.

"I'm from the old school that says a valve should open when it is supposed to."

"Idle workers and idle machinery spell early retirement for me." Reilly, the plant manager, emphasized. "If the valves don't get here on time, we have an idle machine. If service doesn't get here on time, we have an idle machine and idle workers."

The purchasing agent volunteered, "I, and I'm sure you, want the best of all worlds. However, I want most a competitive price from a supplier with a good track record."

Ultimately, the purchasing agent is likely to place the order, but not before the opinions of the others have been considered.

Who Makes the Buying Decision?

Those who are consulted or are in some way involved in the industrial buying decision are commonly called *buying influences*. It is important that the salesperson know who they are and which buying factors are of greatest concern to them.

Purchasing is a well-defined activity in large organizations and in many medium-sized organizations. People are assigned responsibility for purchasing decisions, and written policies and procedures are developed. In small organizations responsibility and procedures are not always as clearly stated. In all organizations more than one person or department is usually involved in the buying decision.

Knowing who influences the buying decision is as important as knowing who makes the final decision. Usually you'll be able to figure out who the most likely buying influences are for the kind of product or service you sell. As you gain experience, you'll also develop perception in discovering the less-obvious buying influences.

Purchasing agents, also called *purchasing managers* and *buyers,* are the professional buyers for many organizations. They usually sign the purchase order, which is the contract that binds the sale. Their clout varies. Some are powerful; others are paper shufflers. Until you discover otherwise, assume the purchasing agent is powerful. This translates to: Don't cross the purchasing agent.

For many industrial products another buying influence specifies the product and the purchasing agent specifies the source. These buying influences are usually people whose jobs may be affected by the purchase or who have special knowledge about the purchase being considered. It is usually necessary to get the opportunity to talk with the buying influence—an engineer, office manager, plant manager—but protocol dictates that you go to the purchasing department first. Bypassing the purchasing department is called *back-door* selling and should be attempted only as a last resort, if at all.

Good purchasing agents seek advice from others in the organization before making purchase decisions, particularly nonroutine ones. Often, company policy dictates that this be done. For major purchases, such as computers and production machinery, a committee of people representing several areas of expertise and

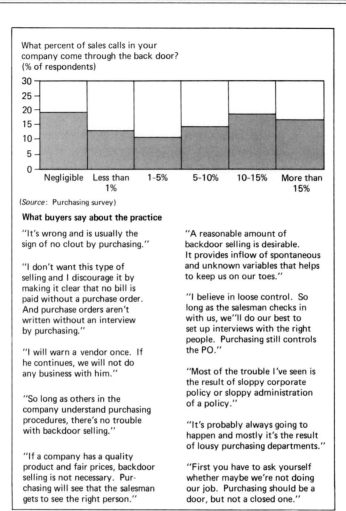

What percent of sales calls in your
company come through the back door?
(% of respondents)

(Source: Purchasing survey)

What buyers say about the practice

"It's wrong and is usually the
sign of no clout by purchasing."

"I don't want this type of
selling and I discourage it by
making it clear that no bill is
paid without a purchase order.
And purchase orders aren't
written without an interview
by purchasing."

"I will warn a vendor once. If
he continues, we will not do
any business with him."

"So long as others in the
company understand purchasing
procedures, there's no trouble
with backdoor selling."

"If a company has a quality
product and fair prices, backdoor
selling is not necessary. Purchasing will see that the salesman
gets to see the right person."

"A reasonable amount of
backdoor selling is desirable.
It provides inflow of spontaneous
and unknown variables that helps
to keep us on our toes."

"I believe in loose control. So
long as the salesman checks in
with us, we"ll do our best to
set up interviews with the right
people. Purchasing still controls
the PO."

"Most of the trouble I've seen is
the result of sloppy corporate
policy or sloppy administration
of a policy."

"It's probably always going to
happen and mostly it's the result
of lousy purchasing departments."

"First you have to ask yourself
whether maybe we're not doing
our job. Purchasing should be a
door, but not a closed one."

EXHIBIT 15.3
BUYERS LOOK AT BACKDOOR SELLING   (*Source: Purchasing*
magazine, November 21, 1979, p. 67. Copyright by Cahners
Publishing. Reprinted by permission.)

concern makes the final buying decision. For reorders of supplies and materials,
purchasing usually acts unilaterally because the buying influences already gave
their advice when the original decision to buy was made. Purchasing agents
usually involve others in the purchase decision when the perceived risk is high.

The Factors Considered

Buyers for industrial customers buy for one reason: It's their job. If they make too
many bad buying decisions, they are out of a job. Until machines become responsible for buying, some emotion will affect the buying process. However, for the

most part, industrial buyers behave rationally, not emotionally, when involved in a buying decision. They are concerned primarily with price, quality, and service.

Price While price is a consideration in most purchase decisions, quality and service will not usually be sacrificed for price alone. Price is often more important in buying accessory equipment and some MRO supplies, even if it means forgoing some quality, because these items do not affect the quality of the product being produced. Standard products tend to be more price-sensitive. When two equally reputable firms are competing for the sale of a standard product, the salesperson for the firm with the lower price is likely to get the order. Price is not as important a factor for infrequently purchased products as it is for frequently purchased ones. A slightly lower price for component parts can affect the customer's income statement considerably. If a manufacturer can save 10 cents on a part that goes into the production of 100,000 units a year, profit increases by $10,000 a year.

The purchasing agent is usually more concerned about price than are others influencing the buying decision. Price is an easily quantifiable measure of a purchasing agent's performance. For example, during austerity periods, the word may go out to hold the line on expenses or cut them by 5 percent. This puts the pressure on the purchasing agent to be even more price-conscious.

Quality Industrial customers usually specify the level of quality they want. In its broadest sense, quality also includes specific product features. Engineers determine the standards for many industrial products. However, other buying influences also are involved in drawing up specifications for some products. The secretary might specify a typewriter with memory; a warehouse manager might specify the maximum width of materials handling equipment.

Price and quality are usually related. Better materials, finer workmanship, and additional features cost money. If your product meets or beats competition, you're in the running for the sale as far as quality is concerned. But remember, your customer may not pay one penny more for quality levels that exceed specifications.

Service Service is a broad term with dimensions that depend on the kind of industrial product sold and the customer's perception of what constitutes good service. Delivery is important for all kinds of industrial products. A product of the highest quality and lowest price that is delivered later than promised can create all kinds of problems for the customer. Reliable delivery is especially important for major equipment, components, and some MRO items.

When the customer orders a machine for delivery on a specific date, planning for the entire organization will be geared toward that machine and that date. The buying firm will hire additional production workers to operate the machinery, and the firm's sales force will be out selling in anticipation of the increased output provided by the machine. Any delay in delivery could result in idle workers, lost sales, and a number of other problems for the customer. Likewise, the importance of reliable delivery of components should be obvious. The finished product can't go out the door until *all* parts are in place. The lawn mower without a blade, the television without a picture tube, and the belt without a buckle are useless. If these components are not available, production stops.

Manufacturers demand a guaranteed supply. They are interested in deliveries beyond the first one. This is why they may be as interested in your production capabilities as they are in your product. It is also the reason manufacturers are hesitant to give all their business to small firms, especially ones without long-standing reputations for reliability.

Technical support services are also commonly expected by customers of industrial goods, both before and after the purchase. In many cases, the prospect has either no engineering department or a limited engineering department. You'll have an edge in getting the sale if you can fill the void.

For machinery it's important that you, perhaps working with your company's application engineer, participate in the design of the machine, supervise the installation, and help train the operators. Technical support can also tip the scale for selling industrial coatings, advertising, data processing, and many other industrial products and services.

KINDS OF SELLING SITUATIONS

The ideal selling situation is to be first and last. Be the first to satisfy an industrial prospect's new need and continue to satisfy it through repeat sales. Of course, this is not always possible. If the need has already been filled by another supplier, you have to either replace the supplier or get a piece of the action. Let's see what these different situations might mean to you.

New Need

New companies and old companies both have new needs to be filled. A new law office needs office supplies. Somebody has to get the business. A new factory needs machinery. Somebody has to get the business. A new warehouse needs materials handling equipment. Somebody has to get the business. These new businesses are aware of these needs and you should be, too. Don't wait until their doors open for business. Too late. No business is conceived the day before it flies. It takes months or years of planning before it is operational. If you can't be in on the conception, be in on the planning. Most new enterprises have all their suppliers lined up far before their opening.

Use the prospecting sources mentioned in Chapter 6 to find out what's new or, better yet, what's going to be new. Check with local and state industrial development commissions to find out what progress they're making in bringing new businesses into your territory. Use your industrial and commercial real estate contacts to find out about property that's for sale. Follow the newspaper and other publications to get additional clues.

Existing companies also have new needs to be filled. Companies must continually change to keep up with all the changes taking place around them—competition, customers, laws. Change creates new needs that require new products and services to satisfy them. Until the mid-1960s only a few million shares of stock were traded on the New York Stock Exchange daily. Brokers handled transactions manually. In the late 1960s volumes began to double and triple. Some brokers went out of business because they could not keep up with the paperwork. Others made changes. The agents of the changes were the computer salespeople who filled the new need to handle increased stock transactions.

You don't have to wait until a company or an entire industry has its back up against a wall to fill a new need. You can help your customer discover the new need before the crisis stage. This increases the probability that your product or service will be the successful candidate for filling the need because you knew about it first.

Almost everything that happens creates a chain reaction of other happenings. Don't just observe the first link; try to anticipate what the whole chain will look like. An event can create prospects you never dreamed about. The Occupational Safety and Health Act (OSHA), the oil crisis, and the deregulation of air rates are examples of events that brought about countless changes in the way organizations operate. Each change spells new opportunities for the industrial salesperson who recognizes it.

Repeat Sales

Products requiring continual replenishment need repeat sales to an industrial customer. They include MRO items, raw materials, processed materials, and parts. Fixed-asset products may be purchased again from the same supplier, but this kind of purchase is usually satisfying a new need—additional, larger, more efficient.

Once you have gotten the initial order, you are looking for the cumulative effect. You want the reams of newsprint to keep rolling into the *Daily Gazette,* the mouthwash to keep flowing into Dr. Toothacher's office, and the salt to keep pouring into the Squiggley Pretzel Company. You have to defend this business against competition. If your competitors are aggressive, they'll try to take your repeat business away from you. It they're any good, they might do it. Be sure that you keep in close touch with every customer's business so that you can spot any changes in requirements.

Sometimes, sellers and buyers agree to blanket orders for repeat sales. *Blanket orders* are purchasing agreements commonly used for frequently purchased products, especially MRO supplies. The buyer estimates normal requirements for the period (usually a year), and the seller assures availability. Price and price adjustment procedures are stipulated. Some types of blanket orders are called *systems contracts.*

A Piece of the Action

As stated earlier, industrial buyers usually don't want to have all their eggs in one basket. They prefer to have more than one supplier, particularly for component materials and parts. In this way, continual supply is better assured and a more competitive environment is created. At the same time, they want to purchase significant volumes from suppliers so that they are considered important customers and can recieve quantity discounts. As you can see, these objectives are contradictory. When you hold all of a customer's business, you hope the company continues to maintain a one-supplier philosophy and you try to keep it sold on this philosophy. When you are on the outside looking in, you have to wait for the prospect to change philosophy or you have to help change it through your selling skills.

Just as small accounts grow into big accounts, a small piece of the customer's business can also grow. It is natural to be discouraged when you can't get an order from a company that has a long-standing relationship with your competitors. If there is enough potential, it's worth your persistence because circumstances do change. Pittsburgh Brewing Company, for example, had bought cans for its hearty Iron City beer from only one supplier for twenty years. While reevaluating its operation, it decided that it would be wise to open its business to more than one supplier to get a more competitive price and to become less dependent. Likewise the United States, highly dependent on Persian Gulf oil supplies, has been seeking other oil suppliers as well as alternative energy sources to avoid dependence. Exhibit 15.4 shows why General Foods likes to have more than one supplier.

EXHIBIT 15.4

JELLO DOESN'T GROW ON TREES

General Foods does a lot of buying before it can produce and sell its wide variety of products, which includes Jello, Raisin Bran, Kool-Aid, and Gravy Train. The forty-five-person purchasing department is responsible for buying 80,000 pounds of raisins, 1.4 million jars, and half a million corrugated cases a day. Additionally, it purchases millions of dollars worth of sugar, rice, plastic bottles, and so forth.

Price is important in the buying decisions for these products, but probably more important is a reliable supply. Just as you can't get solar heat without sunshine, you can't get Raisin Bran without raisins or jello puddings without tapioca starch.

General Foods doesn't like to have all its eggs (it needs them, too) in one basket. It tries to have at least two suppliers for every item it purchases. Years ago it realized the danger of having only one supplier. Celanese, the only domestic company selling tapioca starch, decided to get out of the business. Since tapioca starch is the base for all Jello puddings, General Foods saw big trouble ahead. It solved the problem by finding a buyer for Celanese's tapioca starch business and awarding the buyer a five-year tapioca starch contract.

Source: N. R. Kleinfield, "How a Company Does Its Shopping," *The New York Times*, Jan. 17, 1982, p. F1.

LOOK BEYOND THE SALE

Derived demand in the industrial setting means that the demand for industrial products is the result of the demand for consumer products. We have said that industrial sales are made to businesses and other kinds of organizations, all of which ultimately produce products or services for people like us. When we stop needing their products and services, there is no reason for their existence. Buggy whip factories closed when the automobile came on the scene. Why? There were no more buggies. Ford closed its Mahwah, New Jersey automotive assembly plant. Why? There was a reduced demand for Ford trucks and automobiles. Every supplier of these closed businesses is affected.

What does all this mean to the industrial salesperson? You can hope that whoever buys from your customer continues to buy. Once the buying chain is broken, you're in trouble. However, you can do more than hope; you can help by using your problem-solving ability and your creativity. You've probably seen Du Pont's advertisements for Dacron. Du Pont is directing its advertising to you, the consumer, so that you'll want garments made of Dacron. That's so your clothing store will buy clothing made of Dacron from the apparel manufacturer, who will then buy Dacron from Du Pont. If consumers don't want Dacron, no one else in the distribution channel wants it. Many companies direct their promotional program beyond their immediate customers to help pull the product through the distribution channel. You, too, can think of ways to reach your customer's customer.

A chemical company could not sell its vinyl acetate latex to a regional paint manufacturer. The paint manufacturer already had two suppliers with whom it was pleased. The chemical company wanted a piece of the action but could not offer any price or quality advantages. It decided to spend most of its marketing efforts helping the paint company sell its end product—gallon cans of latex paint sold by paint stores. With the purchasing agent's approval, the chemical company's representative talked with the paint company's marketing manager. He found that the paint company's biggest hurdle to selling more paint was convincing paint dealers that latex paint was as durable as oil-based paint. Using a paint scrub tester, an inexpensive machine with abrasive brushes, he made a presentation to the paint company's management. This test clearly showed the durability of latex paint. The prospect was impressed and granted the representative one more presentation. This time the representative offered free paint scrubbers and booklets entitled "One Hundred and One Things You Always Wanted to Know About Latex Paint, but Never Dared to Ask" to the paint company for its dealers to use at the point of purchase. In return, the representative asked for the sale of one tank car of vinyl acetate latex and got it. This rep got a piece of the action by looking beyond the sale.[1]

WHAT PRICE RECIPROCITY?

Reciprocity is the practice of doing business with firms that do business with you. There's a wide range of reciprocal philosophies among firms. Most firms will at

[1]Adapted from R. Karl von Leer, "Industrial Marketing with a Flair," *Harvard Business Review,* November–December 1976, pp. 117–124.

EXHIBIT 15.5
DERIVING DEMAND   (*Source:* Du Pont.)

least grant a sales interview or encourage a bid from one of their customers. And often this relationship will be given some weight in the buying decision. Some firms, though, attempt to exclude all other suppliers when their customer is selling the product or service they need. As the following scenario illustrates, reciprocity can be costly to the buyer and can be overcome by the seller.

The owner of a dry cleaning business bought all of his business and personal insurance from a local insurance agent. He did this because the agent was a good customer. The dry cleaner refused to talk to any other insurance agent because he wanted to remain loyal to his customer. Finally, an insurance agent made him listen.

AGENT: Is it possible you may be paying too much for your insurance?

DRY CLEANER: All insurance policies cost about the same and Chip Behrens is a good customer.

AGENT: May I look at your policies to see if he's giving you the best rates?

DRY CLEANER: Sure.

AGENT: (*after reviewing policies*): How much cleaning business does your agent give you?

DRY CLEANER: About two hundred dollars a year.

AGENT (*after determining that he could provide the same coverage for much less than the competition*): You'll have to get your agent to change his shirt seven times a day and have his suit dry-cleaned about three times a week to break even for the year.

The dry cleaner bought the insurance. This transaction actually happened; similar transactions happen frequently when salespeople help their prospects discover the price of reciprocity.

Reciprocity does not enter into many selling situations, but when it does, it can be a tough barrier to a sale. If your competitor is being favored by reciprocity and is competitive in all other aspects, the barrier might be insurmountable. Of course, reciprocity might work favorably for you when it is your firm that buys from your prospect. You have to use caution and diplomacy even in situations where reciprocity is not an issue. (See Exhibit 15.6 for some silly examples of diplomatic errors.)

EXHIBIT 15.6

MISTAKES TO AVOID

- Ordering prune juice when having breakfast with a representative of the Florida Orange Growers Association
- Whistling "You Deserve a Break Today" when waiting to see your prospect at Burger King headquarters
- Flicking your Bic to light the cigar of Zippo's purchasing agent
- Talking about your Honda's great gas mileage when calling on a Ford dealer
- Telling a mortician the government should spend more money on health care

BIDDING

Bidding is a procedure in which the buyer specifies what is needed and invites a number of suppliers to formally ask for the order. Many industrial users, especially those that have government contracts, require bids. Municipal, state, and federal agencies require bids for most of their purchases. A town that needs a new school bus, for example, will invite school bus suppliers to bid for the business. The town will specify such things as size and safety requirements. Generally, the supplier meeting the specifications and offering the lowest price makes the sale.

You have to stay on top of any business that may be let out to bid. Buyers advertise for bids from responsible suppliers. They also develop approved bid lists that include the names of suppliers who have the capabilities of satisfying their needs. Your company will probably be on the approved list if you have had previous successful dealings with the buyer.

Sometimes you'll have the opportunity to work with the buyer in determining the specifications for the product. Here's where you can put your knowledge and problem-solving talent to work by having the features of your product become part of the specifications. This may disqualify some competitors from the bidding process because they can't comply with the specifications. Get the buyer to specify a variable-speed motor and disqualify all single-speed—motor suppliers, or get the buyer to specify aluminum construction and disqualify those suppliers whose products have only steel or plastic construction.

DISTRIBUTION STRATEGY

Industrial products are sold primarily by manufacturers directly to end users, by industrial distributors, and by manufacturers' agents. Some manufacturers sell through both their own sales force and distributors or agents. When this dual distribution is used, the manufacturer's sales force usually sells to large customers, sells only certain kinds of products, or sells in concentrated markets. Smaller customers, the remaining products in the manufacturer's line, and the more geographically dispersed markets are sold through distributors or agents. One adhesives manufacturer uses distributors for its chemical adhesives but sells all other adhesives directly to users. A manufacturer of motors sells its large motors directly to users but uses distributors for small motors.

Regardless of whether you sell as a direct factory representative or as a distributor or agent, what we have discussed in this chapter pertains. However, a dual-distribution strategy does create a greater need for cooperation and coordination between the manufacturer's and the distributor's salespeople. Many manufacturers take extra steps to assure a favorable relationship with their distributors. They train distributors' salespeople, provide technical support for distributors, accompany distributors' salespeople on difficult sales calls, and even obtain orders for the distributors.

As a salesperson for a manufacturer, you may be expected to work closely with distributors to help them make sales. Manufacturers that stress these close ties often credit their salespeople with all sales made in the territory—theirs and the distributor's. This encourages a cooperative effort rather than a competitive one that may create conflict if each salesperson were to compete for the same customer.

RECAP

Selling to the industrial market involves challenges that vary with the category of the industrial good sold. The categories are major equipment, accessory equipment, raw materials, component materials and parts, MRO supplies, and services.

Most organizations have a person or a department responsible for purchasing industrial goods. This person is usually called a purchasing agent. Other employees commonly influence the purchasing decision. Industrial buyers generally make rational buying decisions, based primarily on price, quality, and service.

You should try to be the first to discover and fill a new need that arises. Then efforts should be directed toward continually filling the need through repeat sales. When competition has already filled the need, try to get a piece of the action.

Ultimately, sales to the industrial buyer depend on sales to the industrial buyer's customers. Creative salespeople look for ways to help their buyers increase this demand. Regardless of how well selling skills are executed, there are times when reciprocity can frustrate all attempts to make a sale.

Manufacturers sell directly to the industrial market and sell through distributors. When a dual-distribution strategy is used, cooperation and coordination become important elements of the salesperson's task.

REVIEW QUESTIONS

1. How does accessory equipment differ from major equipment?
2. What are MRO supplies?
3. What are component parts?
4. What is a buying influence?
5. What is back-door selling?
6. To what extent is price an important consideration to the buyer of industrial goods?
7. Why is delivery an important service consideration for all kinds of industrial goods?
8. When is the best time to call on a prospect with a new need?
9. Why might a prospect offer you a piece of the action?
10. How can you sell against reciprocity?
11. How do you find out about the opportunity to bid for a sale?
12. Explain dual distribution.

DISCUSSION QUESTIONS

1. Which category of industrial goods would you prefer to sell and why?
2. Are there any similarities between back-door selling and bypassing your supervisor? Explain and comment on the similar dangers.
3. Discuss those situations where you use buying influences in purchasing a consumer good.

LEARNING EXPERIENCES

1. Flip through *Thomas's Register* at your library. Observe how many manufacturers of component materials and parts there are.
2. List all the products and services a typical college purchases and try to categorize them.

CASES

THE ELECTRONIC TYPEWRITER

Issac Asimov, author of over 200 books, loves the IBM Selectric typewriter. At last count he had five of them. He's not alone. There are millions of them adorning desks in offices throughout the world. The Selectric's grand entrance in 1961 ushered in the decline of manual typewriters. At last count, IBM had sold more than 9 million of them.

However, the Selectric and other electric typewriters could also be approaching their Waterloo. Electronic typewriters and word processors are the harbingers of the much-touted "office of the future."

Electronic typewriters cost hundreds of dollars more than electric ones. They automatically center lines and make corrections. It is said that no typist can outtype them. Electronic components, including silicon chips, are dominant; they replace the 2500 mechanical parts found in the Selectric. The chip is the memory that stores what you type. There is no more need to use correction tape or tear that error-laden page from the platen; just rearrange, delete from, and add to what is stored in the memory, and the machine automatically prints the corrected copy.

What excites many people—and scares others—is the capability of electronic typewriters to double as computer terminals.

Questions

1. Into which category of industrial goods does the electronic typewriter fall? Explain.
2. Who are the buying influences?
3. Which benefits would you stress?

YORKTOWN SUPPLY

Yorktown Supply is a distributor of paints, coatings, and equipment. It stocks and sells a wide assortment of products: primers, custom-mixed paints, brushes, wire wheels, masking tapes, protective clothing, air compressors, and spraying equipment.

Its main customers are factories, which use its products primarily for maintenance, and autobody shops. Its sales force averages fourteen years of experience and regularly attends training seminars conducted by the manufacturers of the products it sells. In this business it's important that the salesperson be a problem solver for the customer because there is such a variety of application procedures. The salespeople are experts in recommending the proper spraying equipment.

Marie Riccio, an eighteen-year veteran of the Yorktown Supply sales force, called on Lansing Manufacturing for the first time to survey its needs. She noticed that everything was freshly painted, including equipment and fixtures that were not intended to be painted. When talking with Steve Madden, the maintenance supervisor, Riccio found that atomized air spraying equipment was used for Lansing's painting. Riccio explained how airless spraying equipment would eliminate the fallout that is apparent in the Lansing factory. Madden said, "We buy everything from Neddam Distributing Company. Sorry."

Questions

1. What category of industrial products would spraying equipment sold to autobody shops fall into?
2. What category of industrial products would spraying equipment sold to factories fall into?
3. What category of industrial products would paints sold to factories fall into?
4. What is the next step Marie Riccio should take?
5. Could reciprocity be a factor? Explain.

SIXTEEN

CHAPTER OBJECTIVES

To explain the major concerns retailers have about the products they buy

To describe the various kinds of buying responsibility you will encounter

To show the importance of selecting the right number of the right retailers to sell your product

To emphasize the mutual dependence of buyer and seller as they try to meet their objectives

To point out the many ways you can help the retailer move merchandise from the store's shelves

To stress the need for meaningful sales calls to existing customers

CHAPTER OUTLINE

382

SELLING TO RETAILERS

You can't sell from an empty cart.

Anonymous

American consumers spend about a trillion dollars a year. That's $1,000,000,000,000. They are spending most of that money at the stores of the nearly 2 million retailers in the United States. Before you buy from a retailer, the retailer has to buy from someone else—the salesperson who fills the cart. The next time you shop, observe the thousands, or millions, of dollars' worth of merchandise sitting on the shelves and hanging from the racks. There was a lot of buying and selling effort to get the merchandise there. This chapter focuses on those selling positions responsible for moving merchandise from the factories to the stores where people want to buy it.

RETAILERS AS CHANNEL MEMBERS

Manufacturers sell to retailers directly and through wholesaling middlemen. The distribution strategy used depends on the type of product, the kind of retailer, the potential size of the order, and other aspects of the overall marketing strategy. Apparel and furniture usually are sold directly to the retailer; many food items (particularly frozen foods) usually are sold through food brokers; and convenience goods such as stationery supplies and health and beauty aids are generally sold through wholesalers. Manufacturers often use dual distribution—their own sales force for large retailers and a wholesaler for small retailers. (See Exhibit 16.1.)

Regardless of the channel used, retailers are the final link in the chain between the manufacturer and the consumer. They sell primarily to individuals for personal use and consumption. They range in size from the corner grocery store or yarn shop to Macy's, the world's largest store, and the multiunit international chains, such as Sears and K mart.

As different as retailers are from one another, they have one thing in common: They buy to resell. They want to buy. If they don't buy, they can't sell. Retail buyers are always searching for sellers of merchandise that will satisfy the needs of their customers.

MAJOR CONCERNS OF RETAILERS

Retailers are distinguished from most other types of customers in that they are interested in different things. Remember that they are in the business of buying and reselling. They don't buy for the fun of it, as consumers often do. They buy what they think will make the cash register jingle and make their income statement look most attractive. Their major concerns that are related to your dealings with them are turning over inventory, having a positive cash flow, and showing profit.

Inventory Turnover

Retailers are not in business to stock inventory; they want to sell it. They stock it only so that they have it to sell. Generally, the faster the inventory is sold, the better it is for all concerned. The sooner the merchandise is sold, the sooner the retailer gets sales dollars into the register, and the sooner the suppliers' salespeople can make sales to replenish the inventory.

EXHIBIT 16.1
THE MOST COMMON CHANNELS

MANUFACTURER ─────────────────────────────→ RETAILER

MANUFACTURER ─────────────→ WHOLESALER ─────────────→ RETAILER

MANUFACTURER ─────────────→ BROKER ─────────────→ RETAILER

The relationship between the amount of inventory the retailer has on hand and the amount of sales is called *inventory turnover* (or stock turnover). It is computed by dividing the average dollar amount of inventory for the period (usually a year) into the sales for the same period. If sales are $400,000 and the average inventory is $100,000, the turnover ratio is 4.0 ($400,000 ÷ $100,000). Or you can say that the retailer's inventory turns four times.

Turnover ratios vary with the type of merchandise and the type of retailer. In selling to retailers, you should be aware of:

1. The importance of turnover to your retailers
2. The method used to compute turnover
3. The average turnover rates for the type of merchandise you are selling and the retailer you are dealing with
4. The documented (if possible) turnover rate for the product you are selling

Cash Flow

Turnover affects cash flow. Simply stated, when there is more money coming into the business than going out, there is a positive cash flow. When there is more money going out than coming in, there is a negative cash flow. Many retailers have temporary cash-flow crises caused primarily by seasonal sales variations. Others have constant crises of various origins which often eventually lead to their downfall.

Slow turnover is a major cause of negative cash flow. The turnover slowdown could be the result of decreased sales, increased inventory, or both. Regardless, the retailer's ability to buy additional merchandise is limited. Usually the solution to the problem is an increase in sales and more attention to both inventory levels and the composition of the inventory.

You should learn how to recognize a retailer's cash-flow problem and the cause of that problem. Additionally, you should be aware of how you might be able to help improve the situation. You might be able to get trade credit (credit from your company) for a creditworthy customer. Also, if you sell seasonal merchandise and your company has a dating-order plan, you can encourage your customer to take advantage of it. A *dating order* allows the customer to take delivery before the start of the selling season and pay for it later, usually in three equal payments. When the proper amount and assortment of merchandise is purchased, the retailer is paying invoices with consumer dollars rather than the store's cash reserves.

Profit

Bottom-line talk is rampant today, even in nonfinancial conversation. To the retailer the bottom line is what remains from the sales dollar after paying for the merchandise purchased from the supplier and the expenses incurred in operating the business. Let's look at an abbreviated income statement (Exhibit 16.2) to see what this means.

EXHIBIT 16.2
INCOME STATEMENT I

		Percent of Net sales
Net sales	$300,000	100
Less cost of merchandise sold	195,000	65
Gross margin (profit)	105,000	35
Less expenses	75,000	25
Net profit	30,000	10

As you can see, it's what happens above that determines what the bottom line will look like. Add $30,000 in net sales to the top line, don't change the other percentages, and see what happens (Exhibit 16.3).

EXHIBIT 16.3
INCOME STATEMENT II

		Percent of net sales
Net sales	$330,000	100
Less cost of merchandise sold	214,500	65
Gross margin	115,500	35
Less expenses	82,500	25
Net profit	33,000	10

Notice that the bottom line increases by $3000 in net profit as a result of the increase in sales. You can see that the retailer wants merchandise that's going to help increase sales.

Often, sales can be increased without a significant increase in expenses. Let's see what this would look like if the original dollar amount of expenses ($75,000) remained constant while net sales increased (Exhibit 16.4).

EXHIBIT 16.4
INCOME STATEMENT III

		Percent of net sales
Net sales	$330,000	100
Less cost of merchandise sold	214,500	65
Gross margin	115,500	35
Less expenses	75,000	23
Net profit	40,500	12

In this case $10,500 additional profit dollars find their way to the bottom line.

As you can see, increasing sales and reducing expenses improve profits for the retailer. Profits can also be improved by lowering the cost of merchandise sold (*your* selling price is the retailer's *cost*). Let's try this alteration. We'll just change the percentage of the cost of merchandise sold on the original income statement from 65 percent to 60 percent (Exhibit 16.5). This change brings about a $15,000 increase in gross margin and net profit.

EXHIBIT 16.5
INCOME STATEMENT IV

		Percent of net sales
Net sales	$300,000	100
Less cost of merchandise sold	180,000	60
Gross margin	120,000	40
Less expenses	75,000	25
Net profit	45,000	15

From these examples you can see what the retailer is looking for, or should be looking for, from the merchandise you sell: increased sales and lower costs to produce higher gross margins.

If your merchandise sells fast from the retailer's shelves and yields a competitive gross margin, the retailer's major concerns should be satisfied to the extent that you, the seller, can satisfy them.

WHO DOES THE BUYING?

Authority for buying depends on the kind of retailer you're dealing with. The owner makes the final buying decision in most small stores. A person called a *buyer* makes the final buying decision in most larger stores. A buying committee makes the major buying decisions, especially for new products, for most large retail chains.

Owners

The owner of a small store is usually involved in most, if not all, operating decisions, and buying is usually the number-one decision. Often the owner makes unilateral buying decisions. Sometimes key employees are asked for their opinion or consent or actually make the buying decision for certain merchandise categories. Many stores have employees who have worked for previous owners. These employees, in particular, make or help make many buying decisions for small retailers.

Buyers

Large stores are divided into departments. This makes it easier for their retail customers to locate merchandise and makes the store easier to manage. A buyer is responsible for buying and selling merchandise for one or more departments.

Each buyer is authorized to buy a stated dollar amount of merchandise for a specific time period. He or she actively looks for merchandise that the store's customers will want. Trips to trade shows where many vendors' products are displayed (see Exhibit 16.6), trade journals, and the on-premises presentations of salespeople are the principal sources of information used for making the buying decisions.

The buyer usually makes the final decision. If there is an assistant buyer, you should be aware of the influence he or she might have on the buying decision. Also, the buyer sometimes has to get approval from a merchandise manager, especially when the cost exceeds the merchandise budget for the buying period or exceeds a specified dollar amount.

Buying Committees

Large multiunit retailers commonly have a centralized buying office. A buying committee that includes people representing other divisions assists the merchandise division members in making the decision to add or delete products from the chain's merchandise assortment.

EXHIBIT 16.6
THE MART CENTER IN CHICAGO, WHERE MANY RETAILERS SHOP BEFORE THEY BUY   (*Source:* Mart Center.)

The first hurdle is getting the buying committee to accept your product. Many vendors have national accounts salespeople who are responsible for selling to the buying committees of retailers such as K mart, Penney's, and Safeway. In those cases where you are responsible for getting your product into the chain stores in your territory, you must work closely with the buyer, department manager, or store manager. You must determine how much influence this person has in getting your product on the shelves.

Some chains give their store managers buying authority in some merchandise categories so that they can meet the special needs of their community. Where authority is not given to local management, you have to encourage local managers to carry your message to the central buying office.

Once your product has been approved or listed by a chain, orders still might be channeled through the central buying office. However, each store usually will have some say in the quantities and assortments ordered.

One of the functions of the salesperson is to stimulate the local retail units to place orders with the chain's warehouse.

MANAGING SALES

How many people do you know who buy $40 dress shirts? have an $800 sewing machine? have a garden tractor? Probably not too many. How many buy $20 shirts? have sewing needles? have a garden rake? Probably quite a few. Would people buy more $40 shirts, $800 sewing machines, and garden tractors if more stores sold them? Probably not. Where do they prefer to buy the $40 shirt, at the corner drug store or at a high-fashion apparel store? Probably at the apparel store. These are the kinds of questions that a salesperson has to deal with in deciding on the market representation needed for the products sold to retailers.

The intensity of distribution depends on the kind of product you are selling. Some products need more exposure than others. Price, frequency of purchase, and the distance people will customarily travel are important determinants in the number of retailers that should carry your product. You want intensive distribution for low-priced, frequently purchased products such as most groceries and health and beauty aids. An increase in the number of stores carrying your product will probably bring about an increase in sales.

Many higher-priced, less frequently purchased products lend themselves to *selective distribution*. For example, you want the right number of the right retailers stocking your product. Assume your market analysis shows that ideally two stores in a small city should sell your product to give it proper market coverage, and six stores are prospects. It is unlikely that all six stores would want your brand, because retailers usually want to be somewhat different from their competition. What if four stores want to carry your product? An immediate reaction might be "the more the merrier." Will additional sales be made or will sales be divided among four retailers instead of between two? The disadvantage in dividing sales is that your product may not be sold as actively by all the retailers because it will not be a significant part of each retailer's business. You may decide to select the two (or perhaps three) retailers who will do the best marketing of your product.

Apple Computer, Inc., terminated its buying agreement with Computerland, the largest chain of computer stores, in order to control the location of retail outlets carrying its products. "What if you have five stores on the same corner?" said an Apple spokesperson. "We simply don't feel that the uncontrolled addition of outlets is something we can continue to live with."[1]

Of course, the decision may not be as easy as in the example given. You may have a selling job to persuade two retailers to carry your product. It depends on what you are selling and how well-known and salable your brand is.

Exclusive distribution presents still another test of your management and selling ability. For the garden tractor, the expensive dress shirt, and the sewing machine that does everything but cook dinner, you may want only one retailer selling your product in each area because there just aren't enough prospects to go around. Both you and the retailer are mutually dependent. The retailer is apt to promote the product actively because only the one store will benefit from the promotion. You must be sure to select a retailer who will cooperate with your company's entire marketing effort. In all but the legal sense you must establish a partnership with the retailer.

Managing sales goes beyond selecting the right number of right retailers. Selling the right amount and right assortment of merchandise is equally important. Many retailers will rely on you to advise them on the proper balance of sizes, colors, and styles of merchandise. Some will even want you to keep track of the stock levels and order the required replenishment stock. Keep in mind that there are potential bad effects of both underselling and overselling.

Underselling causes the retailer to face out-of-stock situations. When this happens, the retailer either loses the sale or substitutes a competitive brand. You lose either way. This is averted by forecasting normal demand requirements and safety stock to meet unexpected demand between order periods.

Overselling can also cause problems. It may affect the retailer's inventory turnover and cash flow. What you gain by overselling today you may lose through a smaller sale the next time the retailer reorders. More important, overselling can weaken the retailer's financial position and cause the store's eventual failure. Depending on the kind of product sold and your company's policy, other problems may also appear:

1. Perishable products will rot.
2. Fashion merchandise loses value as it sits on the shelves beyond the life of a fashion.
3. The retailer will have to take unplanned markdowns, thus reducing gross margins.
4. Your company will have to take back unsold merchandise.

Any of these may hurt your relationship with your customer and the image of your product.

---

[1]Andrew Pollack, "Apple Cancels Dealings at Computerland Chain," *The New York Times,* Apr. 20, 1982, p. D13.

BECOMING A PARTNER

There's great satisfaction in watching your customer's business grow. The bigger the role you play in this growth, the more you will benefit. Your success depends on your customer's success. And you probably have a greater opportunity to participate in your customer's success than in any other kind of selling.

A long-term relationship is best established by showing a sincere concern for the retailer's business. Go beyond just selling your merchandise. Often you can advise your customer on various business matters that will help this customer's business. As a result of your contact with other retailers, you will spot new ideas and trends that can be shared with your customers. New accounting practices, merchandising techniques, and inventory systems are among the many areas of mutual interest. Retailers new to the business are particularly interested in your business knowledge. Vendor salespeople commonly help new retailers secure financing, find other vendors, and get their business launched. This kind of assistance makes partnerships. See Exhibit 16.7 for an example of a company that has become a partner with its customers.

SELLING THROUGH, NOT TO

Most retailers stock hundreds or thousands of different products from dozens of manufacturers. Your product will be one of many. Convincing the retailer to buy your product is only the first step in the selling process. Your product must be actively sold once it is in the store. This is most likely to happen when your product is in the proper location, the retailer promotes it, and the retail salespeople are trained to sell it. The situation depicted in Exhibit 16.8 must be avoided.

EXHIBIT 16.7
A LOVEABLE PARTNERSHIP

The Loveable Company of Norcross, Georgia, is in the foundation business in more than one way: budget bras and basements. The company recognized that the drab bargain basements of department stores where its garments are sold were not conducive to merchandising its bras. The answer: Replace the drabness with new displays, bright lighting, and colorful carpeting in those stores wanting this kind of help.

Loveable set up Dream Departments in five major department stores at no cost to the retailers. The cost of future ventures was on a shared basis. Both Loveable and the refurbished stores have experienced significant sales gains from this merchandising innovation.

Source: Sally Scanlon, "Why Department Stores Ought to Love Loveable," *Sales and Marketing Management,* June 1978, pp. 53–55.

EXHIBIT 16.8

The corner grocer had almost half the shelves in the store stacked with jars of mustard. When his friend commented on his abundance of mustard, the grocer led him to the celler storage area and proudly pointed to additional cases upon cases of mustard.

His friend commented, "You must sell a lot of mustard."

"Not me," replied the grocer, "but the salesperson who sells me mustard sells a lot of mustard."

Space Allocation

Your product starts its journey to eventual possession by the consumer by being available at the store. Where it is located in the store makes a difference. If it is in a back-room storage area or in an undercounter storage bin, it's more likely to be stored than sold. Countless studies show that highly visible merchandise sells better than hidden merchandise. The eye level is the buy level.

You must understand where your type of merchandise sells best in a store and then make sure it gets there. Impulse items sell best if they are located on main aisles or near the cash register. Many other items sell best if they are positioned on shelves at eye level. Both the amount of space and the location are important.

Promotional Effort

Much of your company's promotional program requires the retailer's cooperation and support to be effective. Your sales will increase if you can spark the retailer's enthusiasm for cooperative advertising, displays, and other types of promotional support your company offers.

A good *cooperative advertising program* can be beneficial to both the manufacturer and the retailer in helping to move merchandise off the shelves. Your product is featured in the retailer's advertisement, and your company pays a percentage of the cost of the advertisement. The total dollar amount your company will pay depends on the amount of merchandise the retailer buys from you. Assume that your company reimburses 50 percent of the advertising cost on 2 percent of sales and that the retailer purchases $10,000 worth of merchandise. You could reimburse $200 (2 percent of $10,000) on $400 of advertising.

Not all retailers are interested in cooperative advertising. Some do not like the restrictions placed on their advertisement by the manufacturer. Others actively seek good cooperative advertising support when making buying decisions. As in any selling situation, you must determine what is important to the customer. If cooperative advertising is unimportant to your customer, you must decide if you should sell its merits or forget it and concentrate on other benefits. If it is important to your customer, you must show how favorably it compares with your competitors' programs. It's important to remember that cooperative advertising—or any promotional support offered—can help you get your product *on* the shelves and help the retailer get it *off* the shelves.

Displays and space allocation are closely related concerns. In *space allocation* you are concerned with where merchandise is located and how much space is provided for it. *Displays* affect how it is presented. Displays bring attention to the merchandise. Through proper arrangement, the merchandise itself can provide the necessary impact. End-aisle displays found in supermarkets are examples of this.

Signs, mobiles, racks, shelf extenders, counter cards, and cases are among the many display aids used to help visualize and draw extra attention to the merchandise in the store. Because they don't always have room for all display material available to them, retailers must be selective. Some display material is sold to retailers, and some is given to them. Regardless, you must convince the retailer that your display material should be used in the store. Free material might end up in the back room unless you personally set it up.

Trade promotions present another opportunity to move merchandise. They are usually some form of price reduction that the retailer is encouraged to pass along to the consumer. The most common are off-invoice allowances, bill-back allowances, and free goods. *Off-invoice allowances* are direct reductions from the invoice. *Bill-backs* are retroactive payments to the retailer for purchases made during the promotional period. *Free goods* are items given with the purchase of a specified number of units or cases, for example, one free with ten.

As with cooperative advertising and displays, trade promotions are effective only if the retailer cooperates. The trade promotion is intended to sell more merchandise to the consumer, not just more to the retailer. It is hoped that the retailer will lower the price of the merchandise and increase sales. Many times, retailers will increase their purchases to get the trade allowance but will not pass the savings on to the consumer. You do not gain from this. Your increase in sales to the retailer during the promotion will be offset by decreased sales during a subsequent period.

Training

Your customer usually has several salespeople selling your product as well as competing and complementary products. Anything you can do to make these salespeople more knowledgeable about *your* product and how to sell it should increase *your* sales. This is a two-step process. You must convince your customer that this training is beneficial and then provide the training.

There are many approaches to training. Some companies have training schools that their customers and their customers' employees are encouraged to attend. The oil companies have used this method for decades. McDonald's requires that all its franchisees and management personnel in its company-owned locations attend Hamburger University, and Midas Mufflers requires attendance at Midas Institute of Technology. Other companies sponsor occasional dealer clinics that customers and their employees are urged to attend. Manufacturers of technical

EXHIBIT 16.9
DISPLAYS HELP
TO SELL

products customarily sponsor traveling clinics. Homelite trainers travel over 100,000 miles a year bringing product and service knowledge about their chain saws to customers and customer service people.[2]

Even if your product is not conducive to clinics or training schools, you can still develop training programs. Of course, you will need your company's support and your customer's agreement to carry them out. One of the best ways to train a customer's employees is to have them read merchandise tags and labels and any other literature that describes the merchandise. Some vendors offer rewards (with the customer's permission) to store employees who show a certain level of product knowledge.

Use the training facilities and aids that your company has available and develop your own creative training programs. Retailers should be receptive to your offer to help train their employees because they themselves are placing increased emphasis on employee training. Montgomery Ward, John Wanamaker, and May Department Stores are among the larger retailers that are paying tens of thousands of dollars to outside training firms. You can offer it for nothing, but make sure it's worth more than that.

SERVICING CUSTOMERS

In most of these sales positions your primary responsibility is getting repeat business from existing customers. This involves providing a high level of service to assure that your company and its products are helping customers meet their objectives. Just calling on a customer is not enough. There must be a purpose for your call. There are entirely too many salespeople out there calling on customers only because it's Monday again, saying "How's everything? Need anything today?"

Good service can be provided only if you plan your calls. This includes planning the frequency of calls and planning what you expect to accomplish during each call. The customer must be conditioned to realize that every time you arrive there is a purpose for the call. That purpose could be to analyze product movement statistics, explain a new promotional program, report on competitive activity, introduce a new product, or offer other worthwhile information and aid to the retailer. Of course, making a sale is always of paramount concern during the call.

RECAP

Retailers act as buyers for consumers. They want to buy merchandise that will sell quickly and deliver a profit. The owner usually buys for small stores. Designated people called buyers buy for departmentalized stores. Buying committees usually make the major buying decisions for multiunit stores.

---

[2]"Homelite's Travelling Clinics," *Sales and Marketing Management*, Dec. 12, 1977, pp. 14–16.

You must sell to retailers who will do the best job in representing your product in the marketplace. Once a retailer has agreed to carry your product, your task is not finished. A favorable partnership relationship must be established, and effort must be directed toward helping the retailer actively promote and sell the product to the consumer.

Plans must be made to provide service that will maintain and enhance the business relationship. This involves planning the frequency of calls and the content of each sales interview.

REVIEW QUESTIONS

1. What are the channels of distribution commonly used for reaching the consumer?
2. What is inventory turnover?
3. What is a dating order?
4. How can you help a retailer improve cash flow?
5. Who else might influence the buyer's decision for a departmentalized retailer?
6. What is selective distribution?
7. What are the dangers of overselling?
8. Why is it important to sell through the retailer?
9. What should the salesperson do to help the retailer move merchandise from the shelves?
10. What is cooperative advertising?
11. What should be included in planning your sales calls?

DISCUSSION QUESTIONS

1. Which would you find more challenging—finding new retailers to sell your product or helping existing accounts sell more to their customers?
2. Discuss why it is more important for salespeople selling to retailers to manage sales than it is for those selling to consumers and to industrial users.

LEARNING EXPERIENCES

1. Ask the store owner where you shop to describe the best salesperson who sells to him or her.
2. Ask the same store owner, or another, how much attention is given to turnover ratios and cash-flow analysis.

CASES

STRAPPED FOR TIME[3]

Consumers prefer metal watchbands (leather straps represent only 23 percent of the market). Jewelers want to concentrate on high-priced, high-margin watches and diamonds. They don't want to devote valuable space to slow-selling leather watch straps that traditionally yield low profit margins. Therefore, most retailers relegate leather watch straps to under the counter or the back-room storage area, only to be seen when asked for by a customer.

Fear not, you importer of leather watch straps. Your straps carry premium price tags, which jewelers like; watches are selling like hot cakes; leather is in fashion. Go out and sell your straps.

Questions

1. In approaching jewelers, what selling points would you stress?
2. Is it important to get this product on top of the counter?
3. How could you get the straps properly displayed?

[3]Adapted from Thayer C. Taylor, "Hirsh Gets Its 10 Precious Minutes," *Sales and Marketing Management*, Nov. 12, 1979, pp. 39–40.

SUPER SALES

The supermarket business has changed considerably, and most of the changes have affected the job of the suppliers' salespeople. Supermarket operators used to stock most new products coming down the pike, especially those of well-known producers.

The typical supermarket stocks between 10,000 and 12,000 products. Many, however, are reducing the number of products carried. Instead of carrying five or six brands of an item, some are carrying two manufacturers' brands, a private brand (their own or a wholesaler's brand), and a generic product (no name). They are also reducing the number of sizes and flavor variations.

Supermarkets have gross profits of around 20 percent and net profits of around 1 percent. This means that for every dollar they take in, they pay the supplier 80 cents and pay out 19 cents for expenses, leaving them about a penny for profit. They've been adding more general merchandise such as housewares and home furnishings, which usually have gross profits in the 30 percent range, to increase gross profit margins.

Questions

1. How have these changes affected the selling effort of the packaged foods salesperson?
2. Does the addition of general merchandise affect how the salesperson for general merchandise manages his or her sales? Explain.

SEVENTEEN

ETHICS AND THE LAW IN SELLING

> Always do right. This will gratify some people, and astonish the rest.
>
> Mark Twain

Like every other human activity, selling has a code of conduct. It varies from industry to industry and from area to area, but it is always there. There is the free, spontaneous adherence to morality in the marketplace—*ethics*. There is also forced adherence to morality by threat of penalty, i.e., *law*. Contemporary selling is guided by both.

The early origins of selling were rife with shell-game tactics. In spite of plenty of evidence to the contrary, selling was generally thought to be—and indeed often was—a game of outsmarting buyers and competitors. *Caveat emptor* was the rule of the day.[1] But this has changed greatly. Today there are laws and organizations to protect buyers, and there are publications to inform them. There are better business bureaus and small claims courts. Moreover, a rising wave of consumerism has sparked an evolution of stricter business ethics and merchandising morals. This chapter will give you a basic understanding of selling ethics and familiarize you with some of the major laws governing the selling profession.

---

[1]*Caveat emptor* is Latin for "let the buyer beware."

400

SELLING INTEGRITY

Even in the early days there were plenty of sellers who took pride in their integrity. Enlightened self-interest is not a recent discovery. The difference is that in contemporary selling, unethical or illegal conduct is apt to be the exception rather than the rule. Sales training today follows the principle that selling is an honorable and purposeful profession. It counsels against shortcuts, deception, and exaggerated product claims. The service approach is emphasized to further the twin interests of buyer and seller. It is a win-win game where everyone benefits and no one loses.

Of course, there are plenty of exceptions, but the growing recognition of integrity in the marketplace is one of the most significant business developments of our modern era. The modern salesperson is encouraged to seek customers, rather than just orders, and to earn their continuing patronage through legitimate service. Selling integrity has come into its own.

ETHICS FOR THE SALESPERSON

A salesperson's ethics are concerned with a number of relationships:

1. Ethics in dealing with customers and prospects
2. Ethics regarding competitors
3. Ethics in representing management
4. Ethics in relations with management

EXHIBIT 17.1
HOW TO
ALIENATE
BUYERS AND
LOSE MARKETS

Simpson Trusts Us

A young stockbroker was talking to a senior partner of his firm. "We've been sitting on the Simpson discretionary account for three months without an investment."

"Still sit on it, Charlie," was the senior partner's reply.

"We could be making a lot of commissions if we activated the account."

"But with a discretionary account we have a moral responsibility, Charlie. Simpson trusts us and we cannot betray that trust. Anything else is not only unethical, but shortsighted. What's good for the client is what's good for us."

The senior partner was pointing out to his young associate the long-range wisdom of adherence to ethics in business.

Ethics in Dealing with Customers and Prospects

Ethics really do pay off in selling. Misrepresentation, exaggeration, or cutting a corner may gain a sale, but never a customer. Cultivate customers, and the orders will take care of themselves. (See Exhibit 17.2.)

Ethics Regarding Competitors

In football, a clean, hard tackle is idealized. In selling, working aggressively to get an order that might have gone to a competitor is highly acceptable. Just keep it

EXHIBIT 17.2
A CODE FOR SELLERS

1. Tell the truth. That's how you earn credibility.
2. Don't exaggerate your claims. If you do, in time the customer will not believe your truths.
3. Never promise more than you can deliver. It makes the delivery easier.
4. Dedicate yourself to advancing the buyer's legitimate interests through what you sell.
5. Don't sell a product or service to a buyer that, in the buyer's place, you would not buy yourself.
6. Retain the buyer's confidence. It is not only good ethics but good business as well.
7. Never forget that you are in a service profession. Meet buyers in a spirit of service to them.
8. Remember that your sale is not complete till the buyer has been satisfied with what you sold. Following up to assure this not only is ethical but sometimes leads to other prospects.
9. Respect customer complaints and handle them accordingly. A complaint is a chance for you to correct a source of dissatisfaction and retain the customer. The customer who makes a legitimate complaint renders you a service.
10. If you turn out to be wrong in fact or act, admit it and correct it.
11. Speak no ill of your competitors, your company, or your associates.

---

clean. Otherwise, it might boomerang. Sharp, clean competition is good for helping the community, expanding markets, and gaining advantages for the buyer.

Knocking competitors is, of course, shortsighted. It is negative selling. Negative selling can shrink total markets and diminish acceptance for the generic product or service, both your own and that of your competitor. The following dialogue between a seller of gas heaters and a homeowner explains how.

PROSPECT: Thanks for calling, but I've decided on Imperial.
SELLER: Imperial? Didn't you hear about how an Imperial caused an explosion in Silver City and killed two kids?
PROSPECT: Really?
SELLER: Yessiree! I've got the newspaper clipping. Now with our heater, that can't happen because . . .
PROSPECT (*interrupting*): Just a minute. You give me pause. Maybe I'd better reconsider whether I want a gas heater at all.

What if a competitor knocks you, your product, or your service? There is only one way to deal with rumor or misstatements: facts. Counteract false information with true information, as in the following example.

A food processor's purchasing agent tells an additive seller, "I'm hesitant about doing business with you. I've been told you have to be watched closely for coliform counts."

The salesperson calmly replies, "I don't know who told you that, Mr. Greentree. But the answer to rumor is facts, isn't that so?"

"Of course."

"Well, here's a sample copy of the report our quality control department sends you with each shipment. A complete microbiological analysis of the shipment you're receiving. Not just coliform count, but much more."

The factual response to a deprecating rumor reported by a buyer is even stronger when supported by proof. Your selling case actually is strengthened.

Ethics in Representing Management

Sales representatives also have been known to speak disparagingly of their own companies or sources. This is bad judgment. As a salesperson, broker, or agent, no matter what you think about your source, your company, your management, your company policies, or your associates, keep it to yourself. Like a family, there may be disagreements within the fold, but you must present a solid front for the outside world. A buyer is apt to be skeptical about buying from a source when the representative expresses misgivings about it. On the other hand, a buyer is encouraged to buy from a source whose representative is enthusiastic about company, product, people, and policies.

Ethics in Relations with Management

**EXHIBIT 17.3
WOULD YOU BUY
FROM THIS
SOURCE?**

Integrity in relations with management (or source, in the case of an independent agent or broker) is another mark of the professional salesperson. As the main link between source and buyer, you are called upon to supply information on competition, buyer attitudes and preferences, credit information, and many other varieties of intelligence. This should be done conscientiously. For example, to tell management inaccurately that company prices are a major factor in sales resistance—in order to encourage reducing prices—would be highly unethical. It is your moral responsibility to cooperate fully with all company programs and to submit all reports accurately and on time. That is implicit in the representation agreement. Management and sales representatives are expected to work together wholeheartedly, honestly, and sincerely to further their mutual interests.

A particular area where management has a right to expect ethical conduct is in your diligent use of *time* and your respectful handling of *company equipment* and *money*.

Time   In the final analysis, the company pays its sales representatives for sales. However, since time in most cases is an essential ingredient in the making of sales, you are expected to devote a proper amount of time to selling and related activities. Indeed, selling is an ill-chosen calling for anyone who needs to be closely supervised and watched about putting in enough time. This is especially pertinent if you operate away from headquarters. A successful career in selling requires initiative and self-motivation. This spells freedom, and it is one of the main attractions of the selling profession.

Is it ethical for you to moonlight? Since management has contracted for your prime time and is paying for it, no moonlighting assignment should be undertaken without management's approval. Whether this approval is forthcoming or not is quite apt to depend on the nature of the out-of-hours work and how it affects your regular prime-time performance. Repeat: As a salesperson you are paid for performance rather than for time. Most companies frown on moonlighting.

Company Equipment   The representative who hands dog-eared literature over to a prospect or allows a company vehicle to become slovenly or be in disrepair is not living up to what the company deserves. Treat company equipment, vehicles, literature, samples, sample carriers, and all other company equipment as if it were your own. Your company or source will appreciate it.

How about using company vehicles for personal use? This is strictly a matter of company policy and is generally stated at the time of employment. Follow the company policy in this, as in all other matters.

Money   In some categories of selling, the salespeople actually handle the company's money. The ethics in this are too elemental to discuss. However, there is another, more critical area involving the company's money. That is *expense control.* The more profitable your company or source is, the better is your opportu-

EXHIBIT 17.4
WATCH YOUR SELLING EXPENSES

404

nity for personal prosperity. Remember that if your company works on a net profit of 5 percent, it takes $20 of sales to balance the waste of a dollar in expense.

Other Ethical Matters

There are many other matters of ethics in selling. Some of them are bribery, gifts, excessive entertainment, price favoritism, and kickbacks.

Bribery Bribery has gotten into the news in the past few years because of the payment of large sums to buyers or intermediaries in international trade. For example, the prince consort of a European nation admitted receiving $1 million for aiding the consumation of a major government purchase contract. Several officials of American companies were forced to resign because of their unethical conduct in making large payoffs in foreign countries to sell their wares. This is not an open-and-shut question. In our American culture, bribery is unethical, in some cases even illegal. But there are countries where payment to someone other than the buyer is an accepted fact of life. In these cultures, the seller who does not honor this custom is working uphill. The American seller is faced with the awful choice of whether to conform to this custom or to lose orders that mean jobs to American workers.

The level of bribery the average salesperson is more apt to run into is the case of the buyer for a company or institution who either seeks payoffs or gives the business to another seller who offers bribes. Related to outright cash or percentage-of-purchase bribes are other, less pointed practices of questionable ethics: gifts, lavish entertainment, and other incentives way beyond the value of the business at stake and unrelated to quality, service, or price. The self-respecting salesperson with a long-range career objective does not participate in these practices. It is better to lose an occasional order than to become completely demoralized. Unreasonably lavish entertainment must, of course, not be confused with the business lunch and other modest amenities.

Price Favoritism and Kickbacks To discriminate among buyers of ''like quantity and quality'' not only is unethical but, in the section on law in this chapter, will be seen to be even illegal. However, buyers often do get favorable treatment, if not on the invoice, then through under-the-table kickbacks, extra service, and similar tactics. Generally speaking, these evasions are more common in small business than big business. They also vary in prevalence from industry to industry. In most cases, it is company management, rather than the sales representative, that sets policies on equity in customer treatment.

THE SALESPERSON AND THE LAW

In selling, there are legal standards as well as ethical standards. Ethical standards are molded by the customs of a society. Legal standards usually originate in a similar fashion but are formalized by statute.

Following are some of the more important federal laws that have an influence on selling activities. Also, new laws are passed continually. Competent sales management follows these legislative changes and keeps sales representatives informed.

The Uniform Commercial Code

The Uniform Commercial Code (UCC) and its predecessor, the Uniform Sales Act, are the major laws that affect selling activities and practices. The code is lengthy and detailed. Students of selling should be aware of the major areas that are covered. Sales management should be aware of the details as they affect the company and specific jobs.

With the exception of Louisiana, all states have adopted the UCC.[2] Essentially, Article 2 of the code focuses on the relationship between the salesperson and the buyer. Here are some of the most important aspects of the law:

1. *Definition of a sale:* The code clearly states that the salesperson has the authority to legally obligate the company he or she represents. If he or she makes an offer and it receives an unqualified acceptance, there is a contract. The contract does not have to be in writing to be binding. However, the code does differentiate between a genuine offer and an invitation to negotiate; if the salesperson quotes prices, terms of sale, delivery dates, etc., and the buyer accepts, it may be binding.
2. *Warranties and guarantees:* The code distinguishes between express warranties and implied warranties. An express warranty is stated in the contract. An implied warranty is one that is implied by law but not specifically stated in the contract. For example, a new house may have a one-year warranty. The contract may specifically *express* the electric, plumbing, and heating systems. *Implied* would be all other aspects of construction, i.e., the foundation, the sills and joists, the roof, etc. In many sales contracts, both express and implied warranties may exist. Both are legally binding.
3. *Obligations and performance:* The code states that once the terms of sale have been spelled out, both the salesperson and the customer are obligated to perform according to those terms. The performance must be in accordance with the standards common to the particular industry.
4. *Financing:* The salesperson must be completely familiar with and communicate to the buyer the legal aspects of credit used in financing the product or service. This includes all costs of credit: service charges, annual percentage rates, prepayment penalties, etc.
5. *Risk and property rights:* The UCC applies to those areas not spelled out in a specific contract. It becomes applicable when problems relating to the sale arise—problems such as who is responsible for and what to do about damaged goods, insurance claims, or credit difficulties.

[2]Ronald A. Anderson and Walter A. Kumpf, *Business Law,* South-Western, Cincinnati, Ohio, 1975, p. 444.

EXHIBIT 17.5
NOT ALL CONTRACTS NEED BE IN WRITING (*Source:* Rhoda Sidney/Monkmeyer.)

Cooling-Off Laws

Most states, the District of Columbia, and many cities have passed *cooling-off laws*. Although the specific provisions of these laws vary, the primary purpose is to provide consumers with an opportunity to reconsider a buying decision. The major targets of the cooling-off laws are decisions made under the persuasive influence of a salesperson. Door-to-door sales are specifically cited in most of the laws.

The typical cooling-off statute includes the following provisions:[3]

1. Sales covered are those which are made outside the seller's regular place of business.
2. The sale can be cancelled within three days after the transaction by mailing the seller written notice.
3. A notice-of-cancellation statement must be given to the buyer.
4. Many states exempt sales under a certain amount, usually $25.
5. Usually, there is no penalty for cancellation, although some statutes permit a penalty of 5 percent of the cash price, or the down payment.

[3]C. Robert Patty, *Managing Salespeople*, Reston Publishing, Reston, Va., 1979, p. 21.

EXHIBIT 17.6
A NOTICE OF CANCELLATION STATEMENT
MUST BE GIVEN TO THE BUYER AT THE
TIME OF SALE (*Source:* Craig Callan.)

Antitrust Laws

There are four antitrust laws that concern salespeople: the Sherman Act of 1890, the Clayton Act of 1914, the Federal Trade Commission Act of 1914, and the Robinson-Patman Act of 1936. The *Sherman Act* outlaws every contract, combination, or conspiracy in restraint of trade or commerce when a state boundary is crossed. This law proved difficult to enforce, so in 1914 Congress passed the *Clayton Act,* which essentially outlaws price discrimination, i.e., special treatment to the buyer by comparison with other buyers of like quality and quantity. The Clayton Act again proved difficult to enforce, particularly with the advent of large retailers, so in 1936 Congress passed the *Robinson-Patman Act* to amend the price discrimination section of the Clayton Act. The Robinson-Patman Act was originally intended to cover only transactions with large retailers. However, it was written in such general terms that through the years it has become more generally applicable. The act prohibits price discrimination between buyers of products of like grade and quantity if the effect of such discrimination is to impair competition. The charge of discrimination may be against either party to the transaction, the seller or the buyer. For this reason, it is customary for chain store buyers, for example, to refuse to accept a merchandising offer without having the seller sign a guarantee that this offer is being made on equal terms to buyers of like grade and quantity.

The Federal Trade Commission Act of 1914 states that unfair competition is illegal. A false, misleading, or deceptive label or package would be a case of unfair competition, as an example. Because of this act, a number of administrative laws have developed. A very practical approach to this area was provided in 1975 by *Business Week*. It is shown in Exhibit 17.7 and is still useful for the student of selling.

Pyramid Selling

Pyramid selling is a form of multilevel selling which basically involves misrepresentation and sometimes fraud. Pyramiding involves *head-hunting,* a term used to describe the practice of recruiting people willing to invest in an inventory of products, with little concern for their ability to sell. Little time is spent in trying to convert the recruits into successful salespeople. Therefore, few goods are actually moved to the consumer. Rather, the new salesperson is encouraged to recruit additional salespeople to invest in the product.

Laws Relating to Credit

Salespeople should be familiar with the *Debt Collection Practices Act* (1977) and the *Truth in Lending Law* (1969). The Debt Collection Practices Act prohibits

EXHIBIT 17.7
THE TEN DON'TS OF ANTITRUST

1. Don't discuss with customers the price your company will charge others.
2. Don't attend meetings with competitors (including trade association gatherings) at which pricing is discussed. If you find yourself in such a session, walk out.
3. Don't give favored treatment to your own subsidiaries and affiliates.
4. Don't enter into agreements or "friendly" understandings on discounts, terms or conditions of sale, profits or profit margins, shares of the market, bids or the intent to bid, rejection or termination of customers, sales territories, or markets.
5. Don't use one product as bait for selling another.
6. Don't require a customer to buy a product only from you.
7. Don't forget to consider state antitrust laws as well as the federal statutes.
8. Don't disparage a competitor's product unless you have specific proof that your statements are true. This is an unfair method of competition.
9. Don't make either sales or purchases conditional on the other party's making reciprocal purchases from or sales to your company.
10. Don't hesitate to consult with a company lawyer if you have any doubt about the legality of a practice. Antitrust laws are wide-ranging and subject to changing interpretations.

Source: Business Week.

practices of harassment such as late-night phone calls, threats of violence, and use of profane or obscene language. The Truth in Lending Law is designed to assure full disclosure of credit terms to the consumer. The finance charge and the annual percentage rate of the credit must be stated, as well as any other costs that are related to the use of the credit.

Laws Relating to Specific Products

There are several laws that have been passed which relate to specific products. The first is the *Pure Food and Drug Act,* passed in 1906, which prohibits adulteration and misbranding of foods and drugs sold in interstate commerce. This law was subsequently expanded into the *Food, Drug and Cosmetic Act* in 1938. This act prohibits adulteration and sale of foods, drugs, cosmetics, and therapeutic devices that endanger the public health. The *Fur Products Labeling Act* (1951) prohibits misbranding, false advertising, and false invoicing of furs and fur products.

The *Automobile Information Disclosure Act* of 1958 requires that all automobile dealers post suggested retail prices on new cars.

The *Magnuson-Moss Warranty–Federal Trade Commission Improvement Act* of 1975 provides for disclosure standards for written consumer product warranties and defines the standards for such warranties.

There are a number of other laws relating to specific products or services which a salesperson in a specific industry should become familiar with.

Green River Ordinances

A number of cities across the United States have so-called Green River ordinances which relate to nonresident door-to-door salespeople who plan to sell goods or services to residents. In most cases, they require that door-to-door salespeople register with municipal authorities and obtain a license to sell. The specifics of these ordinances vary from city to city, so it is wise for a salesperson to check with authorities in each.

RECAP

Ethics and law affect the job and the decisions of a salesperson. Ethics are concerned with a number of selling relationships, including dealing with buyers, behavior toward competitors, relations with management, and representation of management.

There are several federal laws which have an influence on sales activities. We discussed the Uniform Commercial Code, cooling-off laws, antitrust laws, laws relating to credit, laws relating to specific products, and the Green River ordinances.

REVIEW QUESTIONS

1. A salesperson's ethics are concerned with four selling relationships. What are they?
2. How do you deal with a situation in which a competitor has said untrue things about your product or service?
3. Why is it shortsighted to knock a competitor?
4. Name three points on which management expects ethical conduct on the part of salespeople.
5. Is there a yardstick to indicate where business amenities end and bribery begins?
6. Do buyers ever receive preferential treatment by a seller? How?
7. What does the Uniform Commercial Code say about warranties and guarantees? about financing? about risk and property rights?
8. What does a typical cooling-off statute indicate?
9. Name the intent of the Robinson-Patman Act.
10. Basically, what does the Federal Trade Commission Act of 1914 cover?
11. What is pyramid selling?
12. Name two laws relating to credit. What does each prohibit?
13. Are there any statutes relating to specific products? What are they?

DISCUSSION QUESTIONS

1. Do you think that there are times when it would be justifiable to knock competitors? Explain.
2. How do management and sales representatives depend on each other? Discuss.
3. Discuss the ethical responsibilities of salespeople in regard to working time.
4. How, beyond making sales, can a sales representative help a company's profits? Discuss.
5. Discuss bribery in selling. Give your views on both direct and indirect devices to influence buyers beyond quality, price, and product feature-benefits.
6. Opponents of the cooling-off laws think they give the consumer an unfair advantage to shop around for a better deal after having signed a legal contract. What is your feeling on this?
7. Considering the laws outlined in this chapter, would you want to see additional laws or fewer laws governing the actions of salespeople? Defend your answer in terms of selling as a profession.

LEARNING EXPERIENCES

1. Go to a library and look through the most recent editions of the *Business Periodical Index* to get an idea of what is being written concerning ethics. What does this tell you about the importance of ethics in contemporary society?

2. Scan several of the articles and select the one that most interests you. Present a summary of the article in class and follow up with your opinions about it.

CASES

HARLAN MACHINE TOOL CORPORATION

Harold Kraus, sales representative for Harlan Machine Tool Corporation, was in a dilemma. Olson Brothers was in the market for a computerized lathe. Olson was the biggest machine tool buyer in Harold's territory, but he had never sold Olson a nickel's worth. The reason was a mystery. Carl Troy, the purchasing agent, was always friendly to Harold and listened politely to his presentations. But practically all Olson's machine tool purchases were going to Universal Machine Tool Company. Harold decided to discuss the problem with George West, his sales manager. The following dialogue took place.

WEST: Would you say, Harold, that our line is equal to Universal's in quality, completeness, and service?

KRAUS: I'd say we're superior on quality and equal on the other counts.

WEST: How about your presentations? Is your message getting across to Troy?

KRAUS: I really believe so, George. He even pays a minor complement to one of our products once in a while.

WEST: Let's talk about the lathe he's going to buy. How does ours compare with Universal's point by point.

KRAUS: Just about equal. When I first presented our lathe literature to Troy, he said we were in the running.

WEST: How about prices, Harold?

KRAUS: That's what bugs me. Our price is lower, and I thought Troy would be pleased. He only said, "Good. Price is one factor we'll consider." George, do you think Troy is getting a special price under the table?

WEST: Not from Universal. They're a very ethical house. Sue Grand, the president, would never tolerate that kind of thing. But let's try another tack. Who calls on Olson for Universal?

KRAUS: A fellow named Ernie Sommers.

WEST: How long has he been calling on Troy?

KRAUS: A couple of years. They got none of the business till he showed up. Now they're getting most of it.

WEST: Would you call Sommers a good rep, Harold?

KRAUS: That's another strange one. He's not that strong with other accounts. He's a personable, outgoing fellow, but I don't think he's that hot a salesman.

(*A week later, Kraus came into West's office quite excited.*)

KRAUS: Do you know what, George? I found out why Universal is getting

Olson's business. There's a special relationship between Sommers and Troy. They go out on the town together regularly and Sommers pays the tabs!

QUESTIONS

1. What might Kraus do to counteract this unfair competiton? For one thing, his expense account does not provide for expensive on-the-town outings.
2. Is there any way that sales manager West can help Harold sell the lathe?

GREEN VALLEY SPRING WATER

Sara Smedley has just become a sales representative for Green Valley Spring Water, Inc., a relatively new company aiming to extend distribution in the metropolitan New York City market. Since she formerly represented a food company in the area, she knows and is known to many buyers. Now she is in the office of Robert's Supermarkets, a ten-store local chain in the Bronx, talking to owner Robert Watson.

ROBERT: I'd like to take your line on, Sara, but I just haven't any more shelf space. I've got three lines of spring water now.

SARA: Tell you what, Robert. Give us an end display for four weeks and I can get you a twenty-five percent special discount off the regular wholesale list. How's that?

ROBERT: You're getting close, Sara. I'll tell *you* what: twenty-five percent off the regular wholesale list for four months and leave it to me to promote—with or without displays.

SARA: You've got a deal, Robert. But let's keep it quiet. You're the only chain in the Bronx getting it.

Questions

1. Is this transaction legal or not? Be specific. Look up the appropriate laws to substantiate your answer.
2. If the transaction is illegal, who is liable, Green Valley Spring Water or Robert's Supermarkets?

EIGHTEEN

CHAPTER OBJECTIVES

To understand the principle of selling productivity

To learn how to get the most out of:
Your territory
Your time
Your customers
Your telephone
Your postsale activities
Your aftercalls
Your follow-ups
Your company management

CHAPTER OUTLINE

Selling Productivity: Managing Yourself
    Getting the Most out of Your Territory
    Getting the Most out of Your Time
    Getting the Most out of Your Customers
    Getting the Most out of Your Aftercall
    Getting the Most out of Your Telephone
Gain by Being Managed
    Join the Team
    Cooperate with Your Management
    Fill Out Those Reports
    Gain by Training
    Ask for Help
    Be a Partner to Your Management
Recap
Review Questions
Discussion Questions
Learning Experiences
Case
    Central Permaweather, Inc.

MANAGING YOURSELF AND BEING MANAGED

Increased rewards come from increased productivity. Increased productivity comes from working smart—not just working hard.

Anonymous

EIGHTEEN

One farmer gets twice as much yield per acre as a neighbor. One factory turns out twice as much product per worker-hour as another. One store sells three times as much per square foot of display space as does its competitor. Productivity is the name of the game. It applies in selling as in everything else. Twenty percent of all salespeople are estimated to account for 80 percent of all sales. This is because the 20 percent have higher rates of selling productivity than the 80 percent. They operate in a way that gets them more effective selling time (actual interviews, not traveling or waiting time), a higher ratio of closings to calls, and more dollars of sales per day, per week, per year, and per mile. The measure is not just how much you sell, but how much you sell for the effort you expend. Your selling productivity depends on how well you manage yourself and how well you take advantage of the services which your management provides to help you sell.

In this chapter you will learn how to be productive as a salesperson—how to make your best effort and how to make your best efforts pay off.

416

SELLING PRODUCTIVITY: MANAGING YOURSELF

There are only two ways to increase your sales—sell more customers or sell customers more. The key is selling productivity—getting a bigger yield of customers out of your territory, getting a bigger dollar sales yield out of your customers. That is the main difference between the sellers in the 20 percent group who make 80 percent of all sales and the other 80 percent who are estimated to make 20 percent of all sales. The sellers in the former group are more productive because they manage themselves better. They get more sales production out of each sales call, each hour, and each mile. This is the sum of five components:

1. Getting the most out of your territory
2. Getting the most out of your time
3. Getting the most out of your customers
4. Getting the most out of your aftercall
5. Getting the most out of your telephone

Getting the Most out of Your Territory

A territory is more than an area. It is a market—a mix of people, business establishments, residences, prospects, and customers. If you sell in the field, you are a *territory manager*. One thing your productivity depends on is how thoughtfully you determine where to go, in what order, and when. Review the chapter on prospecting. Pick the parts of your territory where your most likely prospects are. Establish a coverage policy. For example, will you do better to high spot over your whole territory or to concentrate on one section at a time and then go on to the next? Make a 3 × 5 card for each prospect. Map out where you will go each day of the week, each week of the month. Divide your prospect cards into batches by sections of your territory. Each night make a list of the calls you plan to make the next day. Then play position like a billiard player. For example, you are told that a prospect cannot see you today, and you make a date with that prospect for the next Tuesday. Then, for the rest of the time you are in this part of your territory, try to make follow-up dates for the next Tuesday. These follow-ups and the other calls you will schedule for yourself will give you a fully concentrated territory plan for next Tuesday, with a minimum of wasted time and travel. Keep your cards in a box, in a conventional card file, or even batched together with elastic bands for each day of the week, for next week, for the week after next, for the third week, the fourth week, and next month. This provides a tickler system to keep track of which calls you should be making and approximately when. Each week as you plan your itinerary, you move cards ahead to the proper file section. The tickler file is a simple method for guiding your itinerary planning with a minimum of effort or memory strain. Of course, if you have a date on Thursday at 9:30 A.M. with the biggest prospect in your market, when you set up the appointment write it down in your diary in big red letters.

Play the clock as well as the calendar. For instance, a food service seller calling on restaurants and retail bakeries has found that in her territory the best time to see restaurant buyers is between 9 and 11 A.M. in advance of the noon lunch rush

or between 2 and 4 P.M. before the restaurant buyer becomes absorbed with dinner matters. The bakers can be seen at various times, including very early hours. So this salesperson plans each day to see bakers before 9 A.M. and between 11 A.M. and 2 A.M., when restaurant buyers are too busy to receive salespeople.

Getting the Most out of Your Time

It has been estimated that the average salesperson spends 32 percent of the week in traveling and waiting for buyers; 24 percent on paperwork, meetings, and details; 5 percent on service calls; and only 39 percent actually face to face with prospects.[1] Time is the most precious commodity a salesperson has, and time management is critical to selling productivity. If you can raise the 39 percent *real* selling time to 52 percent, you will be increasing your sales potential by more than 33 percent. Broadly speaking, time is the only thing in which all people are created equal. Regardless of what you did not inherit, you are guaranteed 60 minutes to the hour, 24 hours to a day, and 365 days each year. There are two things you can do with this legacy. You can save it prudently, and you can spend it wisely. That is time management.

Saving Time   If you would save time, start by seeing where it goes. Keep a log of what you do with your time for a week. Analyze the total number of hours consumed by each activity. Then ask yourself what you did with your time that was not worth doing. Stop doing it. Ask yourself what you did with your time in terms of your personal and career objectives. Rearrange your priorities. If you are like everyone else, these and similar questions will expose a treasure trove of potential time savings.

Spending Time   The most important rule to guide you as you plan how to spend your time is the *Pareto principle,* also called the *80-20 rule.* Vilfredo Pareto, a nineteenth-century Italian economist, discovered that nothing numerical breaks down into equal components. Although the distribution of a whole into its percentage parts is not uniformly 80 percent–20 percent, it is nevertheless so unbalanced that 80-20 has, in liberal interpretation, become the symbol of the Pareto principle.

EXHIBIT 18.2
GET THE MOST OUT OF YOUR TIME

For example, 23 percent of all male adults are estimated to consume 81 percent of the beer marketed; 16 percent of the homes consume 62 percent of the cake mixes; 17 percent of the homes buy 79 percent of the instant coffee; 11 percent of the male adults buy 74 percent of the breath fresheners; 13 percent of the male adults buy 89 percent of the digestive aids sold. The major portion of a restaurant's business comes from a small percentage of the items on the menu. Eighty percent of television viewing is concentrated on 20 percent of the telecasts. The major portion of sales made are closed by a disproportionately smaller percentage of the salespeople in the profession. (See Exhibit 18.3.)

[1]*Source:* McGraw-Hill Research, August, 1977.

There are three essentials to intelligent time planning: Program your time, plan your time expenditures strategically, and spend your time selectively.

Program your time   List your objectives for each day the night before, for each week the previous weekend. Set your goals for the month and the year as well. Now, remembering Pareto, rank these objectives (such as prospects to sell) in order of value. Put the biggest and best prospects at the top of the list, the smallest at the bottom. Let this ranking guide your scheduling of calls.

Plan your time expenditures strategically   Diligent prospecting and intelligent preapproach increase your selling productivity. The better your overall prospecting and, in particular, your qualifying, the better will be your selection of prospects to sell. The better your preapproach, the more successful will be your approaches. Advance work, like referencing and other door-opening devices, will increase your ratio of interviews to approaches. Superior qualifying will increase your ratio of closings to interviews. This is strategic planning of time. And don't forget paperwork. Keep ahead of it daily and, above all, save it for off-selling hours. The secret of dealing with paperwork is to handle each item only *once* and

EXHIBIT 18.3
THE PARETO PRINCIPLE: THE WHOLE IS THE SUM OF UNEQUAL PARTS

move it on its way to its destination, to scheduling for handling later, or to the wastebasket.

Spend your selling time selectively Selective selling, one of the most constructive developments in today's selling, is the ultimate Pareto. It is the policy of fishing where the big ones are biting. A sugar company, making a time study of its personal selling, was surprised to learn that the amount of time its salespeople were spending with individual customers and prospects bore no relationship to the size or potential size of the account. A system was inaugurated under which sellers received route sheets that scheduled four calls on an A account, to three calls on a B account, to two calls on a C account, and one call on a D account. There was a land-office increase in sales. Another company, encouraging its salespeople to be more selective in terms of selling cost versus buyer potential, saw its number of accounts drop to one-fourth of the former total with a threefold increase in dollar sales! A liquor seller observed that getting its line into a leading dealer's store resulted in calls from other dealers in the same market. Selective selling is vital to time management for greater selling productivity. Analyze your market to locate the pressure points of volume buying, and balance your routing to give them their proper weight in the investment of your selling time.

EXHIBIT 18.4
FISH WHERE THE BIG ONES ARE BITING

Getting the Most out of Your Customers

Satisfied customers are a veritable fountain of additional business and leads to still more business. Nothing surpasses customer satisfaction for repeated purchases and references to new prospects. Three subparts of the selling process assure your getting the most out of your customers: postsale and postsale followup, continuing follow-up, and suggestion selling.

Postsale and Postsale Follow-Up "Selling customers more" begins with the closing of the first sale to a buyer. This phase of the selling process is called the *postsale*. It means leaving no detail neglected in making sure the customer's satisfaction is indeed complete: attention to delivery and service details, warranty forms, and similar matters. You will not sell more to a customer later if you fail to ensure that the customer is not only thoroughly pleased with what he or she bought and with the way the transaction and post transaction were handled but also is conspicuously aware of it. That is why one highly successful real estate salesperson arranges for a house buyer, on arriving at the new home, to find flowers with a message of welcome, the local newspaper, utilities and phone connected, and a supper sent in the first night. This seller never makes a cold call. Every customer sold refers this real estate agent to other prospects.

Then there is the postsale follow-up. Shortly after the purchase, visit or phone the buyer to inquire as to the buyer's enjoyment of the product or service. Buyers like this interest and acceptance of responsibility. In addition, if there is any question or if anything has gone wrong, you can deal with it. Repeat: The first

EXHIBIT 18.5
HOW TO AVOID HAVING TO MAKE COLD CALLS

step in getting more business from and through your customers is making sure of the customer's enthusiastic satisfaction through postsale and postsale follow-up.

Continuing Follow-Up   Selling productivity turns more prospects into buyers, more buyers into customers, and customers into bigger customers. Continuing follow-ups bring repeat orders, sales of additional items, and other prospects. Every car buyer is a prospect for a replacement purchase in the future, and the way to get the inside track is to maintain a continuing relationship with that buyer. Every suit buyer is a prospect for another item of apparel. Every razor buyer will need more blades.

Suggestion Selling   All buyers have latent needs and wants, of which they may not even be aware. Widening the patronage of a customer is another element of selling productivity. We are not talking about pressure selling. We are describing a legitimate service that results from superb product or service knowledge coupled with keen perception of the customer's usage and possible additional usage of what you sell. A simple example of suggestion selling occurs when the department store salesperson sells a lamp and suggests an appropriate lamp shade to go with it. A salesperson for a printing firm suggests a new-employees' welcome manual to a manufacturer along with an actual draft of the copy—and gets the order. An office supply salesperson notices that a customer is overloaded with old records. She gives the buyer an article from an accounting publication that explains what to keep, what to discard, and when to do it. The customer appreciates this service initiative and buys a quantity of kraft storage files to use in following the article's advice. When, in contrast to these positive examples, an automobile service station operator neglects to recommend a needed new battery and the motorist's car later goes dead on the road, this decidedly is not good service in the customer's interest.

Says Robert L. Daniels, vice president of Garrett Industrial Company of Los Angeles: "No matter how well you think you're handling an existing territory, there is probably more business waiting to be plucked from existing accounts than in all the new accounts you could call on in the next six months. There is always more potential where you already are than where you're planning to go, at least in the early stages."[2]

EXHIBIT 18.6
THE PIGGYBACK
SALE

THE PIGGYBACK SALE

"You made the right choice," said Dan Brink to his appliance customer. "The X341 model was designed for a kitchen like yours." With this, he handed over the receipt; after the closing amenities, the customer left the showroom.

Carl Devalle, the department manager, sauntered over to Dan and congratulated him. "Good going, Dan," he said. "I watched you. You're getting better all the time. However," he added with a friendly smile, "you missed one thing."

"What's that?" asked Dan, all ears.

"A chance to make a piggyback sale."

"A piggyback sale?"

[2]"Where Are the Markets?" *Industrial Distribution*, April 1982, p. 41.

"Yup. When it's all bottled up, why not ask the customer what her next appliance acquisition is apt to be? The worst that can happen is she won't know. But she actually thanked you for the way you took care of her on the refrigerator, and you have the inside track on her next purchase. If she says a new dishwasher is next, ask her if she'd like you to keep an eye out for a special sale. You'd be surprised at how she might like that. In fact, there are many cases where the customer names the next appliance and winds up buying it right then or soon after."

"Sounds good," said Dan thoughtfully. "I'll try it next time. Piggyback sale, eh. M-m-m-m-m."

"Do you know the secret of a piggyback sale, Dan? Well, generally speaking, the best prospect of all is the customer you've already sold."

Getting the Most out of Your Aftercall

If you want to raise your selling productivity, take full advantage of three opportunities after each sales call: aftercall analysis, aftercall recording, and aftercall communication.

Aftercall Analysis   This is the selling game's instant replay. It is the salesperson's analysis of what went right or wrong and why, as a basis for improvement. Did you get the order? What was the key? What was the high point of the interview? What feature carried the sale to the closing? Could you have sold more than you did? How? Or, conversely, did you fail to close? Why? What was the turning point? What was the prospect's main reason for not buying? How about emotion-based resistance? Was the setting right? Were you talking to the right person? Were you sufficiently prepared? Was your approach a ho-hum crasher? Was your presentation convincing? Did you stress the right product or service features? Did you relate them to the prospect's interests? Did you have the answers to the prospect's objections? Did you talk too much and not listen enough? Did you make a sound effort to close? Did you pick the right time to close? This aftercall analysis by instant replay is what makes a good salesperson better. It is a vital key to the raising of your selling productivity.

EXHIBIT 18.7
INSTANT REPLAY
IS THE ROAD TO
IMPROVEMENT

Aftercall Recording   The best time to update a prospect card, to note vital information, or to fill in a report form is right after the interview when the facts are fresh in your mind. For most notes on your prospect card, such as a product feature that was well-received or an objection that stymied the closing, a code number or an abbreviation generally will suffice. The link between today's result and tomorrow's improved productivity is often contained in the note you mark on your prospect card. A note on the name of a child or a hobby may be helpful. A point of departure or difference in the interview can provide a natural pickup for the next call.

Aftercall Communication   In many categories of selling, a letter or phone call after the sales interview can have a positive effect. In a purchase of substance, like a house or an insurance policy, this communication should be a standard part of your postsale. If the sale was not closed, but is moving in the right direction, a letter reviewing the plus points as they relate to the prospect may speed up the closing or ease the way for a close on the next call. Another time for an aftercall communication is when the seller has new information that will help the prospect over a resistance hurdle which came up during the sales interview. For example, a shipper objected to a corrugated container because of insufficient vertical-stress resistance. The salesperson phoned the buyer a few days later to report on tests conducted in the plant laboratory as a result of the buyer's misgivings. The report was favorable and the seller was invited to come back for another meeting. Never underestimate the power of the telephone and the mail. Selling is persuasion, and you cannot persuade without communicating.

Getting the Most out of Your Telephone

One of the greatest boons to your selling productivity is your telephone. Although selling in person is the name of the game, the phone can help you arrange to see your prospect in person. There also are instances when the telephone can extend your contact reach. And there are some points on which the phone call is a good bet on its own, certainly more effective than a letter. The phone shrinks distances, enabling you to make contacts otherwise difficult or impossible. It increases the frequency of your contacts, when this is desirable. It is not impeded by inclement weather. It is more personal than a letter because it is a two-way exchange. It sometimes gets you into places you cannot get into in person, even though you may still have to encounter a sentry. It is easier to keep the subject on a productive track during a phone call than in a personal meeting, since the telephone is not as conducive to extraneous conversation. Finally, when you initiate the call, you have the advantage, if you follow proper guidelines. In short, the telephone multiplies your selling effectiveness beyond the limits of miles and hours.

Beyond its already-mentioned uses, the phone can also help you to:

EXHIBIT 18.8
NEXT BEST TO BEING THERE—SOMETIMES BETTER

- Prospect
- Do preapproach research
- Qualify leads
- Get references
- Maintain contact with customers and prospects between personal visits
- Obtain inventory fill-in orders from regular accounts
- Flash merchandising news to buyers speedily when a written communication is inadequate or a response is required
- Motivate inactive accounts
- Make add-on sales to buyers
- Collect overdue balances
- Follow up and reinforce direct mail

Here are some suggestions on how to get the most out of your phone.

1. *Call at the right time*   For example, don't try to compete with the morning mail, and remember that an executive is more apt to be receptive after lunch than before.

2. *Call from the right place*   Be sure you will not be interrupted or distracted.
3. *Think before you dial*   Think about what you plan to say and how you plan to say it.
4. *Make notes on what you will say.*
5. *Listen*   Give the buyer a chance to speak.
6. *Take notes*   Don't take a chance on losing a key to the closing.
7. *Confirm it*   The unhurried reflection after the call on how to phrase your case, not possible in the rapid fire of a personal interview, means your next shot can have bull's-eye pertinence to the prospect's interests. Your letter can summarize your case if the call went favorably. It can offer counterlogic if it did not. You will, of course, recognize whether the situation suggests skipping the letter and confirming the facts in person.

Marginal Account Handling   As discussed earlier, for most companies 80 percent of their accounts yield only 20 percent of their business. These are the marginal accounts, and they are often neglected intentionally or unintentionally. It may not be practical to call on these small accounts in person, but they can be phoned. This is *telemarketing,* a growing activity in business today. For example, with telemarketing a greeting card company can reach remote outlets with current card selections as easily as it reaches its large, urban customers.[3]

GAIN BY BEING MANAGED

There is a science of *followership* as well as leadership. It often is the critical factor in victory. Your management—or source, if you sell as an independent agent or broker—can contribute much to your success in your selling career. It pays to take advantage of this. Here are some of the ways the intelligent salesperson cooperates with management and gains by being managed.

Join the Team

Be a company person, a member of the team. Selling is a poorly chosen career for a loner. If your company or source is worth your time, it deserves your loyalty. Moreover, buyers react favorably to sellers who are enthusiastic about what they sell and its source.

Cooperate with Your Managment

Teamwork is a two-way street. Live up to your part of the contract. In addition to monetary considerations, management supplies you with products or services to sell, information, promotional support, training and education, equipment, guidance, and sometimes leads. In return, you give management complete cooperation by following through on instructions, respecting company policies, actively

---

[3]"The Telemarketing Manual [a Bell System insert]" *Business Week,* May 17, 1982.

participating in company programs, providing dependable answers to requests for information, and conserving selling costs.

Fill Out Those Reports

Reports and records are a nuisance, but an essential to organization and management. They prevent misunderstandings. They aid memory, saving mental energy for creative work. When the individual report you send in is combined with other sellers' reports, they add up to management's recognition of problems that must be solved (often for the benefit of the salespeople), trends to be watched, and opportunities to be commercialized. One seller's opinion or experience may not seem significant. But when it is buttressed by similar expressions from many salespeople, it signals management to do something about it. Fill out those reports, and get them in promptly. They constitute the intelligence lifeline between factory and field. They help management to help you.

Gain by Training

One of the greatest stimuli to raising your selling productivity is the training provided by your management and the continuing development program that goes with it. Take advantage of this. Make the most of the bulletins, information releases, and other aids to better selling supplied by headquarters. The most advanced senior salesperson gains from training and development programs just as the recent recruit does. Remember the old maxim: "As long as you're green you grow, when you get ripe you rot." (See Exhibit 18.9.)

Ask for Help

It pays to consult your supervisor on difficult prospects or problems. You will obtain an objective, seasoned view, often aided by previous experience with the same kind of prospect or problem. Sometimes, your supervisor actually will make a sales call with you to help you solve the problem.

EXHIBIT 18.9

ADVICE FROM AN AVON REPRESENTATIVE

"I read every word of any material I receive from Avon. . . . I'd feel foolish just taking out jars and bottles and not knowing what to say about them!"

Needless to say, this comes from a star Avon salesperson, who does a good job of managing herself and gaining by the support and guidance she receives from the Avon management.

Be a Partner to Your Management

Never forget that you and your management are partners with a common goal. Your management wants to help you to do a better job and to profit by doing so. Exhibit a reciprocal attitude. Be a dedicated member of the team, participating wholeheartedly in all company programs. It is the only road upward in your selling career.

RECAP

Modern selling represents the culmination of a long road of trial and error from which an increasingly scientific discipline has evolved. Research on how to increase selling productivity has commanded and continues to command prime attention on the part of the selling profession: how to make two sales from the effort that might have made one, or $2 instead of $1 from the same number of hours, the same number of calls, and the same number of—or even fewer—miles.

Along with attention to improving selling productivity has gone recognition of the importance of improving service to buyers. The two objectives go hand in hand. Buyers do indeed benefit from intelligent selling. Among other things, selling cost is a significant component of most product or service costs. There is nothing more costly in marketing than the cost of a sale that was not made. The buyer pays for this in the price of the product or service bought.

If you are skilled in self-management and cooperate with company or source management, you are following the high ideals of contemporary selling.

REVIEW QUESTIONS

1. What is selling productivity?
2. What is a piggyback sale?
3. What is meant by playing position in territory management?
4. Name an important record for a salesperson to keep. Describe this record and tell how to use it.
5. What is the average salesperson's biggest problem in time management?
6. What is the Pareto principle? How does it relate to selling?
7. What has a strong bearing on your ratio of sales interviews to approaches? of closings to sales interviews?
8. What is the principle of selective selling?
9. What three subparts of the selling process assure your getting more business out of your customers?
10. What is suggestion selling?
11. What is the aftercall?
12. Why are reports and records essential in business?
13. What are some of the things your telephone can help you to do in selling?

DISCUSSION QUESTIONS

1. In what way is a salesperson also a territory manager?
2. Discuss time and the distance between buyers as factors bearing on self-management. What can you do to make the most of the distances encountered and the limits of time?
3. How important are the postsale and postsale follow-up in selling?
4. Discuss the importance of the telephone in selling.
5. Suggestion selling has been called "high pressure." Do you agree with this criticism? Defend your opinion on this.
6. Would you rather be a company sales representative on a company payroll or an independent sales agent? Why? What are the advantages and disadvantages of each?
7. What are the relative advantages and disadvantages of selling by phone, by letter, and in person? Under what circumstances would you use each?
8. What can you gain by being managed by your company?

LEARNING EXPERIENCES

1. You are a new sales representative for a women's sweater manufacturer, responsible for Connecticut, Rhode Island, western Massachusetts, and Vermont. Your company has been in business only three years, and this is new territory. Your customers will be department and specialty stores. How would you go about setting up a territory coverage plan broadly for the year and specifically for a week? As you write up this plan and schedule, use your imagination for any facts not supplied.
2. Interview the owner or manager of a local, independent hardware store or home center. Find out the answers to these questions:

   • How often are orders placed for various specific products?
   • Under what circumstances and to what degree are orders placed directly with a salesperson visiting the store, by telephone, or by mail?
   • Are more orders placed by phone or by mail or with the sales representative in person on reorders? For products not previously bought?
   • Does the buyer prefer to place orders by phone, by mail, or directly with the salesperson? Why?

   On the basis of your survey, write a report to your sales manager on how you would plan to reach independent hardware or home center outlets with your new line of metal files. You have an established market with dealers for your line of handsaws. Use your imagination for any facts not supplied.
3. Role playing. Let one member of the group act as a prospect who has come into a furniture store to buy a sofa. Another member of the group is to take the part of the furniture salesperson. The scene opens with the prospect deciding to purchase a certain sofa. The salesperson will try to increase the sale. Use imagination for any facts not supplied above. Let the salesperson explain his or

her strategy. Let the prospect tell why this strategy would or would not have been successful. Then let the group comment in open discussion.

CASE

CENTRAL PERMAWEATHER, INC.

Carolyn Small has been engaged to represent Central Permaweather, makers and marketers of a patented central system of air-conditioning, cooling, heating, and humidity control, to open up the northern California market. The Central system is a little more costly to install than most competitive systems, but it is a superior means of all-year-round air control with a lower operating cost than most competitive systems. In the midwest, where Central is established, it has enjoyed a better acceptance of its industrial system than of its residential system. Carolyn has been on the job now for three months, after a three-week training period at headquarters. Her results have been disappointing. She has been mainly approaching residential buyers because she figured the approach would be easier and this residential business would give her a faster start in writing some orders. Carolyn's immediate superior at Central is field sales manager Jim Stewart. She has not seen him since the training period, though she has received a few letters of encouragement, suggesting patience and asking if Carolyn has any special problem. Carolyn has not asked for help because she is not quite certain what the problem exactly is and she keeps hoping that tomorrow will be better. She is apprehensive of getting involved with headquarters at this time, lest her sorry record lead to her dismissal before she gets going.

Questions

1. Is Carolyn Small right in not asking Jim Stewart for help?
2. What are some possible explanations of why Jim Stewart has not taken the initiative in visiting Carolyn in the field or calling her in to headquarters?
3. Using your imagination for facts not stated above, why do you believe Carolyn is unable to get the northern California market going? What are some of the possibilities?
4. What suggestions would you make to Carolyn about her self-management? Detail your answer fully, relating it to questions of territory and time management and ways to overcome the time and distance hurdles. Again, use your imagination for facts not stated above.

NINETEEN

CHAPTER OBJECTIVES

To familiarize you with the basic guidelines for organizing the sales force, as well as with the influence of three management theories on organization

To describe the basic functions of recruiting and selecting salespeople

To examine the basic methods of compensation, including straight salary, straight commission, and combination of salary and commission or bonus

To familiarize you with the major types of training needs of new and existing salespeople

To explore the needs and ways of motivating the sales force

To examine the nature of evaluating the sales force

CHAPTER OUTLINE

SALES MANAGEMENT

Are you motivated to really do a stellar performance at your job?

Are you being treated fairly by your boss?

Was your last performance evaluation fair?

Are your salary and/or commissions enough to keep you going with enthusiasm?

Have you been trained so well that you know your product like the back of your hand?

NINETEEN

Above are some of the questions that will face you as a salesperson. The answers are in large part the responsibility of sales management.

There are many aspects to sales management which could easily fill a textbook, perhaps even a set of texts. They include organizing, planning, sales forecasting, budgeting, time and territory management, recruiting, selecting, training, motivating, compensating, controlling, and evaluating. In this chapter we are going to focus on organizing, recruiting and selecting, compensating, training. motivating, and evaluating. These are the most basic sales management functions and most directly affect the beginning salesperson.

430

ORGANIZING THE SALES FORCE

There are a number of theories of organization and management and they generally are based upon two basic approaches: the *classic* or traditional work-centered approach and the *progressive* people-centered approach. A third approach uses some principles of both the classic and the progressive approaches, depending upon the circumstances and situation. This is called the *contingency* approach. The classic approach to organizing is usually characterized by a style of management best described as theory X, the progressive approach is characterized by theory Y, and the contingency approach is theory Z.

These three theories are explained so that you will be familiar with them. They express clear-cut differences in leadership styles. In real life, however, sales managers may use a combination of these types; there is often overlap. Dr. David Merrill, president of TRACOM Corporation, a Denver-based psychological and research firm, sums it up well this way:

> I had a theory that most successful managers would be highly assertive. I have not been able to prove that, however. There are some very quiet, nonassertive people who are very successful managers. Unfortunately, many managers believe in the mythology that leaders pound tables. We have a macho stereotype in our culture.[1]

The Classic Theory

Under the classic theory, jobs are divided into specialized tasks. Management's job is to coordinate and control these tasks so that the company's objectives can be met efficiently. Authority is clearly established in a hierarchical fashion, and channels of authority and communication are also clearly established.

Classic theory is based upon a set of assumptions that management theorist Douglas McGregor calls *theory X*.[2] Theory X can be briefly described as follows:

• The average human being has an inherent dislike of work and will avoid it if possible.

• Because of this human characteristic of dislike of work, most people must be coerced, controlled closely, directed, and threatened with punishment to get them to put forth adequate effort toward the achievement of work objectives.

• The average human prefers to be directed, wishes to avoid responsibility, has relatively little ambition, and wants security above all.

The Progressive Theory

The progressive theory is based upon assumptions that McGregor calls *theory Y*,[3] which can be described as follows:

• The expenditure of physical and mental effort in work is as natural as in play.

• External control and the threat of punishment are not the only means of

---

[1]Perry Pascarella, "Try Versatility," *Industry Week*, May 3, 1982, p. 68.
[2]Douglas McGregor, *The Human Side of Enterprise*, McGraw-Hill, New York, 1960, pp. 33–34.
[3]Ibid., pp. 47–48.

bringing about effort toward job objectives. People will show self-direction and self-control in pursuing job objectives to which they are committed.

• Commitment to objectives is a function of the rewards associated with their achievement.

• Under proper conditions, the average person learns not only to accept responsibility but to seek it.

• The capacity to exercise a relatively high degree of imagination, ingenuity, and creativity in the solution of organizational problems is widely, not narrowly, distributed in the population.

• Under the conditions of modern organizational life, the intellectual potentialities of the average human are only partially utilized.

The Contingency Theory

Many practicing managers think there are shortcomings with each of the theories as they are stated. Usually, the criticism is that theory Y is too idealistic and perhaps too naive. Critics feel that there are times when people do want to be controlled and when they wish to have structure, although not necessarily all the time. However, strict adherence to the basic assumptions of theory X would prove too restrictive for many organizations and many people. Theory X, furthermore, is often incongruent with the personalities of successful salespeople, who are frequently self-starting, self-motivated, and self-directed. What this personality type needs in most cases is guidance, some structure, consideration, and motivation.

The contingency theory, sometimes called *theory Z* by contemporary management writers, allows the manager to alter his or her approach contingent upon several variables: the type of job the employee performs, the maturity and level of responsibility the employee demonstrates, and the present state of the organization in which the employee works.

The management approach that works best will fit the situation and take the variables into account. Most important, it will be characterized by open communication with the salespeople, rather than relying on written memos and directives as the only way of communicating. The good sales manager is a good listener and works to create an atmosphere of cooperation, one where the salespeople will feel free to openly discuss their problems.

Recognition of good performance is important to motivation of salespeople. The effective manager knows this and is quick to give you praise and credit when it is due. Further, he or she knows how to hand out praise fairly and in direct response to a job well performed. In this style of management, you are treated like an individual, like a human being. The interest that the sales manager shows you is genuine.

Basic Guidelines for Organizing

There are several things that management must take into account in organizing a sales force: function (type of customer), geography, product type, span of man-

432

agement, and need for flexibility. Any single factor may be the basis of organizing the force, although usually it is a combination of several factors.

Function refers to organizing on the basis of the essential nature of the work. If a company had two methods of distributing its product, to the wholesaler and to the retailer, the selling jobs would be divided according to this difference. *Geography* is a fairly obvious basis of organizing: One division or department may handle the northeast, another the mid-Atlantic states, a third the southern states, and so on. If there were several different product lines, as there often are, then organizing may be based on *product type*.

Span of management and need for flexibility add other possible dimensions to the organizing task. *Span of management* refers to the number of salespeople one sales manager can effectively supervise. For example, one company may find, based upon its experiences, that no more than eight to ten salespeople can be effectively handled by a manager, keeping in mind the need for motivation, feedback, communication, etc. Flexibility means being able to adjust the organization to meet changing demands. The *need for flexibility* should be considered in organizing to allow the organization to respond to change. (See Exhibit 19.1.)

RECRUITING AND SELECTING SALESPEOPLE

Recruitment is a minor variation of the standard sales process. The salesperson sells a product or a service; the recruiter sells job opportunities. Sales is the lifeblood of an organization, and having an ample supply of new salespeople is essential to fill openings created by expansion, promotions, and retirements. Management's major task in recruiting is to generate a pool of potential salespeople which is as large as possible so that the best can be selected to fill available positions.

EXHIBIT 19.1
GUIDELINES FOR ORGANIZING THE SALES FORCE

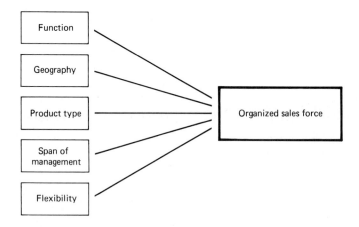

Sources of Salespeople

The well-managed sales organization will keep tabs on several sources of employees so that there will always be a ready supply of applicants. The effectiveness of each source will depend on the job description: Some jobs are more routine than others and may be filled with persons who have less education. Others may require a college or even an engineering background. Consideration must also be given to people who will have the potential for future management positions. Some of the sources which are used to recruit salespeople include:

1. Present employees' friends, relatives, and acquaintances
2. Employees in other departments who may wish to get into sales positions
3. Salespeople from similar and related industries
4. College and university placement offices
5. Advertisements placed in professional journals and newspapers
6. Professional placement services which specialize in selling jobs
7. Word of mouth and centers of influence

The task in the recruitment process is to communicate the job opportunities to as many sources and people as possible. A large pool of interested applicants provides management with the best conditions for selection.

The Selection of Salespeople

Management must select those salespeople who are most suited to selling the firm's product and handling the firm's customer. Each selling job has special needs, and these needs must first be clearly specified in a detailed description of the selling job.

The Job Description   A good job description is the basis of the selection process. Without this, the task becomes hit or miss. A job description is based on a *job analysis* and a *job specification*. Job analysis is the process of determining the skills, knowledge, abilities, and responsibilities that the prospective salesperson will need to successfully do the job. Additionally, it is analyzing these responsibilities as they differentiate a particular job from other jobs. The job specification relates more to the human qualities needed to perform the job. These include education, training, experience, judgment, initiative, physical effort, physical skills, and communication skills.

Because the job description serves as a guideline to selection, it is generally in writing so that it can be referred to. Exhibit 19.2 shows a sample job description.

Once management has an accurate job description, it must gather corollary information about the applicants so that a suitable match can be made. The usual sources of information about applicants are the résumé, the application, employment tests, the employment interview, and reference checks.

The Résumé   The résumé should provide information about your job objective, skills, credentials, educational background, and work experience. A résumé may be sent in advance, delivered in person, or attached to your application.

**EXHIBIT 19.2
SAMPLE JOB DESCRIPTION**

**The Powers Regulator Company
Skokie, Illinois
Job Responsibilities—Sales Engineer**

The Sales Engineer, in general, shall be responsible for the promotion and sale of all Powers' products in his territory. He shall, by his efforts, ethics, personality, and sales ability, establish and maintain The Powers Regulator Company as a highly respected and trusted supplier of control equipment in the heating, plumbing, and air-conditioning field in his territory. He shall bear in mind at all times that it is he who his customers look on as The Powers Regulator Company and, in view of this, conduct himself accordingly. His final objective is to sell Powers' equipment at a profit and to obtain for Powers the largest possible percentage of available control business at a profitable price.

SPECIFIC DUTIES:

A. Promotion of Sales–General (Contract and Specialty)

1. Call regularly on all architectural, consulting engineer, and mechanical contractor accounts in territory.
2. Promote the use of pneumatic controls on all projects. When advisable, promote the use of pneumatic electronic and/or electric controls.
3. Assist consulting engineers in writing control specifications, and up-grade the use of temperature control.
4. Keep informed on new projects in the planning stage, and make preliminary sales effort with architect and engineer. Sell Powers to owner, if necessary, but with architect's permission.
5. Initiate direct mail sales effort where of value.
6. Maintain the Powers advertising brochure as a sales tool, including testimonial letters from customers in territory, and pictures of prominent buildings with Powers control.
7. Regularly check all existing jobs in territory to see if owners and maintenance men are satisfied, and use these for references.
8. Make demonstrations of Powers equipment, both new and old products, to customers at regular intervals.
9. Advise Branch Secretary of new names and their classification to be added to mailing list as well as changes in address, etc., to keep list up to date. Include maintenance men and owners of existing systems on mailing list.
10. Assist Branch Installation Manager in holding schools for maintenance men.
11. Call on all institutions, hospitals, and industrial plants to sell Powers, and establish Powers as a supplier of specialty items through the wholesalers.
12. Call on all plumbing and heating wholesalers in territory, become acquainted with wholesaler territory salesmen to promote specialty sales, and as valuable sources of information and assistance on contract sale.

EXHIBIT 19.2 (cont.)

B. Contract Sales

1. Bidding
   (a) Initiate request for approval letter when Powers is not specified.
   (b) Take off and estimate control system.
   (c) Prepare the mechanical contract bidder's list; estimate price approved by Branch Manager.
   (d) Prepare quotation and distribute to bidders.
   (e) Attend bid openings.
   (f) Contact low mechanical bidder after opening, and attempt to get commitment for control sub-contract.
   (g) Determine exact time when mechanical contractor is to receive his contract and be there at that time to negotiate for control sub-contract.
2. Maintain close and persistent follow-up to obtain order for control sub-contract.
3. Obtain all pertinent job information from contractor such as name of general contractor, valve body styles, sheet metal and electrical sub-contractor names, job site shipping address, approximate dates material is needed, etc. Pass this information on to Installation Manager.
4. Prepare Contract Order Report.
5. Prepare Production Department Material Report.
6. Prepare schematic drawings, valve damper schedules, damper size verification letter, and material orders, and turn over job to Installation Manager.
7. Act as liaison between our construction department and mechanical contractor through completion of job and warranty period.
8. See that final corrected schematic drawings and maintenance booklets are in the hands of building operating engineer.
9. See that operating engineer understands system operation and our equipment. This is the second job of selling.
10. Check to see that all details of construction are complete and system is properly calibrated by construction department.
11. Send statistical data to Skokie.

Source: C. Robert Patty, *Managing Salespeople,* Reston Publishing Company, Reston, Va., 1979, pp. 174–175. By permission of Reston Publishing Company, Reston, Virginia.

The Application   A good application is designed to provide basic information which can be used for prescreening the applicant. For example, if the job description calls for a college degree as a minimum qualification, this question will be part of the application. If you have not completed college, you may be eliminated from consideration at this stage.

Additional questions on the application are useful for drawing tentative inferences. For example, applications may have questions about outside activities, extracurricular activities in school, and other accomplishments. If you fill in these

436

areas, the employer usually feels you are an active, energetic person. Follow-up questions to verify these feelings are then planned as part of the interview.

Employment Testing   Testing is often part of the selection procedure for sales applicants. Selection tests are usually developed by industrial psychologists, and employers generally consult with such a person in using them. The guidelines on employment selection procedures set forth by the Equal Employment Opportunity Commission (EEOC) state that tests designed to measure eligibility for employment must demonstrate evidence of content validity. This means the abilities and personal qualities tested must be proved to be related to abilities and qualities used on the job.[4]

Typical employment tests measure or evaluate the following general areas:

- *Aptitude:* Includes general intelligence or special aptitudes like sales
- *Achievement:* Measures job knowledge or a specific skill, such as mathematical ability
- *Personality:* Measures basic personality characteristics demonstrated to be related to success in selling
- *Vocational interests:* Measures likes and dislikes of people as related to sales occupations

Test results are not ends in themselves and are generally used in addition to other information that has been collected about the applicant.

The Employment Interviews   A good interview should be an information exchange between you and the company's representative. The interview should have two purposes: to allow the firm to gather information about you and to allow you to gather information about the firm. A well-conducted interview follows a structure, or pattern, of predetermined questions. The interviewer should have outlined beforehand what information is needed to make a sound employment decision and should use that outline as a basis of questioning.

Interviewers must be familiar with the 1964 Civil Rights Act as amended, and you should be too. This act specifies that minorities, older people, women, and the handicapped must have a fair and equal opportunity to be employed. No sales position can be labeled male or female, black or white, young or old. In addition, every requirement in the job description must be justified. Height, weight, and age must relate to the requirements of the job and cannot be used to discriminate.

Reference Checks   Reference checks are used by management primarily to verify information that has been gathered and presented during the interview. In many cases, employers find it more direct and convenient to check references by phone rather than by letter, since most references will be more candid about an applicant if they do not have to put their opinions in writing.

---

[4]See *Guidelines in Employment Testing Procedures,* United States Equal Employment Opportunity Commission, available from the Superintendent of Documents, U.S. Government Printing Office, Washington, D.C., 1977.

When you select references, use people who know you well and can speak positively about your job performance or potential. Former employers and former teachers are often good references. Before listing your references, be sure to ask the persons you have selected for their permission. Not only is this good manners, but it also gives your references advance warning so that they can be prepared to respond to inquiries about you.

COMPENSATING SALESPEOPLE

One of the major responsibilities of sales management is the development and carrying out of a workable compensation program. The primary purpose of such a plan is to promote the most efficient and productive use of the sales force. Specifically, a good compensation plan should accomplish the following objectives:

1. Motivate salespeople to perform at their best level by providing an incentive with sufficient clarity so that it will encourage selling and related job responsibilities and reward outstanding performance.
2. Provide an equitable relationship between the work being done and the level of compensation. It is important that this relationship be perceived as equitable by the sales force.
3. Attract and retain desirable salespeople, and provide sufficient stability to allow adequate support and economic security.
4. Provide a means whereby management has the flexibility to maintain an optimum balance between costs and sales.
5. Be clear, easy to understand, and relatively easy to administer in order to minimize the costs of implementation and administration.

Methods of Compensation

There are several methods of compensating salespeople: straight salary, straight commission, and a combination of salary and commission or bonus.

Straight Salary This is the simplest method of compensation, although not the best for most salespeople. If you are on a straight salary plan, you are hired at a predetermined amount, such as $200 per week. The advantages to the company are simplicity, ease of administration, and specified financial commitments. The advantage to you is that you can count on making so much per week. The disadvantage to both parties is that straight salary provides no motivation or incentive for extra effort or excellent performance. A salesperson with $1000 sales per week would earn the same as a salesperson with $5000 sales per week. Also, straight salary provides no cost flexibility for management. Payroll costs would be fixed at $200 per week times the number of salespeople, regardless of whether gross sales were $10,000 or $50,000 per week.

Straight Commission This method of compensation provides for some of the shortcomings of the straight salary method. The commission-on-sales method is based on determining compensation as a percentage of net sales for the pay period. As an example, if your net sales (gross sales minus returns) were $2550 for the week, and your commission was 10 percent of net sales, your earnings that week would be $255.

The commission method of compensation is excellent for motivating salespeople. It provides a direct relationship between output and reward. It also provides management with payroll cost flexibility, which is not found in the straight salary method. The major disadvantage of commission sales is a lack of economic security for the sales force, which, in turn, can make it difficult for management to retain good salespeople. Some firms offer salespeople a weekly *draw,* which is money advanced from future commissions. But draws are funds owed to the company, not salaries. Because of the disadvantages of straight commission, most sales managers offer a commission as *part* of a compensation program.

Salary Plus Commission or Bonus A plan combining salary with a commission or bonus capitalizes on the advantages of each method and at the same time minimizes the disadvantages of each.

The *salary-plus-commission* method is a common method of compensation in selling. In this case, the base salary is usually lower than it would be in straight salary. Similarly, the rate of commission may be lower. However, the combination should provide the opportunity for an outstanding salesperson to earn a higher-than-average salary. The commission rate is usually calculated on the average projected sales in order to bring the total compensation to a level which meets the objectives of a sound compensation program.

The *salary plus bonus* consists of a lump sum of money paid for outstanding performance. It is important that the criteria for outstanding performance be measurable and known to the salespeople in advance if the bonus is going to work as an incentive. Bonuses may be paid for meeting or exceeding sales quotas, for selling a specified product mix, for opening a new account, for developing a new selling technique, or any number of other activities that the company may want to encourage.

A number of companies use combinations of salary, commission, and bonus in order to maximize the positive effects of all methods. Exhibits 19.3 and 19.4 show the results of a survey of alternative compensation plans and selling expenses as a percentage of company sales.

TRAINING SALESPEOPLE

A good training program will encourage, motivate, and educate each new employee. Moreover, it should provide for continuous training for existing employees. Product knowledge must be kept current, and the fundamentals of selling should be repeated frequently, lest they be forgotten. Methods commonly used in the training of salespeople include on-the-job training, classroom instruction, coaching, observation, videotaping (for self-analysis), home study, and special courses provided by outsiders.

EXHIBIT 19.3
ALTERNATIVE SALES AND COMPENSATION PLANS

	Percent of companies using plans				
	All industries		Consumer products 1980	Industrial products 1980	Other commerce industry 1980
Method	1980	1979			
Straight salary	20.4	21.4	15.3	19.7	31.8
Draw against commission	7.2	6.3	8.2	7.2	6.1
Salary plus commission	28.6	27.8	17.3	32.2	24.3
Salary plus individual bonus	27.9	29.3	35.7	26.9	22.7
Salary plus group bonus	5.6	4.8	9.2	5.1	3.0
Salary plus commission plus individual or group bonus	10.3	10.4	14.3	8.9	12.1
Total	100.0	100.0	100.0	100.0	100.0

Source: "Annual Survey of Selling Costs," *Sales & Marketing Management,* February 1981. Reprinted, by permission of the publisher, from *Executive Compensation Service,* "Sales Personnel Report," 26th edition, 1981/1982, © by American Management Associations. All rights reserved.

Jack Falvey, managing director of Intermark, a sales consulting firm, feels that if salespeople want to learn more, they must accept the challenge of teaching themselves on every call.[5] Thus sales training becomes a continuous, lifetime process and is a joint responsibility of management and you, the salesperson.

Training time for new sales employees is usually divided between company orientation, market and industry orientation, selling techniques, and product knowledge. On the average, companies place most emphasis on developing their trainee's knowledge of products or services that they will be responsible for selling. The average amount of time spent on gaining product knowledge is 40 percent of total training time.[6] Other averages are 20 percent on selling techniques, 15 percent on market or industry orientation, and 10 percent on company orientation.[7] However, these averages conceal very wide variations among individual firms. For example, a manufacturer of specialized industrial components that recruits graduate engineers devotes 90 percent of its sales training program to engineering and product knowledge and only 10 percent to all other categories. (See Exhibit 19.9.)

The need for retraining present employees has been well-established and exists in almost all companies. Retraining, or continual training, increases sales productivity by decreasing turnover, enhancing customer relationships, decreas-

[5]Jack Falvey, "Speaking from Experience; Sales Training Never Ends," *Training and Development Journal,* November 1981, p. 41.
[6]David S. Hopkins, *"Training the Sales Force: A Progress Report," The Conference Report,* The Conference Board, New York, 1978, p. 4.
[7]Ibid., p. 5.

EXHIBIT 19.4a
SALES FORCE SELLING EXPENSES* AS A PERCENTAGE OF COMPANY SALES

Industry	Compensation		T&E expenses		Total	
	1979	1978	1979	1978	1979	1978
Consumer goods						
Apparel	3.3%	5.2%	N.A.	0.7%	3.3%	5.9%
Durable goods	1.1	1.9	0.8%	0.8	1.9	2.7
Ethical pharmaceuticals, surgical supplies & equipment	3.6	5.6	1.0	2.9	4.6	8.5
Food	1.7	1.7	0.8	0.7	2.5	2.4
Major household items	2.2	2.4	0.4	0.7	2.6	3.1
Proprietary drugs & toiletries	1.8	2.0	0.5	0.7	2.3	2.7
Industrial goods						
Aerospace products	N.A.	1.5	N.A.	1.1	N.A.	2.6
Automotive parts & accessories	2.5	3.0	0.9	1.6	3.4	4.6
Building materials	1.2	1.2	0.5	0.6	1.7	1.8
Chemicals	2.1	1.9	0.9	1.3	3.0	3.2
Computers	4.8	4.4	1.0	1.6	5.8	6.0
Containers & packaging materials	1.8	1.2	1.1	0.6	2.9	1.8
Electrical materials	2.2	3.1	0.9	0.7	3.1	3.8
Electronics	1.7	2.6	0.8	1.2	2.5	3.8
Fabricated metals (heavy)	1.6	1.4	0.5	0.5	2.1	1.9
Fabricated metals (light)	1.8	2.3	0.6	1.2	2.4	3.5
Fabrics	1.3	1.5	0.2	0.7	1.5	2.2
Instruments	2.0	3.9	1.2	1.5	3.2	5.4
Iron & steel	0.8	0.7	0.1	0.3	0.9	1.0
Machinery (heavy)	1.9	2.1	0.7	0.9	2.6	3.0
Machinery (light)	2.1	3.7	1.0	1.4	3.1	5.1
Office & educational supplies & equipment	11.0	7.5	1.0	1.1	12.0	8.6
Paper	1.1	1.5	0.6	0.8	1.7	2.3
Printing & publishing	6.1	6.9	1.8	2.5	7.9	9.4
Rubber, plastics, & leather	1.0	1.4	N.A.	0.6	1.0	2.0
Tools & hardware	2.3	1.7	0.9	0.8	3.2	2.5

Note: Includes only salespeople's total compensation plus their expenses, that is, travel, lodging, meals, and entertainment. It should be noted that some of the differences between years reflect changes in the organizations that reported data. Because of insufficient data, the following industries are not included in this year's listing: automobile & truck, glass & allied products, and petroleum. Percentages in this table are percentages of sales by the sales force.

N.A.—Not available, sample too small.

Source: American Management Assns., *Executive Compensation Service*. Reprinted, by permission of the publisher, from *Executive Compensation Service*, "Sales Personnel Report," 25th edition, 1981/1982, © 1980 by American Management Associations. All rights reserved.

EXHIBIT 19.4b

TOTAL SELLING EXPENSES AS A PERCENTAGE OF SALES IN
MAJOR INDUSTRIES

Industry	1979	1978	Industry	1979	1978
Consumer goods			**Industrial goods (cont.)**		
Apparel	11.2%	9.4%	Containers & packaging		
Durable goods	5.1	5.3	materials	2.7%	2.6%
Ethical pharmaceuticals,			Electrical materials	5.6	4.8
surgical supplies			Electronics	4.4	5.7
& equipment	13.5	10.5	Fabrics	4.0	1.1
Food	5.4	5.2	Fabricated metals (heavy)	3.4	2.7
Major household items	2.8	4.9	Fabricated metals (light)	4.0	4.2
Proprietary drugs and			Instruments	7.3	5.5
toiletries	16.1	16.0	Iron & steel	1.4	1.2
			Machinery (heavy)	4.3	3.8
Industrial goods			Machinery (light)	5.5	6.8
			Office supplies		
Aerospace products	N.A.	4.1	& equipment	10.0	15.2
Automotive parts			Paper	2.1	1.7
& accessories	4.0	4.1	Petroleum	N.A.	6.3
Building materials	2.8	2.3	Printing & publishing	10.4	9.5
Chemicals	4.2	4.4	Rubber, plastics, & leather	1.7	2.9
Computers	19.4	9.5	Tools & hardware	5.6	9.1

Note: Selling expenses cover cost of median compensation of salespeople and sales management, travel, lodging, meals and entertainment, advertising, and promotion. One of the major difficulties encountered in gathering such information is that wide differences exist between companies in the definition of selling expenses and the costs included in such figures. In addition, some of the differences between years reflect changes in the organizations that reported data. Because of insufficient data, the following industries are not included in this year's listing: automobile & truck, glass & allied products, and petroleum.

N.A.—Not available, sample too small.

Source: American Management Assns., *Executive Compensation Service.* Reprinted, by permission of the publisher, from *Executive Compensation Service,* "Sales Personnel Report," 25th edition, 1981/1982, © 1980 by American Management Associations. All rights reserved.

ing selling costs, and increasing sales. There is an ongoing need to train salespeople concerning product changes and, of course, new products. (See Exhibit 19.10.)

MOTIVATING SALESPEOPLE

One of the most difficult but important jobs of sales management is motivating the sales force—motivating you and the other salespeople to produce at your peak potentials and abilities. Motivation is often difficult because of the differences between the needs of different salespeople. A device that turns you on may be the very thing that turns someone else off. You might be primarily motivated by money, and another representative might be most motivated by personal recognition.

Companies rely on many different techniques in attempting to spur their sales personnel to success. Among the most common devices are opportunity for advancement and promotion, supervisor's encouragement and personal contact, individual incentive bonuses, and commission pay incentives. Other sales force motivators include overall compensation, participation of salespeople in goal setting, advanced training and development programs, travel-prize contests, attendance at sales meetings and conventions, group incentive bonuses, and merchandise-prize contests. Exhibit 19.5 shows a ranking of major sales-force motivators, based on information supplied by 127 senior sales and marketing executives.

Personal recognition is considered a critically important ingredient by most companies. A substantial number of companies are taking special pains to publicize superior performance. Frequently, outstanding performers are cited in company house organs or at special award ceremonies. Others assign their top-ranking salespeople key roles in meeting with customers in special well-publicized projects.

EVALUATING SALESPEOPLE

Accurate and objective evaluation is closely related to motivation and unquestionably related to the continued success of a company. The job of evaluating salespeople is essential because the future of the individual salesperson (you) is involved and the success or failure of the company's overall marketing strategy is involved—no sales, no revenue.

The evaluation process consists of four steps:

1. Analyzing the job and writing the job description
2. Determining performance measurements
3. Measuring and evaluating the actual performance
4. Recommending areas for improvement

The usual criteria for measuring job performance include sales results, customer relations, job knowledge, company relations, and personal characteristics.

The evaluation of sales results includes measurement of your individual dollar sales volume or unit sales volume, gross margin, the number of new accounts secured, the number of sales presentations made, and your territorial market share. The evaluation of customer relations includes such things as your availability to the customer, your skill in customer problem solving, and your ability to successfully provide customer service and assistance.

An evaluation of your job knowledge takes into consideration your prospecting ability, your ability to overcome objections, the effectiveness of your sales presentation, and your knowledge of the product's features, markets, customers, and competition. Evaluation in terms of company relations includes your awareness of your job requirements, your ability to work well with other departments, your ability to recognize problem areas, and your ability to communicate effectively with management. An evaluation of personal characteristics usually includes the

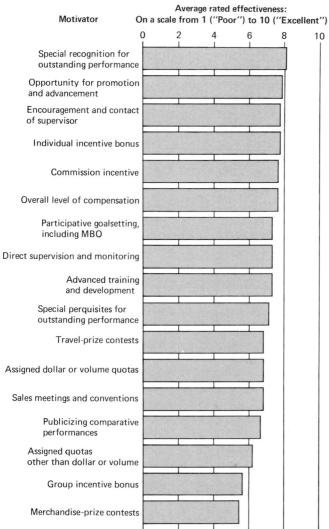

Average rated effectiveness:
On a scale from 1 ("Poor") to 10 ("Excellent")

Motivator

| | 0 | 2 | 4 | 6 | 8 | 10 |

Special recognition for outstanding performance

Opportunity for promotion and advancement

Encouragement and contact of supervisor

Individual incentive bonus

Commission incentive

Overall level of compensation

Participative goalsetting, including MBO

Direct supervision and monitoring

Advanced training and development

Special perquisites for outstanding performance

Travel-prize contests

Assigned dollar or volume quotas

Sales meetings and conventions

Publicizing comparative performances

Assigned quotas other than dollar or volume

Group incentive bonus

Merchandise-prize contests

Note: Based on judgments of 127 senior sales and marketing executives as to the relative effectiveness (on a scale of 1 to 10, ranging from "poor" to "excellent") in stimulating superior performance on the part of members of a manufacturing company's sales force.

EXHIBIT 19.5
SALES FORCE MOTIVATORS IN ORDER OF EFFECTIVENESS
(*Source:* Conference Board Report IB64, "Sales Force Motivation," 1981, p. 5. Reprinted by permission of The Conference Board.)

EXHIBIT 19.6
DO YOUR PERSONAL CHARACTERISTICS MEASURE UP?

appropriateness of your appearance, your judgment, your enthusiasm, your dependability, your verbal communication skills, your imagination, and your drive.

Successful evaluation programs are those that provide for continual observation and feedback, as well as for periodic formal evaluations. Day-to-day observations by a concerned supervisor are particularly important for you as a new salesperson and useful in helping you perfect your routine. This type of evaluation should be positive and approached in the same manner as good coaching. Formal evaluations, on the other hand, are done at periodic intervals. They provide for a time to sit down and carefully go over your performance from the broader perspective that a time period allows. They also are typically presented as positively as possible so that the result will be motivating. (See Exhibit 19.7.)

For an evaluation program to be effective in improving performance, it helps if you, the salesperson, have an opportunity to participate. Both parties should agree on the objectives, the means of attaining them, and the way such attainment will be measured. The program should be based on realistic objectives that reflect actual conditions—the territory, the competition, your sales experience, and the company's assistance. Most of all, you should be committed to the attainment of these objectives.

EXHIBIT 19.7

SAMPLE EVALUATION FORM

Sales personnel evaluation form
for
periodic reviews

Name of salesperson _____

 Annual sales volume in dollars _____

Rank the employee in each of the items using the rating scale of 5 for excellent and 1 for below average

	Rating				
Item	**Excellent**		**Average**		**Below average**
	5	4	3	2	1
Ability to solve customer problems					
Ability to service customer accounts					
Knowledge of product features and uses					
Knowledge of market and competition					
Ability to prospect					
Ability to work with other salespeople					
Ability to work with other departments					
Ability to manage own time					
Ability to manage sales territory					
Personal appearance					
Initiative and enthusiasm					
Creativity and imagination					
Dependability and stability					
Ability to secure new accounts					

Any rating of 3 or below should be explained in writing in the space provided on the back of this form. The supervisor and the salesperson should jointly develop means of improvement.

Signature of Evaluator

_____ Date_____

EXHIBIT 19.8
DIRECT OBSERVATION IS PART OF THE EVALUATION PROCESS
(*Source:* Craig Callan.)

EXHIBIT 19.9

EXAMPLES OF TRAINING PROGRAMS FOR THE NEWLY HIRED

A Food Company

"When a new sales representative is hired, a three-to-four-week initial training and orientation program is provided prior to his or her assuming the duties of a regular sales route or territory. This program consists of the following:

Day 1. Receive welcome to company, sign up for insurance, taxes, benefits, and so on. Be introduced to office personnel, review training about to occur, obtain company car, answer all questions, and be issued with training kit.

Days 2–5. Work in field with experienced sales reps to see what the job is about and to learn parts of the job. At night, read parts from 'trainee kit.' (The 'trainee kit' is a box of materials that includes everything a new sales representative needs to work in the field. It also has information about company operations, product information, the food industry, history of the company, sales policies and procedures, and so on.)

EXHIBIT 19.9 (cont.)

Days 6–10. Visit regional manufacturing plant, meet with department heads for all marketing-related services, and learn how the product is made. Work with regional trainer on selling skills, and continue working on trainee kit at night.

Days 11–15. Work with experienced sales rep in the field, learning how to do the job.

Days 16–20. Start learning a specific sales territory that the trainee will take over within a week or two.

On the morning of Day 6, we sit down with the trainee and ask: 'Now that you have seen what the job is about, is it what you expected and will you be happy doing it?' If any kind of a negative reply is received at this point, we discuss it fully and provide the opportunity for a graceful 'parting of the ways,' if the trainee wishes. Five to ten percent of the trainees do leave at this point—and we have helped to reduce costly turnover at the one- to three-year point with this method.

Throughout the training period the persons doing the training are constantly evaluating the trainee. The trainee is told this and is provided with sample copies of the evaluation forms that are being used by his or her evaluators.''

A Tobacco Products Company

''Newly hired sales personnel generally receive basic training over the first three months of employment. Training is the direct responsibility of each individual sales manager and includes orientation training, that is, introduction to the company's product line, marketing strategy, promotion, pricing, industry orientation, and administrative and sales procedures.

Training consultant specialists are retained by the home office to assist in the preparation of training materials and programs as well as to advise individual managers on techniques and methods of individualizing training and development programs.

Training is expanded to a continuous program of individual self-development which is based on the concept of setting goals, measuring performance against goals, analyzing reasons why goals are not attained, and action planning for self-improvement to meet future goals.

Training consultants continually work with sales managers in other important areas, which include motivation, professional selling skills, attitude development, time and territory management, and the development of effective work habits.

Initially, training is accomplished individually or in small groups. New sales people are then assigned to experienced sales representatives for dual and joint-call experience. After sufficient exposure to experienced sales execution, new sales people are gradually involved in a new selling situation until capable of independent field work. Periodic joint calling with the sales manager continues the practical learning experience.

Each new employee is also scheduled to participate in a minimum of 16 hours of formal classroom training per year conducted by the central office training consultants. This program assures consistency and helps control the quality of training. In addition, each salesperson receives a package prepared by an outside organiza-

EXHIBIT 19.9 *(cont.)*

tion—a self-study, motivation and sales training program which reinforces for eight to twelve weeks in the field what has been learned in the classroom.''

A Forest Products Company

''Persons hired as sales trainees join the company without being assigned to an operating division. Within a few days to a few weeks in a group of five to ten (maximum), they begin the Marketing Personnel Development program, a basic group sales-training program. During the next nine weeks they learn:

• Company organization, policies, procedures; the business of each operating division. During a four-day classroom lecture session, corporate department heads and representatives of all organizational units of the company (service, products, manufacturing facilities, markets, field selling efforts, and so on) discuss the nature, function and objectives of their units.

• The technology of pulp and paper manufacture. A four-day lecture, including programmed instruction and supported by slides and sound movies, teaches the important properties of industrial papers and how these properties are achieved, controlled and measured in manufacture. A three-day tour of an integrated pulp and paper mill concludes this instruction.

• The nature of major markets for the company's products. Sales and sales management representatives discuss major markets for each division.

• Selling skills and communication skills in general (approximately two weeks). Films followed by discussion, printed programmed instruction, recorded cassettes (a commercially packaged program), and role-playing exercises before CCTV camera and recorder provide instruction and application to develop selling and persuasive communication skills. Case problems indigenous to the company's operating divisions supply the framework for selling exercises.

• Principles of time and territory management. Programmed instruction, supplemented by lecture and discussion, develop the principles of sales time management in accordance with profit opportunities.

• This program concludes with a week or two of individual meetings and interviews between trainees and division management personnel interested in adding to their sales staff. Thus begins a competitive selection process, the outcome of which both trainee and division management can influence. Upon accepting the invitation of a division to join it, the trainee now begins a six- to nine-month program of on-the-job training and instruction to learn how to sell specific products to particular markets.''

An Office Equipment Company

''The training program is student paced and approximately 44 weeks in duration. Fourteen of these weeks are in the formal classroom environment. The program is broken into:

• *Marketing Environment.* This four-week class is the first formal training for new hires. It is intended to teach basic selling techniques utilizing structured sales calls,

EXHIBIT 19.9 (cont.)

business knowledge, company business practices, basic computer concepts and applications.

• *Marketing and Systems Design*. During this six weeks, they concentrate totally on the technical aspects of our product line. Programming techniques, application aids, teleprocessing, and hardware considerations are presented.

• *Applications School*. This two-week class concentrates in detail on event-response and manufacturing applications.

• *Advanced Marketing Techniques*. This two-week 'sales school' is intended to be the finishing school for all marketing reps before they assume territory responsibilities.

• *Advanced Systems Training*. This is the 'sales school' for our systems engineers, giving them extensive training on advanced data processing techniques, including the marketing and technical areas."

A Chemicals Company

"Our new field salespersons are recruited on the campus. After screening at headquarters, successful candidates report to one of 26 field sales offices. Almost immediately the new salesperson breaks in on an office sales job (sales order handling), at the same time receiving basic training in telephone skills, order entry, and basic company orientation. He or she goes through a self-study (programmed) instruction course on chemistry and distribution and traffic functions. After 30 to 60 days, the candidate is now ready for the next step.

Four times a year, a three-week training session is conducted at headquarters. This consists of a one-week chemistry course and two weeks of basic company orientation, basics of business, and office selling skills. Our salesperson now returns to his or her field office.

For the next six months, the salesperson performs an office sales job and is rated accordingly. Here the individual is in constant phone contact with customers and, at the same time, participates on occasion in some field calls with field sales people.

Following successful completion of the office assignment, the salesperson attends a one-week field sales session at headquarters, oriented toward doing the field sales job. Subjects include territory analysis, account analysis, account strategy, legal aspects, pricing and, of course, call skills and presentations.

Some of our people then have temporary field assignments (60–90 days). Here the project consists of making market surveys or implementing new promotions. It gives the new field salesperson valuable experience in polishing call skills.

The whole process requires 12 to 18 months, depending on the progress of the individual."

Source: "Training the Sales Force: A Progress Report," *Conference Board Report 737*, pp. 10–12. Reprinted by permission of The Conference Board.

EXHIBIT 19.10

OBSERVATIONS REGARDING THE CHANGING ATTITUDES OF SALES TRAINEES

"I see the salesmen in our industry becoming more educated and more professional in future years. Most have come up through the ranks from retail to distributor to factory. The future sales representatives will be college educated and come directly into the sales force.

The training will be affected accordingly. They will demand more sophisticated training that is in tune with their abilities and needs"

—Manager of marketing manpower development and training,
a household appliance manufacturer

"The question of attitude is not one of what we will expect but, rather, one of what we anticipate: 'Make me feel good about me and my job.' The challenge is to accommodate effectively and channel the human resources toward increasing sales"

—Marketing officer, a bank

"Because of improvements in secondary education, people being recruited for positions in our industry will be more knowledgeable and, perhaps, more demanding regarding training methodology, opportunities for growth and development, and so on. The effect on training programs and methods will be the incorporation of more self-paced, as well as elective, programs and less structure."

—Vice president, a pharmaceuticals company

"We expect that new sales positions in the industry will have to be filled with people whose expectations for an enriched job program will be higher than those in the past. In effect, the expectation to participate in a psychically rewarding sales experience will be higher. This will require the development of more professionalism, with emphasis on the development of programmed materials which more fully integrate the sales requirement to the capabilities of the organization and vice versa. The development of selling aids, merchandising materials, and related programs will be a prime concern for the company, as opposed to a methodology that has previously stressed independent creativity and personal selling."

—Vice president, a paper converter

"There is no question that attitudes have changed among younger people. It is most evident in the areas of motivation and participation. While the ability to earn money is still a prime motivating factor, the knowledge that the sales representative is making a meaningful contribution to the company and for society is equally as strong a motivating influence. And, because this force is so strong, new sales representatives expect active participation in the company. Consequently, in our training programs and methods we will have to be more direct, more willing to discuss company policies, and less assured that new employees will accept the status quo simply because things have always been done that way."

—Director of hiring and training, an insurance company

"The principal difference experienced during recent years in recruiting for sales positions has been the basic lack of enthusiasm or desire to choose a selling career. Efforts have and will continue to be made to demonstrate the professional aspects of a selling career, and more emphasis will necessarily have to be placed in training programs to strengthen and fortify the convictions of the trainee relative to the professionalism of selling."

—Marketing director, a machinery producer

"Several of the divisions in our company are leaning more and more toward hiring experienced salespeople rather than those right out of college. I think we will be hiring people with more 'practical' education. I think they will be coming along with more mature

EXHIBIT 19.10 (cont.)

attitudes, a higher sense of dedication to work and, overall, a more mature approach to business and to life.

In this whole area I am rather optimistic. It could mean more sophisticated and comprehensive training programs accomplished with better results in less time."

—Director of marketing and sales training, a packaging company

"The future applicant will be better educated and much more critical of the status quo. Such things as 'time in grade' for promotion will not be as readily accepted by the future salesperson as it has been in the past. The question: 'Where am I going, and when?' will have to be answered. Techniques such as career pathing will have to be initiated and implemented by present sales managers. The entire area of social change will have particular emphasis on the future employment of sales people, with equal employment opportunities being the major area of concern. Obviously, the existing sales management will have to be aware of these attitude changes and learn to cope with them in order to maintain successful operations."

—Director of planning and marketing research, a food company

Source: "Training the Sales Force: A Progress Report," *Conference Board Report 737,* pp. 26, 27. Reprinted by permission of The Conference Board.

RECAP

The more important aspects of sales management are organizing, recruiting and selecting, compensating, training, motivating, and evaluating. Three management theories affect the approach of management: the classic, progressive, and contingency theories. Function, geography, product type, and need for flexibility provide the basic guidelines for organizing.

Recruitment and selection are distinguished by basic function. Recruiting provides large sources of potential salespeople; selection is the process of identifying the most qualified of the group.

The primary purpose of a successful compensation program is to promote the most efficient and productive use of the sales force. This is accomplished through the following five objectives:

1. Motivation through incentives
2. Balance between work and compensation
3. Attraction and retention of staff
4. Balance between costs and sales
5. Clarity and ease of administration

The common methods of compensation presented are straight salary, straight commission, and combination of salary and commission or bonus.

Training programs within companies are designed to encourage, motivate, and educate each new employee. Such programs usually cover company orientation, market and industry orientation, selling techniques, and product knowledge.

Motivating salespeople is one of the most important aspects of sales management. Companies rely on several techniques to spur their sales force to success. Among them are the opportunity for advancement, supervisor's encouragement, individual incentives, commission incentives, and personal recognition.

Another management function is evaluation. The evaluation process consists of four steps:

1. Analyzing the job and writing the job description
2. Determining performance measurements
2. Measuring and evaluating actual performance
4. Recommending areas for improvement

REVIEW QUESTIONS

1. What is the difference between the classical approach and the progressive approach to management?
2. What is the contingency theory?
3. When organizing the sales force, what things are generally taken into account?
4. Distinguish between recruiting and selection.
5. What are several sources which can be used in recruiting potential salespeople?
6. Why should a job description be written before the selection process begins?
7. What are the basic methods of compensating salespeople?
8. What is the essential purpose of a training program?
9. What are the most common devices used to motivate salespeople?
10. Is personal recognition an important motivator?
11. What are the four usual steps in evaluating?

DISCUSSION QUESTIONS

1. Taking into consideration the basic assumptions of theory X and theory Y, describe how you would react to each of the theories. Under which theory would you work harder? Why?
2. Do you think that personal appearance should be considered in the selection process? Or do you feel that it is not as important as many think?
3. Review the basic types of motivators. List them in terms of their importance to you. Why do you feel you would respond more to some than to others?
4. In order for an evaluation program to be successful it must be motivating. How might management assure that a training program will be motivating?

LEARNING EXPERIENCES

1. Go to your college or university placement office and ask for a copy of a personal interest or a vocational interest test. Ask if you can take either or both of the tests. After they have been corrected and you have seen the results, comment on the validity of the tests from your own point of view.
2. Search the help-wanted advertisements of the largest newspaper in your area and in the classified section of the *Wall Street Journal*. Concentrate on sales jobs. What type of experiences and qualifications are companies looking for? Can you detect any themes or trends?

CASES

AUTOMATED BUSINESS SYSTEMS

Automated Business Systems sells complete office and accounting systems to business and professional offices. Its success in the field has been due to its ability to completely revamp the office, accounting, and financial systems of clients in such a way that cost savings in the first three years generally pay the fee.

Generally, once a prospect has been identified and qualified, ABS sends its sales team to the client's premises. The sales team consists of three sales representatives, called *consultants,* who carry the project through to its close. The consultants usually spend several weeks gathering data on existing procedures and needs and future demands due to potential growth. Then they analyze their findings, write up the report, customize the presentation, present the program, handle objections, and close. Once the system is sold, their major responsibilities for this particular client end, and they repeat the process for a new prospect.

The sales representatives for ABS are paid on a salary, with a bonus awarded to any team that has an outstanding year. This method has worked well in the past, but there are indications that there are problems with it now. There has been concern about a general lack of morale, and management suspects that not all sales representatives are pulling their own weight. The greatest concern is that several of the top salespeople feel their superior performance is not being properly recognized. In fact, one of the staff was overheard saying, "No more ten- and twelve-hour days for me. I've finally caught on. Take it easy—eight to four—and you'll be appreciated just as much."

Questions

1. Do you feel this is a serious enough problem to merit changes in management methods?
2. How would you begin to determine what is wrong with the present methods?

3. What type of motivational programs do you think should be considered in this case?

MONEY IS ALL IT TAKES—OR IS IT?

Tim Zeppler has been a salesman for Electronics 128 for six years. For the last two years he has been the top producer in his district. Therefore, it really didn't come as a surprise to anyone when he was invited to be interviewed for the sales manager's position.

The interview was going well. Zeppler had always liked Ms. Rodwell, the regional vice president of the company. And Rodwell was clearly impressed with Zeppler: his high energy level, his sales record, his technical expertise, and his excellent overall appearance. But she was a bit concerned by Zeppler's response to one question—a question which Rodwell felt was critical. Rodwell had asked ''What two or three things do you think are most motivating to salespeople? That is, which management strategies do you feel would make them put out their best effort?''

Zeppler quickly responded, ''That's easy, Ms. Rodwell. Money is the best motivation. I'd rank it first, second, and third in importance if you're interested in getting people to perform at their best.''

Questions

1. Do you agree with Zeppler? Why or why not?
2. What other forms of motivation do you feel should be used by managment?

TWENTY

CHAPTER OBJECTIVES

To familiarize you with the number of job opportunities in sales for people with different aptitudes and abilities

To familiarize you with general levels of compensation and the opportunities for advancement in sales careers

To help you prepare for a sales career: preparing for employment, writing a résumé, finding the jobs, conducting yourself during the interview, and following up on the interview

CHAPTER OUTLINE

GETTING STARTED IN SALES

Start where you are with what you have.
George Washington Carver

Never before in our economic history has such a high percentage of Americans been involved in sales. Today, more men and women are involved in distributing and servicing products than are required to produce them.[1] This has been called the age of distribution. Certainly one of the most significant economic revolutions of the past century has been the rapid growth of sales.

You come into contact with salespeople every day. They're practically everywhere. What this means is a large number and a great variety of career opportunities. In this chapter we're going to deal with some of the statistics of career opportunities in selling. And then we're going to take you through the process of getting started in sales. This involves pre-interview preparation, writing a résumé, finding the jobs, conducting yourself during the interview, and following up on the interview.

[1]William E. Hopke, *The Encyclopedia of Careers*. J. C. Ferguson Publishing Company, 1978, p. 423.

SALES PROVIDES A VARIETY OF OPPORTUNITIES

You're familiar with many of the types of jobs in selling—door-to-door salespersons, life insurance agents and brokers, manufacturers' representatives, property and casualty insurance agents, real estate agents and brokers, and salespeople in the retail and wholesale trades. (These sales occupations account for more than 90 percent of all the jobs in sales; more than 60 percent are in retailing.)

Another major group of salespeople, in addition to those we've already mentioned above and in Chapter 15, are those who handle stocks and bonds. These people are usually called *registered representatives* or *account executives* and are employed by stock exchange members of securities firms. There is keen competition in the financial services field. The salesperson must really be sharp and must constantly study corporation reports and activities to be in a position to advise intelligently.

Many other types of salespeople distribute sundry objects and services which surround each of us each day, from clock radios, pocketbooks, and candy to business stationery, telephone books, and computer systems. In fact, this book was sold by a representative. Thousands of people work for publishing houses selling books to elementary and secondary schools, as well as to colleges and universities. The sales representatives call on teachers and principals (elementary and secondary) and on professors, deans, and department chairpersons (college and university). Opportunities in sales abound. (See Exhibit 20.1.)

SALES CAREERS REQUIRE VARYING APTITUDES AND ABILITIES

The level of skills, aptitudes, and abilities required for sales jobs varies widely. Some types of selling call for people who have an aggressive approach and who are extroverted. Other selling requires quieter, low-keyed people who can employ a carefully planned soft-sell approach. Some selling jobs demand that you meet the same customer repeatedly; others require you to call on prospects who are nearly always strangers. Some kinds of selling make physical demands on your strength and stamina; others can be handled by phone. Some jobs demand that you travel around a great deal, perhaps being out of the office for days, weeks, or even months. Other kinds require you to be at the same job location every hour of every day. Some selling jobs demand a person with a high IQ; others are best suited for those with average intelligence. Some types of selling jobs require a lot of education and training before you can function fully and successfully. Other selling jobs can be handled with very little training and education. Some jobs are most suited for those who have reached maturity; others are best fitted for young people.

This list could go on and on, but you get the point: There are many types of selling jobs calling for a wide variety of people with different skills, aptitudes, and personalities. The conclusion is obvious: Nearly anyone can find some position in selling that suits her or his needs and motivations.

EXHIBIT 20.1
PROJECTED AVERAGE ANNUAL JOB OPENINGS, 1970 TO
1985 (IN THOUSANDS)

Occupational group	Projected average annual job openings 1970–1985*
Professional and technical workers	204.0
Managers and administrators, except farm	344.2
Salesworkers	316.5
Clerical workers	794.7
Craftsmen and foremen	342.1
Operatives	307.5
Service workers	428.8
Laborers, except farm	20.3
All occupations	2753.0

Source: The Conference Board, 1976.
*Details may not add to total due to rounding.

BUT WILL I BE HAPPY?

Bruce had that familiar feeling of apprehension. He knew the feeling well, and he was getting to the point where he knew its cause. It was indecision. No, not the easy-to-dismiss type like "which movie shall I go to?" or "where shall I spend my spring vacation." This was more strongly rooted because the outcome of his decision was

EXHIBIT 20.2
THERE'S A CAREER PATH FOR EVERYONE

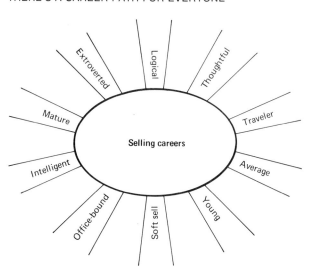

more consequential. Bruce was trying to decide what he was going to do come spring when he received his degree.

There seemed to be plenty of opportunities. The campus placement office had a full schedule of interviews with companies visiting the campus, and when he had glanced at it last week, he noticed that there were a variety of positions. In fact, he had stopped by to see the placement counselor, a Ms. McKey. But he wasn't sure that Ms. McKey knew what she was talking about; she had suggested that Bruce consider a career in sales. It didn't make sense; Bruce had never considered himself the salesperson type. However, he had heard that there were a lot of openings and that the pay was good. And he had heard that it could be a good starting point for a management position in the future. He had majored in marketing. If only he knew where to begin. "There must be some logical way to go about finding a job that matches your interests and ambitions," he thought.

There is a way. In this chapter we'll go through the logical steps to finding a sales job that matches your interests and ambitions.

EMPLOYMENT PROSPECTS ARE GOOD

Employment prospects for selling jobs are good because of two factors. One factor is the continued growth of our population projected for the remainder of the twentieth century. Estimates vary, of course, owing to the different assumptions about the birthrate, but most forecasters see the population ranging from 240 million to 300 million by the year 2000. Exhibit 20.3 shows four different projections through the year 2050 published by the U.S. Bureau of the Census.

The second factor is the long-range trend for a greater percentage of the working population to enter sales and related service occupations each year. For example, in the past decade the percentage of sales workers employed in wholesale trade, life and casualty insurance, real estate, and manufacturing trade showed a greater-than-average increase. The percentage of direct selling to the consumer showed some increase. The slowest-growing field was in retail sales, which, as we mentioned earlier, is the largest field of sales.

Exhibits 20.4 and 20.5 summarize the sales growth. The total number of more than 316,000 annual openings for all types of salespeople between 1970 and 1985 is broken down to 100,000 attributed to growth and 216,500 attributed to attrition. The total number of salespeople by 1985 is projected to be 6,167,000, up from a 1980 count of 5,862,000.

Growth in the sales field will also be due to improved business methods. Orders will be processed more rapidly and efficiently because of electronic data processing. New demonstration techniques will improve presentation. Although automation may reduce employment in some areas of our economy, competition for sales and the need for personal contact in this field should protect the jobs of salespeople, particularly in the more professional, higher-level sales jobs. Only in certain lines—retail sales of groceries, drugs, fast foods, and low-cost variety items—should the effect of automation be felt. But this should encourage the

Millions

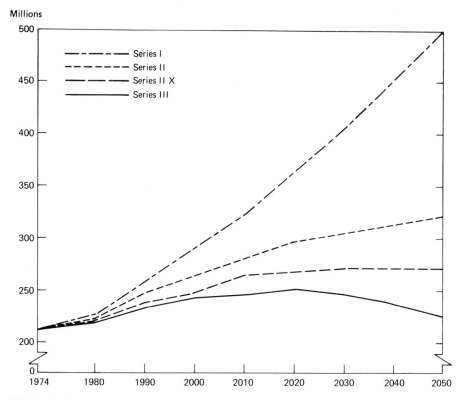

EXHIBIT 20.3
U.S. POPULATION PROJECTIONS TO 2050   (*Source:* U.S. Bureau of the Census.)

recruitment of increasingly more skilled and sophisticated salespeople. The size and complexity of average sales should increase.

COMPENSATION IN SELLING IS COMPETITIVE

Salaries for salespeople are competitive and are classified by the U.S. Department of Labor as being among the top ten occupations.

Generally, the lowest-paid salespeople are those in retail selling. If they are excluded from the statistics, the salaries of salespeople would be among the highest of all occupations. As we mentioned in Chapter 1, many successful salespeople earn six-figure incomes. For example, the 1980 *Occupational Outlook Handbook* states that earnings for experienced securities salespeople averaged more than $30,000. In the wholesale industry, median salaries for the highest-paid salespeople ranged from $27,000 in food products to more than $53,000 in paper products. Manufacturers' representatives are also highly paid. Salaries for inexperienced salespeople ranged from $15,400 to $22,500 (1978 dollars adjusted).

EXHIBIT 20.4
PROJECTED AVERAGE ANNUAL JOB OPENINGS, 1970 TO 1985

| | Average annual job openings 1970–1985 | | |
| | | Job openings due to: | |
Occupation	Total	Growth	Attrition
Salesworkers	316,500	100,000	216,500
Insurance agents, brokers, and underwriters	23,700	10,900	12,800
Real estate agents and brokers	26,900	8,900	17,900
Sales representatives, manufacturing	16,800	6,600	10,200
Sales representatives, wholesale	31,200	13,500	17,700
Salesclerks, retail trade	175,500	42,300	133,200
Salesworkers, retail trade	21,400	7,700	13,700
Salespeople, service and construction	14,000	6,600	7,400

Source: The Conference Board, 1976.

EXHIBIT 20.5
EMPLOYMENT IN 1960 AND 1970 AND PROJECTED 1980 AND 1985, OCCUPATIONS INCLUDED IN STUDY (IN THOUSANDS)

| | Employment | | | | Average Annual Growth Rate, % | | | |
Occupation	1960	1970	1980	1985	1960–1970	1970–1980	1970–1985	1980–1985
Salesworkers	4112	4608	5862	6107	1.1	2.4	1.9	0.8
Insurance agents, brokers, and underwriters	328	412	523	576	2.3	2.4	2.3	1.9
Real estate agents and brokers	234	316	414	450	3.1	2.7	2.4	1.7
Sales representatives, manufacturing	443	394	476	493	1.7	1.9	1.5	0.7
Sales representatives, wholesale	493	635	810	837	2.6	2.5	1.9	0.6
Salesclerks, retail trade	2031	2190	2782	2825	0.8	2.4	1.7	0.3
Salesworkers, retail trade	408	407	497	523	0.8	2.0	1.7	1.0
Salespeople, service and construction	140	151	219	250	0.8	3.8	3.4	2.7
Stock and bond sales agents	35	103	141	153	11.4	3.2	2.7	1.7

Source: The Conference Board, 1976.

SALES CAREERS OFFER OPPORTUNITIES FOR ADVANCEMENT

The proof of the value of a sales background may be seen in the increasing trend to select company top executives and presidents from the sales department. The sales management network itself, which includes branch sales managers, territory managers, regional sales managers, the director of marketing, and the vice president of sales and marketing, also provides opportunities for career growth.

In most types of sales, qualified salespeople will find that their volume of sales, and thus their commissions, show steady growth as their experience and time on the job grow.

THE WORK OF SALESPEOPLE IS IMPORTANT

During periods of prosperity, the salesperson's efforts contribute significantly to high levels of business. A generally high volume of sales maintains full employment and contributes significantly to increased purchasing power. In times of recession, the salesperson creates greatly needed economic activity by stimulating buying efforts. The emphasis usually shifts to conservation and economy, but the need for new, related products and services arises (witness the field of energy conservation goods and services). It has been said that a good salesperson is rarely out of work.

THE FIRST SALES TEST

A real opportunity exists for you to apply the principles we've discussed throughout this book. Landing the first job can and should be thought of as the first sale—in this case *the product is you*, more particularly your personal characteristics, education, training, and career potential. The *prospect* is the potential employer(s) you are going to contact. Prospecting, preapproach and approach, presentation, handling objections, and the close all have applications to the process of getting a job.

Preparing

Thinking of yourself as a product might sound odd, even unemotional and calculating, but it creates a mental attitude which can be very useful in preparing for the job-search process. This somewhat detached mental attitude is useful because it allows you to objectively evaluate your strengths and weaknesses, likes and dislikes, education and training, and previous job experience from the point of view of the employer (the prospect). It allows you to concentrate on those facets about yourself that are of interest to the employer.

You can learn a lot about yourself if you begin by dividing a blank sheet of paper with a vertical line down the middle. Head the left column with *strengths* and the right column with *weaknesses*. Then try some brainstorming, writing descriptive words about yourself in the appropriate column. Strengths may be any number of things that you think are positive characteristics about yourself. Examples might be industriousness, self-discipline, honesty, self-motivation, and independence. Weaknesses might be poor ability to work under structure, procrastination, and short attention span. The point of this exercise is to be able to articulate your positive features while acknowledging your weaknesses. Once you have acknowledged your weaknesses, you can devise a plan for working with them so that they don't become handicaps.

Arrange your strengths in order of importance, not to you, but to a prospective employer. Remember, you are really working on creating a package to present yourself as a very employable commodity. You are listing your salient features and positioning yourself among the competition (the other job applicants) in the job market. Your success in selling yourself will depend upon your preparation and the way you present yourself.

You can repeat this process for likes and dislikes. That is, divide the paper in half with *likes* as one heading and *dislikes* as the other heading. Again, brainstorm and honestly develop the two lists. Typical likes might be being with people, reading adventure stories, participating in sports, and going to the theater. Typical dislikes might include being alone for long periods of time, watching sports on TV, and being with overly talkative people. Finish this list as completely and as candidly as possible.

In completing the two lists, remember that it is important to list anything that comes to mind. This is not the time to try to decide whether a characteristic or a like relates to success in a career in selling. That decision can be made later. Besides, very often a characteristic you feel is not related to success in selling, because of your previous stereotype of salespeople, may in fact be an important characteristic for some type of professional sales position. Remember, we've said over and over in this book that the field of selling includes a great variety of situations which provide opportunities for many different personality traits and characteristics.

Don't try to cheat in making up the lists. Be honest in listing your likes and dislikes, strengths and weaknesses. If, after further study of job openings and companies who are hiring, you feel that you should stress one characteristic and minimize another, that's O.K. That's simply presenting your characteristics in a positive manner. That's selling. Similarly, if you have a weakness that will be a handicap in many types of selling jobs, figure out a way that you can work to eliminate it or build it into a strength. As an example, if speaking in front of groups is a weakness which you have and which you feel will handicap success in selling, take a course in public speaking at a college; join one of the several public groups, like Toastmasters; or be creative and join a drama or theater group.

Of course, if after thoroughly preparing and completing all the brainstorming lists, doing your job-market research, etc., you end up with a composite picture of one who has no talent for sales, you should seriously consider whether it will be a successful career field for you.

Education, Training, and Previous Employment

In order to be prepared for the interview (the presentation) and for writing the résumé, you should make additional lists about yourself under the headings education, training and skills, and previous employment. At this time you may also want to create headings for outside activities and honors and awards. The secret of success at this point is to be complete and honest—leave nothing out and don't worry yet about order of importance. Rearranging and editing will come later when you write the résumé.

Often students question whether certain job experiences have value or bearing on a prospective job, such as a job in sales. The general rule of thumb is to list it if in doubt. Whereas on the surface the job may not be related to any job you aspire to, often it contributes to a pattern regarding the type of person you are. If, for example, you were going to college while working twenty or thirty hours per week, a picture begins to emerge about you—a picture of an industrious person who likes to remain active and busy. This is the proof of one of the characteristics you may have listed on your strengths-weaknesses list earlier.

Writing Your Résumé

After you have gone through the steps we've outlined above, it's fairly easy to write a résumé. A résumé is basically an outline of yourself, particularly those positive things about you that are of interest to prospective employers. One personnel executive states that "the résumé is a written sales presentation that creates a first impression of your abilities and experiences. The mere physical appearance of your résumé could mean the difference between getting or not getting a job."

Résumés must be carefully organized, written, and typed; have no grammar, spelling, or typing errors; and be professionally reproduced on quality paper.

Here is the type of general information that is usually included in a résumé:

- Your name, address, and telephone number.
- Your career or occupational goal.
- Your education. Usually, do not include high school if you have a two- or four-year college degree. Under your college, list your major and minor subjects and the degree you received. Your grades or class rank, if good, should also be listed along with academic awards or honors.
- Other significant education or experiences.
- Professional memberships, certificates, licenses, and awards.
- Special skills, attributes, or characteristics helpful for the position sought.
- Recent graduates with little or no job experience may wish to list job-related academic courses and extracurricular activities.
- Language abilities, published works, and other achievements.

Here are some hints that might help you write an effective résumé.

- Avoid putting anything in your résumé that might create a bias in the employer's mind. This includes age, race, religion, national origin, height, weight, and membership in certain organizations.

• Arrange the information on your résumé to catch the employer's eye. List your most important assets early in the résumé. Make your layout easy to scan—don't crowd everything in to fit on one page. Cut out nonessentials or go to a second sheet.

• Be concise and use a telegraphic writing style. For instance, the sentence ''I was responsible for developing the weekly work schedules for all personnel in the department'' can be best written ''Developed work schedules for department personnel.''

• Keep your résumé clear, concise, and positive. And above all else, be honest.

In writing the résumé, the last step for attaining positive results is to prepare a cover letter to be sent with the résumé. The cover letter should be brief, typed on good-quality paper, and a personal prelude to the facts in the résumé. It should tie in particular skills to the job you are applying for. The cover letter should be addressed to the prospective employer by proper name and title. The cover letter should always be sales-oriented, showing the prospective employer the *benefits* of hiring you and what you can do for *that firm* in *that position*.

Finding the Jobs: Prospecting and the Approach

There are a number of ways of prospecting for job opportunities. The first place to look, the place that usually comes to mind for most of us, is the help-wanted section of the newspapers. Also, most professional journals have employment sections that can be useful, as does the annual edition of the *College Placement Journal,* which is in the career placement office of most colleges and universities.

Many people do not realize, however, that many job openings are not advertised. Also, the advertised job openings are often the same openings that are listed with employment agencies, although in some cases employment agencies will have some listings that are not advertised.

Most companies, particularly the larger ones, depend on a flow of job seekers by way of letters, phone inquiries, and walk-ins. (Walk-ins are job seekers who simply walk into the personnel office to apply for a job. Those who succeed, however, are normally well-prepared ahead of time and have copies of their résumés with them.)

Letters are an inexpensive way to make the initial contact. Consider letters as your own direct-mail campaign. Even though your chance of getting an interview through this method is lower than through responding to an advertised job opening, the increased numbers give you greater exposure. That is, you may get a response of 30 percent for ten advertised jobs, resulting in three interviews. You may only get a response of 10 percent from your direct-mail campaign, but if you've mailed out a hundred letters, that's ten interviews.

Obviously, you've got to select the companies to mail the letters to. There are a number of source directories which will give you the essential information needed to get started. A partial list of some key sources follows. Your librarian will be pleased to help you locate additional ones.

• *College Placement Annual.* Lists companies in the United States and Canada that are seeking college graduates. Published by the College Placement Council.

- *Dun and Bradstreet Million Dollar Directory.* Lists more than 30,000 companies whose net worth is over $1 million.
- *Dun and Bradstreet Middle Market Directory.* Lists more than 30,000 companies whose net worth is between $500,000 and $999,999.
- *Standard & Poors' Register of Corporations, Directors, and Executives.* Lists products and services, officers, and telephone numbers of more than 35,000 corporations in the United States and Canada.

In addition to the names and addresses you obtain from the directories, be sure to add any additional names you may be able to think of from your own contacts and experiences, including leads that you may get from teachers, relatives, and friends.

Once you have selected the prospects from the directories, you should prepare a *cover letter* to be mailed with each résumé. Begin the letter with the name, address, and title of the person to whom the letter is intended. Don't use "Dear Sir" or "Dear Madam" unless it is absolutely unavoidable. A personal touch is critical to the success of your campaign. Usually, the person you will want to address the letter to is the person who has the authority to hire, for example, the sales manager. You can get this name from the sources we've listed above or, if unavailable from these sources, by telephoning the company switchboard and asking for the correct name.

A number of job seekers have had success with the walk-in approach. As mentioned above, this can be successful if the applicant is well-prepared ahead of time, having familiarized himself or herself with the company and, of course, carrying a carefully prepared résumé. The walk-in approach is more time-consuming and more costly than other approaches. But it can be effective, particularly if you are concentrating on one particular geographical area. As is the case in all sales situations, your appearance will be particularly important when using this approach: It is the first impression you will make.

Conducting Yourself during the Interview: The Presentation

We've stressed throughout this book how important planning is to success in selling. In this case, your plan should include a review of your qualifications and preparation for the interview itself.

Review your qualifications   Go over the process of self-analysis outlined earlier in this chapter, and in this case keep an eye toward the particular company or companies with which you will be having interviews.

Prepare for the interview   Develop some knowledge and some questions about the company that will show interest. Anticipate questions that may be asked of you during the interview. Knowledge about the company can come from general reading and from the directories listed earlier in the chapter.

Prepare questions   Pertinent questions about the company will help you to demonstrate your knowledge and interest, something which most employers

EXHIBIT 20.6
AN EMPLOYMENT INTERVIEW   (*Source:* Freda Leinwand/Monkmeyer.)

consider important in making a selection. Here are some examples of questions you might ask:

• Where does your typical sales trainee wind up in five years? in ten years?
• What kind of training do you provide for new employees?
• What kind of training and development do you provide for employees who have been with you for several years?
• Do you have a policy of promotion from within?

Anticipate questions   Preparing for questions you may be asked will help you answer more articulately and authoritatively. The list below is only intended to give you an idea of the types of questions that are often asked. Think about how you might answer these questions and about what additional questions you might encounter.

• Where would you like to be in 5 years? In 10 years?
• In what school activities have you participated? Which did you enjoy the most?
• In what type of position are you most interested?
• Why do you think you would like to work for our company?
• What jobs have you held? How were they obtained? Why did you leave them?
• What courses did you like best? least? Why?
• Why did you choose your particular field of work?
• What percentage of your college expenses did you earn? How?

- What do you know about our company?
- What qualifications do you have that make you feel you will be successful in your field?
- What are your ideas on salary?
- Do you prefer any specific geographical location? Why?
- Why did you decide to go to the particular school you attended?
- How did you rank in your graduating class?
- What do you think determines a person's progress in a good company?
- Why do you think you would like this particular job? this particular company?
- How did your previous employers treat you?
- What have you learned from some other jobs you have held?
- What interests you about our product or service?
- Do you feel that you have done the best scholastic work of which you are capable?
- Do you like routine work?
- Do you like regular hours?
- Will you fight to get ahead?
- What is your major weakness?

Interviewing Tips   At the interview you will face the test, but it will be made easier because of all the preparation you've already gone through. Several suggestions will help ensure the success of the interview:

- *Take pains to present the best possible appearance.* C. L. Blackfan, vice president of marketing at BF Goodrich, says, "It may come as a surprise, but should not, that the most successful salesmen are those who look and act like salesmen. A recent survey indicates that physical appearance does play an important part."[2]
- *Be punctual.* Many employers consider tardiness a poor work habit. You'll be off to a bad start if you're late to the interview.
- *Shaking hands.* Whether you're male or female, if the interviewer makes the first move, respond with a firm handshake. And practice your handshake to ensure that it is appropriately firm.
- *Establish and maintain eye contact.* Many people interpret lack of eye contact as weakness or shiftiness.
- *Watch your posture.* Poor posture is often a sign of lack of interest and lack of self-respect or self-confidence.
- *Ask questions about the company, its product or service, and its policies.* As we've mentioned above, this will be interpreted as a sign of interest in the company.
- *Don't criticize past employers.* This usually backfires and makes you look like a person who has trouble fitting in with others, even if this wasn't the case.
- *Don't understate your past jobs—simply describe them.* Many applicants make the mistake of underselling their previous job experiences. Don't. Often the prospective employer can see merit in your previous jobs that you can't.

[2]Blackfan, C.L., "Salesmen in a Declining Economy," *Industrial Marketing,* December 1979, p. 81.

EXHIBIT 20.7
START THE INTERVIEW ON THE RIGHT FOOT

• *Express appreciation for the interview.* Remembering the usual social amenities will help maintain a positive impression.

• *Clarify or restate your position, if necessary.* This is really handling objections. If the employer seems concerned about something in your past, be sure you explain it in such a way that it will not remain a point on which to reject you.

Follow Up on the Interview

In most cases, you will not be offered the job during the interview. Most employers must interview several applicants before making a final selection. Your task, therefore, is to use this time to stand out from the others. This is done in the follow-up phase. We suggest the following:

The Follow-Up Letter   Immediately after the interview, write the interviewer a follow-up letter. Include at least four things:

1. Express appreciation for the interview and confirm your interest in the position.
2. Add any important information about yourself that, based upon the interview, would merit emphasis.

3. Express your willingness to provide any further information about your qualifications that might be needed.
4. Assume a positive attitude toward hearing from the interviewer.

The Follow-Up Call   Several days after the interview, plan another follow-up, if it is needed. Most interviewers will let you know at the close of the interview approximately when the selection will be made. For example, "We will let you know by the fifteenth of the month." Immediately after this date, if you have not heard, follow up by telephone. In those situations where a decision has not been made, you will have the advantage of bringing your name back to the interviewer's attention. In situations where the job may have been offered to someone else, there is often the possibility that the person refused. Thus your call may serve to be most convenient to the interviewer. In those cases where you have been rejected, you will at least know where you stand, and will be able to concentrate on other prospects. If you don't get the job, don't be discouraged. Review your presentation and refine it. Rejection doesn't mean you aren't qualified—only that someone else was more qualified or better prepared or even that the prospective employer made an error in judgment.

RECAP

In this chapter you've become familiar with information and methods useful in starting a career in sales. You have seen statistics that verify the opportunity for many jobs, been shown that sales careers require people with different aptitudes and abilities, and been shown that it is a field with high incomes.

   Getting a job is the first real sales test. You should thoroughly prepare by listing your strengths and weaknesses, likes and dislikes, education, training, and previous employment. After this self-analysis, you must prospect for job openings, write a résumé and cover letter, and conduct yourself appropriately during the interview. Finally, follow-up activities will help you to close the first sale—your job.

REVIEW QUESTIONS

1. As an occupational grouping, approximately how many annual job openings are in sales?
2. Over 90 percent of sales jobs are in which general areas?
3. What are the reasons that the projection for sales jobs is so favorable?
4. What are the major steps you should go through to successfully land a selling job?
5. What type of information should be included in your résumé?
6. What is the purpose of a cover letter?
7. What are the ways of prospecting for job opportunities?
8. List the sources of basic information about companies.
9. What is the walk-in approach? What can you do to ensure its success?

10. Why is it helpful to ask questions during an interview? What are some questions you might ask?

DISCUSSION QUESTIONS

1. We have said that sales occupations require people with different abilities and aptitudes. From your own experience, discuss several types of successful salespeople and why they have done well in their chosen lines.
2. Discuss why appearance is so important in a job interview. What would be appropriate dress? How would body language, handshake, facial expression, and eye contact affect the impression you make?
3. In a résumé, what is the general rule of thumb about listing jobs which have no direct bearing on job objectives?

LEARNING EXPERIENCES

1. Go to your college library and placement office and compile a list of publications that are available which list potential employers. Discuss how you could narrow down this potential list of thousands to a select one hundred.
2. Interview three personnel administrators in your community. Prior to visiting them, develop a questionnaire regarding the characteristics that they feel are most important in selecting sales trainees.
3. Using your local phone directory, compile a list of potential employers for aspiring salespeople.
4. Using the information presented in this chapter, prepare a résumé and a cover letter for a position in sales.

CASE

CASEY SEEKS A NEW CAREER

Casey joined a national retailer when he graduated from Northern University. After a year of on-the-job and classroom training, he was made manager of the furniture department. This was a stepping stone to assistant store manager, the position he has held for the past seven months. He has done well, and his salary is moving along steadily, but now he has decided that this is not the career for him. He enjoys the contact with the public that retailing affords but it is not in his nature to spend all his working hours in one location. He enjoyed the freedom of movement he had in an earlier selling job. He plans to capitalize on that and look for a job in sales. He thinks that his three-plus successful years in retailing will be considered an asset and his knowledge of furniture will be useful if he can get a job in that field—perhaps selling to retailers. His logic makes sense, both to him and to others he has talked to. Now all he has to do is figure out how to get himself back into the employment market.

Questions

1. Where would you suggest Casey begin?
2. How can he find out where the job openings are?
3. What advice would you give him in preparing for the interview?

INDEX

INDEX

477

478

480

482

486